# Emperor Yang

# of the Sui Dynasty

SUNY Series in Chinese Philosophy and Culture

Roger T. Ames, editor

# Emperor Yang of the Sui Dynasty

## His Life, Times, and Legacy

Victor Cunrui Xiong

State University of New York Press

Published by
State University of New York Press, Albany

© 2006 State University of New York

For information, address State University of New York Press,
194 Washington Avenue, Suite 305, Albany, NY 12210-2384

Production by Michael Haggett
Marketing by Michael Campochiaro

**Library of Congress Cataloging-in-Publication Data**

Xiong, Victor Cunrui.
 Emperor Yang of the Sui dynasty : his life, times, and legacy / Victor Cunrui Xiong.
  p.  cm.—(SUNY series in Chinese phiolosophy and cultrue)
 ISBN 0-7914-6587-X (hardcover : alk. paper)
 ISBN 0-7914-6588-8 (pbk.:alk.paper)
1. Sui Yangdi, Emperor of China, 569-618.  2. China—History—Sui  dynasty, 581-618.  3. China—Kings  and  rulers—Biography.  I. Title.  II. Series.

DS749.29.S85X56  2005
951'.016'092—dc22

2004027813

ISBN-13: 978-0-7914-6587-5 (hardcover: alk. paper)
ISBN-13: 978-0-7914-6588-2 (pbk.: alk. paper)

10  9  8  7  6  5  4  3  2  1

# Contents

# Maps and Tables

## MAPS

## TABLES

## Appendix 1 Tables

## Appendix 2 Tables

# Weights and Measures

## Length

| | Sui | | Tang |
|---|---|---|---|
| | pre-607 | post-607 | |
| 1 *cun* 寸 = | 2.951 cm | 2.355 cm | 3.11 cm |
| 10 *cun* = 1 *chi* 尺 | 29.51 cm | 23.55 cm | 31.1 cm |
| 5 *chi* = 1 *bu* 步 (Tang) | | | 1.555 m |
| 6 *chi* = 1 *bu* (Sui) | 1.7706 m | 1.413 m | |
| 10 *chi* = 1 *zhang* 丈 | 2.951 m | 2.355 m | 3.11 m |
| 2 *zhang* = 1 *duan*ᵃ 段 | 5.902 m | 4.71 m | 6.22 m |
| 4 *zhang* = 1 *pi* 疋 | 11.8 m | 9.42 m | 12.44 m |
| 5 *zhang* = 1 *duan* 端 | 14.76 m | 11.78 m | 15.55 m |
| 360 *bu* = 1 *li* 里 (2160 *chi*) | 0.637 km | 0.509 km | |
| 1 *li* (1800 *chi*) | | | 0.56 km |

## Area

| | Sui | | Tang |
|---|---|---|---|
| | pre-607 | post-607 | |
| 1 *mu* 畝 = 1 square *bu* × 240 | 752.4 m² | 479.17 m² | 580.33 m² |
| 100 *mu* = 1 *qing* 頃 | 75,240 m² | 47,917 m² | 58,033 m² |

## Capacity

| | Sui | | Tang |
|---|---|---|---|
| | pre-607 | post-607 | |
| 1 *sheng* 升 = | 594.4 ml | 198.1 ml | 594.4 ml |
| 10 *sheng* = 1 *dou* 斗 | 5.944 l | 1.981 l | 5.944 l |
| 10 *dou* = 1 *shi/hu* 石/斛 | 59.44 l | 19.81 l | 59.44 l |

## Weight

| | Sui | | Tang |
|---|---|---|---|
| | pre-607 | post-607 | |
| 1 *liang* 兩 = | 41.76 g | 13.92 g | 37.3 g |
| 16 *liang* = 1 *jin* 斤 | 668.19 g | 222.73 g | 596.82 g |

Sources: Wu Chengluo 1937, 64–98; Liang Fangzhong 1980, 542–46.

# Dynastic Powers in the Han-Tang Period

---

**Western Han** (206 BC–AD 8)
**Xin** (AD 9–23)
**Eastern Han** (AD 25–220)
**Three Kingdoms** (220–280)
  Wei, Shu, and Wu
**Six Dynasties** (229–589)
  Wu, Eastern Jin, Liu-Song, Qi, Liang, and Chen
**Western Jin** (265–316)
**Eastern Jin** (317–420)
**Southern and Northern Dynasties** (420–589)

| **Southern Dynasties** | **Northern Dynasties** |
|---|---|
| Liu-Song (420–479) | Northern Wei (386–534) |
| Qi (479–502) | Eastern Wei (534–550) |
| Liang (502–557) | Western Wei (535–556) |
| Later Liang (555–587) | Northern Qi (550–577) |
| Chen (557–589) | Northern Zhou (557–581) |

| Sui (581–618) | Tujue (552–) | | | Koguryŏ (37 BC–) | Gaochang (497–) | Tuyuhun (329–) |
|---|---|---|---|---|---|---|
| | Eastern | | Western | | | |
| | Main | Abo branch | | | | |
| | | | | | Qu Qiangu 麴乾固 (561–601) | Kualü 夸呂 (540–591) |
| | | | | P'yŏngwŏn (559–590) | | |
| | | | | | | Shifu 世伏 (591–597) |
| | | | | | | Fuyun (597–635) |
| | | | | | Qu Boya (601–613) | |
| | | | | Yŏngyang (590–618) | | |
| | | | | | Qu ? (614–619) | |
| | | | Datou (576–603) | | | |
| | | | Tongyehu 統葉護 (617–628) | | | |
| | | | Duliu 都六 (603–605) | | | |
| | | | Shegui (605–617) | | | |
| | Tuobo (572–581) | | Chuluo (603–611)† | | | |
| | Shabolue (581–587) | Abo (581–587) | | | | |
| | Mohe 莫何 (587–588) | Nili (587–603) | | | | |
| | Dulan (588–599) | | | | | |
| Wendi (581–604) (Kaihuang; 581–600; | Bujia/Datou (599–603)* | | | | | |
| Renshou: 601–604 | Qimin (599–611) | | | | | |
| Yangdi (604–618) (Daye: 605–618) | Shibi (611–619) | | | | | |
| Gongdi (617–618) | | | | | | |
| **Tang** (618–907) | | | | | | |

*Datou declared himself Bujia qaghan in 599 and supposedly extended his power over entire Tujue territory.
† In 611, Chuluo submitted himself to Yangdi.

# Acknowledgments

First and foremost, I owe an intellectual debt to scholars of Sui studies. Especially worth mention are Yamazaki Hiroshi and Arthur Wright. Yamazaki's work on Sui Buddhism and bureaucracy has laid a solid groundwork for the study of Sui religion and officialdom. Wright's seminal article on Yangdi's personality inspired me to explore the story of Yangdi and his reign.

In the course of writing this book, I have received assistance from friends and colleagues. I am particularly thankful to Professor Gao Mingshi of National Taiwan University who sent me his recent books on traditional Chinese and Sui-Tang education; and to Professor Kominami Ichirō of Kyoto University who was kind enough to provide me with copies of Japanese articles that are hard to come by in the States but essential for my studies. I am indebted to George Demetrakopoulos of Western Michigan University and Robert Mory of the University of Michigan for their valuable suggestions on the earlier versions of the manuscript.

I greatly appreciate the support I have received from Western Michigan University, its College of Arts and Sciences, and in particular, its History Department, which provided me with funding for research through its Burnham-Macmillan Fund.

I am grateful to Ms. Nancy Ellegate, acquisition editor at SUNY Press, for the effective and professional way she handled my manuscript, and to the two anonymous reviewers for their insights and encouragement, which made its publication possible.

Lastly, I wish to thank my wife, Li Xiaoqing, for her consistent support.

# Part I

---

## From Prince to Sovereign

# Introduction

When Emperor Yang, commonly known in the sources as Yangdi 煬帝, ascended the throne of the Sui in 604, he held dominion over a vast, populous, and prosperous Chinese empire. The Sui dynasty (581–618), in which Yangdi grew up and spent his entire adult life, was a dynamic, transitional period, and one of pivotal importance. Since scholars past and present have often treated it as a prelude to its successor dynasty, the Tang (618–907), it is a very underrated period in Chinese history.

Indeed, the Sui, a comparatively ephemeral regime, seems to pale before the splendor of the Tang, the pinnacle of medieval Chinese civilization.[1] Enduring for almost three centuries, the Tang extended its political power and military might into Central Asia, the Korean Peninsula, and northern Vietnam. Considered by many as China's golden age of medieval arts and literature, the Tang is notable for its unsurpassed poetic tradition and its spectacular achievements in calligraphy, architecture, painting, and craftsmanship. Occupying a crucial position in the history of philosophy and religion, the Tang heralded the renaissance of Confucianism, and witnessed epochal developments in both Buddhism and Daoism. Symbolic of the material achievement of the Tang age, its capital Chang'an, at the center of an extensive urban network, was, at its height, the most populous and civilized metropolis on the face of the earth, and a magnet for traders, pilgrims, and students from as far as Sasanian Persia, Sogdiana, Korea, and Japan.

Nonetheless, the brilliance of the Tang civilization was essentially founded on the bedrock of the Sui legacy. The most significant Sui contributions to that dynasty were the sophisticated political, economic, legal, and military institutions. At the center of the Tang political system were the top echelon Three Departments—the Department of State Affairs with its Six Boards, the Secretariat, and the Chancellery—as well as the second-tier central government agencies of the Nine Courts. All these were adopted in toto from the Sui. The local administration of the Tang was a two-tier, prefecture-county system, which had evolved during the Sui when the first Sui sovereign, Wendi, streamlined the cumbersome three-tier system of the prior regimes. The pre-

3

dominant land-tenure system during the first half of the Tang was that of equal fields, which the Tang took over from the Sui with little alteration. Among extant primary sources, the *Tang Code* stands out as a milestone in Chinese legal history. Yet the Tang legal system as recorded in the *Tang Code* was modeled on its Sui predecessor. Furthermore, the organization of the military forces in the first half of the Tang was characterized by a unique garrison system, known as *fubing* 府兵 (militia), a system that had its roots in the Sui and earlier dynasties. The great metropolises of the Tang—Chang'an and Luoyang—and the great transportation network—the Grand Canal—were among the most valuable tangible assets the Sui bequeathed to posterity. Built at tremendous cost to the Sui, they contributed substantially to the flourishing of the Tang economy.[2]

Whatever sense of indebtedness the Tang may have owed its predecessor, the Sui, it is usually given (if at all) to the first Sui emperor, Wendi, to the point of completely ignoring the contributions of his successor, Yangdi. Nevertheless, as the second Sui ruler, Yangdi played a significant part in shaping the Sui legacy the Tang inherited. After being on the throne for more than thirteen years, Yangdi died a violent death at the hands of his minions in Jiangdu 江都 (Yangzhou, Jiangsu) in the third month of 618 as his mighty empire crumbled. Traditionally considered a tyrant, Yangdi was blamed for the decline of the Sui empire's fortunes and the eventual fall of the dynasty. Ascribing his incompetent rule to his debaucheries and extravagances, scholars are inclined to compare Yangdi to the most notorious sovereigns in Chinese history, such as King Jie 桀 of Xia and King Zhou[a] 紂 of Shang.[3] But unlike King Jie and King Zhou[a], Yangdi, for all his vices, can lay claim to a number of great achievements.

In spite of his enormous impact on the Sui, Yangdi has received woefully inadequate attention in terms of biographical coverage in primary literature. To be sure, biography figures very prominently in the rich tradition of Chinese historiography.[4] But the standard histories, the mainstay of that tradition, in most cases, only summarily chronicle the life of the sovereign in his *benji* 本紀 or "basic annals." As a substitute for imperial biography, the main function of the basic annals in medieval times was to provide a chronological framework for the entire period of the reign in question. Consequently, as expected, Yangdi has no proper biographical entry in the standard history for the period, *Sui shu* (History of the Sui dynasty).

Serious modern studies of Yangdi and his reign are surprisingly few. The most influential work in English on the Sui period is a book-length study by Arthur Wright of Yale, the leading Sui scholar in the West: *The Sui Dynasty: The Unification of China, A.D. 581–617*, which provides the basis for the Sui chapters in volume three of *The Cambridge History of China*. While it is a brilliant, lucid survey of Sui history, with many profound insights, it gives relatively little coverage to the second emperor. Moreover, as is pointed out by its Japanese translators, Nunome and his collaborator, the book suffers from numerous factual errors and textual misinterpretations.[5]

In China, the small number of modern biographies on Yangdi reflect the diverse views of the Yangdi scholarship. Some of them join traditional scholars in chastising Yangdi as a tyrant while others endeavor to rehabilitate him. For example, the short biography by Han Guopan of Xiamen University, a leading Sui-Tang historian in China, essentially accepts the traditional condemnatory view.[6] Much of its analysis is couched in the Marxist terminology of class struggle due to the ideological limitations of the 1950s. At the other end of the spectrum is the revisionist biographical study by Hu Ji. As an apologist work, it is driven by a mission to set the record straight for the "great tyrant," rather than the need for impartial reassessment.[7] A third approach is found in the recent biography by Yuan Gang, which is aimed at the general readership, and attempts to present a more balanced view.[8]

In Japan, Yangdi, as the object of biographical research, has attracted little serious academic attention. Perhaps the best-known Japanese work on Yangdi is *Zui Yōdai* written by the leading sinologist Miyazaki Ichisada. Though intended as popular history, it contains a number of perceptive insights, especially regarding the rise of the Yang house. The lack of the academic apparatus is its main drawback, which makes further pursuit of various topics in the book difficult.[9] Another Japanese work worthy of note is the book on the Sui-Tang transition by Numome Chōfū, a top scholar of Sui-Tang China. Although its coverage of Yangdi is brief, it is more academically oriented, and offers a long-term perspective through a comparative study of Yangdi and Tang Taizong 太宗.[10]

While academic interest in Yangdi persists, a serious monographic study of Yangdi and his reign based on both primary and secondary literatures has yet to be written. This book represents an attempt to fill that lacuna. In view of the scant attention given to Yangdi as a biographical subject in modern and traditional literatures, it is essential to reconstruct his life with an aim to revealing his personality. Since Yangdi is inseparable from the Sui empire he reigned over, and vice versa, it is crucial to closely examine his impact on and interaction with the world around him—the political, economic, military, religious, and diplomatic aspects of a fascinating but poorly understood age of medieval China. Consequently, this book adopts a hybrid approach, one which focuses on the story of Yangdi as much as on the age he lived in.

In this study, I avail myself of all the modern works cited above, in addition to other secondary studies on Yangdi and in related fields in the Chinese, Japanese, and Western languages. But the main focus of my research is on early traditional sources that contain abundant primary information, notably, the *Sui shu* and the *Zizhi tongjian* (Comprehensive mirror for aid in government). As the standard history of the Sui, the *Sui shu* constitutes the most important source for Yangdi studies. Its three component parts—the basic annals, biographies, and treatises—all contain vital information relating to Yangdi and his reign.[11] The *Sui shu* project was first proposed to the Tang court in 621 by Linghu Defen 令狐德棻, a court official who had witnessed the tumultuous Sui era of Daye and the fall of the Sui dynasty. In the following year, court historians were commissioned to compile the *Sui shu* together with the histories of five other pre-Tang dynasties, namely, the Northern Wei, Northern Zhou, Liang, Northern Qi, and Chen. In his edict on the project, Gaozu 高祖 (Li Yuan; r. 618–626) not only gives his endorsement, but also underscores the didactic function of official historiography: to "penalize the wicked and encourage the kindhearted, to learn a great deal about the past and use it as a mirror for the future."[12] This emphasis on didacticism is rooted in an age-long historiographical tradition dating back to the times of the *Chunqiu* 春秋 (Spring and Autumn annals). But within the same tradition, didacticism is balanced by another characteristic that values professional honesty. So Gaozu concludes his edict thus: "[Those assigned to write the histories] must meticulously verify their findings, make extensive references to the past sources, aim at creating the definitive work, and write with candor."[13] This latter characteristic is brought into focus by the progenitor of the standard histories, Sima Qian 司馬遷 of the Western Han, who was applauded by later historians for his courage to comment candidly and unflatteringly on the Han court.[14]

Failing to come to fruition under Gaozu, the *Sui shu* project was revived in very much the same spirit under Taizong (r. 626–649), and its basic annals and biography chapters were brought to completion under the general editorship of Wei Zheng 魏徵. Its ten treatises (*zhi* 志) in thirty *juan*, popularly known as *Wudai shi zhi* 五代史志 (Treatises of the Five Dynasties), were completed and incorporated into the *Sui shu* much later, after the death of Wei Zheng and Taizong.[15]

Since the *Sui shu* was written by a number of scholars over a long period of time, discrepancies are unavoidable. The historians' comment sections, appended to basic annals and biography chapters, often carry strong moral overtones. Their criticisms of Yangdi's deviant behavior in hyperbolic language reflect Wei's penchant to portray Yangdi in the most negative light, in order to justify his overthrow and to caution the ruling emperor Tang Taizong against following the same road. However, these critical remarks are not always congruous with the contents of the chapters themselves, which are often written with greater detachment. Of the ten treatises, those on food and money (*shihuo* 食貨), and punishment and law (*xingfa* 刑法), are generally more condemnatory of Yangdi than other treatises and the basic annals, showing the authors' bias and the editor's apparent failure to reconcile inconsistencies among chapters. The *Sui shu* is further disadvantaged by the loss of a great part of the Sui archives and the Sui Imperial Library. Moreover, official historiography in general has its own limitations. Not only is the process of deciding what to include and what to exclude in a standard history often tainted by personal and institutional prejudices, the numerical data cited could be inaccurate. Government censuses inevitably underestimated population sizes due to large numbers of unregistered people. While figures on Sui troops tended to be closer to reality, those on foreign troops and rebel forces are less reliable.[16]

Although suffering from lack of uniformity of style and occasionally exaggerated commentary and other related blemishes, the *Sui shu*, on the whole, is regarded as one of the better written standard histories for the medieval period. The chief authors of the basic annals and biographies, Yan Shigu 顏師古 and Kong Yingda 孔穎達, both top Early Tang scholars, are noted for their extraordinary erudition. In spite of imperfections, the ten treatises are especially valued for their thematic coverage of the cultural, socioeconomic, and geopolitical aspects of a long span of five dynastic periods—Liang, Chen, Northern Qi, Northern Zhou, and Sui.[17]

Another standard history of interest, which contains a number of biographies of Sui personages and two Sui basic annals chapters, is the *Bei shi* (*BS*), (History of the Northern Dynasties) by Li Yanshou 李延壽, who was also involved in the writing of the ten treatises of the *Sui shu*. Relevant accounts in this work provide contexts of Sui events and can help verify *Sui shu* records. But the *Bei shi* is best used as a supplemental source, since its Sui records are often truncated versions of *Sui shu* accounts.[18]

The great annalist history, *Zizhi tongjian* (*ZZTJ*), completed under the direction of the Song scholar Sima Guang 司馬光, has extensive coverage of the Sui period. The greatest value of this monumental work lies in the fact that, although written even later than the Tang dynasty, its authors, Sima Guang et al., had access to a whole range of primary, traditional sources that are no longer extant. In spite of its didactic commentary, the *ZZTJ* is known for its attention to detail and superb scholarship, and is above all a reliable source of historical information.[19] However, since the most reliable primary source on court events—the court diary—was no longer available for the Daye 大業 period, the task Sima Guang and his associates set themselves of reconstructing Yangdi's life and reign became much more difficult and error-prone.[20] They had to resort to private or miscellaneous histories for primary information, which sometimes contained exaggerations. In view of this, I give particular attention to verifying the veracity of those spurious-looking accounts in the *ZZTJ* by comparing them to other sources.

I also quote (not infrequently) a number of other traditional sources, for example, the *Tong dian*, for information on institutions; pre-Sui standard histories, such as the *Wei shu, Zhou shu, Bei Qi shu, Song shu, Nan Qi shu, Liang shu*, and *Chen shu*, for records on the period of division;[21] and Buddhist sources such as the *Fozu tongji* and *Guoqing bailu*, and Daoist sources such as the *Yunji qiqian*, for coverage of religious events and influences. Since these sources are much less significant to the present study, they will not be treated in detail here. Instead, they will be selectively discussed in terms of authorship and style, in individual chapters when the appropriate occasion arises.[22]

Other sources of primary information are archaeological finds. Due to its relatively short duration, the Sui dynasty never attracts much attention from archaeologists. Only occasionally has archaeological information become available for elucidating the socioeconomic history of the Sui dynasty. For instance, the long-term archaeological investigations of Sui-Tang Chang'an and Luoyang provide more accurate layouts of these two capital cities, with which Yangdi was closely associated. Sui and Early Tang epitaphs and other epigraphic materials, either preserved in antiquarian collections or archaeologically excavated, are often invaluable for verifying and complementing the standard histories.[23] The survey of the Sui Grand Canal conducted by Chinese scholars in the early 1980s is a worthy endeavor to explore the historic routes of that transportation network constructed under Yangdi. The economic documents discovered from Turfan and Dunhuang offer a starting point from which to reconstruct the economic life of the Sui.[24] But archaeology does have its own intrinsic limitations. So far, archaeology has not been very helpful in providing evidence of political changes during the relatively short-lived Sui dynasty. Even excavated textual information is extremely limited in its usefulness for studying the age in question. The Turfan documents, indispensable for research on the Tang local economy, offer no direct information on the Sui. Epitaphs, whether from Sui-Tang times or earlier, are similarly constructed eulogies that usually start with the genealogy of the deceased, followed by a chronological account of his bureaucratic career, and end with elegiac remarks. Useful as they are for verifying official titles, dates, and localities, they add virtually no information to the less glamorous side of the deceased. In view of this and of my emphasis on documentary research, archaeology assumes only a minor role in the current investigation.[25]

The present book is composed primarily of two parts. Following a chapter on the Yang family and the rise of Yangdi's father, Part I provides a narrative account of the life of Yangdi: from child to prince, and from heir apparent to emperor. Part II adopts a multifaceted approach to Yangdi and his reign from the perspectives of such diverse aspects as the pursuit of construction projects, the structure of the civil bureaucracy, and the military administration, as well as matters dealing with education, ritual, law, religion, economic policy, and relations with neighboring powers. The book ends with an epilogue that analyzes Yangdi's place in history and reassesses his life, times, and legacy.

# 1

## The Making of a Crown Prince

Yangdi, né Yang Guang 楊廣, was born in 569 into a powerful aristocratic clan of North China.[1] The sources trace its origin to Yang Zhen 楊震, a most illustrious figure of the Eastern Han, from Huayin 華陰 in Hongnong 弘農 (in Shaanxi). But information on the ancestors after Zhen is murky until the times of Yangdi's grandfather, Yang Zhong 楊忠, who, according to some accounts in the standard histories, once made his home in Wuchuan 武川 Garrison (west of Wuchuan, central Inner Mongolia). As one of the six strategic frontier outposts known as the Six Garrisons in Northern Wei times, Wuchuan is considered the crucial geographical element for the all-powerful Wuchuan clique in Western Wei times. But the traditional genealogy of the Yangs contains erroneous, perhaps fictitious information, and the Yangs' connections with Huayin and Wuchuan are challenged by some scholars. Nevertheless, what matters most is not so much the verifiability of such connections as the assumption the Yangs held of them, and the perception it created. It is in that sense that I treat Huayin as the native place of the Yangs where they located their choronym, and Wuchuan as a key geographical name Yang Zhong was identified with.[2]

Known in his youth for his poise and intelligence, Yangdi was the favorite son of the Yang family. He was endowed with a remarkable talent for literature and loved the pursuit of knowledge. He could have easily succeeded as a career official at court. But the course of events in his lifetime led him to a more important role in history.[3]

The age he lived in was one of extraordinary transformation. Following the breakup of the Han empire in the late second and early third centuries, China had been in a continual state of political fragmentation, with the

9

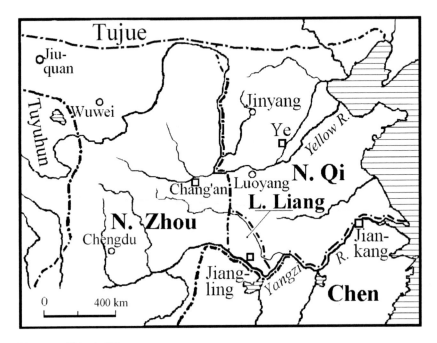

MAP 1.1   China in 572

exception of a brief period of reunification under the Western Jin during
280–311. By the time of Yangdi's birth, China proper was governed by four
separate political entities. Yangdi's home state, the Northern Zhou, was based
in Chang'an (Xi'an, Shaanxi). To its east was the Northern Qi, based in Ye 鄴
(southwest of Linzhang, Hebei, and south of Beijing). To the south was the
Chen, based in Jiankang 建康 (Nanjing). Sandwiched between was the
lesser power of Later Liang 後梁, based in Jiangling 江陵 (Jingzhouqu,
Hubei), a client state of the Northern Zhou with some degree of autonomy.
In the vast steppes of present-day Inner and Outer Mongolia north of the
Northern Zhou and the Northern Qi dwelt the Tujue (Turks), a nomadic
people who often came south to raid the settled communities of North China
(map 1.1). Starting in the late 570s, however, a unifying process was underway. It was Wendi, Yangdi's father, who was instrumental in setting in motion
that process and brought it to completion. Having played a major role in the
577 annexation of the Northern Qi, he officially usurped imperial power to
ascend the throne as the founding sovereign of the Sui dynasty in the second
month of 581.[4]

## Young Prince

While pursuing his dream of unification and conquest, Wendi 文帝 (Yang Jian 楊堅) appointed his sons, including Yangdi, to key administrative and military positions, and conferred upon them princely titles, in an attempt to strengthen the power base of the Yang family. As a young prince, Yangdi, under the tutelage of his appointed mentors, would come of age and gain his initial political experience.

Born into wealth and power, princes were among the most privileged members of society. Concerned that too much material comfort would hinder the development of character and competence, their fathers would deliberately resort to harsh ways to discipline them. In accord with tradition, they often required imperial princes, as part of their upbringing, to reside in principalities or places of assignment far away from the capital. This was intended to toughen them up for survival in the real world in the future, and to shore up imperial authority in the provinces. Wendi happened to be one of the most exacting sovereigns in history who strongly believed that physical discipline and austerity were preconditions for bringing up worthy offspring. Thus Yangdi, though favored by his parents because of his handsome looks and quick intellect, was posted away from the capital as early as 580. It is likely that he was at that time created commandery duke of Yanmen 雁門 thanks to his father's meritorious deeds. Many years later Yangdi still recalled the crucial moment in his life when he was about to be separated from his parents:

> The late emperor (Wendi) set me up in the west audience hall, then ordered Gao Jiong 高熲, Yu Qingze 虞慶則, Yuan Min 元旻 et al. to send Wang Zixiang 王子相 (Shao 韶) to me from the court. At that time, [Wendi] admonished me, "Since you are young and inexperienced, [I] have ordered Zixiang to mentor you. Matters big and small can all be trusted to him. [You] must not get close to mean fellows, nor must you distance yourself from Zixiang. If [you] follow my words, [you] will render a good service to your country, and establish your reputation. If you do not follow my words, [you will] ruin your dukedom (the area he was in charge of) and yourself in no time.

With these stern warnings, Wendi sent his favorite son far away to his place of assignment at the tender age of twelve (eleven). In 581, on the occasion of the founding of the Sui, Wendi upgraded his son's status to that of imperial prince, placing on his shoulders much weightier administrative posts—Bingzhou 并州 area commander and president of the Branch Department of State Affairs of Hebei Circuit. At that time, Yangdi was thirteen (twelve).[5]

Because Yangdi was still a minor, mentoring officials like Wang Shao were constantly on hand to groom and edify him. Once, when Wang was away on a mission, Yangdi created miniature ponds and set up three artificial hills in his princely residence. On his return, Wang locked himself up in chains to remonstrate with Yangdi, who was forced to immediately stop the project. To Yangdi, the kind of prohibitive surrogate parenting provided by the likes of Wang Shao could only add to the trauma of having to live away from his parents at a young age for a considerable length of time. Furthermore, the long distances that separated the princes from their parents offered no physical protection from parental furor. They still had to face severe punishment for their transgressions. Wendi deprived his third son Yang Jun 楊俊 of all his official posts as a consequence of his wasteful and indulgent behavior. When General Yang Su 楊素 tried to persuade Wendi to reconsider his decision, he answered, "I am the father of five sons. If I should follow your suggestion, then why don't we create a different set of legal codes just for the sons of the Son of Heaven?" Wendi took even harsher punitive measures against his fourth son, Yang Xiu 楊秀, for his extravagances and his violation of accepted ritual standards.[6]

From Wendi's severe treatment of Yang Jun and Yang Xiu and from other evidence we can infer that Wendi habitually enforced strict discipline among his sons. Without doubt, Yangdi, like his brothers, lived in constant fear of the imperial wrath. Apparently, Yangdi understood very well that, for the sake of self-preservation, he should suppress his desires for luxury and women. Later, the prospect of becoming heir apparent provided the added incentive to maintain his image as a dutiful, monogamous son living a simple life, an image that would prove decisive in helping him capture the throne.

## THE CONQUEST OF THE LATER LIANG

The first significant political event that took place during Yangdi's early life as an imperial prince was the conquest of the Later Liang, brought about by his father Wendi. The Jiangling area in the middle reaches of the Yangzi had been home to the semi-independent state from 555. Although the Later Liang had been subjected to varying degrees of control by the Western Wei and Northern Zhou, it maintained its autonomy. After the founding of the Sui, Wendi selected a princess of the ruling Liang sovereign, Xiao Kui 蕭巋, as Yangdi's consort. Wendi also thought of arranging a marriage between Yangdi's sister, Princess of Lanling 蘭陵, and Xiao Kui's son, Xiao Yang 蕭瑒, although it did not come to pass. The purpose of Yangdi's marriage was, among other things, to infuse Southern aristocratic blood into the Yang lineage. In the light of the intermarriage between the two families, Yangdi's mother Empress

Wenxian 文獻 urged Wendi to relax his vigilance against the Xiao clan. Consequently, Wendi abolished Jiangling Area Command.

The Later Liang began to enjoy greatly increased independence. But politically, Xiao Kui still had to maintain close ties with the Sui. His position can be understood by the treatment he received during his visit to the Sui capital Daxingcheng 大興城 in 584. At a suburban ritual in his honor, he was allowed to wear the crown of celestial connection and the gauze robe in dark purple—the typical regalia for a sovereign. But once he was inside the newly built Daxing Basilica 大興殿, the central structure of the Palace City, for an audience with Wendi, he was placed in a subordinate position, facing north. It is recorded, however, that sovereign and vassal made obeisances together. The Later Liang sovereign's position resembled that of a vassal king, who, despite his dynastic title, acknowledged the overlordship of the Sui sovereign.[7]

In 585, Xiao Kui died. As Wendi was getting closer to executing his plans of a Southern invasion against the Chen, he began to reassess the relationship with the Later Liang. The Liang constituted a key strategic area if a coordinated attack on the Chen was to be launched. Now that Kui's successor Xiao Cong 蕭琮 took power, Wendi was concerned about the Liang's loyalty. So Wendi summoned Xiao Cen 蕭岑, the uncle of the Liang sovereign, to the Sui court where he was kept hostage, while reviving Jiangling Area Command to closely monitor developments in the Later Liang. If the abolition of the area command in 582 was a gesture of goodwill to Xiao Kui, its revival in 585 signified Sui's distrust of his son, Xiao Cong.

In the eighth month of 587, at Wendi's request, Xiao Cong traveled to Daxingcheng for a visit while Wendi dispatched an army under General Cui Hongdu 崔弘度 to the Later Liang area. Wendi's blatant show of force raised fears among the Liang aristocracy, who led a population of more than one hundred thousand to escape to the Chen. Using this as a pretext, Wendi ordered his troops to occupy Jiangling. The Later Liang, a sovereign state for thirty-two years, ceased to exist. With the Liang region firmly under his control, Wendi sped up the preparation for the Southern invasion, an operation in which Yangdi was to play a decisive role.[8]

Wendi had had his sights on the Southern regime of Chen as early as 581 when he appointed two field marshals to lead a military operation against the Chen. But it did not go well. In early 582, the Chen returned Hushu 胡墅 (southwest of Luhe, Jiangsu) north of the Yangzi, a city seized from the Sui a year before, in exchange for an armistice. The death of the Chen sovereign Xuandi 宣帝 (r. 569–582) thereafter provided the Sui with an excuse to call off the whole operation. However, Wendi never gave up his hope of unification. In his 585 letter to Xiao Cong, Wendi subtly implied that, despite the appearance of a cordial relationship between Sui and Chen, their border areas had yet to be pacified. By 587, it had become clear that the Southern invasion was now Wendi's top priority.[9]

Looking for the right man to lead the Sui expedition, Wendi turned his attention to Yangdi. In spite of his young age, Yangdi seemed to have already gained much administrative experience, having served in a number of key military and civil posts. He was appointed to his first major military position as early as the second month of 581, as Bingzhou area commander (*zongguan* 總管), while receiving the prestigious title, pillar of state (*zhuguo* 柱國), which was later upgraded to superior pillar of state (*shang zhuguo* 上柱國), the highest prestige title in the nation.

The term *zongguan* was a legacy of the Northern Zhou dynasty. It referred to a kind of local military district with some functions of a civil administration, as well as to its commanding officer. Under normal circumstances, a *zongguan* corresponded to a *zhou* 州 (prefecture) in area. However, three *zongguan* (area commands)—Luozhou 洛州 (mainly in present-day Henan), Bingzhou 并州 (in present-day Shanxi), and Yizhou 益州 (the Southwest)—functioned as super area commands; each of them took charge of dozens of area commands. In 582, Wendi replaced these super area commands with the circuit (*dao* 道), with its head office known as the Branch of the Department of State Affairs (*xingtai sheng* 行臺省), and converted Luozhou 洛州, Bingzhou, and Yizhou [Super] Area Commands into Henan 河南, Hebei 河北, and Xinan 西南 Circuits, respectively.

In 583, Wendi converted Xinan Circuit to Yizhou Area Command and abolished Henan Circuit. Prior to the annexation of the Later Liang, in 585, Jiangling 江陵 Area Command was revived. In 588, Huainan 淮南 Circuit was created with its core area in Anhui south of the Huai River. With the conquest of the South in 589, Wendi abolished Huainan Circuit, created Yangzhou 揚州 Area Command, and converted Hebei Circuit back to Bingzhou Area Command. By then, the system of the four super area commands, known also as *da zongguan* 大總管 (superior area commands) was in place. These four superior area commands—Bingzhou (North), Yizhou (Sichuan), Jiangling (later called Jingzhou 荊州) (the middle Yangzi valley), and Yangzhou 揚州 (South)—covered essentially all key areas outside the capital region in China proper. Since most of these superior area commands were placed under the control of Sui imperial princes, it seems that the rationale for setting them up was to greatly extend the Yang clan's control over the provinces while enhancing the military powers of these princes.[10]

Yangdi was the top administrator of the Bingzhou area whether as [superior] area commander of Bingzhou, or president of the Branch Department of State Affairs of Hebei 河北 Circuit (*dao*) until 586 when he officially reached maturity at eighteen (seventeen). In the tenth month of that year, he was appointed to the critical post of governor of Capital Prefecture (Yongzhou *mu*

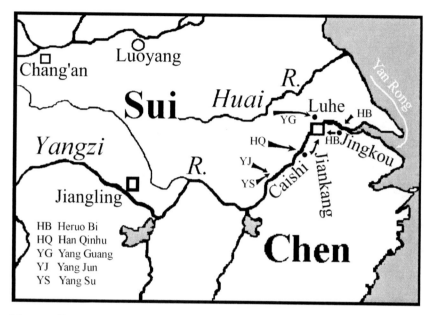

MAP 1.2 The conquest of Chen, 589

雍州牧). In 588, as the war against the Chen was imminent, he was appointed leader of the newly created Huainan Circuit, obviously to prepare for an administrative takeover of Chen territory.

Later in the same year, Yangdi was put in charge of the Southern expedition. Three men were appointed field marshals to lead the invasion—Yangdi, his younger brother Yang Jun, and the veteran general Yang Su. But Yangdi was made unambiguously the commander-in-chief of the Sui army. Now at age twenty (nineteen), he found himself in command of the largest military force ever gathered under the Sui, an army half a million strong, and the best field commanders in the country, including Han Qinhu 韓擒虎, Heruo Bi 賀若弼, Wang Shiji 王世積, and Yan Rong 燕榮 (map 1.2).[11]

## THE SOUTHERN EXPEDITION

To unite China proper by conquering the rival regime south of the Yangzi was Wendi's main strategic goal. Wendi justified his action by what he believed to be his moral authority. He once said to Gao Jiong, "As the parent of the masses, how can I fail to save them just because we are separated by a narrow band of water?" Prior to the Southern advance of the Sui expeditionary forces, Wendi

issued a denunciatory edict against the Chen regime, in which he characterized the Chen sovereign as an evil ruler who committed murders, oppressed
his people, forced women into court service, and squandered money on lavish
palatial projects.[12]

In synchronization with his father's propaganda campaign, Yangdi issued
his own denunciative document against the Chen.[13] Compared with his
father's official edict, Yangdi's piece took the less formal form of a personal
letter. As someone who prided himself on his literary talent and achievement,
Yangdi may well have personally penned the document.

Both documents served the purpose of providing justification for the
Southern invasion. Yet they were distinctly different from each other. Wendi's
was a call to arms issued to his generals, in an attempt to thoroughly discredit
the Chen sovereign Chen Shubao 陳叔寶 through ad hominem attacks while
boosting the morale of the Sui army. Yangdi's piece was addressed to Chen
generals and ranking officials, especially, Chief Minister Jiang Zong 江總, one
of the most respected among them. It was thus much less personal and never
mentioned Chen Shubao by name.

Intended for different audiences, these two documents showed variations
in style and content. Wendi's was more down-to-earth, going little beyond a
pro forma enumeration of the Chen sovereign's vices. Yangdi's, apart from
denouncing the alleged crimes committed by the illegitimate sovereign,
stresses the inevitability of destiny, the inauspicious portents for the Chen, and
the vast strategic and military superiority of the Sui army. Overall, Yangdi not
only brought into focus certain supernatural elements, but also made his arguments logically.

The fact that Yangdi was allowed to write this denunciatory document as
a companion piece to that of his father seems to herald the significant role
Yangdi would play in the Southern expedition, which provided him with an
opportunity to gain political and military experience.

As Yangdi got closer to the center of power, inevitably he began to come
into close contact with Wendi's right hand man, Gao Jiong, who became
increasingly involved in both his political career and personal life. The Tang
historian Du You 杜佑 regards Gao Jiong as one of the Six Sages since antiquity, whose crucial advice to their sovereigns was instrumental in helping
them achieve political dominance. Gao Jiong was closely associated with the
Wuchuan group, the military elite of the Western Wei which claimed among
its members Yang Zhong, Wendi's father, and Dugu Xin, a man of extraordinary political prominence in sixth century China. Gao Jiong's father Gao Bin
高賓 served as a close adviser to Dugu Xin 獨孤信. Wendi married Dugu
Xin's daughter (Empress Wenxian), who had close personal ties with the Gao
family. At court, Wendi was on intimate terms with Jiong, addressing him as
"Dugu," a name shared by his own wife and bestowed upon the Gao family

by Dugu Xin. So thanks to his familial and political connections that went back to earlier generations, Gao Jiong was never considered an outsider by Wendi. In fact, Wendi had an unconditional trust in him, placing him in charge of some of the most important tasks during his reign. On Wendi's orders, Gao Jiong headed a group of high court officials to plan and build the new capital, Daxingcheng, and Wendi acted upon his advice to weaken the Chen's defenses.[14] At the time of the Southern expedition, Wendi appointed Gao Jiong aide-de-camp to the marshal (*yuanshuai zhangshi* 元帥長史) to assist Yangdi in military matters. But key strategic planning of the three armies (i.e., the expeditionary forces) all emanated from Gao Jiong. Clearly, although Yangdi was the de jure commander of the Southern expedition, Gao Jiong was its de facto commander.

The invasion was finally launched in the first month of 589. It proceeded smoothly. Soon the Sui forces stormed into Jiankang, the Chen capital, and captured Chen Shubao, who was hiding in a well within the palace in the company of his favorite concubines. One of these was named Zhang Lihua 張麗華. Bewitchingly charming, she was believed to be the femme fatale who had led the Chen sovereign astray. Defying an order from Yangdi, Gao Jiong had her summarily executed.[15] This is not to suggest that during the Southern expedition Yangdi was merely a figurehead. While there is not much record of his direct involvement in the military operation, once in Jiankang he did appear to be the man in charge. He was a fair-minded administrator, dispensing justice and restoring order, for which he was widely praised. It was on his orders that Gao Jiong and Pei Ju 裴矩, a court official who was to become Yangdi's chief adviser on foreign policy, took over the government archives of the Chen and sealed off its treasury.

In the fourth month of 589, a triumphant Yangdi returned to Daxingcheng. Wendi traveled to Lishan 驪山 in the eastern suburb to greet him and the victorious army under his command. An elaborate ceremony was held at the Ancestral Temple in the Imperial City to present the prisoners. Yangdi was awarded one of the most prestigious titles, defender-in-chief or *taiwei* 太尉. This must have been the proudest moment in his young life of about twenty-one (twenty) years. Proving equal to the organizational and administrative tasks assigned him, Yangdi impressed the rank and file, and won the complete confidence of the emperor. Above all, the expedition of 589 marked his rise as a major political figure at court.[16]

## SOUTHERN ASSIGNMENT

After the Southern expedition Yangdi went back north to continue his original post in Bingzhou, while his younger brother Yang Jun was put in charge

of the newly acquired Southern territory as commander of Yangzhou Superior Area Command. But the latter choice could not have been more inap-
propriate. A devout Buddhist, Jun was benevolent, forgiving, and loving. He
had once asked permission to become a monk. Wendi not only refused, but
ordered him to assist his brother Yangdi in the Southern expedition. Jun commanded a combined army and naval force of more than one hundred thousand but he refused to attack the Chen forces for fear of killing and harming
lives, regardless of General Cui Hongdu's urging. Fortunately for Jun, the
enemy forces surrendered anyway. A poor commander of troops, Yang Jun
turned out to be an equally disappointing peacetime administrator. Although
the Sui treated the surviving court nobles and ranking officials of the former
Chen well, maintaining order in their home territory was no easy task. In the
eleventh month of 590, numerous rebellions broke out, led by local rebel
leaders, such as Wang Wenjin 汪文進 and Gao Zhihui 高智慧. Before long,
the entire former Chen territory rose in arms against the central government.
The rebel armies, varying in size from several thousands to tens of thousands,
savagely attacked county offices and captured county magistrates, disembow-
eling them and consuming their flesh. The Sui court had to send in its most
decorated general, Yang Su, to suppress the rebellions. Unlike Yang Jun, who
abhorred killing, Yang Su, notorious for his cruelty, was a perfect match for
the rebels.[17]

After all the rebellions were put down, at the end of 590, Yang Jun was
ordered to change places with his elder brother, Yangdi. No doubt the decision was based on sound reasoning. Yangdi, who had served successfully as
commander-in-chief of the expeditionary army, was more likely to help consolidate central authority in the South and respond decisively to future disturbances. By now, Yangdi had not only come of age, but also had come to
admire Southern culture. He must have felt quite comfortable with the new
appointment.

It is highly likely that Yangdi's wife, Lady Xiao 蕭氏 (later Empress Xiao
蕭后), daughter of the Later Liang sovereign Xiao Kui, was at first the main
source of his Southern influence. Lady Xiao was born in a second month into
the Liang sovereign's family. According to a custom in the South, second-
month newborns were bad luck, and should not be raised. So her uncle Xiao
Ji 蕭岌 adopted her. Soon both her uncle and aunt died, and she was transferred into the custody of her uncle on the maternal side, Zhang Ke 張軻.
While living with the Zhang family, Lady Xiao experienced abject poverty.

When Wendi decided to select a Liang princess as Yangdi's bride, Lady
Xiao was the last on his mind. Divinations were conducted on all of Xiao
Kui's daughters. Since Lady Xiao was the only one whose results were auspicious, she was chosen. She descended from a genteel émigré family with ancestors hailing from Lanling, in present-day Shandong in the North. In their new

home territory in the South, the Xiaos of Lanling, as they came to be known, became one of the most influential aristocratic clans. When Wendi looked for a bride for his favorite son, aristocratic pedigree, which was Lady Xiao's most valuable asset, was a major consideration. Intermarriage with the first family of Jiangling served a strategic purpose as well. It would help to bring the Later Liang further into the orbit of the Sui.

Born of a Southern aristocratic family of Han descent, Lady Xiao was a woman of gentle disposition who never tried to interfere in her husband's affairs. Later, when she became aware of her husband's immoral conduct, she wrote a critical essay not to remonstrate with him, but to admonish herself. Over the years, Yangdi appreciated the companionship of this exemplary woman of the South, who was dutiful, supportive, and self-effacing, and praised her womanly virtues and self-cultivation. Bright and learned, she was known for her love for literary composition. As a devoted Buddhist, she shared a common religious background with her spouse and his family. Her virtuousness won the respect and favors of Wendi. One of the skills she mastered was divination. Her prediction about the fall of Crown Prince Yang Yong 楊勇 prompted Wendi to discuss, with Gao Jiong, Yong's deposition. Yong would have fallen from favor had it not been for Gao's persistent opposition.[18]

Her unassuming presence notwithstanding, Yangdi's wife must have exerted a strong cultural influence at home. Yangdi himself was a master of divination and physiognomy. But professional diviners were low in the social hierarchy and divination had never been included in the curriculum prescribed for Yangdi either as a young noble of the North or an imperial prince. In all likelihood, Yangdi learned his divinatory skills from Lady Xiao, who had been in close contact with the downtrodden and the poor while growing up in the South, where a strong belief in the supernatural was common. Yangdi also conversed fluently with his wife in the Wu dialect of the South. For a Northerner, a high level of competence in this dialect was no mean feat: It required years of early exposure. Yangdi probably picked it up at an early age from Lady Xiao, whose grandfather Xiao Cha 蕭詧 grew up at the court of Liang Wudi 梁武帝 in Jiankang, a Wu dialect area, before setting up his own court in Jiangling.

However much Yangdi may have been indebted to the popular culture of the South, it was Southern high culture, particularly its literature, that held the greatest attraction for him. The North and the South had followed quite different courses of development in literature since the Luoyang débâcle of the early fourth century. The Northern émigrés like the Xiaos of Lanling had brought their literary and artistic traditions south with them and laid the groundwork for the flowering of Southern literati culture, which reached a much higher level of sophistication than the North. Yangdi showed great admiration for the Southern literary tradition. His poetic style testifies to a strong influence of the palace style (*gongti* 宮體) of the Liang, which was dominant in Southern poetry. While it is not certain where Yangdi learned his Southern style, the long years he spent with Lady Xiao predisposed him to favor the Southern tradition. Lady Xiao's great-grandfather was the literary giant Xiao Tong 蕭統, the compiler of the authoritative literary collection *Wenxuan* 文選, whose brother Liang Jianwendi 梁簡文帝 (Xiang Gang 蕭綱, r. 549–551) was the progenitor of palace style poetry. Lady Xiao showed herself to be a worthy inheritor of the rich Southern literary tradition through her "Rhapsody on My Wishes" ("Shu zhi fu" 述志賦), the only piece of her writing that has survived.[19]

During his decade-long residence in the South as the highest military commander and civil administrator from the North, Yangdi's affection for the South only grew stronger. He apparently came to admire the architectural style of the Liang and Chen, and would adopt it in his luxuriously built new city Luoyang. Years later, when the courtiers Dou Wei 竇威 and Cui Zujun 崔祖濬 (Ze) unwittingly used disparaging expressions to describe the people of the South in their works commissioned by the court, Yangdi passionately defended Southern culture, calling the South the "famous metropolis under Heaven" where were gathered "learned erudites and accomplished Confucians" with unrivaled scholarship. Yangdi gave vent to his indignation by ordering a good flogging for both Dou and Cui. Eventually, the South became a determining factor in a number of crucial decisions he made after his accession: the building of the second capital; the completion of the Grand Canal; and the shifting of the center of his activity from the North to Jiangdu in the last years of his reign. But, despite his attachment to the South, Yangdi was destined to return to the capital in the North, where the stage was set for a succession battle.[20]

## The Koguryŏ Interlude

It is not known for sure when Yangdi began to covet the post of crown prince. But a key military event—Wendi's campaign against Koguryŏ in the Northeast—greatly improved his odds for appointment to that post. The main obstacle to the appointment, Gao Jiong, was to fall in the aftermath of the campaign.

Sui-Koguryŏ relations had been deteriorating after the 589 Sui conquest of the Chen. Fearing that a similar fate might befall him, King P'yŏngwŏn 平原 of Koguryŏ (r. 559–590) started to strengthen his country's defense and build up grain reserves. Thereupon, Wendi sent him an intimidating letter to express his displeasure, in which Wendi criticized Koguryŏ for expelling the

Mohe and encircling the Qidan 契丹 (Khitans), another nomadic people west of Koguryŏ with customs similar to those of the Mohe. The relations among these powers were marked by frequently shifting alliances, and at times all had tributary ties with the Sui court. Recent events, however, indicate that Koguryŏ was becoming a dominant power in Manchuria. Before Wendi took any military action, P'yŏngwŏn died, and his son Yŏngyang 嬰陽 (Wŏn 元) (r. 590–618) succeeded him. Through his envoy, Wendi conferred on Yŏngyang the hereditary title of commandery duke of Liaodong 遼東郡公, and at Yŏngyang's request Wendi appointed him king of Koguryŏ. But Yŏngyang was already the de facto sovereign of Koguryŏ even without Wendi's endorsement. By requesting a Sui investiture, Yŏngyang apparently intended to construct a harmonious relationship with the Sui. However, despite his professed desire for peace, in 598, Yŏngyang led an army of warriors from Mohe 靺鞨 (Malgal), a nomadic power north of Koguryŏ, to raid Liaoxi 遼西 (in southern Manchuria), which was within the boundaries of the Sui. What Yŏngyang hoped to gain in encroaching upon Sui territory is not clear, but his aggressive action triggered a violent response from Wendi, who not only invalidated Yŏngyang's official titles, but also threatened military action. Probably, because of its refusal to accept the major political change in East Asia politics—the Sui conquest of Chen—Koguryŏ had to face the military might of a united Chinese power.[21]

With almost unanimous support at court Wendi launched the Liaodong 遼東 campaign with a two-pronged attack on Koguryŏ in the sixth month of 598. A ground and naval force of three hundred thousand was mobilized under the command of Prince of Han 漢王 Yang Liang 楊諒 and Gao Jiong. Ironically, Gao Jiong had been the main opponent of the operation.

The movement of the Sui land forces was hampered by inadequate food supplies and widespread disease. The naval forces under the ex-Chen general Zhou Luohou 周羅睺 suffered crippling losses in heavy storms while attempting to cross the Yellow Sea from the Shandong Peninsula to invade Pyongyang. Between its departure in the sixth month and its humiliating retreat in the ninth, the Sui expeditionary army lost 80–90 percent of its men. The failure of the campaign must have left an indelible mark on the mind of Yangdi. A decade later, it would provide him with a key rationale for starting his own campaign of conquest against Koguryŏ.[22]

Meanwhile, the campaign, in conjunction with other developments, sowed the seeds of dissension between Yang Liang and Gao Jiong. This led to an unexpected outcome: the downfall of Gao Jiong himself. The irony is that although the Yang Liang-Gao Jiong conflict resulted in the latter's removal and paved the way for Yangdi's rise, Yang Liang himself later became Yangdi's most dangerous enemy.

## THE SUCCESSION CONTROVERSY

Until the tenth month of 600, Yang Yong stood directly in the way of Yangdi's career path. The rivalry between these Yang brothers evolved into a life and death struggle that over time led to Yong's downfall. But the undoing of Yong was a long and complex process that resulted from the interplay of a number of factors: Yangdi's cunning maneuvering; Empress Wenxian's petty jealousy; General Yang Su's denigration; Wendi's paranoiac suspicion; and Yang Yong's own recklessness.

Wendi's decision to select Yang Yong as crown prince was based on careful considerations. Like his younger brother Yangdi, Yang Yong was known for his love of learning. Moreover, he was generous, benevolent, simple, and honest. Wendi began to groom him for the position very early. As soon as Wendi assumed regency over the Northern Zhou sovereign, he assigned Yang Yong to govern the former Northern Qi area. After the founding of the Sui, Wendi intentionally allowed him to get involved in major decisions on political and military affairs of the state. When Yang Yong offered his critical suggestions, Wendi always listened carefully and often acted upon them. The blood bond that existed between Yong and his brothers—all of whom were born by the same mother—seemed to prevent the brothers from challenging his position. The same bond would oblige Yong to treat his brothers decently after their parents were gone.[23]

But Wendi's trust in the crown prince began to erode. It started with a minor event that roused Wendi's suspicion. At the time of a winter solstice, court officials had an audience (*chao* 朝) with the crown prince. For Wendi, *chao* was an exclusive term reserved for the sovereign. In the case of the crown prince, the proper term should have been *he* 賀 (to congratulate). What Yang Yong had done was a breach of the ritual code and a transgression against imperial authority. In a separate event, Wendi ordered a select number of officers of the Guards of the Crown Prince's Residence (*zongwei* 宗衛) to be transferred to the Palace City, and Gao Jiong, whose son was married to Yang Yong's daughter, responded by expressing concern that the security of the Eastern Palace, the crown prince's residence, might be compromised. Wendi was furious because he regarded the Eastern Palace as a competing center of power that potentially posed a threat to the Palace City, his own residence.

The process of Yang Yong's downfall accelerated when he fell out of favor with his mother, Empress Wenxian. Of Northern non-Han extraction, she was strong-willed, meddlesome, and domineering. As befitted her role as the family matron, she had arranged the marriage between Yang Yong and Lady Yuan 元氏. But, much to the chagrin of the jealous empress, Yang Yong kept a large number of concubines, and was particularly infatuated with one of them, Lady Yun 雲氏. After Lady Yuan's death, Yun began to take her place, a practice not only frowned upon in Northern culture but abhorred by Empress Wenxian, because of a deep-rooted prejudice against concubines in Northern society.[24]

Meanwhile Yangdi became aware of the rift between his mother and the crown prince, and it whetted his desire to replace his older brother. To win over his parents, Yangdi carefully cultivated his image as a monogamous husband. He allowed a few concubines in his entourage, but only cohabited with Lady Xiao. All the children he fathered by his concubines were given away. He would show up with simply dressed servants at court in carriages drawn by plainly harnessed horses. When he intimated to his mother that he had inadvertently incurred the wrath of the crown prince, he won her sympathy.

Yangdi's exemplary behavior, his deference and obedience to the empress, and the fear that the crown prince's brothers would be in harm's way after the empress died—all this provided the rationale Empress Wenxian needed to replace the crown prince. Yangdi, meanwhile, with the help of his underling Yuwen Shu, secured the crucial assistance of General Yang Su, whose opinion carried much weight with the emperor.[25]

Like Wendi, Yang Su was from a Huayin choronym. Despite his many literary accomplishments, Yang Su was best known as a soldier. His rise to fame began during the Northern Zhou campaign against the Northern Qi in 577. Now as vice president of the right of the Department of State Affairs, Yang Su was sharing power with the most influential figure at court, Gao Jiong, vice president of the left of the same department. For the tripartite alliance of Wenxian, Yangdi, and Yang Su to succeed, Gao Jiong, Yang Yong's perennial protector at court, had to be removed first. But the task was difficult if not impossible, so long as Wendi continued to trust him. Previously, officials attempting to malign Gao had incurred Wendi's wrath and lost their own positions. The opportunity came when Gao Jiong's wife died. At Empress Wenxian's urging, Wendi offered to find Gao Jiong another wife. Gao Jiong politely turned him down, citing his advanced age and devotion to Buddhism as two main reasons not to remarry. Soon, Gao Jiong's favorite concubine gave birth to a boy. Wendi became displeased with Gao when Empress Wenxian reminded him that by declining the imperial recommendation for a wife while keeping in semisecret his own concubine, Gao had deceived the emperor.

Then came the ill-fated Liaodong campaign of 598, in which Gao time and again overruled Yang Liang's suggestions. When the empress heard Yang Liang's grievances, she disclosed them to the emperor. In the process, Wendi went through a perception change regarding his most trusted minister. Now he became increasingly wary of the prospect of a Gao Jiong-Yang Yong alliance. Convinced of his criminal intent, Wendi punished Gao by stripping him of all his official positions. Later as more evidence of Gao's conspiracy was discovered, he was disenrolled and reduced to commoner status.[26]

Yangdi, residing in the South, normally visited the capital once a year, and was far away from the center of the action. Still he played his part in the tripartite alliance through bribing one of Yang Yong's favorite retainers in the Eastern Palace, Ji Wei 姬威, who secretly spied on the crown prince and reported directly to Yang Su.

Painfully aware of the steps his mother and brother had taken against him, Yong consulted an astrologer, who confirmed his fear, and predicted that the crown prince would be deposed. A panicky Yong had bronze and iron weapons melted down to make ritual paraphernalia, and set up a commoners' village in the Eastern Palace with humble structures and bare furnishings. He would visit the village every now and then, in the hope of counteracting the prediction. But these desperate attempts did not stop his precipitous decline.

It was Yang Su who made the next decisive move against Yang Yong. By Wendi's request, Yang Su monitored Yang Yong's activity during the emperor's absence from the capital. Upon Wendi's return, Yang Su gave a very unfavorable report on the crown prince. Not only had Yong shown an unwillingness to obey the imperial edict to go after those associated with the Liu Jushi 劉居士 incident, he also complained of his treatment at the time of the uprising against the Northern Zhou. Yong even suggested that he had helped his father capture the throne. By using such dramatic expressions as agitated, furious, shaken, and tearful, Yang Su portrayed a disgruntled crown prince who openly defied imperial authority.[27]

Ji Wei then testified about Yong's hubris, extravagance, and usurpative ambitions and provided damaging evidence that proved Yong's evil intent towards Wendi. According to Ji, after a session with an old woman diviner, Yang Yong allegedly said, "The taboo day (death) of our respected father is in the eighteenth year (598). The time is near." Wendi, who had long been contemplating the possibility of deposing Yang Yong as crown prince, was in tears. The reports given by Yang Su and Ji Wei prompted him into action.

Another strong rationale for Yang Yong's removal was his possible adulteration of the imperial line by allowing Lady Yun to usurp the position of the primary wife. To upgrade a concubine, let alone a concubine of lowly birth, to the status of a primary wife was a violation of tradition in the North. When Wendi and Empress Wenxian (Dugu) married Yang Yong to Lady Yuan, what was foremost on their minds was the decent pedigree of her father, Yuan Xiaoju 元孝矩. But Yang Yong cared little for the woman chosen by his parents. By contrast, Lady Yun, the woman Yong did love, was the product of an illicit liaison of a lowborn commoner, named Yun Dingxing 雲定興. Wendi referred to him as "that moron," and showed great displeasure with Yang Yong's obsession with his daughter. Suspecting that Yang Yong had a hand in causing the death of Lady Yuan, Wendi severely reprimanded him. Allegedly, in a moment of rage, Yong uttered a death threat to Yuan Xiaoju, which convinced Wendi that he himself was Yong's intended victim.

In view of the deep-rooted bias Wendi and his empress harbored against Yun, and their perception of Yang Yong as a serious threat to the throne and to the other princes, they would depose Yang Yong no matter what. With Gao Jiong no longer by his side to offer opposition, Wendi immediately initiated the deposition process. In the tenth month of 600, Wendi, in full military attire, mounted the Wude Basilica 武德殿 in the Palace City, as armored warriors stood in formation. When Yang Yong was summoned to the imperial throne, he feared for his life. Wendi's close adviser, Xue Daoheng 薛道衡, announced in stern language the imperial decision to depose him as crown prince, and to reduce him and his offspring to commoner status. As part of the standard scapegoat mechanism, some of the key figures in the Eastern Palace administration were subjected to various punishments, ranging from decapitation to confiscation of family assets.

In the eleventh month of 600, Yangdi, thirty-two (thirty-one), was officially appointed heir apparent. He departed from his beloved South for the capital in the North, and moved into the Eastern Palace. As for Yang Yong, the ex-crown prince, he was physically placed in the Eastern Palace, at the mercy of his younger brother.[28]

## STRUGGLE AGAINST THE OTHER BROTHERS

Yangdi was crown prince for fewer than four years, from the eleventh month of 600 to the seventh month of 604. Little has been recorded about his activity in this period. It would seem that he continued to play the role of the filial son and caring husband. His ever suspicious father would hardly tolerate any deviation from model behavior. Anxious to please his father, Yangdi requested that Eastern Palace officials forsake the convention of addressing themselves as subjects to the crown prince. The apparent rationale was that, although they worked for the crown prince, they should pledge their undivided allegiance to the emperor. Often concerned about the strong presence of the Eastern Palace, Wendi immediately approved the request. This gesture clearly set him apart from his elder brother Yang Yong, who as crown prince had displeased Wendi through receiving officials from a south-facing seat, a position symbolic of imperial power.[29]

Halfway through his essentially uneventful crown prince years, Yangdi, in the eighth month of 602, witnessed the passing of his birth mother, Empress Wenxian née Dugu at 59.[31] According to the *Zizhi tongjian*, Yangdi bemoaned her death in public, crying bitterly in the presence of his father and palace maids until he fainted away. The same source hastens to add that in private, Yangdi drank, ate, talked, and laughed as if nothing had happened. He even asked to have fat and dry meats and fish smuggled into the Eastern Palace.

Consistent with the negative portrayal of Yangdi in traditional historiography, Sima Guang and his associates attempt here to "expose" Yangdi's hypocritical and unfilial behavior. No doubt, his exaggerated public display of sorrow showed the histrionic side of his character. But his refusal to practice abstinence from food and drink while in mourning, if the record is believable at all, may be attributed to a careless refusal to conform to the established custom. To traditional scholars, the violation of the food taboo provides grounds for condemnation. However, for all his ambivalent feelings about his demanding father, he had no reason to harbor any resentment towards his mother, who, more than anyone else, had been instrumental in putting him in the Eastern Palace. It is not known whether Yangdi's public display of grief was a calculated move. But to express extreme sorrow on such an occasion as was expected of a filial son would no doubt impress Wendi, for whom Wenxian had not only been his life-long companion but also his closest counsel on matters of state.[31]

For Yangdi, the loss of his mother who had constantly safeguarded his interest in front of the emperor may have significantly increased his sense of insecurity. Now he had to rely solely on his father's judgment for his own political survival. The potential challengers to his succession might still come from any of his brothers except Yang Jun, Prince Xiao of Qin 秦孝王, who had died of poisoning at the hands of his jealous wife in the sixth month of 600.[32]

Of the three surviving brothers, Yang Yong was always perceived as a threat to Yangdi's current status as heir apparent. While Yang Yong was kept in captivity in the Eastern Palace, its main occupant, Yangdi, did everything in his power to prevent his release. Convinced that he had committed no crime to deserve the deposition, Yang Yong repeatedly requested an audience with Wendi to voice his grievances. Yangdi intercepted the request every time. In desperation, Yang Yong even climbed a tree to cry out his plea for an audience. At Wendi's request Yang Su launched an investigation, and reported: "Yong is deranged and confused, having been haunted by crazy ghosts. He is hopeless." As a member of the tripartite alliance, Yang Su was not interested in improving Yang Yong's situation at all.

In the struggle against Yang Yong, Yangdi enjoyed a clear advantage—his direct control over his rival's physical movement. The same cannot be said of his fight against the other two brothers. The one Yangdi considered the most menacing was Wendi's fourth son, Prince of Yue 越王 Yang Xiu 楊秀. Handsome looks, martial skills, bravery, and an awe-inspiring presence at court made him stand out among the Yang brothers. But Wendi was concerned about his fate precisely because of these qualities: "Xiu will inevitably come to a bad end.

So long as I am alive, there should be no worries. But when left with his brothers, he will surely rebel."[33]

Yang Xiu did not hide his displeasure with Yang Yong's deposition. Yangdi, seeing in Yang Xiu a potential troublemaker, wanted to discredit him. However, stationed in the remote Shu 蜀 area in the Southwest, Yang Xiu was apparently beyond his reach. Eventually, Yang Xiu stumbled through his own folly. When his extravagant behavior violated the established ritual code, Wendi condemned him. An awe-stricken Yang Xiu pleaded in self-deprecating language, "Humble as I was I received imperial favors. Posted to my princedom I failed to obey the law, and deserve to die 10,000 times." Yangdi and other princes were moved to tears by these words, and asked for leniency.[34] A stone-faced Wendi responded: "Formerly, when the prince of Qin (Yang Jun) was wasteful with money and material, I admonished him as a father. Today Yang Xiu has harmed the people, and I should discipline him as a sovereign." When a court official came to Xiu's defense, an infuriated Wendi threatened to have his tongue cut off and even suggested decapitation as Xiu's punishment. Wendi then decided to assign a number of high officials to prosecute Xiu instead. While the prosecution was underway, Yang Su turned in two pieces of incriminating evidence. One was an effigy with two hands tied together and a nail driven through the heart. Su found it at the foot of Mount Hua 華山. On the effigy were written the names of Yang Jian (Wendi) and Yang Liang and a prayer to curse them. The other was a call-to-arms document, denouncing Wendi's rebellious ministers, and thievish son. Although both were supposed to have been the work of Yang Xiu, the sources allege that Yangdi created the effigy and Yang Su forged the document.[35] In response, Wendi reduced Xiu to commoner status and had him imprisoned in the palace.[36]

The remaining fraternal challenge to Yangdi was Prince of Han 漢王, Yang Liang, who had governed the key Bingzhou area from 597, where he had under his jurisdiction fifty-two *zhou*-prefectures. Like Yang Xiu, he was unhappy about the deposition of Yang Yong. When Yang Xiu fell from favor, Yang Liang was particularly upset. As a favorite son of Wendi, Liang was granted special permission to govern his realm without having to comply with codes and statutes. As he began to make military preparations for eventualities, he gathered tens of thousands of close followers, in the name of beefing up Northern defenses against the Tujue. He gathered a large number of warriors for his private army, and developed a close bond with military commanders under his jurisdiction. When his army was defeated by the marauding Tujue forces, Wendi disenrolled more than eighty of his generals, banishing them to the Southern frontier area for punishment. Yang Liang, who had escaped punishment himself, attempted to retain them because they were his men. An angry Wendi reprimanded him, "Once I am gone, if someone wants to make a rash move against you, he will capture you like a chicken in a coop. What is the use of using your buddies?"[37] In spite of his wrath, Wendi never wavered in his support of Yang Liang, who was to become the only serious threat to Yangdi's accession after Wendi's death.

Intensely suspicious, Wendi had deliberately kept Crown Prince Yang Yong in a weak position. After the founding of the Sui dynasty, Yong was hardly involved in any major military campaigns or policy decisions. He had waited insecurely for his father's death and his own accession. Denied the chance to prove his worth, Yang Yong was powerless to defend himself when his mother connived with Yang Su and Yangdi to remove him. Although everyone involved should bear his or her share of the blame for the fall of Yang Yong, ultimately it was Wendi who set the trap for his oldest son. By concentrating so much military and administrative power in Yangdi, Wendi created, perhaps at first subliminally, a powerful competition for Yang Yong, and unwittingly enhanced Yangdi's position in his bid for the post of crown prince and the throne. Focusing on the weaknesses and alleged misconduct of the crown prince, Wendi was compelled to depose him in favor of Yangdi in the light of the latter's success in government, his rising reputation, and model behavior.

At the time of Yang Yong's fall, an official of the Eastern Palace by the name of Li Gang 李綱 risked his life to give the emperor a warning: "Since antiquity, seldom has the deposing of the oldest son [as heir apparent] happened without jeopardizing the state." That advice went unheeded.[38]

# 2

## Yangdi and His Reign

### THE ACCESSION

As the Renshou period approached its end, Yangdi came closer to making his dream of ascending the throne a reality. However, being the officially appointed successor was no guarantee of succession. Wendi could revoke his heir apparent status at a moment's notice. Fortunately for Yangdi, as Wendi grew older his trust in the crown prince deepened. Increasingly intolerant of the humidity and heat in the Palace City in Daxingcheng, Wendi in the last years of his life often spent summers in the suburban Renshou 仁壽 Palace to the west.

In the spring of 604, Wendi made his last trip to Renshou and he never returned. Prior to his departure, the diviner Zhangqiu Taiyi 章仇太翼 (Lu 盧 Taiyi) warned him of the danger of the trip. A furious Wendi threw him into jail and vowed to have him decapitated. During his absence, Wendi entrusted all state affairs down to the last detail to Yangdi. In the fourth month, Wendi fell seriously ill. On the tenth of the seventh month, lying in bed with tears in his eyes, he bid farewell to his ministers, and ordered the release of the diviner Zhangqiu Taiyi.[1] Then two accidents happened that triggered violent responses from the dying emperor and nearly changed the course of history.

To prepare for eventualities at the time of his father's death, Yangdi employed his old ally Yang Su as his eyes and ears around the emperor. In response, Yang Su wrote a secret report on the situation but it was delivered to Wendi by mistake. After reading it, Wendi became incensed. Meanwhile, the crown prince, who had been summoned from the capital to attend on his father, made ill-timed sexual advances to Lady Chen 陳氏 (also known as

29

Xuanhua 宣華), a highly influential young woman, who was Wendi's favorite consort. Emboldened by his father's weakened condition, Yangdi threw caution to the wind, but his act backfired and almost cost him his political future. Lady Chen managed to escape back into the emperor's room to report the incident. An infuriated Wendi responded by requesting two of his attending courtiers, Liu Shu 柳述 and Yuan Yan 元巖, to summon his oldest son Yang Yong immediately. In view of Yangdi's clandestine activity against the emperor and his criminal intent towards the imperial consort, Wendi decided to replace Yangdi with his older brother as crown prince. But it was too late. Yangdi and his supporter Yang Su arrested Liu Shu and Yuan Yan, replaced the imperial guards with the Eastern Palace guards, and placed two of Yangdi's closest followers, Yuwen Shu 宇文述 and Guo Yan 郭衍, in charge of the emperor's security. They also ordered Yangdi's minion Zhang Heng 張衡 to attend the emperor. After the imperial consorts and all palace maids had been sent away from Wendi's room, Wendi died under suspicious circumstances on the thirteenth of the seventh month (August 13), 604, in what came to be known as the Renshou Palace incident. According to tradition, a testamentary edict was issued, which denounced Yang Yong and Yang Xiu as subversive and evil, and endorsed Yangdi as Wendi's successor.[2]

Traditional scholars believe the edict was a fabrication completed under Yangdi's instructions. Similarly, they believe Yangdi was the true culprit in his father's death, committing patricide through the hands of Zhang Heng. In fact, the issue of patricide is at the center of the traditional judgment of Yangdi's moral character. However, some modern revisionist historians question the authenticity of the record, which, they believe, serves the ulterior purpose of vilifying Yangdi.

Lü Simian bases his skepticism on melodramatic details, such as Yang Su's secret message ending up in Wendi's hands, and on the story of unwanted sexual advances by Yangdi to Lady Chen despite his prior contact with her. It seems that some narrative details may have been fictionalized, but there is not enough textual evidence to negate the essence of the account. Besides, the earlier contact Chen had with Yangdi had not been sexual (Yangdi had given her some gifts, and she had lent support to him in the struggle for the post of crown prince), and cannot rule out the possibility of her resisting Yangdi's sexual advances. Miyazaki Ichisada dismisses the whole story as a later fabrication, basing his argument on discrepancies in records of the event in the basic annals and the biographies.[3] Unfortunately, he offers little textual evidence.

Han Sheng has put forward a painstaking argument in support of this position. First, according to him, the more reliable *Sui shu* account records that Wendi died of natural causes, which the *Zizhi tongjian* accepts. Here the key term the *Sui shu* uses in recording the passing of Wendi in his basic annals is *beng* 崩 (to die), which does not indicate murder. However, in a basic annals chapter, the term is often used as a stylistic device to indicate the passing of a sovereign and not as a technical description of the manner of death. For example, the *Sui shu* records Yangdi died by way of *beng* as well in his basic annals, even though elsewhere it is unequivocal about his regicide. Similarly, although the *Sui shu* records Wendi's death as *beng* in the basic annals, it does not exonerate Yangdi of his role in the death of his father. In the biography of Yang Su, the suspicious presence of Zhang Heng in Wendi's sickroom is clearly indicated.

Second, Han contends, Yangdi's henchman, Zhang Heng, was given the posthumous title of Zhong 忠 (loyalty) by Tang Gaozu, which would not have been possible if Zhang had really been involved in a patricide. However, the title Zhang received was given in consideration of his service to Yangdi, not Wendi. In that sense, Zhong (loyalty) was appropriate since he was killed by Yangdi after offering candid advice.[4]

Third, Han argues that no late Sui and Early Tang comments on Yangdi mention his patricide. Here Han mostly relies on the *Sui shu*, penned by Wei Zheng et al. But there were at least three works bearing the same title. The other two *Sui shu*, one by Wang Shao and the other by Zhang Dasu 張大素, are no longer extant. Wang Shao 王劭, whose *Sui shu* was criticized as unreliable, died before the fall of the dynasty. Zhang Dasu, however, lived through the end-of-dynasty turmoil and died in Taizong's reign. His account might be different from that in Wei's *Sui shu*. Indeed, the early Song encyclopedia *Taiping yulan* quotes a *Sui shu* account (probably Zhang Dasu's) that lends credence to the patricide theory. In addition, there are other extant contemporary records of Yangdi's patricide. The Tang source, *Zhenguan zhengyao* 貞觀政要, quotes Tang Taizong on Wendi's death: "After Wendi was killed by Yangdi, law and government went into decline." Furthermore, a piece of epigraphic evidence dating back to 634 describes Wendi's successor as a usurper. All this clearly attests to the public perception of Yangdi's usurpation in Taizong's time.[5]

Moreover, what befell Liu Shu and Yuan Yan, the two court officials instructed by Wendi to draft the edict to depose Yangdi, cannot be satisfactorily explained by the revisionist theories. Yangdi not only disenrolled and exiled Liu Shu to a remote area, but ordered his own blood sister Princess of Lanling, Liu's wife, to divorce him. Lanling refused and requested to accompany Liu to his place of banishment instead. After Yangdi turned down her request, she died in extreme grief. Yuan Yan was treated in a similar manner. Their prompt and severe punishment can only be understood in the context of Yangdi's usurpative bid for power.

Another suspicious development was the move by Yangdi to keep his father's death a secret for eight days, effectively delaying his own official ascension. What was the rationale behind the delay except that the conspirators needed time to cover up their act? One of the actions Yangdi took in the interim was to attempt to recall Yang Liang 楊諒 from Bing Prefecture with a forged edict by Wendi, which caused Yang Liang to rebel. Why did Yangdi need to forge the edict at all if he had come to power by way of legitimate succession?[6]

In sum, contrary to revisionist arguments, there are neither inexplicable contradictions nor signs of fabrication in the traditional account of Yangdi's patricide.[7] On the other hand, in Yangdi's defense, if he had failed to take preemptive action, he would certainly have lost his position and probably his life at the hands of his father or elder brother. The succession struggle, as is often the case, had become a life-and-death struggle.

With his accession assured, Yangdi moved to attend to some unfinished business. He sent Lady Chen a golden box with the word "Sealed" in his own handwriting written across the seal. When Lady Chen opened it at the urging of the messenger, she found several love knots inside. That night, Yangdi took her to bed.[8] This seemingly isolated incident would have little significance in Yangdi's life had it not been for the fact that Lady Chen was one of the two consorts of his deceased father. The other consort was Lady Cai 蔡氏, also known as Ronghua 容華, with whom Yangdi had his will as well.[9] Both Chen and Cai were legally Yangdi's stepmothers. The sexual escapades Yangdi embarked on around the time of Wendi's death belied his carefully crafted image of a faithful husband. For quite some time Yangdi had to assume the model role he had no reason to like. In gratifying his sexual fantasies, he revealed a hidden side of his personality—his lack of moral restraint.

In describing Yangdi's deviant acts, traditional scholars use the term *zheng* 烝, which implies incest with a close relative of the older generation. The choice of that term suggests Yangdi committed acts of moral depravity of the worst kind.[10] To be sure, polygamy was sanctioned by law, but extramarital affairs were strongly censured. Incestuous relations with the concubines of one's father were particularly prohibited. Yangdi was condemned mainly because of his deliberate violation of one of the most strictly enforced taboo institutions, the incest taboo.[11]

His reckless sexual adventures notwithstanding, Yanagdi never lost sight of what he needed to do to shore up his power. Particularly worried about his surviving brothers, Yangdi forged two imperial edicts: The first one condemned the ex-crown prince Yang Yong to suicide, and the second summoned Yang Liang to the capital. Upon hearing the first edict, Yong refused to take his own life, and had to be strangled. As for the second edict, it failed its purpose because of a technicality.

Before his death, Wendi had made a foolproof secret agreement with Liang, which allowed him to authenticate Wendi's seal on an imperial summons. The telltale sign was an extra dot on the character *chi* 敕 (rescript). The bearer of the imperial summons would also carry half of a unicorn-shaped jade tally, which should be a perfect match with the other half in Liang's possession. Noticing the missing dot on the character *chi* (rescript), Yang Liang realized that Wendi was probably no longer alive. Thereupon he raised the banner of insurgency against his brother. In the ensuing conflict, Liang was defeated and captured by General Yang Su.[12]

## YANG LIANG AND THE YANG YONG LINEAGE

In the seventh month of Renshou 4 (604), Yangdi officially ascended the throne at the Renshou Palace. In the following month, he accompanied the hearse of his father back to the capital where he began to hold court.

As emperor, he had to deal with some lingering problems resulting from his hasty accession, particularly the recently captured Yang Liang and the offspring of the deceased former crown prince. Court officials unanimously recommended death as Liang's punishment. But Yangdi decided to reduce him to commoner status instead, saying, "This emperor believes that 'brothers are rare.' Because of my feelings [towards him, I] cannot bear to say it (denounce him). I would bend the law to spare his life." Yang Liang eventually died in custody.[13]

As for the descendants of Yang Yong, Yangdi kept them alive until the year 607. Yuwen Shu submitted a memorial that virtually requested their elimination. Subsequently, on Yangdi's orders, Yang Yan 楊儼, the oldest son of Yang Yong's, was killed by poisoned wine, and his seven brothers were dispatched while on their way to banishment. Reportedly, they were all buried face down, out of fear their ghosts might haunt the living.[14]

The different ways Yangdi dealt with Yang Liang and the children of Yang Yong point to Yangdi's underlying concern about the security of his power. He regarded Yang Liang as a little brother who had gone astray but did not deserve to die for his crime. It is true that Yang Liang had taken treasonous action against the court, but deprived of his military power, he was no longer a threat. The case of Yang Yong was entirely different. As the erstwhile crown prince and the most viable alternative to Yangdi, Yang Yong had posed a serious challenge, real or imagined, to his accession. Even after his death, that challenge remained so long as his direct male descendants were alive. The decision to exterminate all the legitimate instead of all the surviving male members of the Yang Yong lineage illustrates the reason for the murder: to remove any potential threat to the legitimacy of Yangdi's rule.

## LUOYANG

Not long after his accession, Yangdi started to execute ambitious plans to integrate North and South China, including the building of the Eastern Capital, Luoyang 洛陽; the digging of the Grand Canal; the construction of a national palace network; and touring strategic areas by land and water. Luoyang allowed Yangdi to establish an operational base in the East and constituted an integral part of the imperial residential system composed of Luoyang, Daxingcheng, and Jiangdu. Yangdi would divide his time among these three metropolises, using them as terminuses for his numerous tours, which brought him as far north as the Ordos and southern Manchuria, and as far west as the Gansu corridor.

As soon as Yangdi emerged from the Yang Liang crisis as the victor, he shifted his attention to the East. He officially unveiled his ambitious plan to build a new capital at Luoyang on the twenty-first of the eleventh month in Renshou four (December 17, 604).[15] According to one source, the Luoyang project employed, on average, two million adults every month for corvée labor. Even if we interpret this figure in a most conservative manner, that is, taking two million to refer to man-days of labor, we still end up with close to seventy thousand laborers working on the project on any given day.[16] Working conditions were harsh. About two thousand laborers were needed to haul structural timber on wooden wheels and iron axles from the distant South at the slow pace of 20 to 30 *li* a day before it could be shipped north by water. It often cost hundreds of thousands of man-days to transport a single timber from provenance to destination. Forty to fifty percent of the laborers were said to have succumbed to the crushing weight of the project. Each month, it was reported, from Chenggao 城皋 (northwest of Xingyang, Henan) in the east to Heyang 河陽 (south of Mengzhou, Henan) in the west, vehicles carrying the corpses of laborers were always within view of each other on the road.[17]

In the first month of 606, the Eastern Capital at Luoyang was officially completed at tremendous human and material cost. It immediately became the favorite city of Yangdi, the base of his operations in the North and the premium political center of the nation.

## THE TONGJI CANAL

In the third month of 605, when the Luoyang project was still in full swing, Yangdi initiated two more major public works projects—the Tongji Canal 通濟渠 and Han Conduit 邗溝 projects. As the first section of the Grand Canal, the Tongji Canal ran from Luoyang southeast to link up with the Huai valley to the south. To accomplish this daunting task, Yangdi mobilized a labor force that seemed unprecedented in size. The *Kai he ji* 開河記 (Record of canal digging) records some three million six hundred thousand men between the ages of fifteen and fifty (or fourteen and forty-nine) working on the canal project. They were under the supervision of fifty thousand young warriors. For every five households, an additional underage, elderly, or female laborer was recruited to provide food services. The total number of people involved was estimated to be 5,430,000.[18] However, the source in question, which is replete with accounts of ghostly apparitions, is intended primarily as a work of fiction and is vaguely based on some historical facts.[19] The canal ran through six commanderies—Henan 河南, Xingyang 榮陽, Liang 梁, Qiao 譙, Pengcheng 彭城, and Xiapi 下邳—with a total number of registered households of 775,000 in 609. Multiplying it by 5.17—the average household population for Sui times—we get 4,006,750 as the registered population.[20] It is inconceivable that the local population could support a much larger labor force on a continual basis in addition to the two million workers already engaged in the Luoyang project.

Different from this account, the *Sui shu* and the *Tong dian* record that more than one million adult males and females were mobilized in the construction of the Tongji Canal.[21] This is a more believable figure. Theoretically, the local population could support a labor force of this size without risking immediate economic collapse.

Officially, the canal was completed in one hundred and seventy-one days. In reality, the project probably dragged on for years. With its potential benefit to the economy still years away, the impact of this project on the labor force was devastating. One source records that as the Sui government under Yangdi forcibly recruited male laborers to work on the building of the Tongji Canal, corpses of those starved to death appeared in large numbers.[22]

By comparison, the Han Conduit, another canal project, was a minor undertaking with the purpose of extending the Grand Canal south to the Yangzi valley. It started in the third month of 605, but its completion date is not documented. Of relatively short duration, the project mainly involved dredging, deepening, and widening existing waterways. It employed a relatively small labor force of more than one hundred thousand. The completion of the project allowed the Grand Canal to link up with the Jiangnan Canal 江南河 built in 610, the last southern extension of the canal, which penetrated deep into the former Chen territory and the Yuhang area.[23]

## THE SOUTHERN TOUR OF 605–606

While the country was still hemorrhaging from the large-scale construction projects, Yangdi made his first and most expensive imperial tour of the South in 605–606.[24] The sources record the beginning of Yangdi's journey on the fifteenth day of the eighth month (October 2) in 605, but not his arrival date.[25] A passage in the Buddhist source, *Fozu tongji*, records that he gave an audience to the Tiantai 天台 monk Zhizao 智璪 in Yangzhou 揚州 (Jiangdu) in the ninth month of 605. This suggests that by that date, Yangdi had arrived in the South.[26] Yangdi then started on his return journey in the third month of 606. The precise route of the journey is not documented but it is clear Yangdi did not take the Grand Canal because its Tongji section had yet to be completed. Instead, he probably took the alternative route that went from Luoyang east through the Yellow, Ji 濟, and Si 泗 Rivers to reach the Huai River.[27]

A detailed record of the extraordinary magnitude of the imperial progress on the first Southern journey has survived. For the occasion, an imperial dragon ship was commissioned. Reportedly 45 *chi* 尺 in height and 200 *zhang* 丈 from bow to stern, it was a colossal vessel of four decks. The top level housed a miniature palace system, complete with the main basilica, the inner basilica, and the east and west audience halls. The next two levels below were divided into one hundred and twenty chambers known as houses, ornamented in gold and jade. The bottom level was occupied by attending eunuchs. The vessel for the empress was constructed and decorated in a similar manner, but on a smaller scale. Nine accompanying vessels of three decks known as *Fujing* 浮景 (Floating Scenes) were waterborne basilicas. They were followed by thousands of lesser ships such as the *Yangcai* 漾彩 (Floating Colors) and the *Zhuque* 朱雀 (Vermilion Bird), carrying tributary goods from various court and government offices. More than eighty thousand laborers were hired to haul the ships. Among those, nine thousand dressed in silk towed the key ships that set sail before the *Yangcai*. They were followed by thousands of smaller vessels such as the *Pingcheng* 平乘 (Smooth Ride) and the *Qinglong* 青龍 (Cerulean Dragon). The imperial harem, princes, princesses, court officials, Buddhist monks, Daoist adepts, and foreign visitors were in the entourage. Imperial guardsmen of the Twelve Guards were aboard their own ships with their weaponry and tenting equipment. The whole procession, guarded by cavalrymen moving along the two banks, allegedly extended over a distance of more than 200 *li* 里 . Wherever the procession passed, prefectures and counties within a radius of 500 *li* were requested to contribute delicacies.[28] This record, contained in the punctuated edition of the *Zizhi tongjian*, provides a rare glimpse of the event. The numbers, however, call for caution. According to pre-607 Sui standards, the height of Yangdi's dragon ship of four decks (45 *chi*) is equal to a realistic 13.28 m (10.6 m).[29] But the length of 200 *zhang*, or 590 m (471 m), is inconceivable for a river ship, typically of carvel construction.

As noted, Yangdi took existing, old routes on this trip with more unfavorable conditions than the Tongji Canal. As the much improved replacement route, the Tongji was about 40 *bu* 步 or 71 m in width.[30] Even if the dragon ship were built to the recorded specifications, it would probably be too long to navigate along the Tongji through the valleys and watersheds between the Yellow and Yangzi, to say nothing of the old routes. The editor's comment on the length of the ship in the record, found in the punctuated edition of the source, indicates that in other editions the unit of length *zhang* is replaced by *chi* (1/10 *zhang*). If we use this latter figure, the length would be 59 m (47 m), which was sustainable by the level of engineering current during Sui times. However, the much smaller size would not allow it to hold one hundred and twenty houses (chambers). Thus it is almost certain that these houses were symbolic rather than real.

These inconsistencies in the *Zizhi tongjian* notwithstanding, there is little doubt that this tour was Yangdi's most ostentatious display of luxury ever recorded. From departure to return, it took place between the eighth month of 605 and the fourth month of 606. Judging from records in his basic annals, on his return trip alone Yangdi spent a total of forty days, from the sixteenth of the third month to the twenty-sixth of the fourth month, to travel from Jiangdu to Luoyang. This indicates the return journey was undertaken at a leisurely pace; Yangdi must have broken his journey on numerous occasions. It is also conceivable that the journey was prolonged by the enormous size of his entourage.

The travel to the South did not interrupt state business. On arrival in the South, Yangdi announced an amnesty for the Yangzi-Huai region and the area to its south. He granted a five-year tax exemption for the territory of Yangzhou, and a three-year tax exemption for the area under the former Yangzhou [Superior] Area Command. These area-specific relief measures provided much economic benefit to the South at a time when the North was under increasingly suffocating financial burdens. So Yangdi's Southern trip, for all its extravagances, had its positive side.[31]

## HEIR APPARENT

Upon his return from the South, Yangdi had to face the loss of his oldest son, Crown Prince Yuande 元德 (Yang Zhao 楊昭), who died in the seventh month of 606 at the age of twenty-three (twenty-two). As one of Yangdi's two sons by Empress Xiao, Yang Zhao was appointed crown prince in the first month of 605. In spite of his young age, Zhao already possessed a number of desirable virtues such as frugality and benevolence. Plagued by weight problems Zhao fell seriously ill. A shaman was called in on imperial orders, who gave the ominous diagnosis, "He is haunted by the prince of Fangling 房陵王 (Yang Yong)." Zhao succumbed soon after.[32] By default, his brother Yang Jian[a]

楊暕 became the most likely choice for crown prince. Known for his handsome looks, Jian[a] had been much favored by his grandfather, Wendi, who promoted him to commander of Yangzhou Superior Area Command to take charge of military affairs south of the Huai. He patronized famous literati such as Cui Ze 崔賾 (Zujun) and Wang Zhen 王貞, and demonstrated a strong faith and interest in Buddhism in his invitation letter to the monk Zhizhong 智眾 of the Dongshan Monastery 東山寺 in Suzhou 蘇州.[33] By 607, Yangdi had apparently accepted what appeared to be the inevitable. He promoted Jian[a] first to governor of Yongzhou 雍州牧 at the old capital and then to governor of Henan 河南尹, head of the newly created Eastern Capital. The entire crown prince entourage of more than two thousand was transferred to him.

But before his expected appointment became official, Yang Jian[a] was corrupted by his newly acquired power. He would send out his underlings to search for dogs, horses, and women. Encouraged by Jian[a]'s immoral behavior, his underlings, in the name of their master, brought abducted women into his residence to rape them. Initially, Yangdi hardly took notice of his son's misconduct but Jian[a]'s luck began to run out when an attractive woman, originally meant for Yangdi, was offered to Jian[a]. This aroused Yangdi's sexual jealousy and intense resentment of his son. Then the father-son relationship was irrevocably damaged on a hunting trip. While Yangdi finished the trip empty-handed, his son presented him with a large catch of game. Yangdi was infuriated, especially when his attending officers blamed Yang Jian[a]'s men for keeping the game away. Thereafter, Yangdi started a series of attempts to destroy Yang Jian[a] and his family.

The persecution reached its crescendo after Yangdi was informed of Jian[a]'s illicit sexual relations with the sister of his deceased wife, of his consultation of a physiognomist (*xianggong* 相工) who predicted his rise to royal power, and of his practice of sorcery as a way to deter the three sons of his elder brother Yang Zhao from seizing the post of crown prince before him. On Yangdi's orders, Yang Jian[a]'s advisers and administrative assistants were either executed or banished to remote border areas. His lover was forced to take her own life. As for Yang Jian[a] himself, he was put under the close surveillance of a tiger-brave general (*huben langjiang* 虎賁郎將), who would report to Yangdi every suspicious move. Yangdi was so concerned about his son's threat against him that he staffed Jian[a]'s retinue with only the old and weak.[34]

Yangdi's disillusionment with his second son Jian[a] made the selection of an heir almost impossible. Apart from Jian[a] the only possible candidate was Yang Gao 楊杲. But Gao was too young, and the fact that he was born by a concubine instead of the reigning empress would be an issue should he be named crown prince. To be sure, Yangdi had other male descendants, but they were either dead or not in a position to compete. Yangdi had lost a son while still prince of Jin; he also had sons by other concubines, whom he gave away to impress his mother.[35] It might become necessary to bypass the second generation to select an heir apparent among Yang Zhao's sons. However, with court critics and remonstrators silenced, no one at court would seriously raise the issue of succession. Thus, after the death of Yang Zhao in 606, the court remained without heir apparent for the remainder of the second reign.

## THE TOUR OF THE ORDOS (607)

In 607, perhaps still mourning the loss of Crown Prince Yang Zhao and remaining undecided as to whether or not to appoint Yang Jian[a] as his replacement, Yangdi embarked on the historic overland tour of the Ordos area bordering on Tujue territory.

Certainly, traveling by water was the preferred way for ostentatious display of regal power and wealth, but key areas of strategic interest, especially in the North, were often not easily accessible by water. Thus, Yangdi was more likely to have traveled by land. On his famous 607 trip to the Ordos, Yangdi departed from the capital, Daxingcheng, on the eighteenth (*bingshen* 丙申)[36] of the fourth month, 607 and arrived at the Chi'an Marsh 赤岸澤 (north of Hua County, south Shaanxi) on the twenty-first, where he paid homage to the tomb of Li Mu 李穆, one of his father's comrades-in-arms.[37] After stopping by Yanmen 雁門 (Dai County, Shanxi) and Mayi 馬邑 (Shuozhou, Shanxi), on the fourth day (*xinsi* 辛巳) of the sixth month, he found himself hunting in Liangu 連谷 (north of Shenmu, north Shaanxi), which lay within the boundaries of Yulin Commandery 榆林郡. On the eleventh day (*wuzi* 戊子) of the sixth month, Yangdi reached his destination—Yulin 榆林, located on the south bank of the Yellow River loop that meandered along the northern boundary of the Ordos. The fact that Yangdi paid a visit to this remote area so soon after coming to power, and that the Yulin Palace was located there, signifies the strategic importance of the region as a frontier outpost of Sui China bordering on Tujue territory. Tujue, the most formidable challenge to the Sui court, was foremost on his mind when Yangdi started on this journey (map 2.1). On the twenty-seventh of the sixth month, Yangdi ascended the Northern Loft-building to view fish in the Yellow River, and entertain his court officials with a sumptuous banquet.

The climax of the trip was Yangdi's meeting with Qimin qaghan 啟民可汗 of Eastern Tujue. To impress the Tujue leader, Yangdi had ordered Yuwen Kai 宇文愷, the leading Sui architect, to build a tent of enormous size, reportedly large enough to house several thousand people. Yangdi entered the great tent to hold court in the company of the guards of honor. He then regaled Qimin qaghan and his people with festivities and acrobatic shows.

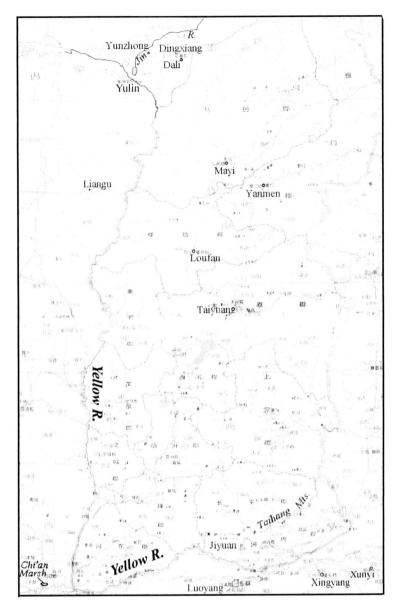

MAP 2.1   Key places visited by Yangdi on his 607 tour

What followed was virtually an exchange of gifts in spite of the assertion in some sources that the barbarians were awed into paying tribute. The Tujue and other Northern barbarians presented oxen, sheep, camels, and horses, and received silk in return. According to the punctuated edition of the *Zizhi tongjian*, the barbarians presented tens of millions of animals and Qimin alone received twenty million *duan*ᵃ 段 of silk.[38] Such quantities, however, were unthinkable at the time. "Tens of millions" (*shu qianwan* 數千萬) of animals is probably an error for "hundreds of thousands" (*shu shiwan* 數十萬), 1 percent of the recorded quantity. As for the quantity of silk, the *Cefu yuangui* records a more realistic "200,000 (*ershiwan* 二十萬) *duan*ᵃ"[39] in lieu of "20,000,000 (*erqianwan* 二千萬) *duan*ᵃ."[40] Even these much smaller quantities may have been exaggerated, since they constituted an enormous amount of wealth in Sui times. These criticisms notwithstanding, there is little doubt that Yangdi treated the Tujue leader very generously. In addition to silk, Yangdi showered Qimin with other personal gifts, including carriages and horses, drummers, trumpeters, banners, and pennants.

On the sixth of the eighth month, the imperial progress departed from Yulin to go north through Yunzhong 雲中 (south of Tumd Left Banner) and upstream along the Jin River 金河 into Tujue territory. It is recorded that Yangdi was accompanied by half a million armored warriors, one hundred thousand horses, and their logistical supplies. His caravan extended over 1,000 *li*. On imperial orders, Yuwen Kai built a sightseeing basilica on wheels. Composed of several detachable parts, this moving basilica was spacious enough to accommodate several hundred guardsmen. Yuwen also constructed a touring city with a circumference of 2,000 *bu* (2,820 m).[41]

Yangdi paid a visit to Qimin in his tent, and returned with him to Sui territory on the thirteenth. On the seventeenth, Yangdi crossed the Loufan 樓煩 Pass (Jingle, Shanxi), and on the twenty-sixth, reached Taiyuan 太原 (southwest of present-day Taiyuan). He then climbed the Taihang Mountains to the east. On the thirteenth of the ninth month, Yangdi arrived in Jiyuan 濟源 (Jiyuan, southwest Henan) where he visited Zhang Heng; he eventually reached Luoyang on the twenty-third. The primary objective of this tour was to secure China's boundary in the Ordos region by consolidating the Sui's alliance with Eastern Tujue at the highest level. An upshot of the journey was the reaffirmation by Qimin qaghan, who was the nominal Tujue leader, of his commitment to the Sui court.

While on the tour, Yangdi made far-reaching decisions concerning domestic politics and public works. He mobilized more than a million laborers to build the Sui Great Wall, executed three top-ranking officials, and ordered the construction of the Jinyang 晉陽 Palace. Yet as always, Yangdi mixed business with pleasure. He went hunting, mountain climbing, and sightseeing near Zhang Heng's home. He took part in festivities in the company of the Tujue and other barbarian chieftains. From departure to return, the whole journey took more than five months. It went on record as one of the most extravagant overland tours that Yangdi had ever made.[42]

## COURT CRITICS

While still on the 607 land tour, Yangdi was criticized by four highly respected court officials for his extravagance. Yangdi reacted impulsively by executing three and ousting one of them. These decisions marked a turning point in Yangdi's political career in terms of relations between sovereign and high officials. To understand Yangdi's rationale, we must examine the evolvement of the top leadership during the second reign.

During the first few years of his rule, Yangdi treated key officials from the previous reign relatively well. The best known of them was Gao Jiong, the most powerful nonroyal court official under his father until 599. Gao had strenuously opposed Yangdi's appointment as crown prince, but Yangdi's early action towards Gao Jiong harbored no malicious intent at all. On the contrary, he appointed Gao Jiong *taichang qing* 太常卿 (president of the Court of Imperial Sacrifices), a key ministerial position.[43]

Another key court official who had similar ups and downs in his political career was Su Wei 蘇威, whose father was Su Chuo 蘇綽, a reform-minded board president of extraordinary power under the Western Wei. Highly recommended by Gao Jiong, Su Wei was one of Wendi's closest advisers. The year 589 was the high point of Su's political career when he was appointed vice president of the right of the Department of State Affairs. After a brief dismissal from office, Su was rehabilitated and appointed president of the Chancellery, only to lose it on account of his lèse majesté. However, Su Wei won back the complete trust of Wendi towards the end of the first reign. Not only was he reappointed president of the Chancellery, he was also reinstated as vice president of the right of the Department of State Affairs. Although Su Wei had never been considered Yangdi's man, Yangdi, upon accession, continued his appointment, and promoted him to vice president of the left of the Department of State Affairs.[44]

Among Wendi's military commanders, Heruo Bi 賀若弼 stood out as one of the most brilliant Sui generals. In the Southern expedition, he had played a pivotal role in conquering the Chen, but he had some weaknesses, among them petty jealousy and contentiousness. He felt bitter about the fact that the highest symbolic prize of the war, the last emperor of the Chen, was captured by General Han Qinhu, not by himself. In spite of the rich rewards and promotions he received, Heruo openly complained about his alleged unfair treatment, which led to his loss of office. When Yangdi came to power, he did not have any intention of reinstating Heruo. Still, when the opportune occasion arose, Yangdi did not mind using his advice.

As a high-ranking official who had rendered meritorious service under Wendi, Yuwen Bi 宇文弲 enjoyed particularly great respect and reputation. He was competent in military affairs and civil administration and played a major part in conquering the Northern Qi for the Northern Zhou court and in subjugating the Chen during Wendi's reign. He had served as commander of a number of area commands under Wendi before he was promoted by Yangdi to president of the Board of Rites.[45]

All of the four key officials noted above, except Yuwen Bi, had been disgraced by Wendi. All of them initially fared rather well under Yangdi. When he embarked on his grandiose tour of the Ordos, he had all four of them in his entourage. But his extravagances—the lavish entertainment of Qimin qaghan and the overgenerous gifts to him, and the major plan to build the Great Wall—worried them. All four were critical of this irresponsible behavior. Su Wei officially remonstrated against the building of the Great Wall. Yangdi ignored his advice and employed a vast labor force to complete the project.[46]

Gao Jiong was initially concerned about Yangdi's love of *sanyue* 散樂 (incidental music). *Sanyue* originally referred to a kind of court acrobatic performance and its music during the Northern Qi and Northern Zhou dynasties. Wendi had dissolved the *sanyue* troupe and sent away its actors and actresses. In 606, on the occasion of the Tujue leader Qimin qaghan's visit, Yangdi reassembled the troupe to stage a spectacular acrobatic performance.[47] Gao then intimated that fondness of [improper] music had caused the fall of Xuandi of Northern Zhou, and the visit of Qimin could have endangered national security. General Heruo Bi also referred to the reception Qimin had received as excessively extravagant. Yuwen Bi, like Gao Jiong, compared Yangdi with Xuandi, and considered the Great Wall project a nonemergency.

When these unflattering remarks were reported to the court, Yangdi pulled off a coup de main that was to redefine his relations with court officials. On the twenty-ninth of the seventh month in 607, he ordered the summary execution of three of the four critics—Gao Jiong, Yuwen Bi, and Heruo Bi. The wives of Gao Jiong and Heruo Bi were enslaved in the palace, and their sons were banished to frontier areas. The same fate probably befell Yuwen Bi's family. The crime of these critics was libel against court policy. Officially, the last of the four, Su Wei, was penalized with dismissal from office because of his close association with the other offenders. But his earlier objection to the Great Wall project was probably a major factor in incurring imperial displeasure.[48]

A main target of Yangdi's critics was his fiscal irresponsibility, which had manifested itself in the construction of Luoyang, the digging of the Tongji

Canal, and the Southern tour of 605. The very fact that Yangdi could get away
with those expensive projects without encountering too much opposition testifies to the security of his position. It is hardly imaginable that those high
officials of the previous reign could pose any threat to Yangdi's rule. By executing Gao Jiong, Heruo Bi, and Yuwen Bi, and by dismissing Su Wei, Yangdi
seems to have acted impulsively and reactively. What is even more surprising
was the lightning speed with which Yangdi translated his impulses into punitive action without even pretending to go through the normal judicial proce-
dures. A confession Yangdi made a few years later may help to explain the
rational basis for his action. Commenting on Xue Daoheng, another out-of-
favor court official of the first reign, Yangdi said, "I used to work with him
when I was young. He looked down on me because of my young age. He,
together with Gao Jiong and Heruo Bi, monopolized power outside the court."
The memory of Gao's and Heruo's hubris and the fear of being outmaneu-
vered by his father's powerful officials were determining factors in Yangdi's
crucial decision to execute them.[49]

Having eliminated some of his top advisers and silenced the rest, Yangdi,
in the first month of 608, initiated another major construction project: the
building of the Yongji section of the Grand Canal. The immediate strategic
objective Yangdi had in mind was to prepare for a large-scale military conflict
with Koguryŏ. Yongji would link the Eastern Capital with Hebei, making it
much easier to transport troops and materiel from the South and the Central
Plain to the Liaodong front in Koguryŏ. The labor force involved is said to
have exceeded a million men and women. Having exhausted the pool of available adult males, the main taxpayers and labor force of the empire, the government began to rely increasingly on females for labor. Meanwhile Yangdi
launched another Great Wall project in the seventh month of 608, in which
he mobilized a male labor force of more than two hundred thousand to extend
the wall eastwards from the Yu valley 榆谷 (west of Yulin).[50] Both of these
projects, launched on the heels of Luoyang and Tongji, attest to Yangdi's open
defiance of his critics and his resolve to realize his strategic vision regardless
of cost.

In a fit of paranoia, Yangdi eliminated Xue Daoheng himself. A literary
talent who had served as Wendi's close adviser, Xue had been summoned from
a provincial post to the capital when Yangdi ascended the throne. Xue once
presented to the court a prose piece entitled "Panegyric on Gaozu Emperor
Wen" ("Gaozu Wen huangdi song" 高祖文皇帝頌), in which he sang praises
to Wendi's achievements in hyperbolic language. Annoyed by the glorification
of the previous reign, which meant, for Yangdi, belittling his own achievement,
Yangdi was determined to frame him. When Xue's close friend, Fang Yanqian
房彥謙, advised him to keep a low profile—to stop socializing and to behave
himself humbly—for the purpose of self-preservation, he did not take the
advice seriously. When he grew weary of the slow process through which some

newly introduced statutes were adopted, he commented casually, "If Gao Jiong were not dead today, these statutes would have gone into effect a long time ago." To that Yangdi responded angrily: "Do you still cherish the memory of Gao Jiong?" On Yangdi's orders, Xue was condemned to suicide at the advanced age of seventy (sixty-nine).[51] But he could not comprehend what he had done wrong, even when faced with death, and was eventually strangled by Yangdi's hatchet men. Yangdi, who could not conceal his schadenfreude, asked rhetorically, "Can he still compose, 'From bare rafters fall crumbs of the swallow's nest'?"[52] As a leading litterateur of his time, Xue had aroused much jealousy in Yangdi, who considered his own literary talent unsurpassed.

Yangdi's distrust of powerful officials was not limited to those who dared to show disrespect and challenge his authority. It was extended to his own closest supporters like Yang Su. Not only had Yang Su been instrumental in bringing Yangdi to power, he had also led the successful campaign against the Yang Liang rebellion, paving the way for Yangdi's initial consolidation of imperial power. Yangdi was never parsimonious in rewarding Yang Su with gifts. But in his paranoid state of mind, Yangdi secretly wished for Yang Su's death. When a grand astrologer (taishi 太史) predicted that a major figure would die in the Sui 隋 area, Yangdi transferred Yang Su's fief from Yue 越 to Chu 楚 to counteract the prophesy. In so doing Yangdi may well have anticipated a fulfillment of the prophesy resulting in Yang Su's death since Sui and Chu were governed by the same celestial domain in astrology. Yang Su clearly expressed his death wish by rejecting medication, and died in 606 not long after Yangdi came to power.[53]

Even Zhang Heng, who had been among Yangdi's small coterie of loyal officials in Wendi's time, fell victim to Yangdi's overly suspicious temperament. As right mentor (you shuzi 右庶子) of the Eastern Palace, Zhang was in charge of grooming Yangdi for succession and was probably involved in Wendi's death. On his Ordos tour of 607, Yangdi even paid a personal visit to Zhang in his country mansion and stayed there for three days. However, Yangdi's perception about him changed completely when Zhang attempted to advise Yangdi to exercise moderation in his construction projects. A displeased Yangdi remarked cynically: "Zhang Heng says that his plans were responsible for putting me on the throne." Eventually, after his concubine reported on his libelous comment on court policy, Zhang was forced to end his own life in 612.[54]

## THE SEVEN NOBLES AND THE FIVE NOBLES

The death of Yang Su and the dismissal of Su Wei from office had a major effect on the top echelon of the bureaucracy. The chief minister system, as refined by Wendi, was now in jeopardy. Both Yang Su and Su Wei had served as the leaders of the Department of State Affairs. When Yang Su died, his office of department president died with him; and after Su Wei was forced to give up his position as vice president of the left of the department, no effort was made to replace him. The most crucial executive agency of the central government was left without an official head for the rest of the reign. Yangdi dealt with other chief ministerial positions in a similar manner. By 612, only one chief minister position remained in service.

Yangdi did not leave these top jobs vacant through negligence. Instead, he deliberately bypassed conventional routes of promotion to central leadership in order to make unofficial appointments. In so doing, Yangdi shifted the decision making power at court to the less secure group of de facto chief ministers. The fact that Su Wei was to be reappointed official chief minister as president of the Chancellery and remain in that position until 616 was made less significant by his concurrent appointment as a de facto chief minister. In all likelihood, the official chief ministerial position he still held was reduced to ceremonial status.

Evidence of a leadership group outside the official chief minister structure was found as early as the seventh month of 606 when top government leaders were involved in civil service recruitment. The official in charge of the operation was nominally, Niu Hong 牛弘, president of the Board of Personnel. However, his power was eclipsed by six other decision makers at court—Su Wei, Yuwen Shu, Pei Ju 裴矩, Pei Yun 裴蘊, Yu Shiji 虞世基, and Zhang Jin 張瑾. Collectively, these six officials and Niu Hong were referred to as the Seven Nobles (*qigui* 七貴) of the Appointment Section.[55] Of these seven top power holders, all but Niu Hong and Zhang Jin were later appointed by Yangdi as de facto chief ministers. Nevertheless, by virtue of his inclusion in the Seven Nobles, Niu Hong was no doubt one of the most influential officials at Yangdi's court. Niu Hong was also a perennial survivor of court politics, thanks to his personality, which was marked not only by a carefulness but also by a transcendence. Even the overbearing Yang Su commented admiringly, "I can match the wisdom of the duke of Qizhang 奇章公 (Niu Hong), but not his stupidity." As the nation's top ritual scholar, Niu Hong served competently, first as president of the Board of Rites and then as president of the Board of Personnel under Wendi, a post he continued to hold under Yangdi. It is believed that among high officials who had served under the previous reign, Niu Hong was the only one who continuously enjoyed the unswerving trust of Yangdi.

The remaining member of the Seven Nobles who received no de facto chief minister status was Zhang Jin, who has left only a scanty record in history. There is no biographical information on him in the sources. As general-in-chief of the Courageous Guard of the Left, Zhang was involved in a number of offensives against the Tujue. Though powerful in his own right, he was clearly inferior in status to the other military figure of the seven, Yuwen Shu.

Su Wei, Yuwen Shu, Pei Ju, Pei Yun, and Yu Shiji, the more influential five members of the Seven Nobles were also known as the Five Nobles (*wugui* 五貴), a group that evolved after Gao Jiong's death in 607. As de facto chief ministers they constituted the inner circle of Yangdi's court.

The only professional warrior of the five, Yuwen Shu was the son of Yuwen Sheng 宇文盛, a Wuchuan commander, who had been awarded the title superior pillar of state and general-in-chief (*shang zhuguo da jiangjun* 上柱國大將軍) by the end of the Northern Zhou, and may be identified as a late member of the Wuchuan 武川 group. Yuwen Shu, as his son, distinguished himself in the wars against Yuchi Jiong and the Chen under Wendi. He was among a handful of staunch supporters of Yangdi before he became crown prince. During Yangdi's reign, he was without doubt the most trusted general. In his dealings with the court, Yuwen Shu was extremely careful, and never made a disagreeable remark. He delivered presents to the court that pleased Yangdi, who continued to shower him with unmatched favors. Because of his special relationship with Yangdi, Yuwen survived a disastrous defeat by Koguryŏ for which he bore a major responsibility. When he died in Jiangdu, Yangdi bestowed upon him posthumously the most prestigious official title—president of the Department of State Affairs (*shangshu ling* 尚書令).[56]

Pei Ju was a member of the Peis of Hedong 河東, one of the powerful aristocratic lineages that were perennially present in the political landscape of medieval China. When he was promoted de facto chief minister, he was vice president of the Chancellery (*huangmen shilang* 黃門侍郎) with a rank of 4a, which made him one of the lowest-ranking officials thus promoted. Even the Six Board presidents and the capital prefect enjoyed higher official status.[57] Primarily responsible for formulating and implementing Yangdi's policy concerning the Northern and Northwestern frontiers, he dealt successfully with Tujue, Tuyuhun 吐谷渾, and the oasis states in the Western Regions. Having followed Yangdi to Jiangdu, he sensed the danger rebellion posed to the empire and reported the situation to Yangdi. Thanks to his report, Pei fell out of favor, only to be reinstated soon after. Ever cautious, Pei Ju, according to his biographer, was among those very few key court officials who survived politically under Yangdi without compromising their moral integrity.

Although Pei Yun could be regarded as a Pei of Hedong 河東 in terms of choronym, his ancestors had lived for generations in the South. His father had been a Chen official who was captured and retained by the Northern Zhou while Pei Yun worked for the Chen. Secretly switching his allegiance to Wendi, he functioned as a covert Sui agent and was well rewarded after the fall of the Chen. Under Yangdi, he was appointed censor-general (*yushi dafu*

御史大夫), in charge of the Censorate, the highest surveillance organization with broad powers to investigate, discipline, and impeach ranking officials. Essentially, Pei Yun became the hatchet man who did Yangdi's bidding. Over time he perfected his skill in deciphering Yangdi's intentions. Always taking his cue from the sovereign, he would either intentionally frame an official under investigation or get him acquitted.

Quintessentially a Southerner, Yu Shiji was an accomplished writer and scholar. His father was a palace cadet (*taizi zhongshuzi* 太子中庶子) under the Chen, a leading official in the crown prince administration. Basically ignored by Wendi after the fall of the Chen, he was appointed vice president of the Secretariat (*neishi shilang* 內史侍郎) by Yangdi. Together with Pei Ju, he was the lowest ranking of the Five Nobles, but as keeper of secret court documents and drafter of imperial edicts for Yangdi, he was virtually the most powerful official at court. His power did not derive from merit or prestige, but from his ready access to the emperor.

Although one of the Five Nobles, Su Wei belonged to a different category altogether. He was one of those rare critics of the court who was to outlast Yangdi himself. Not long after his dismissal by Yangdi in 607, Su Wei was reinstated as president of the Chancellery. Thenceforth, he was more prudent than before. For lack of sufficient data, it is difficult to speculate on Su Wei's survival throughout those turbulent years. Among the personal traits listed in his biography, honesty and cautiousness stand out. Although his argumentative side often irked people, perhaps his cautious side saved him from the ultimate disaster—execution by edict. On the other hand, his patron, Gao Jiong, who was executed, cannot be said to have been incautious; his premature death may be attributed to circumstances beyond his control. Although his harsh criticisms against Yangdi's excesses were not intended for the emperor's ears, they were reported to the court. Yangdi may well have associated these criticisms with Gao's past tenacious fight against Yangdi's rise to power and his defiant killing of Zhang Lihua. However, the determinant factor for Yangdi's decision to take his life was apparently the knowledge that serious complaining against Yangdi emanated from not one but three highly respected court officials from the previous reign. It aroused in Yangdi the fear of a group conspiracy, and triggered his paranoid, impulsive reaction. By contrast, Su Wei, who delivered his rather mild criticism by way of a memorial much earlier, was spared the outburst of the imperial furor.[58]

The institution of the Five Nobles marked a fundamental change to the top leadership. Through promoting officials of insufficient seniority and qualifications to de facto chief ministers, Yangdi succeeded in systematically circumventing officially appointed chief ministers. Both Sui emperors used this mechanism, but to different effects. For Wendi it was a supplement to the official channel of appointment. But under Yangdi, de facto chief ministers functioned as heads of the government in place of the presidents of the Three Departments.

By surrounding himself with sycophantic advisers, Yangdi was not only able to undertake his favorite domestic projects without restraint, putting the economy at risk of ruin through overspending, but also to pursue his international vision.

On the international front, Yangdi advocated a policy of proactive engagement and aggression in areas that had traditionally been within the Chinese sphere of influence and even beyond. He brought Linyi 林邑 (Champa) in Vietnam and Liuqiu 琉球 in the East China Sea to submission by force, and sent imperial missions to remote places like Chitu 赤土 in the Malay Peninsula and Yamato in Japan. He greatly enhanced Sui China's presence in Central Asia through annexing a vast Tuyuhun territory. In the wake of that expansion, he went on a tour of inspection to the Northwest in 609, which brought him to Zhangye 張掖, the Northwestern trading outpost on the Silk Road.

Starting in the early 610s, Yangdi began to shift his focus to the Northeastern state of Koguryŏ, even though Tujue was becoming increasingly a threatening presence on the horizon. His repeated military conflicts with Koguryŏ in the last years of his reign was to become a catalyst for the decline and fall of the Sui dynasty.[59]

# 3

## The Collapse of the Sui

The Sui empire reached the pinnacle of its power in 609 when its population peaked. Thereafter as signs of social and economic stress became increasingly manifest, the empire began to unravel. The agents of change that eventually brought it down were the multitude of rebellions that sprang up towards the end of the dynasty against a background of economic decline and population depletion, as a result of the prolonged, flagrant abuse of power. Serious trouble with law and order began to emerge in 611 on the eve of the first Liaodong campaign. As compulsory military service, corvée labor for public works, and other fiscal impositions grew more oppressive, rebellion broke out with increasing frequency. The total number of documented late Sui insurgencies, big and small, reputedly exceeds two hundred. In all, an estimated four to five million people were involved in armed rebellion against the government, or about one tenth of the Sui population in 609. Roughly, this last violent stage of the dynasty can be divided into three phases based on the magnitude of insurgencies: Phase One (611–613), Phase Two (613–616), and Phase Three (616–618).

The first phase started with relatively small-scale rebellions, and ended with the catalytic event that set in motion the collapse of the empire—the Yang Xuangan rebellion, which took place in 613 in the middle of the second Liaodong campaign. The second phase, starting with the crushing of the Yang Xuangan rebellion, saw the widespread outburst of public wrath against the Sui court, engulfing China in a nationwide turmoil. The third phase was marked by the mass defection of Sui army commanders and officials and their participation in the rebellious effort, which led to the demise of Yangdi and his dynasty[1] (map 3.1).

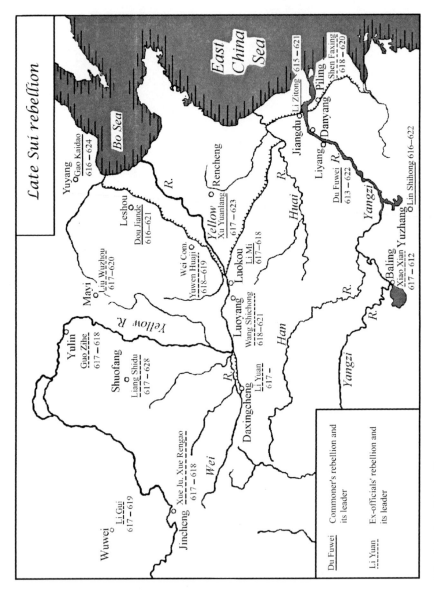

MAP 3.1  Late Sui rebellion

## PHASE ONE (611–613): INITIAL OUTBREAKS AND YANG XUANGAN

Serious civil unrest began as early as 611, almost two years before Yang Xuangan started his rebellion. Extant sources point to the uprising led by Wang Bo 王薄 of Zouping 鄒平 in Mount Changbai 長白 (northeast of Zhangqiu, north Shandong) as the genesis of large-scale organized rebellion. Around the same time, two major rebellions raged in neighboring areas: one led by Liu Badao 劉霸道 to the northwest, in Pingyuan 平原 Commandery (seat: Ling County, northwest Shandong); and the other by Gao Shida 高士達, southwest of Pingyuan in Qinghe 清河 (seat: northwest of Qinghe, Hebei).

The timing and geographical distribution of these rebellions are of vital importance for understanding the primary causes of late Sui popular disturbances. The year 611 was a period of major natural disasters, particularly in the North China plain region east of the Taihang Mountains and south of the Yellow River. More than forty prefectures were flooded. Meanwhile, Yangdi's massive efforts to prepare for the Liaodong campaign began to have a devastating, cumulative impact on an economy already strained by incessant mobilizations of the productive labor force for construction projects. To support his troops on the Liaodong front, Yangdi ordered six hundred thousand laborers to transport strategic grains north on wheelbarrow. The long distance and treacherous road conditions caused delays, and the rice they transported was barely enough for their own consumption. On arriving in Liaodong, the laborers had no rice to deliver to the military, and rather than face severe punishment, they fled. These aggravating developments provided the ideal breeding ground for banditry and rebellion. As for those civilians who did not leave home for the front, "forced on pain of death to meet government requisitions, they had to resort to robbery for survival. In consequence, they began to gather together to form groups of bandits." These bandit groups were often composed of rebel forces who pillaged randomly, sacked cities, and posed a serious threat to local governments; worse still, some grew into major antigovernment forces with tens of thousands of insurgents.[2]

It is no coincidence that a large-scale rebellion erupted in northwest Shandong-southeast Hebei. As the hinterland of the former Eastern Wei-Northern Qi area, this region had seen continuous banditry since Northern Qi times. Extreme hardship brought on by natural calamities and an uncaring government created the ideal conditions for insurgency.

The story of Sun Anzu 孫安祖, one of the early rebel leaders, provides us with a telling example of how submissive subjects were turned into rebels. Sun lived in Zhangnan 漳南, Qinghe Commandery (northeast of Gucheng County, Hebei). In 611, a catastrophic flood inundated his village and destroyed his house. The famine that followed took the life of his wife. Despite his family's mishap, Sun was conscripted for military service on the Liaodong campaign. He begged the county magistrate to excuse him from service due to poverty. But the infuriated magistrate had him flogged. Sun killed the magistrate and went into hiding. The future rebel leader Dou Jiande 竇建德, who was a junior officer in the Sui army, took Sun under his wing. With Dou's support, Sun led hundreds of stragglers and the destitute to start an armed rebellion.[3]

Yangdi ignored these early rebellions in marginal geographical areas like north Shandong. Yet, as long as the underlying socioeconomic conditions failed to improve, the spread of rebellion remained a serious threat.


## The First Liaodong Campaign

In analyzing the reasons behind Yangdi's decision to launch his anti-Koguryŏ invasions, Arthur Wright has produced a sophisticated argument that is similar to Jin Baoxiang's hypothesis about a fan-shaped semi-encirclement by nomadic powers. To Wright, Koguryŏ's increasing threat to China's security was the backdrop against which Yangdi invaded Koguryŏ. There were three possible candidates for forming an anti-Sui alliance with Koguryŏ, namely, Eastern Tujue, Mohe, and Qidan. There was the additional concern that the military power of Koguryŏ might feed into anti-Sui sentiments in the former Northern Qi area. However, the Koguryŏ-Eastern Tujue alliance never materialized while both Mohe and Qidan were minor players in Sui times. Of the seven Mohe tribes, the Boduo 伯咄 was the strongest, but it only had a force of seven thousand men. Another Mohe tribe, the Sumo 粟末, far from helping Koguryŏ against the Sui, often raided Koguryŏ. Each of the Qidan's ten tribes had an army of only one thousand to three thousand. Furthermore, in 605, on the occasion of a Qidan raid into Ying Prefecture 營州, the Sui officer Wei Yunqi 韋雲起, commanding an Eastern Tujue army, routed the Qidan forces and captured forty thousand of the Qidan population. At the time of the first Liaodong campaign, Mohe, in spite of its recent anti-Sui activities, actually joined forces with the Sui in attacking Koguryŏ. While it is true the former Qi area in present-day Shandong was home to the first major anti-Sui rebellions, there is no evidence the rise of Koguryŏ's military power had any direct impact on the rebellions. Instead, they were caused by Yangdi's labor and military levies to prepare for war against Koguryŏ. Being a visionary, Yangdi may well have considered the advantage of establishing long-term security on the Northeastern frontier through invading Koguryŏ. But overall the invasion was driven more by ambition and pride, and by a desire to finish the task his brother

Yang Liang and father had failed to accomplish, than by a rational fear of being encircled by barbarians.[4]

The potential destabilizing effect of domestic rebellion did not deter Yangdi from going to war against Koguryŏ. For him the top priority was to bring that erstwhile colony of Han China, with a people culturally akin to the Han Chinese, into the orbit of Sui. With that goal in mind, he made a number of strategic moves. First, he launched the Yongji Canal project in early 608 that allowed the Grand Canal system to extend north from the Yellow River valley to Zhuo Commandery 涿郡 (seat: in the southwest of Beijing), an area close to Koguryŏ territory. Second, he constructed new sections of the Great Wall to deter attacks by nomadic tribes beyond the Northern frontiers. Third, he cultivated cordial relations with the Tujue leader Qimin qaghan, in the hopes that a friendly Tujue power would not only ease the fear of a second front, but also serve as a deterrent against Koguryŏ. Fourth, he made repeated efforts to procure military supplies.

In the second month of 611, Yangdi made a long journey north by the newly completed Yongji Canal from the South and arrived at the Linshuo Palace 林朔宮 (in the southwest of Beijing) in Zhuo Commandery, which was to become the base of his operation for the following year. Meanwhile, war preparations intensified. In the port city of Donglai 東萊 (Laizhou, Shandong), three hundred ships were commissioned. Corvée laborers drafted from various commanderies were set to work on the ships. A general mobilization order was issued to gather troops in Zhuo. Special forces were organized—ten thousand sailors and thirty thousand archers from the South, and thirty thousand spearmen from Lingnan 嶺南. To transport uniforms, armor, and tents, fifty thousand war chariots were ordered from Henan, Huainan, and the South. Male laborers from the Yellow River valley were mobilized to provide logistical supplies, while those from the Huai and Yangzi valleys were commandeered together with their boats to transport rice from the Liyang 黎陽 and Luokou Granaries 洛口倉 to Zhuo. However, even at this early stage, Yangdi's massive efforts of preparation began to take their toll. His horse tax led to skyrocketing horse prices. The working conditions for corvée laborers on his ship project were so harsh that some of them found their limbs infested with maggots after long stays in water. Their overall death rate was about 30–40 percent.[5]

Ignoring these problems, Yangdi inaugurated his Liaodong campaign in the first month of 612, with a declaration of war. Citing precedents of the Xia, Shang, and Zhou dynasties to justify his invasion, Yangdi denounced Koguryŏ for its liaisons with the Qidan and Mohe, its incursions into Liaoxi 遼西, and the disrespect it had shown the Sui court. He enumerated the crimes of the Koguryŏ sovereign—harsh laws and statutes, heavy taxation, manipulation of politics by key ministers and great lineages, cronyism, widespread bribery, and refusal to remedy wrongs, in addition to bringing great misery to the civilians of Koguryŏ through incessant warfare and endless corvée duties. But these pro forma accusations were too general and vague to serve as an excuse for military intervention.

Although Yangdi talked contemptuously of the Koguryŏ king and scoffed at the tiny size of his realm, he made serious military, economic, and diplomatic preparations for the war in a span of four years. Obviously, he wanted to avoid his father's mistake of underestimating the enemy.[6] The invading armed force of 1,133,800 Yangdi amassed was the largest gathering of troops for a single operation in Chinese history up to that time.[7] A labor force twice as large was responsible for its logistical supplies. Under Yangdi's personal command, in the third month of 612, the Sui army arrived on the west bank of the Liao River 遼水, the natural barrier the Sui army had failed to break through during Wendi's campaign. Relying on the river as the first line of defense, the Koguryŏ army took up its position along the east bank. When the three pontoon bridges constructed by the architect and engineer Yuwen Kai fell short by more than 1 zhang (1 zhang = 2.355 m), the Koguryŏ army unleashed a surprise attack with an overwhelming force. The Sui troops were pushed back to the west bank, having suffered heavy casualties and lost the commanding general Mai Tiezhang 麥鐵杖 who perished while attempting to lead his troops across the river. The engineer He Chou had to work frantically for two days to finally extend the pontoon bridges to the east bank. Sui attacks then resumed. The Koguryŏ defense, after suffering tens of thousands of casualties, collapsed, and the Sui army pushed on to lay siege to the city of Liaodong 遼東 (Liaoyang).[8]

At Liaodong, Yangdi personally directed the campaign as the commander-in-chief of the Sui forces. He laid down restrictive rules to his field generals. Every attack should be coordinated, three-pronged. Any troop advance had to be reported and approved by the emperor. His style of micromanagement was further complicated by a quixotic policy on surrender. No attacks should be launched against surrendering Koguryŏ troops. To implement that policy, he installed in each army a special officer (shouxiang shi 受降使; the commissioner who accepted surrender), who doubled as army supervisor on the battlefield. The shouxiang commissioner—probably variably known as weifu shi 慰撫使 (pacifying commissioner)—was not subject to the command of a field general; instead, he acted on imperial edicts. To halt Sui attacks, the Koguryŏ took advantage of the situation to feign surrender on several occasions The Sui generals, forced to wait for imperial approval for action, lost a number of opportunities to sack Liaodong (Liaoyang). The Koguryŏ were able to hold their own against the Sui onslaught there and in other cities.

The only bright spot of the war was the initial victory scored by General Lai Huer 來護兒, who commanded the naval forces of the Yangzi and Huai to enter the Pei River 浿水 (Taedong River) and defeat the Koguryŏ army near Pyongyang. After his forty thousand warriors charged deep into Pyongyang, Lai allowed them to fall out of formation and loot the city. But his troops were caught in a devastating ambush by the Koguryŏ troops, particularly the five hundred daredevils under the command of Kŏnmu 建武 (Yŏngnyu 榮留), younger brother of the Koguryŏ king. Only a few thousand of Lai's troops survived.[9]

On the Liaodong front, after 305,000 Sui troops in nine armies had crossed the Liao River and gathered on the west bank of the Yalu River 鴨綠水, the Koguryŏ general Ŭlchi Mundŏk 乙支文德 arrived, who made a false offer of surrender and escaped. The Sui commanding officer Yu Zhongwen 于仲文 then launched an attack across the Yalu River despite inadequate supplies of provision and General Yuwen Shu's 宇文述 opposition. Ŭlchi deliberately led the Sui armies deep into Koguryŏ territory. After Yuwen realized that Pyongyang was well fortified, he ordered his exhausted troops to withdraw. On their westward retreat, they were attacked in midstream on the Sa River 薩水 (Salsu), and sustained staggering losses in men and materiel. With the food supply depleted, Yangdi withdrew his army after setting up a tiny Liaodong Commandery, with the captured town Wuliluo 武歷邏 (northwest of Shenyang) as its seat.[10]

Many factors contributed to the failure of the campaign. The overly ambitious recruitment probably worked against rather than in favor of the Sui expedition. At the time, the total number of warriors under arms in the *fubing* system was estimated to be around six hundred thousand. An expeditionary army almost twice its size must have included a large number of poorly trained new recruits, which could only serve to weaken the combat effectiveness of the Sui forces. Furthermore, there was a host of other disadvantages—the terrain and climate, well-fortified enemy cities, and especially an overextended supply line. One of the most devastating weaknesses was the inferior leadership provided by the supreme commander, Yangdi.[11] By tightly controlling troop movements, Yangdi deprived his field generals of the crucial power of making prompt decisions, and took away the element of surprise against the enemy. The idiosyncratic rules he made on surrender turned out to be an additional impediment. Failure to form international alliances against Koguryŏ also significantly reduced Yangdi's chance for victory. In the complex world of power politics in early seventh century Northeast Asia and East Asia, Eastern Tujue was the most formidable force next to the Sui. With the death of Qimin in 611, the relationship with Eastern Tujue deteriorated. Although both Silla and Paekche on the Korean Peninsula were rivals to Koguryŏ, neither contributed to the campaign. The only recorded involvement of foreign forces in this first Liaodong campaign is that of the Mohe troops. But Mohe was a small military power and could not help the Sui tip the balance of war.[12] Greatly outnumbered, the Koguryŏ resorted to guerilla tactics in familiar home territory, and used their capital city to entrap the Sui forces.[13] Against impossible odds, the Koguryŏ repelled the mighty invading army.

## The Second Liaodong Campaign

No sooner did Yangdi arrive in Luoyang than fresh war preparations were underway. Yangdi amassed another invading army in Zhuo Commandery and ordered the repair of the old city of Liaodong to store grain reserves.[14]

In the third month of 613, Yangdi headed for Liaodong Commandery. The strategy he devised for the second campaign was a familiar one. He would lead the main force east across the Liao River. Yuwen Shu and Yang Yichen 楊義臣 would lead an army to storm the capital Pyongyang. General Lai Huer was ordered to lead his naval force from Donglai 東萊 to join the attack from sea. Crossing the Liao River in the fourth month, Yangdi launched a merciless attack on the city of Liaodong. His generals resorted to all sorts of siege warfare techniques, including tunneling and the use of scaling ladders. Casualties were extremely high on both sides, but the Koguryŏ held their own for more than twenty days. Yangdi then ordered more than one million sacks of soil to be dumped at the foot of the city walls to pave the way for Sui warriors. Eight-wheeled, multistoried carriages towering above the city walls were also deployed to allow archers to launch arrow attacks into the city.

Just as the Sui army was about to storm the city, Yangdi received a message that took him completely by surprise. Yang Xuangan, the son of the deceased general Yang Su, rebelled. Horrified, Yangdi made an immediate withdrawal, leaving the bulk of the materiel behind. Fearing that the Sui army had laid a trap, the Koguryŏ did not start a pursuit until two days later. By the time they caught up with the Sui rearguard, the Sui main force had already crossed the Liao River back into Sui territory. Yangdi's second Liaodong campaign came to an ignominious close.[15]

## Yang Xuangan 楊玄感

Different from other rebel leaders, who were members of the downtrodden, Xuangan grew up in perhaps the most prestigious nonroyal family under the Sui. After his father Yang Su died in 606, Xuangan inherited the title of duke of Chu 楚 and was promoted to the post of president of the Board of Rites (*li*'*bu shangshu* 禮部尚書). However, neither power nor prestige could allay his sense of vulnerability in consequence of Yangdi's growing suspicion. He had formulated a plan to take Yangdi's life as early as 609 when the emperor was on an expedition against Tuyuhun. But the plan was not acted upon thanks to opposition by his uncle Yang Shen 楊慎, who argued against the move on ground of the country's apparent unity.[16]

In many respects, the year 613 was perfect timing for Yang Xuangan to go into action. After the disastrous failure of the first Liaodong campaign, the economy was stretched to the limit. Extensive flooding and widespread epidemics had decimated the population in the North. The launching of the second Liaodong campaign only exacerbated the situation. As incidents of banditry and robbery increased dramatically, the semblance of unity vanished. With Yangdi away in southern Manchuria, the two capitals were considered easy targets.[17]

Yang Xuangan raised the standard of rebellion while in charge of transporting provisions from Liyang 黎陽 (near Xun County, Henan) to the Sui troops on the Liaodong campaign. In the sixth month of 613, on entering the city of Liyang, Yang Xuangan publicly denounced General Lai Huer, accusing him of rebellion. The fact that Xuangan initially targeted Lai instead of Yangdi indicates his concern about the lack of public support for his open anti-Yangdi activity. It was then that his chief strategic adviser, Li Mi 李密, laid out three strategies. The best one was to suffocate the Sui armed forces on the Liaodong campaign by cutting off logistical supplies hoping it would prompt a Koguryŏ attack from the east. The second best strategy was to go west and take Guanzhong, an area that would provide resources for long-term survival and natural barriers against invaders. The third strategy was to conquer nearby Luoyang. Yang Xuangan chose the last strategy, believing that capturing the family members of high-ranking officials living in Luoyang would further weaken support for the Sui, while sacking the city would also boost morale among his followers.[18]

It was during the subsequent siege of Luoyang that Yang Xuangan made a public denouncement of Yangdi in a letter to the chief defender of the city, President of the Board of Revenue (*minbu shangshu* 民部尚書) Fan Zigai 樊子蓋.[19] Despite his portrayal of Yangdi as an evil ruler, Yang Xuangan failed to win over Fan Zigai, who put up a tenacious resistance against rebel attacks. To lay siege to the city, Yang Xuangan deployed one hundred thousand troops at the Shangchun Gate 上春門 (Shangdong 上東 Gate during Tang times), the northernmost east gate (map 4.1).[20] During weeks of fierce fighting, the rebel forces were able to pick up a number of key defectors from the Sui cause, including the sons of such senior officers and officials as Han Qinhu, Yang Xiong, Yu Shiji, Lai Huer, Pei Yun, and Zhou Luohou.[21]

Yang Xuangan's troops soon occupied the grounds of the Department of State Affairs (*shangshu sheng* 尚書省), located in the Eastern City, an enclosed area just east of the Palace City. This suggests that Yang did break into the city, but the penetration was limited. There is no record of the rebel army occupying the Palace City where the royal entourage resided, the Imperial City where central government agencies were concentrated, or nonofficial residential areas. In part, the design of the city itself probably accounted for the limited progress made by the rebels within the walled area. Although overall defense of the city relied on its outer walls, the urban area within was compartmentalized into many self-contained, well-fortified divisions. The royal-administrative quarters in the northwest corner of the city were subdivided into several separate walled areas—the Palace City, the Eastern Palace, the Eastern City, the Hanjia Granary 含嘉倉, and the Imperial City.[22] All this could serve as additional barriers that hindered the advance of the rebel troops. Soon, the loyalists under Fan made an effective counterattack while government reinforcements under President of the Board of Justice (*xingbu shangshu* 刑部尚書) Wei Xuan 衛玄 bore down from the Mang/Beimang Mountains 北芒/邙山 north of the city.

Before the main Sui force approached Luoyang, Yang Xuangan declared victory and turned west to march on Guanzhong, on the advice of Li Zixiong 李子雄, ex-president of the Board of Revenue (*minbu shangshu* 民部尚書). This was in fact Li Mi's second best strategy, but its adoption came too late to save the rebels. While en route, Yang Xuangan laid siege to the Hongnong Palace 弘農宮 (in Sanmenxia, Henan) despite Li Mi's urgent plea, losing three days valuable time. After the Hongnong fiasco, the rebel forces were practically destroyed. When Yang Xuangan escaped to Min Township 閔鄉 (east of present-day Tongguan), government forces commanded by Yuwen Shu, Wei Xuan, Lai Huer, and Qutu Tong caught up with him. Frantically, Xuangan moved into Shangluo 上洛 (Shang County, Shaanxi) with a small band of cavalrymen. Several rounds of fighting later, the once mighty rebel force was reduced to only Xuangan and his brother Yang Jishan 楊積善, both without their horses. At his own request, Xuanguan was hacked to death by Jishan, who then stabbed himself. While the head of Xuangan was delivered to the emperor, his corpse was hauled to a marketplace in Luoyang, where it was quartered and, after being exposed in public for three days, ground up and burned. With Yangdi's permission, General Yuwen Shu had the wounded Jishan tied to a wooden shaft, enclosing his neck with a chariot wheel. Officials shot at him until his body was covered with arrows like a hedgehog. He was then dismembered. Xuangan's other brothers either died during the rebellion or were hunted down and killed by the Sui army. The lineage of the powerful Yang clan was exterminated.[23]

The failure of the Yang Xuangan rebellion can be attributed to a variety of factors. But first and foremost was the fact that high-ranking Sui officers continued to demonstrate their fealty to the Sui court and the command structure of the Sui army remained intact. So long as professional soldiers such as Lai Huer and Yuwen Shu, and high-ranking officials like Fan Zigai lent their support to Yangdi, Yang Xuangan stood little chance of toppling the dynasty. Had he followed Li Mi's favored strategy of cutting off logistical supplies of the Sui forces on the Liaodong campaign and coordinating a two-pronged attack against the main Sui force with the Koguryŏ, Xuangan might have been able to significantly improve his odds. Instead, he chose Li's least workable strategy of laying siege to Luoyang, probably because of its proximity. Laying siege to cities was usually considered an undesirable strategy, especially to a city as well-fortified as Luoyang. Forced to give up the siege when the enemy forces were closing in on him, Xuangan laid siege to another city of little strategic significance. His unwise military decisions hastened his destruction.

Yet, in spite of its short duration—from the sixth month to the early eighth month[24]—the rebellion contributed significantly to the downfall of the dynasty. Even though other rebellions had been brewing for quite some time, the Yang Xuangan rebellion was the largest and the best organized insurgent movement. Unlike other rebel groups, which were characterized by random acts of banditry, Yang had a clear vision from the beginning: to topple Yangdi's rule. Forcing Yangdi to withdraw the Sui army from Liaodong seriously damaged its morale and battle readiness. The draconian measures Yangdi took in the wake of the rebellion further isolated him and stoked the already simmering, widespread resentment among the populace. Most significant, the rebellion spawned similar efforts to bring down the government.

## Phase Two (613–616): The Spread of Rebellion

Although the Yang Xuangan rebellion was quickly suppressed, it left Yangdi badly shaken. Undoubtedly, something was seriously wrong with his overall military and economic policy. He urgently needed to implement corrective measures to pacify his subjects if he wanted to stem the tide of rebellion. But instead, Yangdi went out of his way to further alienate the masses. In the months immediately following the suppression of the rebellion, Yangdi was clearly in a mood for revenge and inflicted a reign of terror on Luoyang. Those who had accepted relief rice from the rebels were hunted down and buried alive. In all, thirty thousand people allegedly related to the rebellion were executed and their family members enslaved. More than six thousand people were banished to remote areas. In his relentless pursuit of Yang Xuangan's supporters and sympathizers, real or imagined, Yangdi drove more people to despair.[25]

In the latter half of 613, a number of large-scale rebellions sprang up in the South and the North China plain. The first Southern rebellion of significant size was started by Liu Yuanjin 劉元進 in Yuhang 餘杭 (Hangzhou) with tens of thousands of followers. It was immediately followed by another Southern rebellion under Zhu Xie 朱燮 and Guan Chong 管崇, who joined forces with Liu Yuanjin. The combined rebel army of more than one hundred thousand men was active in the lower Yangzi valley. To their north, Wu Hailiu 吳海流 of Jiyin 濟陰 Commandery (seat: west of Dingtao, Shandong) and Peng Xiaocai 彭孝才 of Donghai 東海 (seat: southwest of Lianyungang, Jiangsu) rebelled at the same time, commanding a joint force of tens of thousands.

Meanwhile, on the North China plain, more insurgent armies, often of extraordinary size, emerged. This area had suffered the worst famines for a long time, disproportionately shouldered the burden of the Liaodong campaigns, and borne the brunt of the suppression of the Yang Xuangan rebellion. In the present-day Hebei-Shandong area, Ge Qian 格謙 declared himself prince of Yan 燕王; Sun Xuanya 孫宣雅 followed suit by naming himself prince of Qi 齊王. Each commanded an army of one hundred thousand. At Mount Changbai 長白山 (northeast of Zhangqiu, Shandong), the rebel army under the command of Wang Bo and Meng Rang 孟讓 exceeded one hundred thousand. In Guanzhong, to cap a catastrophic year of Daye nine, in the twelfth month (January, 614), a monk by the name of Xiang Haiming 向海明 gathered a rebel force of several tens of thousands and declared himself Maitreya, the future Buddha, in Fufeng 扶風 Commandery (seat: Fengxiang County, Shaanxi), posing a direct threat to the main capital where the Ancestral Temple of the Sui imperial clan was located. After a propitious dream, the monk declared himself emperor, adopting Baiwu 白烏 (White Raven) as his reign title. Although this religion-inspired rebellion was soon put down, it did not augur well for the coming year.[26]

As rebellion spread like a prairie fire and threatened to completely disrupt the social order of Sui China, circumstances demanded that the sovereign take decisive military action and address the fundamental grievances that had turned law-abiding subjects into rebels. But apart from dispatching his generals on a few haphazard anti-rebel missions, Yangdi continued to devote his energies to the elusive dream of conquering Koguryǒ.

## The Third Liaodong Campaign

Oblivious to the danger of domestic rebellion, Yangdi had, by the beginning of 614, regained enough confidence to start organizing a third Liaodong campaign. In his declaration of war on King Yǒngyang 嬰陽, Yangdi justified his military action not only on account of the military exploits of ancient sovereigns but also on Yǒngyang's defiance. While Yangdi had held out a glimmer of hope that the king could be cowed into submission before, he now no longer entertained any such illusions. The third month of 614 found Yangdi in Zhuo Commandery again, where he conducted a ritual ceremony to worship the Yellow Emperor, a patron god of war. By the time Yangdi arrived in the frontier town of Huaiyuan 懷遠 (northwest of Liaoyang, Liaoning) in the seventh month, China proper was already engulfed in turmoil; large numbers of newly recruited troops failed to report for duty. The Koguryŏ side also showed signs of exhaustion. Just when the Sui general Lai Huer, upon scoring a major victory, was about to march on Pyongyang, a terrified Yŏngyang hurriedly sent an envoy to surrender. As a token of goodwill, Yŏngyang handed over Husi Zheng 斛斯政, a close associate of Yang Xuangan, who had defected. Yangdi took the opportunity to declare victory and return. Back in Daxingcheng, he ordered Husi quartered outside the Jinguang 金光 Gate. His flesh was cooked and distributed among court officials, who were forced to eat it, and his bones were burned and ashes scattered. But despite all the fuss over Husi's capture, for Yangdi real victory was as elusive as ever. When Yŏngyang turned down his summons to appear at the Sui court, a clear indication of continued defiance, Yangdi became obsessed with the idea of a fourth campaign.[27]

Before he embarked on the fourth campaign, Yangdi went to Daxingcheng to perform some key state rituals. By that time, many people had come to believe that Yangdi's only option for survival was to consolidate his power in the rich and highly defensible Guanzhong area. Prior to Yangdi, Guanzhong had served as the power center for most of the key dynasties. The awareness of its strategic importance had predated the Sui by more than a thousand years. But Yangdi intended to go back east to Luoyang instead. When Director of the Astrological Service Yu Zhi 庾質 warned Yangdi against the move, an irritated Yangdi threw him into jail where he later died. Yu Zhi and his associates offered counsel based on occultist interpretations of disastrous and strange portents. Although generally of low rank, the occultist advisers had direct access to Yangdi who greatly valued their suggestions. The fact that Yangdi not only rejected Yu's advice out of hand, but also silenced the adviser permanently, indicates Yangdi had begun to depart from his own usual practice.[28]

## The Siege of Yamen

By the end of 614, Yangdi entered Luoyang.[29] Using Luoyang as his base, Yangdi went on an inspection tour of the Sino-Tujue borders to the north that led to the traumatic siege of Yanmen in present-day northern Shanxi.

With Koguryŏ still on his mind, Yangdi retreated into Taiyuan on the 18th of the fifth month in 615 (June 19, 615) and proceeded north to the Fenyang 汾陽 Palace (southwest of Ningwu, in north Shanxi) to escape from the summer heat. In the eighth month, he went further north to the frontier area. He had been advised by some officials not to take the trip because of the Tujue threat, but he ignored them.[30] In all likelihood, the trip was part of his strategic plan to deploy Sui forces for an attack on the Tujue.[31] But he was caught off guard when a secret messenger sent by Princess Yicheng 義成 arrived to warn him of imminent attack by Eastern Tujue forces. She was the widow of Qimin qaghan and had remarried to his son Shibi 始畢 qaghan. Despite her lingering loyalty to the Sui, she could not stop Shibi from launching the attack. A frantic Yangdi rushed with his entourage into the city of Yanmen 雁門 (in Dai County, north Shanxi), and sure enough, Shibi led a cavalry of several tens of thousands in a charge against the imperial procession. By then, of the forty-one towns under the jurisdiction of Yanmen, thirty-nine had fallen. One of the commanding officers was Fan Angui 范安貴, who, as is indicated in his epitaph, perished in battle in defense of the emperor.[32] Numerous other officers must have met the same fate. Yanmen was now under siege with its civilian and military population of one hundred and fifty thousand and a food supply of twenty days. The siege of Yanmen brought Yangdi perilously close to death. In desperation, he sent his spy to Princess Yicheng for help. She reacted by dispatching her messenger to Shibi to report an "emergency" situation in the north.[33] Meanwhile, rescue forces from Luoyang and various commanderies had arrived. Subsequently, Shibi lifted the siege.[34]

Although Yangdi survived the siege physically unscathed, two developments during and after the siege hastened his downfall. The first one concerned promotional and material rewards for the soldiers and officers who had defended Yanmen. The second one, directly related to the first one, concerned Yangdi's future invasion plans against Koguryŏ.

When Yanmen was still under siege, Yangdi promised to reward his defense forces with generous promotions and material goods. However, upon return to Luoyang, Yangdi considerably raised the criteria for promotion and withheld material rewards completely. Before Yanmen, Yangdi had been preparing for a fourth Liaodong campaign. During the siege, to boost army morale, Yangdi declared a cessation of hostilities towards Koguryŏ, but once the siege was over he resumed his plan for the campaign. Yangdi's flip-flops, parsimony, and intention to reinitiate the unpopular expedition against Koguryŏ, regardless of prior grave losses of life and property, infuriated the generals and soldiers. After the siege of Yanmen, the loyalty the military had shown Yangdi and the court began to dissolve.[35]

## The Move South

All this time, the social and economic conditions of the populace continued to get worse; war, fiscal impositions, banditry, and famine had reduced many commoners to starvation. They consumed tree bark, ground reeds, cooked earth, and human flesh. Such events happened even though government granaries were well-stocked.[36] This desperate situation provided fertile ground for rebellions that plagued North and South with unrelenting ferocity. Insurgent armies of more than one hundred thousand warriors had become commonplace.[37] In 615, the Zhu Can 朱粲 rebellion broke out in the Jing-Xiang 荊襄 area (Jingzhou-Xiangfan area, Hubei). It boasted an army of several hundred thousands.[38]

On Yuwen Shu's advice, Yangdi arrived in Luoyang from Taiyuan in the tenth month of 615. By the fifth month of 616, the rebel problem had worsened. As Yangdi gathered high officials to inquire about rebellion, the sycophantic Yuwen Shu played down the situation. But Su Wei bluntly pointed to the stark reality that law-abiding subjects had been converted into bandits on a massive scale. Upon suggesting rebels be pardoned and recruited to fight the Koguryŏ, Su Wei, a perennial political survivor at court, was ousted and disenrolled.[39] This episode offers prima facie evidence of Yangdi's unwillingness to come to grips with the rebellions that had assumed uncontrolled proportions. It does not necessarily follow that Yangdi was always oblivious to the serious consequences of the rebellions. In an edict dated the second month of 615, Yangdi made a rare public admission that vagabonds and bandits had caused a major problem even as he attempted to play down its impact by emphasizing that peace had been restored. Yangdi was clearly aware of the dangers associated with the rebellions, but he chose not to be fully informed about them. Meanwhile, his stay in Luoyang became increasingly unpleasant. In the usual gathering of territorial representatives from all over the country at the beginning of 616, more than twenty commanderies did not send in theirs, a telltale sign that the central government was losing its grip on local powers. In the fourth month, a fire broke out in the Daye 大業 Basilica. Fearing it was a bandit attack, a panicked Yangdi rushed into the nearby Western Park and hid in the bushes until the fire was put out.[40]

These events, plus the unpalatable news about the rebels, may have worked to gradually change his perception about the viability of Luoyang as his main residence. He was faced with two options: first, to go west to Daxingcheng in Guanzhong to rebuild his power base and second, to go south to escape problems in the North. Although Yangdi had previously considered the Guanzhong option, once he made a strategic decision to move south, no one could stop him. He was infuriated by one of his most trusted generals Lai Huer, himself a Southerner, who voiced his opposition for strategic reasons. When General Zhao Cai 趙才 came forward with a similar suggestion he was thrown into jail. Ren Zong 任宗 and Cui Minxiang 崔民象, two more remonstrators against the trip, were not so lucky: One was clubbed to death, and the other beheaded.

Yangdi and his entourage departed for the South in the seventh month of 616. En route, when confronted by a couple of self-appointed remonstrators, he had them summarily dispatched. The fact that so many desperate attempts were made to prevent Yangdi from proceeding to the South testifies to the widespread perception that the trip Yangdi was embarking on could lead to disaster. By abandoning the entire North to the rebels, Yangdi was throwing away his Mandate of Heaven. His Southern trip of 616 was his last.[41]

## PHASE THREE (616–618): THE LAST DAYS

We do not know when Yangdi arrived in the South. But we are certain that he had already settled down in Jiangdu by the tenth month, when Yuwen Shu, who had accompanied him, died there. The overall political and military situation continued to deteriorate even as Yangdi was on his way south. Rebel leaders Li Zitong 李子通, Zuo Caixiang 左才相, and Du Fuwei 杜伏威, each commanding a force of several tens of thousands, pillaged the Huai and lower Yangzi valleys. In the eighth month, Zhao Wanhai 趙萬海, leading a rebel army of hundreds of thousands, raided Gaoyang 高陽 (east of Gaoyang, Hebei).[42] A prime reason for the extraordinary growth of rebellion was Yangdi's almost complete lack of initiative in dealing with it. Probably, unlike Koguryŏ or Tujue, Yangdi did not consider the bandit groups worthy adversaries. At least initially, most of them did not have dynastic pretensions. Besides, surrounded by minions who did their utmost to shield him from bad news, Yangdi was not in a position to fully assess the seriousness of the situation. Furthermore, the rebellions, numerous and scattered, made effective suppression extremely difficult.

As 616 gave way to 617, a more menacing trend emerged. An increasing number of Sui generals and high officials revolted. As members of the elite, they were distinguished from plebeian rebel leaders by their existing power bases and privileges. They carved out their own territories and positioned themselves in the scramble for national dominance at a time when China had been reduced to a state of chaotic anarchy. An early example was Tiger-brave General Luo Yi 羅藝 (*huben langjiang* 虎賁郎將, rank 4a), who was in charge of rebel suppression in present-day north Hebei. Luo staged a mutiny himself and became de facto the independent governor of the Youzhou 幽州 area (seat: Beijing). This trend was particularly obvious in the Northern frontier area and the Northwest where mutinous Sui officers were transformed overnight into local warlords. In the second month of 617, Liang Shidu 梁師都 openly revolted in Shuofang 朔方 Commandery (seat: northeast of Baichengzi, north Shaanxi), where he had been serving as commandant of the local Soaring

Hawk Garrison (*yingyang fu langjiang* 鷹揚府郎將, rank 5a). Following his initial success in conquering territory in present-day Shaanxi, Gansu and Ningxia, Liang declared himself emperor of the Liang dynasty.[43] Simultaneously, in Mayi 馬邑 Commandery (seat: Shuozhou, north Shanxi), Liu Wuzhou 劉武周, [cavalry] commander of the Soaring Hawk Garrison (*yingyang fu xiaowei* 鷹揚府校尉, rank 6a), murdered the commandery governor and carved out his own territory in present-day north Shanxi and the Ordos region. Like Liang Shidu, Liu Wuzhou declared himself emperor. In Jincheng 金城 Commandery (seat: Lanzhou, Gansu), Commander (*xiaowei*) Xue Ju 薛舉 set up his own kingdom after imprisoning commandery and county officials. Expanding into Longxi and present-day Qinghai, Xue first declared himself hegemonic prince of Western Qin 西秦霸王, then emperor.[44]

With the collapse of Sui central authority, Shibi qaghan of Eastern Tujue, allegedly commanding one million cavalrymen, became the dominant power in the North and Northwest.[45] He formed lord-vassal relationships with a number of Chinese claimants to power, and conferred the imperial titles Dingyang 定楊 Son of Heaven, and Jieshi 解事 Son of Heaven upon Liu Wuzhou and Liang Shidu, respectively.[46]

Then, the most significant late-Sui rebellion took place in Taiyuan, in the fifth month of 617. It was started by Li Yuan 李淵, a key member of the Sui ruling establishment.[47] At that time, he held the position of regent (*liushou* 留守) of Taiyuan. *Liushou*, in late Sui times, was a kind of ad hoc position created for Yangdi's most trusted officials who assumed regency from a key metropolitan center over vast surrounding areas.[48] It gave Li Yuan dominant administrative and military powers in the region. Most primary sources record that it is Li Yuan's second son, Li Shimin 李世民, who, supported by Li Yuan's close associate Pei Ji 裴寂, persuaded Li Yuan to rebel.[49] This view is challenged by modern revisionist scholars, who believe that Li Shimin's role here was invented by Tang scholars to glorify his past.[50] At any rate, Li Yuan's rebellion was uniquely successful, not only because of its size and its superior organization, but also because of the foresighted decision made by its leaders to move west to capture Guanzhong.[51]

Mutinous activity was not limited to the North and the Northwest. In the South, the new home territory of Yangdi, members of the elite also began to form their own independent regimes. Supported by commanders (*xiaowei*) like Dong Jingzhen 董景珍 and Lei Shimeng 雷世猛, in the tenth month of 617, Xiao Xian 蕭銑, descendent of the royal family of the defunct Later Liang, publicly ended his ties to the Sui and revived the kingdom of Liang at Jiangling 江陵.

Amid these chaotic developments, Yangdi settled down permanently in the South. Anecdotal records indicate that an increasingly distraught and despondent Yangdi often lapsed into a state of maudlin sentimentality. The once ambitious, self-confident, and hubristic emperor resigned himself to fate.[52]

The main source of his bitterness was news of rebel victories, so Yangdi made it abundantly clear that he loathed hearing about them. Thus, close advisers like Yu Shiji took it upon themselves to shield the emperor from bad news. Whenever there was a request for emergency help from a general or a local administrator under rebel attack, Yu played it down and reported, "These rat thieves and dog robbers! The commanderies and counties should hunt them down and wipe them out. I wish that His Majesty would not worry about them."

Taking his cue from Yu, Yangdi went so far as to have the messengers clubbed for spreading wild rumor. So as Yangdi continued to be kept in the dark, a growing number of commanderies and counties fell to the rebels. Then a victory report from General Yang Yichen took Yangdi by surprise. Yang claimed to have defeated several hundred thousand rebels in Hebei, and Yangdi was visibly disturbed by the large number of rebels. Yu Shiji then suggested, "Although there are numerous petty outlaws, they are nothing to worry about. Yichen is the one who commanded a large army to conquer them. If he (Yichen) is at large for long, he will become a great threat." So Yang Yichen, one of the most effective anti-rebel generals, was relieved of his command and his troops were dispersed. This caused an immediate resurgence of rebel activity in the area.[53]

Yangdi's refusal to aggressively address the issue of rebellion led to further deterioration of what was left of central authority. Powerful warlords supported by Tujue remained unchallenged in the Northwest and the North, as was Xiao Xian's Liang dynasty in the South. In addition, a number of rebel groups, led by commoner leaders with dynastic pretensions, rose to prominence. Among these, the most formidable was the rebel army founded by Zhai Rang 翟讓 and now under Li Mi. A top adviser to Yang Xuangan, Li Mi had miraculously escaped his Sui captors through bribery. Basing himself in Henan, he posed the greatest threat to Luoyang, now defended by Yangdi's grandson Yang Tong 楊侗. With allegedly one million followers, Li Mi captured the nearby Luokou Granary 洛口倉, and Luoyang was in imminent danger.[54] Meanwhile, rebel leaders elsewhere seriously eroded Sui control in numerous localities. Particularly strong among these were Dou Jiande, active in present-day Hebei; Gao Kaidao, a former subordinate to Ge Qian, in Yuyang 漁陽 (Ji County, Tianjin); and Du Fuwei who, originally from present-day Shandong, was now based in Liyang 歷陽 (He County, east Anhui) in the South. Taking advantage of this disorder, Li Yuan lost no time in consolidating his hold on Guanzhong. With the help of Tujue, he crushed the resistance put up by Generals Song Laosheng 宋老生 and Qutu Tong 屈突通. By the eleventh month of 617, his forces had captured the biggest prize of the war, Daxingcheng.[55]

To make a smooth dynastic transition, Li Yuan declared a new Sui era, Yining 義寧, and inaugurated a puppet emperor—Gongdi 恭帝 (Yang You 楊侑, r. 617–618), grandson of Yangdi and son of Yang Zhao—in the Daxing 大興 Basilica (renamed Taiji 太極 Basilica under the Tang), the main structure of the Palace City in the capital. Yangdi was named honorary emperor (taishang huang 太上皇) in absentia,[56] which was tantamount to announcing his forced retirement.

Meanwhile, the collapse of the socioeconomic and political order began to affect Yangdi personally. The unexpected deterioration of his security forces set the stage for a mutiny in Jiangdu that would climax in his death. Before then, Yangdi's personal safety had been guaranteed by Wang Shichong 王世充, the most powerful general in the South. After Li Mi started laying siege to Luoyang, Wang Shichong and his troops were sent north in an attempt to rescue the Eastern Capital. The royal guardsmen (xiaoguo 驍果) Yangdi had brought with him from the North now took charge of his security detail. According to a Sui shu passage, a large number of them hailed from Guanzhong and their desire to return to their home area was considered the prime reason for the mutiny. However, this passage probably does not present the whole picture. On the composition of these xiaoguo troops, a passage in the "Shihuo zhi" chapter of the Sui shu offers some revealing information:

> [Yangdi] then visited Taiyuan, and came under siege in Yanmen by the Tujue. The Tujue thereafter dispersed, and [Yangdi] returned hastily to Luoyang. Increasingly, he enrolled recruits to enhance xiaoguo units as replacements for the original recruits.

This is a clear indication that before Yangdi made his last trip south, the xiaoguo units were already staffed with numerous new recruits from the Central Plain area outside Guanzhong.[57] The xiaoguo, regardless of their places of origin, played a crucial role in the mutiny. The first ominous sign of these guardsmen's disloyalty was mass desertion, which increased dramatically in the last months of Yangdi's sojourn in the South.

After Luokou fell to Li Mi, Yangdi completely abandoned any hope of recapturing the North.[58] He began to seriously contemplate moving the capital to Danyang 丹陽 (Nanjing), further up the Yangzi. These developments prompted General Dou Xian 竇賢 to flee west with his homesick xiaoguo troops. Although Dou Xian was captured and beheaded, the royal guardsmen continued to run away in large numbers. Their officers were caught between the extreme measures Yangdi took against deserters and the irrepressible urge of the guardsmen to return home. Sima Dekan 司馬德戡, a tiger-brave general from Fufeng (Fengxiang, Shaanxi) in charge of the royal guardsmen, spoke of the dilemma he and other officers faced:

Nowadays every royal guardsman wants to leave. If I attempt to persuade them, I am afraid that I will be killed first. If I do nothing and the case is later revealed, my family will suffer extermination. What should I do?

The only way out, Sima decided after consulting his colleagues, was to disappear with other guardsmen. Soon he found himself planning with a number of officers and court officials their own escape. As the conspiracy spread, it evolved from a plan for desertion to a plot to assassinate the emperor and terminate Sui rule. One of the disaffected officials was Vice Director of the Directorate for the Palace Buildings (*jiangzuo shaojian* 將作少監) Yuwen Zhiji 宇文智及 who urged the conspirators to avoid the fate of Dou Xian and to pursue their own imperial cause. Huaji 化及, Zhiji's brother, was now nominated leader of the conspirators. Ironically, the Yuwen brothers were sons of the late Yuwen Shu, Yangdi's favorite general. When security officers began to openly discuss plots of rebellion, a palace maid, with Empress Xiao's encouragement, warned Yangdi that a coup d'etat was imminent, but an incredulous Yangdi had her decapitated. No one would ever again risk his or her life to alert Yangdi to the grave danger he was in. The conspirators then took a crucial step to win over the support of the royal guardsmen. Sima Dekan and his associates began to spread the rumor that Yangdi, having heard about the plot of royal guardsmen, had prepared a large quantity of poisoned wine to kill all of them at a banquet and that he only wanted Southerners to stay. Thereupon, the royal guardsmen submitted themselves to the command of the conspirators.[59]

On the night of the tenth day of the third month (April 10), 618, two security officers, Yuan Li 元禮 and Pei Qiantong 裴虔通, both conspirators, were on duty inside the palace. They had intentionally left the palace gates unlatched. Meanwhile, Sima Dekan raised a rebel army of several tens of thousands in the Eastern City, probably a walled area adjacent to the palace, ready to enter the palace. For his own security, Yangdi had selected from official slaves several hundred stoutly-built men as his personal bodyguards. They were housed at the Xuanwu 玄武 Gate, the northern entrance of the palace that often held the key to the safety of the imperial residence. But on that day, a forged imperial edict had sent them out of the palace. The rebel royal guardsmen took over palace security after encountering only minimal resistance. Under the command of Sima Dekan, the rebel troops entered the palace by the Xuanwu Gate.

On hearing the commotion, Yangdi changed his clothes to go into hiding in the Western Pavilion (*xige* 西閣), but was soon captured by Pei Qiantong's rebel troops. The next morning, after Yangdi was paraded in front of the rank-and-file rebels, the rebel leaders ceremonially enumerated his ten major crimes:

1. abandonment of the Ancestral Temple;
2. touring without end;
3. launching frequent foreign expeditions;
4. committing extreme acts of extravagance and lasciviousness;
5. causing adult males to die in war;
6. throwing females and the weak into the ditches (in reference to the heavy corvée service they were forced to perform);
7. ruining the livelihood of the four groups of people (i.e., literati, farmers, craftsmen, and traders);
8. causing banditry and rebellion;
9. trusting only sycophants;
10. covering up errors and rejecting remonstrance.

By then Yangdi's favorite son Yang Gao 楊杲, aged twelve (eleven), was already crying uncontrollably. When Pei Qiantong cut off his head, Yangdi's imperial robe was splattered with Yang Gao's blood. Wishing to die in dignity, Yangdi requested poisoned wine, but it was denied. The rebel officer Linghu Xingda 令狐行達 strangled Yangdi with a silk towel. Yangdi was fifty (forty-nine) years old.[60]

With the help of some palace maids, Empress Xiao made two makeshift caskets out of lacquered boards for the remains of Yangdi and his son. The final irony was that Yangdi, having acquired a reputation as a life-long philanderer, was buried by his wife Empress Xiao, who was faithful to the last. After the founding of the Tang dynasty, Yangdi's remains were reburied in a tomb in Leitang 雷塘 northwest of Jiangdu.[61] When Empress Xiao herself died in 648, on Tang Taizong's orders her remains were buried in the same tomb.[62]

Until the last moment of his life Yangdi was perplexed by the motives of the conspirators, since they were among his most favored court officials and military officers. He did not realize that the palace revolt they instigated was essentially the tragic denouement of a prolonged process of steady decline.[63]

The degeneration had obviously accelerated in 613 after the failure of the second Liaodong campaign in the wake of the Yang Xuangan rebellion. As his melancholy grew, Yangdi became increasingly withdrawn and reluctant to deal with rebellion. While his empire was caving in around him, Yangdi turned to escapism, seeking relief in music, women, and eventually flight away from the troubled area. His final retreat to the South was a symbolic acknowledgment of defeat. It demoralized the military and destroyed what was left of public morale. It came as no surprise that mutinous officers chose that moment to join the fray and set up their own independent regimes. Finally, caught in a world of self-deception, completely isolated from society at large, betrayed by his generals, and abandoned by his bodyguards and servants, Yangdi was left alone with his favorite son to face his executioners.

# Part II

---

## Yangdi and His Empire

# 4

---

# Luoyang and the Grand Canal

This chapter marks a shift in approach and focus from chronological narration to thematic examination of the socioeconomic, political, religious, and international dimensions of Sui China as shaped by Yangdi. We begin with a study of two monumental construction projects—the Eastern Capital Luoyang and the Grand Canal. As the most costly projects Yangdi had ever undertaken, they were also of vital strategic importance, with a long-lasting and profound impact on the Sui and Tang economies.

## THE LUOYANG PROJECT

Little by little late spring in Luoyang arrives,
The brilliance of the season abounds.
Poplar foliage is turning dark,
Peach trees are not yet barren of blossoms.
Into the roof eaves swallows are struggling to enter,
Through the woods birds are flying in confusion.
As for the person guarding the mountain pass,
Thick dew is just descending on his uniform.[1]

These lines by Yangdi capture images of Luoyang 洛陽 in late spring, a city of architectural splendor and natural beauty. The Luoyang Palace inside the city, upon completion, became one of the three primary imperial residences, the other two being the Daxing Palace in Daxingcheng 大興城 and the Jiangdu Palace in the South. As Yangdi's first major construction project,

Luoyang was smaller in scale than Wendi's Daxingcheng. But it was unsurpassed in its extraordinary extravagance. Its prohibitive human and financial cost, and its luxurious architecture contributed to and perpetuated a perception that the building of Luoyang broke the back of the economy and ruined the empire for good. Nonetheless, as the following edict will testify, there were sound strategic, geopolitical, military, and economic justifications for adding the second capital.[2]

## Yangdi's Edict on Building Luoyang

Imperial edicts were often written by court document drafters. This was especially true of the Northern non-Han dynasties where writing formalized edicts in florid language was usually not the forte of the sovereign. Still, unless the sovereign was reduced to the position of a figurehead by powerful court figures, he provided the idea behind the edict. As for the edict in question, the only complete surviving document about the initiation of the Luoyang project, the *Sui shu* in no uncertain terms attributes it to Yangdi. There is no compelling reason to doubt this attribution, especially in view of the fact that Yangdi prided himself on his literary skills.

> Yangdi's Edict on Building Luoyang (December 17, 604)
>
> 1. Yin and yang wane and wax with the changing way of Heaven. People take their proper place in the world, driven by the differentiating force of creation. If the will of Heaven never alters its course, how can creation give rise to the four seasons? If human affairs remain unchanged, how can a government rule its people? Is it not true that the *Book of Changes* says: "[Huangdi, Yao, and Shun were] conversant with change, so that their people never became tired," "change brought about conversance, and with conversance they achieved durability," and "those who possess virtue can endure, and those who possess merit can expand." Moreover, I have been told that [when a ruler is] satisfied with peace yet capable of change, the people were greatly transformed. Consequently, the Zhou royal family of Ji 姬 founded the two Zhou [capitals], in accord with the wishes of King Wu 武王. The people of Yin moved capitals five times, consummating the enterprise of King Tang 湯. If one cannot adjust oneself to the human world and Heaven, how can he accomplish his achievement on the basis of transformation? Benevolent rulers of people and state, beware!
>
> 2. Luoyi 洛邑 (Luoyang) has been a capital since antiquity. Within the precincts of its royal territory, Heaven and Earth merge

with each other, yin and yang work in harmony. Commanding the Sanhe 三河 (Henan, Hedong, and Henei 河內) region, it is safe-guarded by the four mountain passes. With excellent land and water transportation, it provides a whole gamut of taxes and tribute. Thus Gaozu of Han 漢高祖 said: 'I have traveled far and wide under Heaven, and I have only seen Luoyang.' Since ancient times, there was hardly an emperor or a king who failed to notice Luoyang. But what deters [the Sui court] from making Luoyang a capital? Some argue against it because of the incomplete unification of China. Others claim that it would be too costly for the state treasury. There-fore, no edict on the building of Luoyang has been issued [until now]. Ever since the founding of the Sui dynasty, [we] have intended to create a new Luoyang in the Huai-Luo 懷洛 (Huai: Huaizhou 懷州 with its seat northeast of present-day Luoyang, in Qinyang, Henan; Luo: Luozhou, with its seat east of present-day Luoyang) area. Day in and day out time passes. Now when I am here thinking of this, emotional words bring me to tears.

3. Solemnly following the treasured calendar, I reign over the country. Showing respect without fail, I follow the wishes of my progenitors wholeheartedly. Recently, Liang, prince of Han 漢王諒 rebelled, spreading his pernicious influence into Shandong, capturing a number of prefectures and counties. Since [the area] is separated by mountain passes and rivers, the Sui troops from afar will not be able to arrive in time in response to an emergency. Moreover, the erstwhile subjects of Bing Prefecture (the area under Liang's control) have been resettled in Henan, which serves the same purpose as the Zhou reset-tlement of Yin people. In addition, the Southern frontier is far away while the Eastern area is vast. Now is the moment to make the right move. Court officials, high and low, all concur with this view. Since Chengzhou 成周 (old Luoyang) is in ruins beyond repair, the Eastern Capital shall be built on the Yi 伊 and Luo 洛 Rivers. [I] shall hereby create appropriate offices and positions, which will provide the people with leadership.

4. In the beginning, palatial structures were created to make life convenient. Beams and roofs were erected to give shelter from wind and dew. In view of this, lofty towers and spacious edifices are hardly appropriate architectural forms. Hence, the commentary of the *Book of Changes* says: "Frugality accompanies virtue. Extravagance pro-motes evil." Xuanni 宣尼 (Confucius) said: "[I] would rather be frugal than immodest." How can people say that palaces are perforce com-posed of luxuriously designed towers and chambers while earthen steps and painted rafters are not fit for the emperor? Thus we know,

the world does not exist to serve a sovereign, but rather the sovereign exists to govern the world. The people are the essence of the state. With the essence consolidated, the country is at peace. If the people are abundantly provisioned, who else is not? The present construction project must be based on frugality. Efforts must be made to ensure that no walls with carved patterns or edifying buildings will rise from today on. Instead, I will bequeath to posterity humble palaces and simple food. [To that end,] government agencies in charge shall lay down rules and regulations that satisfy me.[3]

Written in traditional style, this edict employs conventional language and devices in reference to the cosmological, historical, and geopolitical aspects of the location with emphasis on the need for frugality. But if we compare Yangdi's edict with those by other sovereigns, we notice they justified the building of a new city in this locale in similar terms. In his edict of 579, Northern Zhou Xuandi 宣帝 talks about the interaction of yin and yang, the dominant powers of Heaven and Earth, and the benefit of tribute and taxes.[4] In his edict more than one hundred years later, Tang Xuanzong 唐玄宗 emphasizes the historic associations of Luoyang, the benefit of taxes and tribute it received, and its unique position as the center of the land that gathered the six qi 氣 (yin, yang, wind, rain, darkness, and brightness), that is, the six sources of vital energy.[5] What distinguishes Yangdi's edict from the others is the stress on the necessity for change as formulated in the Book of Changes, a process of transformation that gave rise not only to new dynasties, but also new capitals. But the idea of using change to justify the building of a new capital had been advanced by Yangdi's father in his edict on Daxingcheng.[6]

In light of the evidence, we can say with assurance that Yangdi's arguments at the beginning of the edict for the transcendental and economic significance of Luoyang are primarily pro forma in style and content. It is in his appreciation of the increasing strategic importance of the area that Yangdi demonstrated remarkable foresight. Luoyang was pivotal for control of the Bing area (Shanxi) in the North and the Southern frontier area in the conquered territory of the former Chen. His younger brother Yang Liang, commander of Bingzhou Superior Area Command, had started a large-scale rebellion that posed a serious threat to Yangdi's rule. The process of suppressing the rebellion, which had spread east into the Central Plain, brought into focus the fact that it was difficult to dispatch government troops to the area. After Yang Liang's surrender, Yangdi, following an ancient tradition, resettled a large number of the Bing population in Henan. A major urban center was needed to keep a close eye on them.

Oddly enough after his lengthy rationale on the strategic importance of Luoyang to the North, Yangdi pays no attention to the South. Instead, he mentions in passing a Southern frontier area (section 3), which was essentially different from the political center of the South in the lower Yangzi valley. Later developments showed that for Yangdi the South held a much greater attraction. To have easy access to the major cities in territories that had formerly belonged to the Chen in the lower Yangzi valley was without doubt one of Yangdi's primary reasons for building Luoyang.[7] The fact that he refrained from focusing attention on the South may be attributed to the lingering perception that the South was a symbol of decadence.

The last part of the edict is devoted to one subject—frugality. Yangdi stresses that the significance of a palace lay in its practical functionality, not its luxurious design, and cites the commentary to the *Book of Changes* and Confucius in support of this argument. In his conclusion, Yangdi set the basic tone for his commitment to frugality and simplicity in implementing his first major construction project (section 4). Yet the focus on frugality was more complicated than meets the eye. It actually conceals an inner conflict, which may be examined in comparison with his effort to downplay the major influence of the South on his decision to build the city.

Although Yangdi was predisposed to undertaking extravagant building projects, these projects would have contradicted the fundamental virtue of frugality Wendi had attempted to inculcate into his sons. After his father's death, in launching the Luoyang project, Yangdi had to face the conflict between established values and natural inclinations. Here, lip service paid to frugality only thinly veils his desire for extravagances. A *Sui shu* passage points to Yangdi's true state of mind:

> Yuwen Kai assumed that what the emperor was really after was grandiosity and extravagance. Consequently, his design of the Eastern Capital was absolutely splendid and spectacular. The emperor was so overjoyed that he promoted Kai to the rank of *kaifu* 開府 [*yitong sansi* 儀同三司] (commander unequalled in honor, a prestige title of rank 1b), and the position of president of the Board of Works ( *gongbu shangshu* 工部尚書, the most powerful position in the building profession, in charge of construction projects for the central government).

As the main architect of Luoyang, Yuwen Kai knew Yangdi's unarticulated desire well enough to build an extraordinarily magnificent city, despite what was said in the edict.[8]

## Luoyang: Construction and Design

In the third month of 605, Yangdi issued an edict to provide an additional rationale for building Luoyang—to get close to the people in order to listen to their advice and grievances; this also served as justification for a future tour of inspection. By this time, the Luoyang project had been underway for several months and the city had begun to take shape. On Yangdi's orders, urban households from Luo Prefecture, and households of rich merchants and major traders from other areas moved into the new city by the tens of thousands.[9]

In the same edict, Yangdi appointed a panel of three court officials to head the project: Gao Jiong, Yang Su, and Yuwen Kai. In reality, Yuwen Kai was the only man in charge. Referred to by Chen Yinke as one of the three great technologists of the Sui dynasty, he was more instrumental than anyone else in creating and actualizing Yangdi's luxurious construction plans (map 4.1).[10] Of Xiongnu descent, Yuwen Kai was, at the beginning of the Sui, marked for extermination as Wendi attempted to eradicate the royal Yuwen family of the

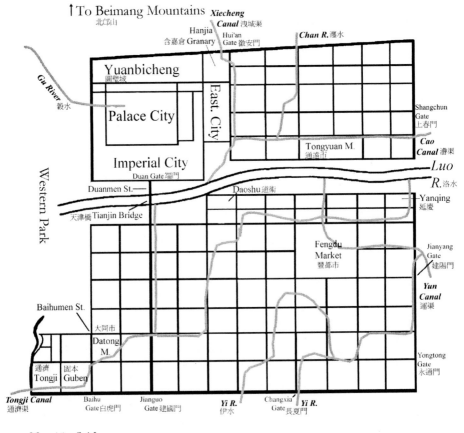

MAP 4.1   Sui Luoyang

Northern Zhou. He was saved only after Wendi realized that he did not descend from the royal branch of the Yuwen lineage. Even before Luoyang, he had already become the first architect of the Sui, undertaking such key projects as the Ancestral Temple, Daxingcheng, and the Renshou Palace.[11]

Court technologists like Yuwen Kai, He Chou, and Yan Pi were often blamed for encouraging Yangdi in his extravagant habits.[12] Although professional duties required these quintessential technocrats at court to perform dedicated technical service rather than engage in remonstration, they did not make the slightest attempt to stop Yangdi from his vices.

The Luoyang project was officially completed on the sixth (*xinyou* 辛酉) of the first month (February 18), 606, just about one year after it had been inaugurated by Yangdi's edict. The new city, now known as the Eastern Capital, was a milestone in the career of its main architect Yuwen Kai. Approximately 47 square km in area, it was slightly larger than one half the size of Daxingcheng. What it lacked in size was more than made up for by its innovative planning and extravagant palace structures. The *Sui shu* describes it thus:

> It (Luoyang) was unrivaled in its extraordinary splendor. Since the emperor, as imperial prince, had pacified the South in person, he assimilated the curvilinear and angular [styles] of Liang and Chen [structures], using them as [architectural] standards. Its walls rose higher than the Mang (or Beimang 北芒/邙) Mountains. Floating bridges spanned the Luo River. Above the golden gate and ivory watchtower[13] were erected winged belvederes. Precipices were collapsed, and rivers cut off to make way for [pillars shaped like] multicolored clouds. Trees were transplanted from south of the [Five] Mountain Ranges (northern Guangdong and Guangxi) to create forestland. The Mang Mountains were enclosed within the Imperial Park.[14]

The unique position of the palace and government quarters in the overall layout of Luoyang is worth noting. Surrounded on the north by the Mang Mountains, on the south by the broad waterway of the Luo River, and on the east by a canal that ran from north to south, the location of these quarters in the northwest corner of the city was in tune with certain geomantic principles, according to which, an optimally located structure should have a hill to its north, a pond to its south, a river to its east, and a road to its west. Although the cosmology of city planning in ancient China came to stress symmetry and axiality, Yuwen Kai positioned the palace and government quarters asymmetrically in their current locations. Some scholars believe this is an indication of the inferior status of Luoyang. However, it seems more likely that this

palace location was selected out of practical consideration. According to
Daxingcheng's convention, the capital city should be bounded on the north by
an extensive imperial park. But in Luoyang, that was impossible since the
northern suburb was a mountainous area that had served as the burial ground
for royalty and nobility since antiquity. Consequently, the Imperial Park was
planned immediately west of the city instead. Locating the palace in the northwest corner of the city allowed it direct access to the park while complying
with the conventional practice that required the placement of the palace in the
extreme north, a practice that violated the prescriptions in the *locus classicus* for
Chinese city planning recorded in the *Kaogong ji* 考工記 (Book of artificers).
Moreover, occupying the highest ground of the city, the palace location avoided
the mistake Yuwen Kai had made in Daxingcheng where the palace, because
of geomantic consideration, was placed in the lowest depression of the urban
area.[15]

The main structure of the palace, Qianyang 乾陽 Basilica, was Luoyang's
most spectacular landmark. Its east-west length measured 30 *jian* 間 (bays) or
approximately 120 m, and its north-south depth measured 29 *jia* 架 (purlin
spaces) or 9 *zhang* (21.12 m).[16] The foundation of the basilica was 9 *chi*
(2.12 m) high, and the height from ground level to rooftop finial was 170 *chi*
(40 m).[17]

To understand the spatial significance of these measurements, we only
have to compare them with those of the Hanyuan 含元 Basilica, the central
structure of the Daming 大明 Palace in Tang Chang'an 長安, built by
Gaozong 高宗 (r. 649–683) to supercede the Taiji 太極 Basilica as the main
court building. As such Hanyuan should be the largest palace structure in Tang
China. Revealed by archaeology to be 55 m by 20 m in area,[18] it was roughly
half the size of Qianyang. As probably the most spacious palatial structure in
Sui times, the Qianyang Basilica was notoriously expensive to build, a fact that
later gave rise to a Tang popular saying, "As soon as Qianyuan 乾元 (Qianyang
under the Sui) was completed, the Sui fell apart."[19]

Immediately south of the Palace City was the Imperial City where government offices were located. Emanating from its main southern entrance was
a thoroughfare that served as an axis. Moving south, it penetrated the city's
residential area, passed through the city's southern entrance and extended
beyond the city limits into the southern suburbs. Known in Tang times as
Dingdingmen 定鼎門 Street, the axial thoroughfare performed a similar function as Zhuquemen 朱雀門 Street in Daxingcheng, that is, to maintain a semblance of symmetry and axiality. However, the axiality of the Luoyang axis
and its southern extension was only relevant to the westernmost part, not the
entire walled area, of the city. Axiality is a key concept in the cosmology of
the Chinese capital city, with the central axis functioning as the *axis mundi*
between Heaven and Earth. The limited axiality we see in Luoyang indicates

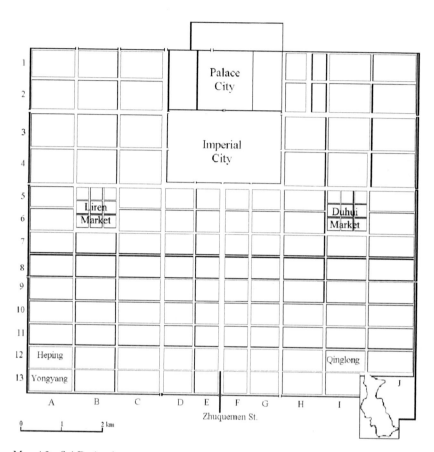

MAP 4.2   Sui Daxingcheng

a compromise between the practical needs of the palace location and the fundamental principle of an age-old tradition. It also shows that, to the planners of Luoyang, the penetrating, straight-line, north-south axis was of greater significance than the symmetrical morphology of the city (map 4.1; map 4.2).[20]

The residential area that lay outside the palace-government area was divided into numerous self-contained units known as *li* 里 or *fang* 坊 (wards). The Luo River, traversing the area from west to east, was responsible for the somewhat irregular distribution of wards. There were thirty ward spaces north of the river and east of the palace. Of these, two wards were combined to create the Tongyuan Market 通遠市, which reduced the number of the northern wards to twenty-eight. To the immediate south of the river were fourteen small

wards, each of which was half the size of a regular ward. To their south were
sixty-six regular size ward spaces. Four wards in the east were merged into the
Fengdu Market 豐都市, and one ward in the southwest was converted into
the Datong Market. That left the southern area with sixty-one regular wards
and fourteen small wards, or a total of seventy-five wards. Adding these to the
twenty-eight northern wards we arrive at one hundred and three as the total
number of wards.[21] This total, however, excludes the six wards in the southwest corner west of Baihumen 白虎門 Street.[22]

Among early firsthand accounts of Sui-Tang Luoyang, the *Liangjing xinji*
(*LJXJ*) (A new record of the two capitals) is probably the most influential.
Completed in the early eighth century, it gives a ward by ward description of
every nook and cranny in Chang'an and Luoyang. Most of this work is no
longer extant. For physical descriptions of the city, we have to refer to much
later sources. One such source is the *Yuan Henan zhi*, which quotes the
*Liangjing xinji* to indicate the dimension of a Sui-Tang Luoyang ward as
300 *bu* by 300 *bu*. The fact that these measurements were identical with those
for Northern Wei Luoyang standard wards suggests that Sui Luoyang's wards
followed local standards instead of the earlier Sui conventions created in
Daxingcheng.[23]

Local tradition also left its mark in the setup of the city's market system.
In Daxingcheng, two marketplaces were planned and located south of the
Imperial City. Symmetrically positioned with reference to the central axis, they
had obvious cosmological implications. In Luoyang such considerations were
absent. Following a long-standing local tradition, three, instead of two, markets
were designed. Two of the markets, Tongyuan and Fengdu, were placed on
either side the Luo River,[24] and the third one, Datong Market 大同市, whose
original locale is not documented—was moved in 610 to a location in the
southwest corner of the city close to the Tongji Canal.[25] These pragmatic locations were a major improvement over those of Daxingcheng's markets, which
were a long distance away from any major waterway.[26]

As the seat of Henan Capital Prefecture, Luoyang had under its jurisdiction eighteen counties: two urban counties (Henan and Luoyang), and sixteen
suburban counties. The metropolitan area of Luoyang boasted a total of
202,230 registered households at the peak of the Sui or approximately
1,045,500 residents.[27] Of these, probably around 40–50 percent resided in the
urban area.[28] Further, there may easily have been an additional unregistered
population of several tens of thousands, including royalty and their entourages,
clerics, the military, and transients. With an estimated population of half a
million or more during its prime, Luoyang, as the second most populous
metropolis in the world,[29] was apparently taking shape as one of the most prosperous urban centers in the nation under Yangdi.

## Yuanxiao 元宵 Festival

The prosperity of Luoyang was best testified by public events that utilized the city grid and its broad avenues. The most memorable one started in Luoyang on the night of the fifteenth in the first month of 610. Under the personal aegis of Yangdi, a large-scale extravaganza was organized to entertain various barbarian tribal leaders on the street outside the Duan Gate 端門, the southern terminus of the Imperial City. According to the *Zizhi tongjian*, acrobatic shows were performed in an area with a circumference of 5,000 *bu* (7,065 m), where a large orchestra of string and pipe instruments, composed of eighteen thousand people, played. The music could be heard dozens of *li* away. From dusk to dawn, lanterns and candles lit up the sky above and the ground below. The event lasted until the end of the month. From then on, the expensive party, on Yangdi's orders, became a recurrent annual event. This, according to tradition, was the beginning of the popular *yuanxiao* festival.

To traditional scholars the *yuanxiao* festival is another example of Yangdi's wasteful extravagance. But the accuracy of this particular record seems questionable. Assuming the space in question was square, the area would be 1,766 m by 1,766 m. Luoyang was a compartmentalized city with more than one hundred walled wards. The only possible space for the performance south of the Duan Gate was the north-south thoroughfare, known as by its Tang name, Dingdingmen 定鼎門 Street, in the sources. As the widest street of the city, it was, according to traditional sources, 100 *bu* (141.3 m after 607) in width. Archaeological digs have revealed it to be narrower, about 90–121 m in width.[30] The space south of the Duan Gate was further confined by the presence of the Luo River cutting through the city. In light of the evidence, the recorded party space was simply not there.[31] Although the *Zizhi tongjian* is generally regarded as highly reliable, it occasionally accepted exaggerated accounts without proper verification. In part this problem was caused by the early loss of court diaries of Yangdi's reign, the factual basis for official court history. Without them, later historians turned to less reliable, private and miscellaneous accounts.[32] By comparison, the more believable account in the *Sui shu* only records Tianjin Street 天津街 (which should be the same as Tang Dingdingmen Street) as the locale of the festivities without providing specific dimensions for the performance area.[33]

Despite conflicting accounts in the sources about the actual scale of the event, there is no denying Yangdi spent an enormous fortune on these parties to entertain and impress his foreign guests. Even though the street space of Luoyang was far more constricted than is allowed for by the *Zizhi tongjian*, it could and did, with imperial blessings, function effectively as public open space for the benefit of its residents.

## THE GRAND CANAL

One of the salient features of Luoyang was the pragmatic positioning of its markets in the vicinity of main water channels, which testifies to Yangdi's keen awareness of the vital role of water transportation in the economy of the city. In fact, under Yangdi, Luoyang evolved into the hub of an unprecedented nationwide water transportation system which came to be known as the Grand Canal (map 4.3). Arguably his greatest legacy, the Grand Canal was also his most criticized and controversial public works project.[34]

Before Yangdi came to power, his father had constructed the first strategic waterway of the Sui—the Guangtong Canal 廣通渠—with a length of more than 300 li (191 km or 153 km based on post-607 standards) in 584, linking Daxingcheng to the Tong Pass area to the east,[35] where the Wei River 渭水 joined the Yellow River.[36] The practical need for this canal arose from the poor navigability of the Wei as a result of the heavy silt its currents carried. This canal served as an alternative route for transporting strategic commodities and was accompanied by a grain reserve system set up on the North China plain and in the Guanzhong area.

Yangdi's more extensive Grand Canal was of far greater strategic significance. It was comprised of two systems: (1) the southern system that traveled from Luoyang east and southeast through the Huai 淮 to reach Jiangdu and Yuhang (Hangzhou) in the lower Yangzi valley; and (2) the northern system that extended from Luoyang northeast to Zhuo Commandery (Beijing).[37]

### The Tongji Canal 通濟渠 (605–611)

As the first strategic waterway of the southern system constructed by Yangdi, the Tongji linked Luoyang with the Huai valley.[38] It was composed of two sections: eastern and western. The eastern section was known as the Bian River 汴水 or Bian Canal 汴渠 in Tang times. The length of the eastern section can be estimated by a reference by the Tang poet Bai Juyi 白居易 to the distance between the Yellow and Huai Rivers—1,300 li (1,430 post-607 Sui li) or about 728 km (1 Tang li = 560 m).[39]

The western section of the Tongji originated at the confluence of the Luo and Gu 穀 Rivers in the Western Park. From there it flowed east into Huaiyi 懷義 Ward in the city's southwest corner. It continued its course east- and northward until it emptied into the Luo River at Yanqing 延慶 Ward, in the northeast corner of south Luoyang.[40] Coursing eastward, the Luo River joined the Yellow River to the east. Further to the east, the eastern section of Tongji, usually considered the canal proper, branched off from the Yellow River at Banzhu 板渚 to begin its journey southeast, linking up Xunyi 浚儀 (Kaifeng),

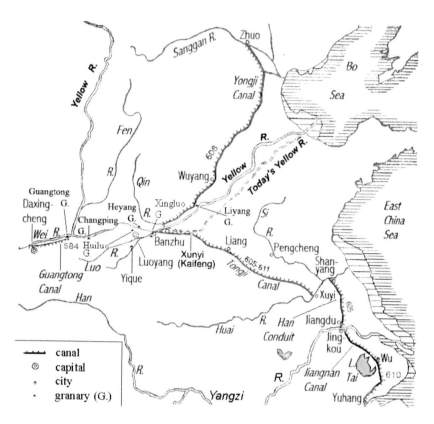

Banzhu 板渚
Changping Granary 常平倉
Daxingcheng 大興城
Fen River 汾水
Guangtong Canal 廣通渠
Guangtong Granary 廣通倉
Han Conduit 邗溝
Han River 漢水
Heyang Granary 河陽倉
Huiluo Granary 回/迴洛倉
Jiangdu 江都

Jiangnan Canal 江南河
Jingkou 京口
Lake Tai 太湖
Liang 梁
Liyang Granary 黎陽倉
Luo River 洛水
Luoyang 洛陽
Pengcheng 彭城
Qin River 沁水
Sanggan River 桑乾水
Shanyang 山陽
Si River 泗水

Tongji Canal 通濟渠
Wei River 渭水
Wuyang 武陽
Xingluo Granary 興洛倉
Xunyi 浚儀
Xuyi 盱眙
Yangzi River (Jiang 江)
Yellow River (Heshui 河水)
Yique 伊闕
Yongji Canal 永濟渠
Yuhang 餘杭
Zhuo Commandery 涿郡

MAP 4.3 The Grand Canal

Yongqiu 雍丘 (Qi County), and Songcheng 宋城/Liang (south of Shangqiu).
Scholars are divided on the canal route between Songcheng and the Huai. One
opinion believes that at Songcheng the canal made a shortcut southward to
join the Huai at the seat of Si 泗 Prefecture (north of Xuyi). This shortcut
argument is primarily based on an eyewitness report by the Tang writer Li Ao
李翱, who traveled along the Tongji on a Southern journey in 808, and
recorded his stopover at the seat of Si Prefecture before he entered the Huai.[41]
Recently it was reported that remains of the original levees of the Sui canal
were still visible on the ground. Tang-Song shipwrecks and other relics have
been uncovered along the route.[42]

   The alternate view believes that after Songcheng, the canal continued
eastward and joined the Si northeast of Pengcheng 彭城 (Xuzhou). The Si in
turn joined the Huai to the South. This Si River counterargument relies on
records of the Tang scholar Li Jifu 李吉甫, and the Song historian Sima
Guang and his collaborators (map 4.4).[43] Furthermore, some argue that since,
according to official records, the project lasted a total of one hundred seventy-
one days, it is difficult to complete it in such a short period if Yangdi did not

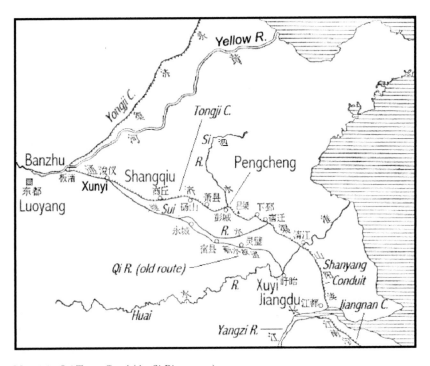

MAP 4.4   Sui Tongi Canal (the Si River route)

utilize existing water channels.[44] The last argument, however, is brought into question by recent research that pushes back the completion date of Tongji to 611.

The exiting water channel the Si River route ran through was a branch of the ancient Hong Conduit 鴻溝. Initially built in pre-Qin times, the Hong Conduit was first created by deflecting the Yellow River at a place north of Xingyang 滎陽. Over time it evolved into a multichannel canal system, and through its many tributaries linked the Yellow valley with the Huai valley. The Si River route followed one of the Hong Conduit's tributaries that ran southeast from Xunyi through Songcheng, eventually joining the Si River at Pengcheng. Known as the Bian River 汴水 in the Six Dynasties period, it was also referred to as the old Bian River in later times.[45]

Since both the Si River route and the shortcut route that ran parallel to and southwest of it were navigable in Sui times, it is difficult to identify which one was the Tongji Canal, concludes Pan Yong, after a field investigation of Sui-Tang canals in 1984.[46] Yangdi seemed to favor the shortcut route, because he located a major palace complex (Duliang) near Xuyi, at its southern terminus.

The project started on Yangdi's orders in the third month of 605; the completion date is not recorded. Many scholars regard the eighth month of the same year, when Yangdi as emperor embarked on his first Southern journey by water, as the completion date of the canal.[47] However, on his return journey, in the fourth month of 606, Yangdi's mode of travel changed from ship to carriage at Yique 伊闕, a place south of Luoyang and way off course from the canal.[48] This clearly indicates that at that time, the Tongji Canal was not operational.

At the time of his second Southern journey, which started in the third month of 610, Yangdi was seen in Dongping 東平 (east of Yuncheng, Shandong),[49] a place more removed from the canal even than Yique. This record seems to suggest that by early 610, Tongji was not yet ready for use. Only on the return trip of his second journey in the second month of 611 did Yangdi take Tongji for the first time. In fact, before Tongji was completed, Yangdi had used an alternative route that went by way of the Yellow, Ji 濟, Si 泗 and Huai Rivers, and the Han Conduit to reach the Yangzi.[50]

## The Han Conduit (*Han gou* 邗溝) (605)

From the lower Huai valley, at Shanyang 山陽 (present-day Huai'an), the Grand Canal resumed its southward extension. According to the *Zizhi tongjian*, Yangdi completed the Han Conduit section of his system with more than one hundred thousand laborers in 605.[51] Before Yangdi, there had been two existing water routes from the Huai to the Yangzi. One was the Han Conduit of Spring and Autumn vintage, which flowed southeast from the Huai to empty into Lake Sheyang 射陽, before emerging south of the lake to join Lake Bozhi 博芝 to the south and then Lake Fanliang 樊良 to the southwest. The conduit continued its course south of the Fanliang until it merged into the Yangzi. Let us call it the Lake Sheyang detour. The second route was the Han Conduit of Eastern Han origin, or the straight route. It originated from the Huai at Shanyang, and then traveled due south to Lake Fanliang where it joined the last section of the Lake Sheyang detour. In Sui times, both Wendi and Yangdi built canals between Huai and Yangzi, utilizing existing waterways. Wendi's canal was called Shanyang Conduit 山陽瀆, and Yangdi's canal, the Han Conduit. Opinions abound regarding the precise identification of the Sui canals. One influential view regards the Lake Sheyang detour as the course of both of the two Sui canals. In other words, according to this view, Yangdi only rebuilt his father's canal, which was in turn based on an existing Spring and Autumn canal. A different view identifies the straight route (the Eastern-Han Han Conduit) plus the section of the Spring and Autumn Han Conduit between Lake Fanliang and the Yangzi as Yangdi's canal; and the Lake Sheyang detour as Wendi's canal. Both the Sheyang Lake detour and the straight route were functional in Sui times (map 4.5).[52] The Han Conduit brought Jiangdu—the de facto capital of the South—into the Grand Canal system. After his death, Yangdi was laid to rest in Hanjiang County nearby.[53]

## The Jiangnan Canal 江南河 (610)

As the last major extension of the Grand Canal in the South, the Jiangnan Canal started from south of the Yangzi at Jingkou 京口 (Zhenjiang). It went south past Qu'e 曲阿 (Danyang) and Jinling 晉陵 (Changzhou), circumvented Lake Tai through Wuxi and Wu 吳 Commandery (near Suzhou), and ended at the seat of Yuhang 餘杭 Commandery (Hangzhou) as it emptied into present-day Hangzhou Bay. The digging of the Jiangnan, more than 800 *li* in length (407 km) and more than 10 *zhang* (23.55 m) in width, began in 610.[54] Before Yangdi could utilize the new canal to visit the Yuhang area, territorial ambitions beckoned him to go by the Grand Canal in the opposite direction. In the second month of 611, he was on his way to the North in preparation for war against Koguryŏ.[55]

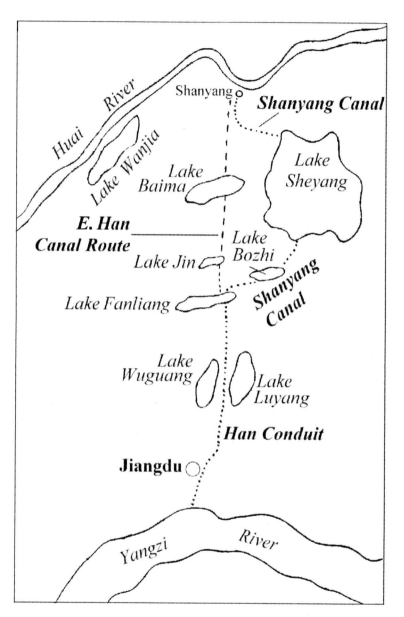

MAP 4.5   Han Conduit

## The Yongji Canal 永濟渠 (608)

To incorporate the Hebei area into this new water transport system, in the first month of 608, Yangdi started building the longest section of the Grand Canal, the Yongji, with a total length of more than 2,000 *li* (1,018 km).[56] To complete the project, Yangdi's engineers again connected existing water routes and improved their navigability. Two rivers were crucial for the initial stages of the project: the Qin River 沁水 originating from the Shaanxi area, and the Qing River 清/水 (Wei River) coursing from central Henan northeastward. The first step was to dredge the section of the Qin from present-day Wuzhi to the Yellow River. The second involved linking the Qin at Wuzhi with the Qing to its east. The canal extended its reach as far north as Zhuo Commandery (Beijing).

For Yangdi, the strategic significance of Yongji lay in its potential for logistical support for his invasion of Koguryŏ. Having issued a threat to its sovereign in 607, Yangdi may have intended to back it up with the canal as an enhanced military supply route to the Hebei area.[57]

## An Overall Assessment

If we add up the lengths of the Tongji (1,430 *li*), Yongji (2,000 *li*), Jiangnan (800 *li*) and Han Conduit (est. 400 *li*), we arrive at 4,630 *li* or 2,357 km as the total length of Yangdi's Grand Canal.[58] In terms of magnitude alone, it was without doubt the grandest navigation system ever undertaken by a single sovereign in premodern history. While the Tongji Canal-Han Conduit section provided the transportation artery between the North China plain and the Huai and Yangzi areas, or between North and South China in general, the southern extension, the Jiangnan, penetrated deep into the South. The Yongji Canal to the North brought Koguryŏ territory, an area targeted by Yangdi for military conquest, within easy reach. Clearly, the four canals that made up the Grand Canal were the result of strategic planning. In the long run, this national transportation system brought about closer economic integration between North and South, and contributed significantly to the historic transformation through which the economic center of China shifted from the wheat growing North China plain to the lush rice regions in the lower Yangzi valley.[59]

In assessing the historical significance of Yangdi's main construction projects, it is impossible to ignore the excessive human and economic cost they incurred. Still, it is undeniable that one of his most enduring projects—the Grand Canal—was to greatly facilitate economic growth in the post-Sui era for generations to come. The Late Tang writer Pi Rixiu 皮日休 expressed the kind of ambivalent sentiment shared among Tang scholars towards these expensive undertakings:

> Therefore, by dredging the Qi River 淇水 and Bian River,[60] and by cutting through the Taihang Mountains,[61] Sui [Yangdi] had inflicted intolerable sufferings on the people under the Sui. Yet [these projects] have provided endless benefits to the people under the Tang. Nowadays, in addition to the Nine Rivers,[62] there are the Qi and Bian Rivers, which provide access to fish traders of Zhuo Commandery in the North, and carry shipments from Jiangdu in the South. The benefits they provide are enormous indeed! These early accomplishments are monumental. Yet it did not require a single [Tang] laborer to carry a wicker basket [of soil], nor a single [Tang] soldier to chisel through a dangerous place. Is it not true that Heaven has greatly benefited us with the help of the despotic Sui [sovereign]?[63]

City planning and canal building were two different types of civil engineering activities, but they were interconnected in the Luoyang and the Grand Canal projects because of the tangible link of Luoyang, the hub of the new waterway network, to the Grand Canal, and because of Luoyang's dependence on the canal for economic prosperity. The construction of Luoyang laid the groundwork for the Grand Canal, which in turn led to a major reorientation of the country's cultural, economic, and political foci to the East and South. With Luoyang at its center, this new canal network, built in four sections over a period of five years (605–611), served as the North-South transport system that closely integrated the key economic areas of the Yellow, Huai, and Yangzi valleys for the first time in history. In the ensuing Tang dynasty, Luoyang blossomed into a thriving metropolis. As the South continued to grow in relative economic significance, the Grand Canal matured into the strategic North-South highway, indispensable for the existence of the central court.

# 5

## The Palace Network

No sooner than [Wendi's] mountain tomb was completed did [Yangdi] start his inspection tours. Now that peace under Heaven had prevailed for a long period, and soldiers and their horses were in their prime, [he] could not help aspiring to the achievements of the First Emperor of Qin 秦始皇 and Wudi of Han 漢武帝. So he began to build and renovate palace structures with unmatched extravagance.[1]

Despite the judgmental, moralistic undertone of these words from the comment section of Yangdi's basic annals in the *Sui shu*, they highlight one important characteristic of Yangdi—his penchant for glory and extravagance. While it is true that Luoyang, the Grand Canal, and, to a lesser extent, palaces at Jinyang, Yulin and Linshuo stood as testimony to his strategic vision, the same could not be said about most of his numerous smaller projects, which only added to the heavy economic burden on the populace without providing much immediate or long-term benefit (map 5.1).

### PALACES AT THE WESTERN AND EASTERN TERMINUSES OF THE TONGJI CANAL

From Guanzhong in the west, to Luoyang in the east, to Jiangdu in the Yangzi valley, Yangdi built a network of more than forty secondary palaces. With Daxingcheng at its core, Guanzhong played host to the western group of Sui palaces in the drainage area of the Guangtong Canal in southeast Shaanxi,

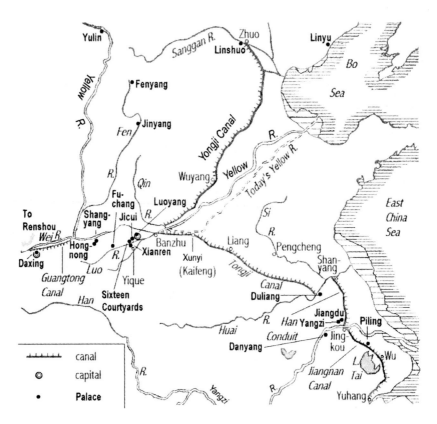

MAP 5.1    Major palaces under Sui Yangdi

including Bushou 步壽 in Weinan 渭南 (present-day Weinan, Shaanxi) and
Xingde 興德 in Huayin 華陰 (present-day Huayin). East of Guanzhong and
south of the Yellow River in west Henan were more palaces: Shangyang 上陽
in Taolin 桃林 (north of Lingbao, Henan), Hongnong 弘農 in Shanxian 陝縣
(Sanmenxia), and Fuchang 福昌 in Yiyang 宜陽 (west of present-day
Yiyang).[2] Unfortunately, little information survives on these palaces. There is,
however, much more textual evidence on palace complexes to the east at the
western and eastern terminuses of the Tongji Canal.

## The Western Park

As the Luo River flowed through the western suburb of Luoyang, its water
was diverted into a channel that ran east towards the city. That channel was

the western section of the Tongji Canal. Encompassing the canal and its surrounding areas was the vast Western Park (*xi yuan* 西苑), variably known as Fanghua 芳華 (Fragrant Flowers),[3] Huitong 會通 (Amalgam), and Shanglin 上林 (Upper Forest) in Sui times and as Jin 禁 (Forbidden) and Shendu 神都 (Divine Capital) in Tang. Within the park were clustered some of the most important suburban palaces ever built by Yangdi.[4] With the Beimang Mountains on the north and the canal coursing through its southern area,[5] the park extended west as far as the Xiao 孝 River, with a circumference of 229 *li* and 138 *bu* (approx.117 km). There were a total of fourteen park gates, which were unevenly distributed. The east side had two gates: Jiayu 孝 (Good Omen) and Wangchun 望春 (Awaiting Spring); the west side had five: Yingqiu 迎秋 (Greeting Autumn), Youyi 遊義 (Excursion's Meaning), Longyan 籠煙 (Cage's Smoke), Lingxi 靈溪 (Numina Brook), and Fenghe 風和 (Harmonious Wind); the south side had three: Qingxia 清夏 (Pure Summer), Xing'an 興安 (Increasing Tranquility), and Zhaoren 昭仁 (Luminous Benevolence); and the north side had four: Chaoyang 朝陽 (Facing Yang), Lingpu 靈圃 (Numina Nursery), Yudong 禦冬 (Winter-Proof), and Yingfu 應福 (Reception of Happiness).

In the Early Tang period, Taizong converted much of the park space for residential use. Consequently, the Tang circumference was reduced to 126 *li* or approximately 71 km (variant: 120 *li*). While there is no precise record on the specific dimensions of the Sui park, the Tang park was of irregular shape, with the length of its east side 17 *li*; its west side 50 *li*; its south side 39 *li* (variant: 29 *li*); and its north side 24 *li*.[6]

The Tang park area was enclosed with a wall 1.9 *zhang* (5.9 m) in height. Although there are no records of a Sui park wall, in view of the conventional practice of walling imperial parks, and of the existence of park gates, a Sui wall must have been erected. It is possible that the Tang continued to use part of the Sui wall even after the enclosed park area had been reduced.[7] The location of the park was planned so as to offer easy access to the emperor residing in the Palace City. But judging from extant documentation, the Palace City did not have an entrance that opened directly onto the park. According to a map the Qing scholar Zhuang Jing 莊璟 copied from the *Yongle dadian*, the Palace City had only one west entrance—the Baocheng Gate 寶城門 (Gate of the Treasured City), which opened onto a buffer zone surrounding the west, north, and east sides of the Palace City.[8] The west side of the Imperial City area, however, had two entrances, the Xitaiyang Gate 西太陽門 (West Sun Gate) to the north and the Gate of Lijing 麗景 (Beautiful Scenery) to the south. The Lijing is the only gate clearly indicated in the sources as leading directly to the park.[9] The two east gates of the park, Jiayu and Wangchun, were in all likelihood located in a section of the park wall that was not adjacent to the walled area of Luoyang.

The enormous size of the park allowed Yangdi to locate in it no fewer than eight palaces, in addition to the resort area known as the Sixteen Courtyards.[10] In Tang times, the reduced park area hosted at least eleven palace complexes. Of those, five were inherited from Yangdi.[11] Situated probably in the southeast part of the park was a lake, known simply as the Sea (*hai* 海) with a circumference of more than 10 *li*. In the lake, three hills were created, each more than 100 *chi* tall, symbolic of the three divine mountains of Penglai 蓬萊, Fangzhang 方丈, and Yingzhou 瀛洲. A profusion of estrades, belvederes, basilicas, and pavilions dotted the hills.

To the north was the Canal of Dragon Scales (Longlin 龍鱗). About 20 *bu* wide, it meandered through the Sixteen Courtyards before it emptied into the Sea. All but one of the Sixteen Courtyards have left their names: Yanguang 延光 (Broad Light), Mingcai 明彩 (Brilliant Colors), Hanxiang 含香 (Fragrance), Chenghua 承華 (Received Flowers), Ninghui 凝暉 (Focused Radiance), Lijing 麗景 (Beautiful Scenery), Feiying 飛英 (Dancing Snowflakes), Liufang 流芳 (Floating Aroma), Yaoyi 曜儀 (Splendid Beauty), Baifu 百福 (Hundredfold Happiness), Wanshan 萬善 (Myriad Charities), Changchun 長春 (Long-lasting Spring), Yongle 永樂 (Eternal Joy), Qingshu 清暑 (Summer Resort), and Mingde 明德 (Luminous Virtue).[12] The main entrance of each courtyard was composed of three gates that faced the canal on the south. Managed by a mistress of rank four, it had its own farm named after the courtyard itself where sheep, pigs, and fish were raised, and garden vegetables and fruits grown. The halls, basilicas, loft-buildings, and belvederes therein were splendidly built. The courtyards competed with one another for imperial favors with their offerings of exquisite and sumptuous food. Yangdi loved to tour the park on horseback on moonlit nights in the company of thousands of palace maids.[13]

In the easternmost part of the park was another lake, which measured 5 *li* east-west by 3 *li* north-south. Known as Ningbi (Dark Green) Pond 凝碧池 in Tang times, it was probably the same as Jicui (Jadeite Green) Pond 積翠池 in Sui. It was made famous by the acrobatic show Yangdi staged for Qimin qaghan. Jicui, as the centerpiece of its namesake palace and the premier beauty spot of the park, was known for its hills, ponds, and green woods.[14]

While the Luoyang project was still underway, Yangdi ordered Yuwen Kai and his associates to construct the Palace of Apparent Benevolence (Xianren 顯仁) to the south of the Sea within park grounds. Located in Shou'an 壽安 (Yiyang, Henan) and renamed Mingde 明德 (Luminous Virtue) in Tang times, the palace extended south to the Zao Brook 皁澗, and north to the Luo River.[15] To its northwest and in the westernmost part of the park, the Hebi 合璧 Palace was to be built in Tang times.[16] Since the Luo River was the natural westward extension of the Tongji Canal, the immediate access of the Xianren Palace to the Luo placed it within easy reach of the canal system (map 5.2).

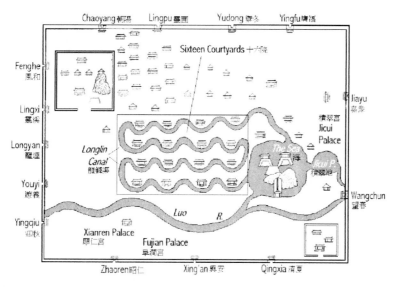

Map 5.2   Schematic map of the Sui Western Park, Luoyang

About 7 *li* from the Baocheng Gate, the western entrance to the Palace City, the Qingcheng 青城 (Green City) Palace was situated. Originally built by Gao Yan in 554 under the Northern Qi, the Green City itself had served the purpose of defense against attacks from the Northern Zhou. Yangdi converted it into a palace. Probably not far from the Baocheng Gate was the Lingbo (Wave) Palace. The more famous structures in Lingbo included the Hanjing (Scenic) Basilica and the She (Archery) Hall. There were also loft-buildings, watchtowers, and more than 10 *li* of moats with or without water.

To the south was the Palace of Fujian 阜澗 (Hills and Brooks), also known as the Ganquan 甘泉 (Sweet Fountain) Palace. Set up by the Secretariat Drafter (*neishi sheren* 內史舍人) Feng Deyi 封德彝, the palace had a circumference of more than 10 *li* and joined the Western Park to the north. Laid out on a hilly terrain it enclosed within it the Baichi Brook 百尺澗 (Hundred Foot Brook), Tongxian Feiqiao 通仙飛橋 (Transcendents' Flying Bridge), and Qinglian 青蓮 (Green Lotus) Peak in its south part.[17] Also inside the park was a Jinghua Palace 景華宮 (Palace of Elegant Flowers). Yangdi is recorded to have ordered his underlings to capture large quantities of fireflies within the grounds of Jinghua for lighting purposes.[18] Three less well-documented palaces dating back to Yangdi's times were found within the park area as well: Lengquan 冷泉 (Cold Fountain), Chaoyang 朝陽 (Facing Yang), and Qiyun 棲雲 (Perching Cloud). Like Jinghua, they do not have a confirmed location.[19]

In the park space outside the palace complexes and courtyards, there were a host of other structures, such as basilicas, halls, and pavilions, with no clear affiliation.

Lying within the Luoyang area but outside the Western Park were palaces such as Tingzi 亭子 (Pavilion), about 12 *li* east of the Shangchun 上春 Gate, Luoyang's east entrance to the north. To its east was the Jirun Pond 積潤池 (Moisture Pond). About 20 *li* further east was the Hualin Garden 華林園 (Floral Grove Garden) with its own ponds and terraced pavilions (*xie* 榭). In addition, there were the Longchuan 龍川 (Dragon River) Palace, and the Pingluo Garden 平洛園 (Smooth Luo Garden); both were located east of the Shangchun Gate as well.[20]

## Duliang Palace 都梁宮

Linking the Luoyang area in the Yellow River valley and the Huai River valley to the southeast was the eastern section of the Tongji Canal, a long stretch of waterway lined with willow trees. At its eastern terminus, where Tongji joined the Huai River in Xuyi 盱眙 (northeast of present-day Xuyi, Jiangsu), was the Duliang Palace with a circumference of 2 *li*. About Duliang, relatively detailed information has survived. Set up in 605, it was located 16 *li* southwest of the Tang county seat of Linhuai 臨淮, and north of the mountains. A triple corridor meandered through the palace grounds. From the west originated seven fountains—their rivulets eventually merged together. Above the east fountain was the Basilica of the Floating Goblet (Liubei 流盃).[21] In the southwest part of the palace on the bank of the Huai River, a fishing terrace was built. On top of a high hill facing the Huai sat the Basilica of Four Prospects (Siwang 四望). Close by ran the Serpentine River (Quhe 曲河) where dragon ships and other large vessels were anchored. In nearby Xuyi County, the Duliang Relay Palace (*yigong* 驛宮), built in 610, served as Yangdi's way station between Duliang and Jiangdu.[22]

## PALACES CLOSE TO THE NORTHERN FRONTIER

Although Hedong area to the north was not linked to the Grand Canal, it was home to some of Yangdi's most elaborate palace complexes. Yangdi had spent his formative years in Jinyang as prince of Jin before his assignment to the South and his promotion to the post of crown prince. For Yangdi this area may have been a place of sentimental attachment as well as strategic significance.

Located northwest of Jinyang (southwest of Taiyuan, Shanxi) was the Jinyang 晉陽 Palace, constructed on Yangdi's orders from 607. When completed it was enclosed by walls of 4 *zhang* and 8 *chi* tall in an area 2,520 *bu* in circumference.

North of Jinyang was the Fenyang Palace 汾陽宮, built by Yangdi in the northern part of Loufan Commandery 樓繁郡 (southwest of present-day Ningwu in north Shanxi) in 608. The original purpose of the palace was to suppress the aura of a Son of Heaven, believed to pose a direct threat to the throne. Located on the Cen Mountains 涔山 where the Fen River 汾水 originated, it offered cool temperatures during summer.

Probably not far from the Fenyang Palace was a cluster of ten architectural complexes, known collectively as the Ten Palaces (*shigong* 十宮), which were built along rivulets and on undulating terrain inside the Changfu Park 長阜苑: Guiyan 歸雁 (Returning Wild Geese), Huiliu 回流 (Returning Current), Jiuli 九里 (Nine Li), Songlin 松林 (Pine Grove), Fenglin 楓林 (Maple Grove), Dalei 大雷 (Great Thunder), Xiaolei 小雷 (Little Thunder), Chuncao 春草 (Spring Grass), Jiuhua 九華 (Nine Flowers), and Guangfen 光汾 (Shining Fen) Palaces.[23]

West of the settled Chinese community of Bing Prefecture was the Ordos area in present-day Inner Mongolia, an area that had been a bone of contention between the Han Chinese and the nomads since antiquity. Yangdi converted the area's Sheng Prefecture 勝州 into Yulin Commandery 榆林郡, which served as the locale for the Sui Yulin Palace (southwest of Togtoh). The palace itself was probably erected by Yangdi, who needed a resting station there to deal with the Tujue and to supervise the much more ambitious construction project of the Sui Great Wall.[24]

To the east, in the southwest of present-day Beijing was the Linshuo Palace 臨朔宮. On his 611 visit there, Yangdi ordered his underlings to provide housing for all of his attending officials, civil and military alike, of rank nine and above,[25] and gave an audience to Tujue's Chuluo qaghan 處羅可汗.[26] Most importantly, the palace served as Yangdi's headquarters from which to mount military campaigns against Koguryŏ.

Further to the east in Beiping Commandery 北平郡, midway between present-day Lulong and Qinhuangdao, Hebei, was the Linyu 臨渝 Palace, the easternmost major palace complex under Yangdi, probably constructed by him as well.[27] To its north were the Great Wall and the vast area of Manchuria.

## PALACES IN THE SOUTH

Yangdi's official residence of the South was the Jiangdu Palace located in Jiangdu (Yangzhou). This main palace complex in the lower Yangzi valley had as its companion structure the Yangzi Palace nearby. It is not known when the Jiangdu Palace was planned and built under the Sui nor are there surviving records of its scale and main structures in Sui times, although the *Zizhi tongjian* talks about its estrades, halls and more than one hundred houses.[28] In Tang times, the city Jiangdu was renamed Yangzhou. Its dimensions were recorded by the Japanese monk Ennin in 838: 11 *li* north-south and 7 *li* east-west, with a circumference of 40 *li*.[29] The city walls, erected in Tang times, enclosed an area divided into two parts, the Minor City (*zicheng* 子城) in the northwest corner, and the Outer City (*luocheng* 羅城). In the southwest part of the Minor City a rammed earth foundation about 100 square m was revealed, which was probably the site of the Jian Loft-building 建樓, later known as Loft-building for Picking Stars (Zhaixinglou 摘星樓), a palatial structure set up by Yangdi.[30] In the last few years of Yangdi's life, Jiangdu became Yangdi's main domicile until his death in early 618 (map 5.3).

To the southeast of Jiangdu was the Piling Palace 毗陵宮, built in 616 in the southeast part of Piling Commandery, probably close to present-day Wuxi. The whole area was a huge enclosure with a circumference of 12 *li*. Inside, sixteen secondary palaces (*ligong* 離宮) were built. Luxuriously constructed and furnished, this palace surpassed its prototype, the Western Park of Luoyang, in grandeur.

West of Jiangdu was the former site of Jiankang. Regarded as the ultimate symbol of decadence, the city had been razed to the ground by Wendi after the Sui conquest of the area. Now rechristened Danyang 丹陽, it became another favorite place for Yangdi, who was willing to ignore its past association with failure and depravity. Not only did he start building the Danyang Palace, he also had plans to relocate the capital there[31] and to construct new palaces further down south in Guiji 會稽 Commandery (north Zhejiang).[32] None of these plans came to fruition due to his untimely death.

In studying Yangdi as a builder of palaces, what we find most striking is his unrivalled appetite for continuous construction activity. On this, the *Zizhi tongjian* offers an insightful observation:

> Not a single day passed without the emperor getting involved in some palace project. Although there were numerous parks, gardens, pavilions and basilicas in the two capitals and the Jiangdu area, [Yangdi] grew tired of them over time. When he toured these places for pleasure, he would look right and left. Not satisfied with any of these, he would be at a loss where to go. In consequence, he gathered maps of mountains and rivers under Heaven, and personally examined them, in search of places of beauty for palaces and parks.[33]

Driven by an irresistible urge to build palaces in such rapid succession, he hardly had time to enjoy most of them. Efforts at curbing this urge were met with violent responses (as in the case of Zhang Heng). For Yangdi, the pursuit

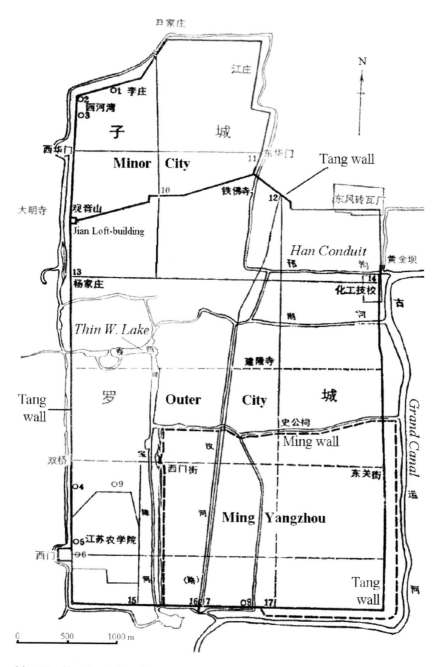

MAP 5.3  Yangzhou in Tang Times

of palace projects was no longer a means through which one realized the primary purpose of providing spacious, luxurious quarters to the inhabitant. Rather it became almost an end itself.

The palatial structures Yangdi created were distinguished by (1) quantity; (2) political, and strategic considerations; and (3) complexity. Although earlier sovereigns are known to have built lavish palaces of complex design and immense magnitude, few could compare with Yangdi in terms of the number of palaces constructed. The more than forty palaces Yangdi built along the waterways from Daxingcheng to Luoyang to Jiangdu are enough to rank him as a builder of palaces far ahead of any sovereign before him in quantitative terms except for the First Emperor.[34] And this does not even include other palaces in the vicinity of the Northern frontier and the South. Based on rather inadequate historical records, during his short reign of less than fourteen years, at least seventy palaces were erected, at an average pace of five per year, and a large number of them were built on an impressive scale as well. But scale itself did not necessarily claim his foremost attention. A case in point is Luoyang, where he focused on the luxurious design of the palace structures and the improved functionality of the city.

None of his palaces seemed to serve the sole purpose of self-aggrandizement in the manner of the Epang阿房 Palace of the First Emperor. Nor were they divinely inspired like the Jianzhang 建章 Palace of Han Wudi. Often strategically located, Yangdi's palaces were created for his personal enjoyment and convenience, even though most of them were underutilized. The Luoyang palace group in the Central Plain and the Jiangdu palace group in the lower Yangzi valley served at various times as centers of his operations. The Jinyang Palace was at the heart of Bing Prefecture, an area crucial for the defense of the two capitals. The Yulin Palace provided a base for conducting frontier diplomacy in the Ordos area, while the Linshuo Palace served as the backstage area of his military campaigns in the Northeast.

In terms of design, particularly worthy of attention were Yangdi's mega-palaces, which, unlike the conventional isolated palace enclosures, were composed of multiple subpalaces, such as the Ten Palaces in the North, and the Piling Palace in the South. Giving expression to grandiosity, he set high standards for complexity of design in architecture.

In creating palace complexes, Yangdi also came under the influence of previous ages. One of his most inspiring examples was doubtless the First Emperor. The three hills of Penglai, Fangzhang, and Yingzhou at the center of the Sea in the Western Park were named after three famous divine Qin mountains, allegedly in the Eastern Sea, where, according to legend, transcendents dwelled.[35] As the First Emperor was uniting China through war, each time he conquered a state, he would build a replica of its palace north of the Qin capital Xianyang. As a result, from the North Slope (beiban 北阪) of

Xianyang in the north, down to the Wei River in the south, and from Yongmen
雍門 east to the confluence of the Jing 涇 and Wei, "basilicas, houses, and
concealed passageways were joined together by rambling pavilioned corridors.
[He] filled them with beauties, and bells and drums (ritual instruments) captured from various states."[36] By locating replicas of palaces of the conquered
states in a designated palace area, the First Emperor may have produced the
prototype of a megapalace conceptually similar to those by Yangdi, who
attempted to emulate him in architectural accomplishment.

As one of the most prolific builders of palaces, Yangdi was caught in a
never-ending cycle, which compelled him to make wasteful use of court revenues for horrendously expensive projects. In the same spirit, he showed utter
indifference to cost when touring or engaging in entertainment activities.
Although certain technical details in textual records on Yangdi's excesses are
found to be inaccurate, nevertheless, sufficient evidence has proved that
throughout his reign, Yangdi had an enduring love for extravagance. Yangdi
was able to give full play to his penchant for grandiosity, thanks to the sound
economic foundation he inherited from the previous reign, and the wealth of
the entire nation he had at his disposal. Surpassing his immediate and distant
predecessors, he brought imperial luxury to a new height. But over time his
extravagant lifestyle would lead to serious economic consequences. His building projects constituted a heavy drain on the nation's resources, and his overall
fiscal irresponsibility contributed significantly to the onset of a prolonged economic crisis nationwide.

# 6

---

# The Bureaucracy

The Sui administrative system created by Wendi was a milestone in the political history of premodern China. In contrast to the cumbersome bureaucratic models of the Southern and Northern Dynasties, Wendi's was a more efficient, better delineated, synthetic system that survived the Sui itself to become the foundation of the Tang bureaucratic structure. Clearly, it is within the framework of this system that we have to examine Yangdi's bureaucratic apparatus. Still, unsatisfied with the status quo, Yangdi introduced a number of major changes to civil administration and the military with a far-reaching impact on the relationship between sovereign and bureaucracy and between central authority and local government.

## CIVIL ADMINISTRATION

### Central Government

Before his rise to power, Wendi saw an atavistic system of bureaucracy in action during his tenure as a key court official of the Northern Zhou. The Northern Zhou system had been created by the Western Wei (535–557) power-holder Yuwen Tai 宇文泰 (505–556), one of the most controversial institutional reformers in history, based on the *Rites of Zhou* (*Zhou li* 周禮). Assisted by his chief court adviser of Han descent, Su Chuo 蘇綽 (498–546), Yuwen Tai initiated a number of institutional reforms to consolidate his power in Guanzhong while attempting to distinguish himself from the Eastern Wei (which closely identified itself with the Xianbei 鮮卑 tradition), as well as from the Liang dynasty in the South that regarded itself as the inheritor of the Han and Wei-Jin legacy. Although stressing his Xianbei connections, Yuwen Tai modeled his reforms on the ancient Western Zhou prototype. At the head of the newly created government was the grand chief minister (*chengxiang*; later, *da chengxiang* 大丞相). Directly under him were the Six Offices, named after Heaven and Earth and the four seasons. The officialdom was classified according to an archaic hierarchical system, composed of nine appointment ranks (*ming* 命), with rank nine being the highest.[1]

On coming to power in 581, Wendi not only ordered the extermination of the surviving male members of the Northern Zhou royal house, but also set out to destroy the Northern Zhou's bureaucratic structure. The *Sui shu* succinctly sums up the dramatic transformation of the officialdom from Northern Zhou to Sui:

> Giving special consideration to the surviving documents of Feng 酆 and Hao 鎬 (Western Zhou), [the Northern Zhou] set up the Six Offices [based on the *Rites of Zhou*] to take charge of government. Their elaborate institutions are commendable. When Gaozu (Wendi) came to power, numerous measures had to start anew. The Zhou offices were again abolished while the Han and Cao-Wei systems adopted.[2]

Why did Wendi introduce such drastic institutional reforms? There are no easy answers to the question since traditional sources provide little information. The most apparent explanation may be sought in the fact that the Northern Zhou system was based on an archaic tradition that was allegedly Western Zhou in origin and not on the political reality of the times. The system clashed with the pragmatism of Wendi. Furthermore, as a usurper, Wendi was anxious to justify his raison d'être as the new dynastic ruler by creating his own identity while distancing himself from the power he had replaced, just like the Yuwens who wanted to differ from the previous Northern Wei. Considering the harrowing experiences the Yangs had gone through under the Northern Zhou, Wendi may well have harbored strong resentment against its royal family and institutions. As a key member of the Northern Zhou court, Wendi's father Yang Zhong 楊忠 had fallen afoul of Yuwen Hu 宇文護, the great power manipulator at court and the chief enforcer of the Northern Zhou system. Wendi himself narrowly escaped Hu's murderous attempts. Although Wudi took Wendi under his wing, he and Wendi had entirely different religious beliefs. After Wudi's death, Wendi had a rather perilous existence at the court of Xuandi 宣帝, who threatened on a number of occasions to exterminate Wendi and his family.[3]

Wendi's thorough reorganization of the central and local administrative systems was to become his greatest political legacy. Ignoring its Northern Zhou predecessor, Wendi's complex new system was based on the Han, Northern Wei, and Northern Qi traditions.[4] The central government was composed mainly of the Five Departments, Six Boards, and Nine Courts. Of the Five Departments, three were in charge of the central government, namely, the Department of State Affairs (*shangshu sheng* 尚書省), the Chancellery (*menxia sheng* 門下省), and the Secretariat (*neishi sheng* 內史省), collectively known as the Three Departments.[5] The remaining two, the Department of the Palace Library (*mishu sheng* 秘書省) and the Department of Palace Domestic Service (*neishi[a] sheng* 內侍省), were in charge of palace affairs and were practically left outside the core leadership.

The functions of the Sui Three Departments are not clearly defined in the sources. Based on the Tang model, ideally, the Chancellery and Secretariat were directly involved in the decision-making process. The Secretariat served as the originator of policy proposals, which were reviewed by the Chancellery before being sent on to the executive branch—the Department of State Affairs—for implementation. But in practice, heads of the Department of State Affairs had major policy making responsibilities. Directly under the department were the Six Boards with broad executive powers. They may also be considered top government agencies even though their role was implementing rather than formulating policy.

Officially ranking higher than the leaders of the Three Departments (chief ministers) and board presidents were the Three Dukes (*sangong* 三公) and Three Preceptors (*sanshi* 三師). Since these were essentially honorary titles under Wendi and did not carry functional powers, their bearers were not top central leaders unless they concurrently held other key functional posts. There were other central government agencies such as directorates (*jian* 監) and courts (*si* 寺), but in terms of policy formulation and execution, these agencies were of secondary significance.

The Nine Courts (*si*) and their predecessors were a tradition that harks back to the Han dynasty. In essence, these central agencies often overlapped the Six Boards in function but were not nearly as powerful. However, unlike the Tang period when the Nine Courts were ranked lower bureaucratically and functioned as subordinate agencies to carry out directives of the Six Boards, the Sui Nine Courts were headed by officials with the same rank as the presidents of the Six Boards (rank three, upper class)[6] (appendix 1, table 1).

Wendi, in the process of overhauling the central bureaucracy, also redefined the relationship between court and central bureaucracy. Under the Northern Zhou, the single most important official was the grand chief minister or chancellor, who was ex officio head of the central bureaucracy. In

consequence, the office of grand chief minister was perceived as a major threat
to the throne. Wendi was personally familiar with its power, having usurped
the throne while holding that office. To eliminate that threat, he permanently
abolished it, and set up an oligarchic leadership under his direct control. Thus,
three departments instead of a single one constituted the central nerve system
of the government. The executive branch of the central government, the
Department of State Affairs, was without doubt the most powerful among the
Three Departments under the Sui. It should have been headed by its president (*shangshu ling* 尚書令). But due to Wendi's distrust of the office, the
presidency only existed in name during his reign. Its two vice presidents (*puye*
僕射) became top executive officers by default. Wendi's concerns about these
powerful officials was clearly shown in an edict he issued to Vice President
Yang Su: "*Puye* are the chief executives of the country, and should not be
allowed to attend to detailed affairs. All they need to do is come to the department every three or five days to discuss important matters."[7]

The two vice presidents of the Department of State Affairs, together
with the heads of the Chancellery (*menxia* 門下) and the Secretariat (*neishi*;
*zhongshu* 中書 under the Tang), made up the top echelon leadership of the
central government, known as chief ministers. As the highest government officials responsible for the formulation of state policy, under normal circumstances, they constituted the emperor's inner circle of advisers.[8] Apart from
regular holders of these top posts, unofficial, de facto appointments of chief
ministers were also made.

As soon as Yangdi fell heir to this complex bureaucratic system, he set out
to reform it, although as sovereign, he had every reason to maintain a semblance of political continuity. Most of Yangdi's institutional reforms at the
central level took place in 607. It was no coincidence that in that year he executed top advisers Gao Jiong, Heruo Bi, and Yuwen Bi, and demoted Chief
Minister Su Wei. The suppression of potential opposition seems to have
cleared the way for Yangdi's plans to reshape the central bureaucracy.

A notable departure from the previous reign was the reorganization of the
ranking system. "Ranks (*pin* 品) one through nine are only divided into upper
and lower classes (*zheng cong* 正從). First and second grades (*shangxia jie*
上下階) [as the subdivisions within a class] are abolished."[9] This is a clear
indication that Yangdi streamlined his father's multilayered hierarchical system
with its ranks, classes, and grades. Since we have found no record of the use
of grades in Sui times in extant sources, we can only guess how the system
worked on the basis of other systems. When Wendi came to power, the official ranking system of the Northern Zhou he inherited was comprised of eighteen classes. Still earlier, the ranking system introduced under Xiaowendi of the
Northern Wei had thirty rungs on the official ladder of promotion. In all likelihood, Wendi reverted to the thirty-rung system of the Northern Wei, while

Yangdi changed it back to the Northern Zhou system of eighteen rungs. The Tang discarded Yangdi's system based on the Northern Zhou model in favor of Wendi's system based on the Northern Wei prototype. Behind these changes back and forth between the thirty-rung and eighteen-rung systems was the effort on the part of the reigning sovereign to distinguish and distance himself from the previous dynasty or reign.

A central theme of Yangdi's administrative reform was the strengthening of the power base of the court at the expense of the central bureaucracy. The powerful office of grand chief minister abolished by Wendi remained defunct under Yangdi. Although he appointed Yang Su president of the Department of State Affairs, the only Sui holder of that office, he distrusted the post so much that after Yang Su's death in 606[10] it became vacant and remained so for the rest of the reign.

Perhaps the most enduring contribution Yangdi made to the central bureaucracy was the restructuring of the Department of State Affairs with its Six Boards, and the Nine Courts.[11] As noted above, under Wendi, the heads of the Nine Courts were in the same rank as those of the Six Boards. In fact, in the hierarchical listing of Sui officials, three court presidents—*taichang* 太常 (Court of Imperial Sacrifices), *guanglu* 光祿 (Court of Imperial Entertainments), and *weiwei* 衛尉 (Court of the Palace Garrison)—were labeled as the top Three Chamberlains (*sanqing* 三卿), ranking above all presidents of the Six Boards except *libu* 吏部 (Board of Personnel). The remaining five board presidents of the *li^abu* 禮部 (Board of Rites), *bingbu* 兵部 (Board of War), *duguan/xingbu* 都官/刑部 (Board of Justice), *duzhi/minbu* 度支/民部 (Board of Revenue), and *gongbu* 工部 (Board of Works) were followed by the lesser Six Chamberlains of the *zongzheng* 宗正 (Court of the Imperial Clan), *taipu* 太僕 (Court of the Imperial Stud), *dali* 大理 (Court of Judicial Review), *honglu* 鴻臚 (Court for Dependencies), *sinong* 司農 (Court of the National Granaries), and *taifu* 太府 (Court for the Palace Revenues).

Yangdi strengthened the role of the Six Boards by promoting all vice presidents (*cheng* 丞) from rank 4b (lower class) to rank 4a (upper class), and by redefining the powers of the *shilang* 侍郎. Before, there were thirty-six *shilang* serving as bureau directors at the rank of 6a. Yangdi reduced the number to six while promoting them to rank 4a. The reinvented *shilang* then served as assistant presidents of the entire Board. Yangdi demoted the chamberlains of the Nine Courts except that of Court of Imperial Sacrifices (*taichang*), from rank 3a to rank 3b, and the vice chamberlains (*shaoqing* 少卿) from rank 4a to rank 4b. These measures paved the way for the functional subordination of the Nine Courts to the Six Boards, a practice institutionalized under the Tang.[12]

Of the original Five Departments, the last one, the *neishi^a sheng* (Department of Palace Domestic Service), was demoted to a directorate (*changqiu jian*

長秋監) under Yangdi. In its place the *diannei sheng* 殿內省 (Department of
Palace Administration) became the newest member of the Five Departments.
Under Wendi there had been a central agency called the Terrace of Censors
(*yushi tai* 御史臺) in charge of surveillance. Yangdi added two more terraces—
*yezhe tai* 謁者臺 (Terrace of Receptions) and *sili tai* 司隸臺 (Terrace of Inspectors)—to create the "Three Terraces" (*santai* 三臺). Both were responsible for
investigation of officials. The *santai* had been in existence in Han times for
the purpose of keeping the sovereign in touch with the administration.[13] The
revival of the institution was no doubt inspired by the Han prototype.
However, it served a different purpose—to tighten the control over the officialdom. As a usurper and a daring reformer who would break many established rules, Yangdi made a calculated but sensible decision to strengthen the
surveillance agencies.

Yangdi grouped five central supervisory agencies together with an assort-
ment of functions as the Five Directorates (*wujian* 五監): *shaofu* 少府 (Imperial Manufactories), a spinoff from the Court for the Palace Revenues (*taifu
si*); *changqiu* (Palace Domestic Service), converted from the Department of
Domestic Service (*neishi*$^a$ *sheng*); *guozi* 國子 (Education) and *jiangzuo* 將作
(Palace Buildings), converted from the National University and the Court of
Palace Buildings, respectively; and *dushui* 都水 (Waterways), converted from
the Terrace of Waterways (*dushui tai*). Under Wendi, unlike the Nine Courts
which were led by *qing* 卿 (chamberlains), the Court of Education National
University and the Court of Palace Buildings were headed by a libationer (*jijiu*
祭酒) and a grand artisan (*dajiang* 大匠), respectively. By permanently grouping them with the directories, Yangdi brought into focus the Nine Courts, a
measure that helped rationalize the central bureaucracy (appendix 1, table 1).

Yangdi did not take too kindly to certain nonfunctioning, fancy titles. He
abolished both the *sanshi* 三師 (Three Preceptors) and *tejin* 特進 (specially
advanced), honorific titles reserved for revered high officials. Neither was
he satisfied with the nine-rank aristocratic system, composed of state prince
(*guowang* 國王), commandery prince (*junwang* 郡王), state duke (*guogong*
國公), commandery duke (*jungong* 郡公), county duke (*xiangong* 縣公),
marquis (*hou* 侯), earl (*bo* 伯), viscount (*zi* 子), and baron (*nan* 男). Yangdi
simplified the system into one of prince, duke, and marquis, which was reminiscent of a similar effort he made in streamlining the ranking system. In so
doing, Yangdi seemed to have attempted to gain better control of the aristocracy or been motivated by a desire to differentiate his reign from that of his
predecessor.[14]

## Local Government

The pre-Sui *zhou-jun-xian* (prefecture-commandery-county) system of local government was a cumbersome and corrupt one. Under this three-tier structure, local government offices proliferated. This prompted one official to compare it to "using nine shepherds for ten sheep." The previous regime of Northern Zhou, after its conquest of the Northern Qi, had a total of 508 commanderies and 211 prefectures. At the beginning of the first Sui reign, according to a *Tong dian* record, there were a total of 310 *zhou* 州-prefectures and 508 *jun* 郡-commanderies.[15] Since Wendi then held the same amount of territory as his Northern Zhou predecessor, these records indicate that the number of commanderies under him remained the same while the number of prefectures increased by almost one third.[16] In 583, on the advice of Yang Shangxi 楊尚希, Wendi instituted bold reform measures to eliminate *jun*-commanderies.[17] Throughout his reign, Wendi added fifty-six prefectures in the North and sixty-one prefectures in the South after the conquest of the Chen. If we deduct abolished prefectures (thirteen in the North and three in the South), we are left with a net gain of 101 prefectures.[18] Since most of the added Northern prefectures were created in or after 583, and none can be confirmed to be earlier than 583, it is highly likely that none of the fifty-six Northern prefectures were included in the total number of 310.[19] Neither were the new Southern prefectures, which were added in 589. To work out the approximate consolidated number for the total of prefectures at the height of the first reign, we add 101 (the total number of added prefectures under Wendi minus abolished ones) and 310, and get 411.

The precise number of counties under Wendi is not documented. But by adding the numbers of Chen counties (438) and Northern Zhou counties after 577 (1,124), we arrive at 1,562 as the estimate total.[20]

Apparently not impressed with his father's system of local civil administration, Yangdi introduced a number of major changes. In 607, Yangdi replaced all the prefectures (*zhou*) with commanderies (*jun*), while maintaining the two-tier system. However, this was not simply a nominal change of nomenclature. In 609, after the *zhou*-level of administration had been abolished, there were a total of 190 commanderies under Yangdi, which was less than one half of the total number of prefectures under Wendi.[21] Meanwhile, Yangdi reduced the total number of counties by almost 20 percent, from an estimated 1,562 to 1,255. Even so, Yangdi's new system still had the highest commandery (prefecture) to county ratio (1:6.6) for a long time, which in itself was indication of more efficient government organization.[22]

Drastic reduction of the size of the local bureaucracy was one of the main achievements of Yangdi's reform of local government. To tighten his hold on the local governments, Yangdi set up an inspection system headed by two inspectors-in-chief, with two *biejia* 別駕 (mounted escorts) in charge of the two capital areas, and fourteen provincial inspectors (*cishi* 刺史) in charge of other commanderies and counties. They regularly made field visits to monitor the performance of the local officials and reported their findings to the court.[23]

Yangdi took measures to demote local officials across the board as well. For example, while an upper *zhou* prefect ranked 3a under Wendi, his equivalent under Yangdi, an upper *jun* governor, ranked 3b. Meanwhile, magistrates of the four capital counties were, contrary to the national trend, promoted from rank 5b to rank 5a.[24] These moves obviously indicate Yangdi's effort to enhance central authority at the expense of local administration.

Guided by the same principle, the administration of the residential wards (*fang* 坊) in the two capitals, now renamed *li* 里, was taken over by the court. Extending his administrative control into the religious sphere, Yangdi ordered that a supervisor (*jian* 監) and an assistant supervisor (*cheng* 丞) be assigned to each Buddhist monastery (*si* 寺), now renamed *daochang* 道場, and each Daoist abbey (*guan* 觀), now renamed *xuantan* 玄壇.[25]

## The Army

When Wendi ascended the throne, the military administration he took over was almost as complex as its civil counterpart. There were prefectural and commandery forces in the provinces, frontier armies charged with defending border areas, and palace guards responsible for safeguarding the court. The most important military forces were, however, those in the network of *fubing* 府兵 garrisons, which were essentially a government-sponsored militia system.[26] Like the palace guards, the *fubing* forces were part of the imperial guard system, only with a different mission. The non-*fubing* palace guards were responsible for the personal safety of the emperor. Though involved in similar duties, the *fubing* forces also served as gate guards and patrols within palace grounds and as vanguards for the imperial progress. Most of them were stationed in strategic points in and around the capital and beyond. No records on Sui *fubing* organization have survived. It seems that its basic unit was probably similar to the *tuan* 團 (regiment) at one thousand in strength, under which was the *dui* 隊 (company) of about one hundred.[27] The much better documented Early Tang *fubing* system had as its basic unit the *fu* 府-garrison with a troop strength that varied from eight hundred, ten thousand, twelve hundred, to fifteen hundred. The total number of Tang garrisons ranged from 594 to 634. Although *tuan* and *dui* continued to exist under the Tang, their sizes were greatly reduced. A Tang *tuan* had about two hundred to three hundred troops at full strength while a Tang *dui* had about fifty.[28]

—

Under Wendi, the *fubing* system, which had first appeared in the Western Wei, came of age. It was composed of twelve central commands known as the Twelve Garrison Commands (*shi'er fu* 十二府) with subordinate units known as Cavalry (*piaoqi* 驃騎) Garrisons, deployed in the capital and other strategic areas. Each Cavalry Garrison had as its commander a cavalry general (*piaoqi jiangjun* 驃騎將軍) and as its deputy commander a chariot and horse (*cheqi* 車騎) general.[29]

Yangdi introduced military reforms to the *fubing* system in 607 that paralleled similar efforts in the civil arena. Of Wendi's Twelve Garrison Commands, only four were known as guards (*wei* 衛). Yangdi converted them into a system of Twelve Guards and Sixteen Garrison Commands. The Twelve Guards now functioned as the twelve central commands of the *fubing*, and its use continued well into the Tang dynasty. Yangdi's Twelve Guards were also part of the Sixteen Garrisond Commands, which included four more non-*fubing* units—Left and Right Imperial Bodyguard (*beishen* 備身) Garrison Commands and Left and Right Palace (*jianmen* 監門) Garrison Commands (appendix 1, table 2).[30] In addition, Yangdi renamed the Cavalry Garrisons (*piaoqi fu*) as the Soaring Hawk (*yingyang* 鷹揚) Garrisons, under the command of the *yingyang langjiang* 鷹揚郎將 (Soaring Hawk commandant) and *yingyang fu langjiang* 副郎將 (Soaring Hawk vice commandant). Furthermore, Yangdi demoted all *fubing* garrison commanders by a full rank from 4a to 5a, and vice commanders from rank 5a to rank 5b.[31]

In local military administration, Yangdi discontinued military prestige titles for high- and middle-ranking officers, and terminated the *zongguan* 總管 (area command or area commander) system in the first month of 605.[32] Under Wendi, four superior area commands (*da zongguan* 大總管), each comprised of dozens of regular area commands, had been created, primarily for the imperial princes, in an attempt to strengthen court control of local military forces. Yangdi had headed Bingzhou and Yangzhou Superior Area Commands before he was promoted to crown prince.[33] In a sense, it was his *da zongguan* experience that made Yangdi a formidable challenger first to the sitting crown prince Yang Yong and then to Wendi himself. The firsthand knowledge Yangdi had of the amount of power at the disposal of a *da zongguan* probably prompted him to move to abolish the entire *zongguan* system.[34]

While overhauling the Sui military, Yangdi instituted a major shift in the Sui defense strategy through redeploying *fubing* forces. Since there is no record on the overall deployment of Sui troops, it has to be estimated by other evidence, such as that on the establishment or abolition of area commands. During the first reign, the security of the capital in Guanzhong had initially been the main focus of Wendi's military strategy. However, it would seem that as Wendi came to concentrate considerable military power in the four superior area commands, Guanzhong itself was left without a dominant military force for its defense towards the end of the first reign, and was even seriously threatened by Bingzhou to its east immediately after Wendi's death.

With the founding of the Eastern Capital at Luoyang, the East became the new center of military power at the expense of Guanzhong. Consequently, in spite of its strategic location and vast riches, Guanzhong became vulnerable to Tujue's attacks from the north, and was left in a weak position to deal with domestic unrest. For the same reason, it became easy prey to the insurgent leader Li Yuan 李淵, who, early in his rebellion, was able to occupy Daxingcheng in short order and consolidate his power before setting out to conquer the rest of China.[35]

## PATTERNS OF RECRUITMENT

To understand the changing dynamics of the Sui bureaucratic system we must examine it in the context of court politics. There is no better way to accomplish that objective than through a systematic study of Sui bureaucratic recruitment practices at the highest level.

In this area, the work of Chen Yinke has been particularly relevant and influential. Studying the evolution of political institutions of the Sui-Tang period, in the early 1940s he advanced his hypothesis on the so-called "primacy of the Guanlong bloc." It argues that, from the Northern Zhou to the Early Tang, court politics was dominated by an aristocratic group with a particular geographical identity, namely, the Guanlong bloc, so named because its members were from *junwang* 郡望 or choronyms in the Guanlong area (primarily Shaanxi and Gansu), that is, the Northern Zhou area before the annexation of the Northern Qi. A choronym refers to a medieval clan of high social station, associated with a certain locality where its eminent ancestors were believed to have been born. The status of a family was often determined through identification of its ancestral lineage with such a clan. Throughout this period, the court actively advanced the interest of the Guanlong bloc through appointing bloc members to key official posts, often at the expense of members of other choronym-defined blocs such as the Shandong bloc (in the former Northern Qi area, particularly, present-day Hebei, Henan, and Shandong) and the South bloc. This hypothesis has been challenged in recent decades with the thrust of the criticism mainly focusing on the Early Tang phase.[36]

Keeping in mind Chen's hypothesis, and other interpretative approaches, we will examine recruitment patterns of Sui ranking officials, exploring their family backgrounds, choronyms and other geographical identities, and their relations with the sovereign. An exhaustive study of Sui bureaucratic appointments at various levels requires major efforts at statistical gathering and analysis, and that is beyond the scope of this book. Therefore, we will focus mainly on the top echelon of the central administration, namely, leaders of the Three Departments and the Six Boards, as representatives of the high-ranking officials under the Sui in terms of bloc identity and lineage background. Only limited attention will be devoted to lower-level central agencies such as the directorates and the courts.

The first issue to address is the composition of bureaucratic recruits in terms of choronym. During Wendi's reign there was a total of fourteen persons appointed to twenty-one chief ministerial posts. Of these twenty-one appointments (including multiple appointments), four (about 19 percent) were made to officials outside the Guanlong bloc. If multiple appointments are excluded, of the fourteen appointees, eleven or 79 percent had Guanlong choronyms, and three or 21 percent had Shandong choronyms. Of the six vice presidents of the Department of State Affairs on record, only one (Gao Jiong; less than 17 percent of total) was from a non-Guanlong choronym. Of the six presidents of the Chancellery, two (Gao Jiong and Liu Ji, or about 33 percent) were from the non-Guanlong bloc of Shandong. Among the nine presidents of the Secretariat, only one (about 11 percent of total) was a non-Guanlong outsider (Li Delin 李德林, also from Shandong) (appendix 1, table 3).

This may be considered prima facie evidence that during the first reign of the Sui dynasty, members of the Guanlong bloc were favored in official chief ministerial appointments. This seems to lend support to Chen Yinke's primacy of Guanzhong thesis.

In making these high-level appointments, Wendi often favored members of the royal house. However, Wendi seemed to draw a line between *shangshu sheng* 尚書省 (Department of State Affairs) and non-*shangshu sheng* appointments: He never appointed a royal to head the *shangshu sheng*. Although traditionally considered chief ministerial positions, the presidencies of the Chancellery and Secretariat held much less power than their counterparts in the *shangshu sheng*. Staying away from royal favoritism, Wendi was in a better position to promote the most capable administers to these crucial executive posts of the central government.

The importance of the Department of State Affairs is further born out by the disparities in Wendi's treatments of the top appointments to the Three Departments. Although each department was supposed to have two leaders, the Department of State Affairs was the only one whose two top positions were continuously filled. Based on appointment and dismissal dates, I have tentatively worked out the appointment periods of the presidencies at the Chancellery and Secretariat (appendix 1, table 4). Presidency A of the Chancellery had brief interruptions between 590/7 and 594/7, and 601/1 and 602/10. Presidency B was interrupted between 587 and 589/6, and was kept vacant after 590/7. The Secretariat's presidential appointments were much more confusing. Presidency A had a long break between 592/7 and 599/6. Presidency B remained vacant after 593/6. In addition there seemed to exist a third presidency (C) in the early part of the first reign, which was at variance with the officially approved structure with two top seats for the Secretariat. These findings, and the fact that the emperor tended to use the top posts at the Chancellery and Secretariat for royal favoritism, but never those at the Department of State Affairs, underscore the less important functions of the two departments.

Apart from official appointments to the top jobs, the Sui sovereign sometimes recruited officials into the inner circle of the court through de facto chief ministerial appointments.[37] Two such appointments made by Wendi were of royal descent—Yang Yong, Wendi's first crown prince, and Yang Xiong 楊雄, a nephew. Obviously the first one was intended to prepare the future emperor for his role in the realm of government. The second one was probably in part based on the appointee's merit—he was a member of the Four Nobles, a powerful group at court that included Gao Jiong, Yu Qingze, and Su Wei.[38] Of the remaining four appointees, all nonroyal, only Linghu Xi 令狐熙 was of Guanlong origin. Chen Mao 陳茂, Xue Daoheng, and Liu Shu were all from the Shandong area. In appointing de facto chief ministers, Wendi seemed to equally favor the two dominant blocs of the North (appendix 1, table 5).

Of the six clans that supplied Wendi's de facto chief ministers, the Linghus of Dunhuang may be considered a local aristocratic one of Tuoba extraction.[39] Three—the Yangs 楊 of Huayin, the Xues 薛 of Hedong and the Lius 柳 of Hedong—were of prominent aristocratic lineage. All the appointees, except the commoner Chen Mao, had a father who had served in a key official position under the Northern Wei or Northern Zhou.

At the lower level of the top leadership were presidents of the Six Boards affiliated with the Department of State Affairs. There were a total of thirty-three appointees of board presidents under Wendi (appendix 1, table 6). Of these, sixteen, or 48.5 percent, were from Guanlong choronyms; and sixteen from Shandong choronyms. Here the evidence suggests that in naming board presidents, Wendi placed equal weight on the two dominant blocs, without consciously favoring the Guanlong bloc.

As for the lineage information of the board presidents, most of them had fathers who had been officials under Northern Wei or Western Wei-Northern Zhou, with the notable exception of Hulü Xiaoqing 斛律孝卿, whose father had served under the Northern Qi. Almost all appointees were of aristocratic lineage. Exceptions include Liu Ren'en 劉仁恩, Feng Shiji 馮世基, Kudi Qin 庫狄嶔, and Guo Jun 郭均, for whom no confirmable background data exists. Although there is no lineage information about Zhangsun Pi 長孫毗, he was likely a Zhangsun of Luoyang and was probably no doubt of noble descent. The only appointee of confirmed commoner status in this group was Li Yuantong 李圓通, who rose to power thanks to his direct access to Wendi as his family servant.

Yangdi did not depart significantly from the established practice of the first reign in terms of choronym preferences, judging by his chief ministerial appointments. If we exclude Yang Da 楊達, the only appointee from the previous reign who did not receive a new appointment, there were six Yangdi appointees, of whom, two or about 33 percent were of non-Guanlong origin. Apart from Xiao Cong 蕭琮 who was from the South, all appointees were direct descendants of Western Wei-Northern Zhou high-ranking officials (appendix 1, table 7).

What differentiate Yangdi's official appointments to chief-ministership from his father's are their conspicuous lacunae. When Yangdi came to power, he inherited Wendi's government and kept the two vice presidents of the Department of State Affairs—Yang Su and Su Wei. Before long, Yangdi promoted Yang Su to president of the department. Probably at this junction, Su Wei was called in to fill the position of vice president of the left of the same department. But no effort was made to fill the position of Su Wei's original position, the vice president of the right. After Yang Su's death in 606, the presidential position disappeared. With Su Wei's dismissal from office in 607, the vice presidency of the left vanished as well.

Of the three appointees to the presidency of the Chancellery, Yang Wensi 楊文思 died in office at the ripe age of seventy (sixty-nine) around 610.[40] After the other president, Yang Da, died in 612, Su Wei became the only president until his downfall in 616. As for the three appointees to the presidency of the Secretariat, two, Yang Yue 楊約 and Xiao Cong, were dismissed at the beginning of the Daye reign, and the last appointee, Yuan Shou 元壽, died in office in early 612. From then on no new appointments were made to fill these vacancies.

So, starting in 607, the most important executive positions in the government, those of vice president of the Department of State Affairs, were vacant. From 612 on, the leading positions in the Secretariat remained unfilled and Su Wei, as president of the Chancellery, remained the only officially appointed chief minister. After Su Wei's dismissal in 616, all official chief ministerial positions were vacant and Yangdi did not make a single appointment to fill them. Instead, he relied on de facto appointees as top leaders of the central government.

In making de facto appointments to chief ministerships, Yangdi did not seem to favor members of the Guanlong bloc at all. Of the total six appointees, only two—Su Wei and Yuwen Shu—may be classified as members of the Guanlong bloc. Yu Shiji was a quintessential Southerner. Pei Yun was from a Shandong choronym, but he was born and raised in the South and was a descendant of an émigré branch of a noble lineage that had moved to the South generations before. So he was in essence a Southerner as well. Although sharing the same choronym with Pei Yun, Pei Ju belonged to a different branch of the same lineage, and its bloc identity was with Shandong.[41] Xiao Yu 蕭瑀, whose appointment seems to be of an ad hoc nature, was a member of the royal Xiao family of the Later Liang, and the younger brother of Yangdi's wife (appendix 1, table 8). Naturally, Xiao should be considered a Southerner. Although Yangdi's appointees were a diversified group with no Guanlong dominance, they were at the same time all of aristocratic lineage. Apart from Xiao Yu who was of Later Liang royal descent, all of them were scions of high officials at the Western Wei-Northern Zhou, Northern Qi, or Chen court.

In the area of board presidents, Yangdi made a total of eighteen appointments. Of these, ten or 55.5 percent were to those from Guanlong choronyms; and seven or 39 percent were from Shandong choronyms. These appointments gave only slightly more weight to the Guanlong bloc than was the case under Wendi. The only major difference between the two reigns is the fact that while Wendi appointed no Southerner to a board president position, Yangdi appointed one (Fan Zigai 樊子蓋), which accounted for 5.5 percent of his total appointments (appendix 1, table 9). The case of Fan Zigai becomes statistically significant when viewed in conjunction with Yangdi's other high level appointments. Xiao Cong, for example, as a Southerner, was appointed by Yangdi to serve as chief minister. Furthermore, although, like his father, Yangdi selected most of his top generals from the Guanlong and Shandong blocs, he did appoint four commanders of Southern choronyms as generals-in-chief of the Sui army—Zhou Luohou 周羅睺 of Jiujiang 九江, Mai Tiezhang 麥鐵杖 of Shixing 始興, Yuan Ziwen 袁子溫 of Danyang 丹陽, and Lai Huer 來護兒 of Jiangdu.[42]

From our survey of Sui recruitments of top leaders, two prevailing themes emerge. The first is the continued dominance of the aristocracy. It persisted even as the abolition of the elitist Nine Ranks system opened the possibility for the career advancement of officials of relatively low social station and for a far more meritocratic government. With few exceptions, all the appointees to chief minister and board president positions were direct descendants of high-ranking officials of an earlier dynasty.

The second is the lopsided bias of choronym distribution among top leaders in favor of Guanlong, a phenomenon that serves as the basis for Chen Yinke's thesis of the primacy of the Guanlong bloc. This Guanlong emphasis, however, may have been the result of the fact that the Guanlong area, especially Guanzhong, was the home territory of the Sui, from where the Sui founder tended to recruit his close advisers. From Wendi to Yangdi, we detect no apparent pattern that consistently favored the Guanlong bloc. While it is true that official chief ministers under both Wendi and Yangdi were predominantly from Guanlong choronyms, that numerical advantage was greatly diminished among appointees to board presidents, and vanished among de facto chief ministers. The Shandong bloc, on the other hand, far from being the target of exclusion, was well represented in de facto appointments.[43]

The bloc that had been initially excluded was the South. There was not a single Southern appointee to a chief ministerial or board presidential position under Wendi. In part, this can be explained by the relatively late addition of the South to the empire, and by the failure of Wendi to pursue an inclusive policy towards the Southern literati in top-level appointments. But Yangdi, known for his strong pro-South sentiment, seems to have made a deliberate effort to promote Southerners to leading positions at court.

In summing up Yangdi's institutional reforms, the *Sui shu* says, "When Yangdi succeeded to the throne, he was bent on reviving the ancient. He set up new offices and divided existing posts, all according to old rules."[44] We see evidence of this in a more clearly defined Nine Courts system, and the revival of the Three Terraces. As a result of these reforms, Yangdi significantly shifted the balance of power between court and bureaucracy and between central and local administration, in favor of the former. He enhanced the power of the court by expanding the independent surveillance activity carried out by the Three Terraces. He consolidated the powers of the Six Boards under the Department of State Affairs and demoted the Nine Courts, setting a precedent that arguably constituted his most important, lasting political legacy to the Tang, whose central executive agencies were organized according to the same concept. His promotion of capital county officials and his direct control of the capital urban wards indicate the special importance he attached to the seats of the central government. By demoting the commandery level officials, Yangdi weakened the power base of local administration, which in the long run also contributed to a stronger central authority.

Although Yangdi introduced the bulk of his reform measures in 607, he instituted numerous additional changes. As the *Sui shu* puts it:

> The emperor, after the statutes of the third year [of Daye] (607), often unexpectedly introduced new posts, which were then subjected to further changes.[45]

Beneath his dominant themes of reform—archaism, rationalization, and centralization—we can detect a driving force for action, which manifests itself in his edict on building Luoyang:

. . . the *Book of Changes* says, "[Huangdi, Yao, and Shun were] conversant with change, so that their people never became tired," "change brought about conversance, and with conversance they achieved durability," and "those who possess virtue can endure, and those who possess merit can expand." Moreover, I have been told that [when a ruler is] satisfied with peace yet capable of change, the people were greatly transformed.[46]

A strong desire for change seems to have compelled Yangdi to keep introducing reforms to the central and local bureaucracies.

As a component of his overall reform of the officialdom, Yangdi initiated military reforms that went far beyond mere terminological changes as claimed by some modern scholars.[47] In compliance with his strategic shift to the East, he created a new defense system with Luoyang at the center, a major departure from his predecessor. While instituting measures to demote provincial civil offices, he significantly lowered the bureaucratic ranks of *fu*-garrison commanders and eliminated all area commands at a time when the Sui military was going through rapid expansion. Through reform, Yangdi not only readjusted the relationship between central and local commands, but also, and more significantly, endeavored to achieve the prime objective of strengthening the military authority of the central court.

In the area of recruitment, Yangdi hired a larger number of top officials from the Guanlong bloc than from the non-Guanlong blocs, a practice he inherited from his father. However, in one key area he deviated meaningfully from the previous reign. While both Wendi and Yangdi used the mechanism of making de facto appointments, it performed different functions. For Wendi, it was a supplement to the existing official chief minister institution, whereas for Yangdi, it served as the main avenue for appointing chief ministers. Consequently, Yangdi's inner circle was much more dependent on the throne than its predecessor, easing the way for the kind of highly autocratic rule that came to characterize his reign. Furthermore, by showing a greater willingness to appoint persons from the underrepresented South bloc, in the area of de facto chief minister appointments Yangdi completely undermined, probably unwittingly, the Guanlong dominance at the top echelon of the government.

# 7

## The Educational, Ritual, and Legal Institutions

As discussed in chapter 6, both Wendi and Yangdi were instrumental in continuously revamping the Sui bureaucratic system. Outside the realm of bureaucracy, they also made significant contributions to the transformation of other institutions. Scholars have long recognized the importance of Wendi in pushing institutional reforms,[1] but they have paid scant attention to the role of Yangdi. Although overshadowed by his father's great achievements, Yangdi vigorously pursued sweeping reforms, often in defiance of the precedents set by his father. In this chapter we examine those reforms in the context of the evolving dynamics of the Sui educational, ritual, and legal systems.

### EDUCATION

The Sui dynasty embodied a critical phase in the evolution of the premodern education system. Two epoch-making changes in education were introduced during the Sui: the abolition of the Nine Ranks system, and the creation of the civil service examination system.

The system of the Nine Ranks and Impartial Judges (*jiupin zhongzheng* 九品中正) had been introduced during the Cao-Wei dynasty to replace the corrupt recruitment practices of the Han dynasty. It placed aspirants to office in nine hierarchical ranks in accord with their talent and virtue. Commandery officials, known as impartial judges, were charged with assessing and ranking the aspirants; a higher recruitment rank would result in a higher official appointment. Initially, it purported to select the most qualified candidates for government office, but during the Six Dynasties period, it became highly elitist, with a narrow focus one's status at birth. Consequently, "there was no one of lowly birth in the upper rank, nor was there anyone of noble birth in the lower rank." The whole system of the Nine Ranks officially ended during the Kaihuang period under Wendi. This development was significant in removing the major obstacle to the emergence of a more merit-based examination system, a system that was evolving at about the same time.[2]

The earliest evidence of the existence of the new system is found in a 587 edict by Wendi: "Every year, various prefectures provide three *gongshi* 貢士 (nominees for office) each." The Sui *gongshi* system awarded degrees in different subjects. Among these, the *mingjing* 明經 (classicist) and *xiucai* 秀才 (cultivated talent) degrees are well documented. Both categories had existed in much earlier times. Under Wendi, there was also the *bingong* 賓貢 (guest nominee) degree, which, according to Gao Mingshi's study, was the progenitor of the *jinshi* 進士 (presented scholar). Gao further hypothesizes that the three *gongshi* recruited from each prefecture were in the three disciplines of *mingjing, xiucai,* and *bingong*.[3] In a sense, the introduction of the *gongshi* may be considered the forerunner to a full-fledged civil service examination system.

In spite of these new degrees, towards the end of his reign, Wendi grew increasingly disenchanted with the state sponsored Confucian education system of official schools in the capital and provinces. This is clearly evidenced in an edict issued in the sixth month of 601:

> Now in the national schools, the number of students has approached 1,000, and at the prefectural and county levels, the numbers of students are not small. But despite their enrollment, [they] spend their time doing nothing. [They] do not possess exemplary virtues nor talents which the state can use. There are good reasons for setting up schools. But [we have] quantity instead of quality. From today forward, [we] should focus on reduction, while making clear our rewards.

Following this edict, Wendi reduced the number of students at the national level to seventy, and abolished all provincial schools. On the same day, he issued another edict glorifying Buddhism and distributing the Buddhist relics among various prefectures. These restrictive measures against Confucianism earned Wendi the judgment that he "was not pleased with Confucian learning and only focused on criminal law."[4]

Yangdi's approach to the official school system was different. Upon coming to power, he shifted to a Confucian-style principle of kingly government. "In the old days, when philosopher-kings ruled all under Heaven, is it not true that the key lay in 'loving the people'?" asked Yangdi rhetorically. In an edict of 605, he paid due respect to teachers and scholars, and pledged his support of the education system. He gathered a large number of Confucian scholars in the Eastern Capital to discuss the success and failure of government. In a symbolic gesture to show his respect for the Confucian tradition, he even conferred the title of the "marquis of sage descent" (*shaosheng hou* 紹聖侯) upon Confucius's descendants. Yangdi's efforts to revitalize the national, prefectural, and county school systems succeeded; history records that these systems surpassed even the high level of achievement reached at the beginning of the previous reign.[5]

While Yangdi continued to give state support to the existing system, a major reform in education took place that introduced the *jinshi* and other degrees. By Early Tang times, the *jinshi* degree was taken for granted. An official record indicates that in 622, the various prefectures sent in four kinds of candidates for official appointment, namely, *mingjing, xiucai, junshi* 俊士 (talented scholar), and *jinshi*. All four of these categories had apparently been inherited from the previous reign of Daye under Yangdi, although by that time, the *bingong* category had already been defunct, probably replaced by the *jinshi* and *junshi*. Concerning the actual process of the replacement, no record survives. In terms of the differences between these categories, Gao Mingshi speculates that the *xiucai* and *mingjing* catered to students of aristocratic birth, while the *jinshi* and *junshi* were aimed at those of humbler family backgrounds. However, the paucity of historical data makes it impossible to substantiate this hypothesis. Judging by the content of the Tang curricula, it would seem that Sui *mingjing* students focused on the study of the Confucian classics while *jinshi* students concentrated more on the study of literary pieces. Initially, the *jinshi* degree probably ranked low among academic credentials, but because of the upper class's interest in literature the prestige of the *jinshi* soared during the Tang.[6]

The *mingjing, xiucai,* and *bingong* degrees under Wendi, and the *mingjing, xiucai, junshi,* and *jinshi* degrees under Yangdi would not have been of great significance had it not been for the fundamental change in the qualification process. A civil service examination system was introduced as early as the Kaihuang period, as is indicated by a *Bei shi* record on Du Zhengxuan 杜正玄. It throws some light on the process required of a nominee for the *xiucai* degree for his appointment in Sui times. First, he had to pass an oral exam on appropriate subjects (*ceshi* 策試) locally. Second, he would sit for a written exam at the appropriate central government agency, which required writing essays in imitation of well-known pieces.[7] Du Zhengxuan's experience underscores not only the literary focus of Sui appointment exams for the *xiucai*, but also the already highly competitive nature of the merit-based examination system in its infancy.[8]

The main suppliers of candidates for the civil service exams were official schools at the capital, prefectural, and county levels.[9] This Confucian-dominated school system received unequivocal support at the beginning of the Sui from Wendi.[10] A central government agency (known as *guozi si* 國子寺 [Court for Education] or *guozi xue* 國子學 [National University] under Wendi, and as *guozi jian* 國子監 [Directorate of Education] under Yangdi) was directly in charge of the three central institutions of education, namely, the National Academy (*guozi xue*, different from its namesake above), the Grand Academy (*taixue* 太學), and the Four Gates Academy (*simen xue* 四門學).

Both the National Academy and the Grand Academy had been key official schools of higher education since Western Jin times. The Four Gates Academy had been first set up under the Northern Wei in Luoyang, deriving its name from the four city gates of the dynastic capital. Initially, its curriculum focused on philological studies (*xiaoxue* 小學). It was during the early Kaihuang period under Wendi that it was promoted to a full-fledged academy. It is believed that students of the National Academy and the Grand Academy mainly studied for the *xiucai* and *mingjing* degrees, while those of the Four Gates Academy the *jinshi* and *junshi* degrees.[11]

## RITUAL

The ancient Chinese concept of *li* 禮 was much broader in meaning than its Western counterpart, ritual. Apart from the religious sense of ritual, *li* encompassed a noble code of conduct, which included propriety, decorum, protocol, and etiquette, and served as the moral foundation of Confucianism. *Li* not only includes officially sanctioned ceremonies but also ritual paraphernalia such as carriages and regalia because their treatment is often emblematic of one's ritual conception. Codified *li* practices were essentially ritualistic because they constituted a crucial, transcendental component of state institutions that can be described as a set of prescribed behavior that is symbolic, nonrational, and mostly recurrent.

Historically, great importance was attached to state ritual, not least because of its perceived power of providing divine sanction for the actions of the sovereign, and for legitimizing his rule. This was especially true for the founding sovereign of a dynasty like Wendi, who said: "In the absence of ritual nothing can be accomplished in terms of power and virtue, benevolence and justice; when it comes to pacifying the above and governing the people, nothing is as good as ritual."[12]

As a usurper, Wendi set himself a daunting ritual task. Apart from enacting existing ritual prescriptions, he again had to distinguish himself, this time ritually, from the Northern Zhou, the regime he had replaced. So he developed a new ritual system based primarily on the traditions of the Northern Wei, Northern Qi, Liang, and Chen.[13]

About Yangdi's concept and practice of ritual, not much information has survived, but there is enough evidence to suggest that Yangdi was not nearly as concerned about ritual as his father. While he attempted to introduce a number of ritual reforms, they were far less sweeping than his reforms in other areas.

## The Five Ritual Categories

In Sui times, state sacrifices were grouped into five categories: ceremonies for auspicious events (*ji* 吉), reception (*bin* 賓) ceremonies, military (*jun* 軍) ceremonies, congratulatory (*jia* 嘉) ceremonies, and ceremonies for misfortunes (*xiong* 凶). In official ritual literature, the *ji* rites are given by far the most prominent place. Subdivided into three classes, the first class of the *ji* rites were the major sacrifices (*dasi* 大祀). They included services to the Lord on High (*haotian shangdi* 昊天上帝), the Five Directional Emperors (*wufang shangdi* 五方上帝), the sun and the moon (*riyue* 日月), the August Earth God (*huangdiqi* 皇地祇), Divine Land (*shenzhou* 神州), She 社 and Ji 稷 (gods of soil and grains), and ancestral spirits at the Ancestral Temple (*zongmiao* 宗廟). The second class, the medium sacrifices (*zhongsi* 中祀), included services to the Five Dipper Stars and the Twelve Chronograms (*xingchen* 星辰), the Five Sacrifices (*wusi* 五祀; rites to the gods of the Five Phases), and the Four Prospects (*siwang* 四望; in reference to landmarks that represent the major directions, including the Five Marchmounts, Four Mountains, and Four Rivers). The third class, the minor sacrifices (*xiaosi* 小祀), included services to the Star of the Center (*sizhong* 司中), the Star of Destiny (*siming* 司命), Wind Master (*fengshi* 風師), Rain Master (*yushi* 雨師), Various Stars (*zhuxing* 諸星), and Various Mountains and Rivers (*zhushanchuan* 諸山川).[14]

Upon accession, Wendi requested Xin Yanzhi 辛彥之, libationer (president) of the Court for Education (*guozi jijiu* 國子祭酒), to create a Sui ritual code, which Wendi intended to be different from earlier ones. It focused on *ji* ritual ceremonies conducted in the capital's suburbs, especially those held in the south and north. In the south suburb there were two key ritual centers, the Round Mound (Yuanqiu 園丘) and the Southern Suburban Altar (*nanjiao* 南郊), located to the east and west of the north-south main street (south of the Taiyang Gate 太陽門), respectively. In the north suburb there were the Square Mound (Fangqiu 方丘) and the Northern Suburban Altar (*beijiao* 北郊).

The Round Mound was the place where biennial services were conducted, on the day of the winter solstice, for the highest ranking of all ritual divinities, the Lord on High, accompanied by numerous lesser deities, notably the

Five Directional Emperors. The Southern Suburban Altar was used for services to Gandi or Ganshengdi 感生帝 (Life-giving God) in early spring. The
Square Mound in the north was used for worshipping the August Earth God
on the day of the summer solstice, while the Northern Suburban Altar was for
worshipping Divine Land in early summer. It was stipulated that all these rites
should use Taizu (Yang Zhong, Wendi's father) as the chief ancillary god.

Yangdi simplified the ritual procedure for worshipping the Lord on High
in his 614 participation in the winter solstice event at the Round Mound. For
convenience, he skipped the purification rite called *zhai* 齋 (abstinence or
retreat), which was supposed to take place in the ceremonial tent (*ci* 次) at the
site.[15] Abstinence performed the crucial function of preparing the ritualist by
way of purification to cross the important threshold from the world of the
profane to enter the world of the sacred. Neglecting this preparatory stage
risked defeating the purpose of ritual and bordered dangerously on the
sacrilegious.

In 605, Yangdi introduced a key change to both the early spring sacrifice
to Ganshengdi (Life-giving God) at the Southern Suburban Altar, and the
early winter sacrifice to Divine Land at the Northern Suburban Altar: He
replaced Taizu (Yang Zhong, Wendi's father) with Wendi as the chief ancillary god.

Historically, a ritual structure, known as the Hall of Brilliance (*mingtang*
明堂), was set up in the southern suburb of the capital for the worship of the
Five Directional Emperors. But debates about its structure had never ceased
since the Han dynasty and they flared up again under the Sui. Because of the
ritual scholars' failure to reach consensus, it was not built at Wendi's capital.
Under Yangdi, attempts were made to revive the structure. But, sidetracked
by the Luoyang project, Yangdi stopped short of erecting it for lack of
commitment.[16]

## Ancestral Worship

From antiquity, the positioning of two key urban ritual structures—the Ancestral Temple (*zongmiao*) and the Altars of State (*sheji* 社稷), both sites for *ji*
ceremonies—in the main capital was of crucial symbolic significance. The
established practice in the Six Dynasties period was to place the Ancestral
Temple on the left (east) and the Altars of State on the right (west) of the
palace. The Northern Zhou, claiming to follow an ancient precedent, reversed
their positions. Wendi, in establishing the Sui Ancestral Temple, reverted to
the more established practice and replaced the five-chamber temple system
with a four-chamber system in accordance with a theory of the Eastern Han
scholar Zheng Xuan 鄭玄. The four chambers were respectively dedicated to:

(1) Gaozu 高祖 (great-great-grandfather) Yang Huigu 楊惠嘏; (2) Zengzu 曾祖 (great-grandfather) Yang Lie 楊烈; (3) Zu 祖 (grandfather) Yang Zhen 楊禎; and (4) Kao 考 (father) Yang Zhong. The last one, Yang Zhong, with Taizu 太祖 (grand progenitor) as his temple title, was also honored as the founding ancestor and would enjoy temple services in perpetuity.[17]

The Sui ancestral temple system went through a major reorganization under Yangdi, who adopted a seven-chamber system. It was believed that this system was a Western Zhou tradition. It had been advocated by the Cao-Wei scholar Wang Su 王肅, the archrival and harshest critic of Zheng Xuan. Following another Western Zhou ritual tradition, at Yangdi's urging, the ritual scholar Xu Shanxin 許善心 and his associates proposed a system in which the spiritual tables of the three founding ancestors, namely, Shizu 始祖 (the initial founding ancestor), Taizu and Gaozu (Wendi), in their individual basilicas, would enjoy continuous sacrificial services. The last two ancestors were allegedly known as *tiao* 祧 (dynastic ancestors) in Western Zhou times. This *tiao* convention, although of ancient genesis, had been recently practiced by the Northern Zhou dynasty and discarded by Wendi.[18]

After the founding of Luoyang, Yangdi became weary of the ritual obligation to make offerings to his father's spirit at the Ancestral Temple in Daxingcheng. He came up with an innovative idea whereby a cenotaph was set up in Guben 固本 Ward in Luoyang. Displaying Wendi's clothes and crowns to symbolize the presence of Wendi's spirit, it served as a kind of surrogate temple where ancestral ritual services were conducted according to temporal requirements. It is worth noting that the location of Guben Ward, west of the central axis, signifies a reversal of the established practice of his father and a revival of the Northern Zhou practice.

In 607, when presented with a request for setting up a formal Ancestral Temple in Luoyang, Yangdi hesitated, concerned as he was with his own place after death should a dual ancestral temple system be founded. He later approved the plan for a separate temple for Wendi, but it was never built.[19]

By siding with Wang Su against Zheng Xuan in his choice of a temple system, and by reviving the ancient *tiao* convention, Yangdi acted in defiance of his father's ritual legacy. Through repeatedly tinkering with the established practice of ancestral worship, he demonstrated a willingness to sacrifice ritual propriety for the sake of expediency.

## Mountain Rites

Codified ritual observances included ritual activities at sacred mountains, particularly the *feng shan* 封禅 rites (*ji* category) at Mount Tai (the Eastern Marchmount), traditionally regarded as the most sacred mountain ceremonies.

The imperial trip to Mount Tai was usually a major ritual event that was undertaken by the most ambitious sovereigns in celebration of their great earthly accomplishments. These, however, were nonrecurrent rites that rarely took place. Wendi in 595 visited Mount Tai to conduct a sacrifice to beg forgiveness for his errors, which were believed to have brought about droughts. In the Mount Tai rite, he followed the ritual procedure stipulated for the Southern Suburban rite (*nanjiao* 南郊). Although Yangdi as early as 594 had petitioned his father hard to pay a ritual visit to the scared mountain, he never did it himself. Instead, Yangdi participated in ritual ceremonies at two other sacred mountains, Mount Heng 恒山 (the Northern Marchmount near Laiyuan, Hebei) and Mount Hua 華山 (the Western Marchmount near Tongguan, Shaanxi). In the first instance, he basically followed the ritual precedent set by his father on his Mount Tai visit. In neither case did Yangdi make special preparations; in other words, his visits to the sacred mountains were side trips away from the main course of his journey.[20]

## Military Rites

There is precious little record of Yangdi's association with the other categories of state rites except *jun* or military rites. There were four basic military rites conducted on the occasion of the sovereign's departure from his palace on an expedition or a tour of inspection: the *lei* 類 (thematic) rite for Heaven (the Lord on High), the *yi* 宜 (expedient) or *yishe* 宜社 rite for the God of Soil, the *zao* 造 rite for one's ancestral spirit, and the *ma* 禡 (Horse God) rite. Yangdi's involvement in three of these—*lei*, *yi*, and *ma*—is well documented.[21]

In early 612, on his first military campaign against Koguryŏ, Yangdi sent his proxies to set up two substitute altars south of Jicheng 薊城 (in the southwest of Beijing) on the Sanggan 桑乾 River, one for the God of Soil (She) and the other for the God of Grains (Ji), to conduct the *yi* rite. Meanwhile, Yangdi participated in the *lei* rite south of the Linshuo Palace (in the Jicheng area). North of Jicheng, another altar was set up where a sacrifice was made to the ancestor of horses in what was apparently a *ma* rite. Prior to the departure of his generals, Yangdi gathered them at the Linshuo Palace and personally bestowed commands upon them. With pomp and circumstance, the Sui expedition forces began to advance, one army a day for a total of twenty-four days in a most elaborate ritual deployment of troops. Later that year, Yangdi conducted another *ma* rite together with the sacrificial ceremony in honor of Huangdi 黃帝 (Yellow Emperor; also known as Xuanyuan 軒轅).[22]

Also featured in the *jun* category were the *dashe* 大射 (grand archery) rite and its byproduct *shou* 狩 (royal hunt) rite, with a focus on the cultivation of the martial spirit. In 607 while visiting Yulin, Yangdi staged an elaborate winter royal hunt ceremony with the purpose of impressing the Tujue leader Qimin and other foreign chieftains.[23]

Yangdi's *jun* rites activities documented here, except for the grand archery and royal hunt rites, were all associated with his preparations for war against Koguryŏ. They attest to his strong belief in ritual potency and his proclivity for utilitarianism in ritual practice.


## The Imperial Carriage System

Immediately after coming to power in 581, Wendi, following a proposal by President of the Secretariat Li Delin, gave the go-ahead to destroy the imperial palanquins and carriages the Sui inherited from the Western Wei and Northern Zhou. There were two notable exceptions: the set of five carriages (*wulu* 五輅), introduced by Li Shao 李韶 in the Taihe 太和 period (477–499) of the Northern Wei and later adopted in the Tianbao 天保 period (550–559) by the Northern Qi; and the set of four horse drawn carriages for the empress, initially proposed by Mu Shao 穆紹 during the Xiping 熙平 period (516–518) of the Northern Wei. Chen Yinke regards this as proof of the Sui dynasty's systematic effort to avoid the Northern Zhou institutions in favor of those of the Northern Qi. The fact that Li Delin, who was charged with the Sui ritual reform, was an erstwhile minister of the Northern Qi familiar with its ritual practices lends support to Chen's argument.[24]

The imperial carriage system that took shape under Wendi was composed of five carriages for various occasions:

1.   the jade (*yu* 玉) carriage in black with its rear decorated with jade ornaments (for sacrificial ritual and imperial matrimony);
2.   the gold (*jin* 金) carriage in red with its rear decorated in gold (for imperial audiences, archery, and feasts);
3.   the elephant (*xiang* 象) carriage in yellow with its rear decorated with an elephant pattern (for travel);
4.   the leather carriage (*ge* 革) in white with leather straps (for imperial inspection tours or military operations);
5.   the wood carriage (*mu* 木) covered in lacquer (for hunting).

In 594, on Wendi's orders, the carriage system underwent some slight changes. Overall, the Sui carriage system was considered a cross between the Western Zhou and Han prototypes.

Once in power, Yangdi began to reform his father's carriage system. He added a set of companion carriages to the five carriages, and appointed a prestigious panel to discuss the issue. Sitting on the panel were powerful court officials Yang Su and Yu Shiji, established ritual scholars Niu Hong and Xu Shanxin, and leading technologists Yuwen Kai, He Chou 何稠, and Yan Pi

闍毗. They carried out lengthy academic discussions that bordered on the pedantic in an attempt to provide rationale for the structures, designs, and usage of the carriages.[25]

Apparently, these discussions sponsored by Yangdi were not very different from previous ones held under Wendi; they all concerned the renovation of the existing carriage system. But while Wendi's carriage system retained some Northern Wei and Northern Qi features,[26] Yangdi's panel ignored the Northern traditions completely. Instead, it referred directly to pre-Qin and Han sources.[27] For more recent precedents, it cited works of the Western Jin such as the third century *Wei zhi* 魏志 (History of the Cao-Wei) by Chen Shou,[28] or works of Southern Dynasties vintage.[29] Interestingly, it ignored the precedents of Wendi's reign as well. The subsequent five-carriage system Yangdi's ritual reformers created was somewhat different from that of Wendi. It provided more specific guidelines for the appropriate number of pennants, ornaments, and drivers. The function of its third carriage—the elephant carriage—was redefined as the vehicle used for the sacrificial rite to Houtu 后土 (the Royal Earth).[30]

It was the creation of the companion carriages (*fuche* 副車) by Yangdi that most strikingly distinguished his system from that of his father. According to the *Sui shu*, Wendi never used companion carriages. After his conquest of the Chen, he ordered the destruction of its companion carriages.[31]

Yangdi, on the other hand, matched each of his five main carriages with a secondary carriage of similar structure and color. However, the companion carriages ranked two classes lower, and had only twenty-four drivers as compared with twenty-eight for the imperial carriages. Apparently, Yangdi and the scholars working for him, by setting up a new companion carriage system, were willing to challenge Wendi's established practice. But the rationale for reviving the companion carriage system lay in historical precedents—the Qin, Han, Liang, and Chen all had their companion carriage systems—and in the fact that it might offer the emperor added security. The First Emperor of Qin was said to have escaped an assassination thanks to his companion carriage.[32]

## Regalia

Upon usurping power from the Northern Zhou, Wendi requested a thorough overhaul of the Northern Zhou royal regalia system, a system Pei Zheng 裴政, vice president of the Court of Imperial Sacrifices (*taichang shaoqing* 太常少卿) criticized for adopting barbarian elements and violating accepted standards. A Sui system was thus created based on the Cao-Wei, Western Jin and Northern Qi prototypes.[33] However, this system was egregiously inadequate. To be sure, on the grand occasion of the New Year audience the emperor would wear the celestial regalia (*tongtian fu* 通天服); and for ritual events such as suburban rites and ancestral temple visits, the emperor would wear the dragon regalia (*gunyi* 衮衣). But other types of traditional regalia were missing, in part due to a lack of information in the North and Wendi's indifference. After the conquest of the Chen, its regalia were taken over by the Sui. However, Wendi, perhaps in the spirit of frugality and simplicity, did not use them. At that time, the standard costume for the court official was a kind of yellow robe, which was no different from a commoner's attire. The emperor, out of convenience, wore the same outfit as well while holding court. The only indication of imperial status were the Thirteen Rings.

Not content with his father's simple system, Yangdi reformed it in accordance with ancient customs. It was believed that the Western Zhou system provided six types of regalia for the Son of Heaven on different occasions: black fur (*daqiu* 大裘), dragon design (*gun* 衮), pheasant design (*bi* 鷩), tiger design (*cui* 毳), rice-grain design (*xi* 希, or *chi* 絺), and plain design (*xuan* 玄 or *yuan* 元). Of these, only the black fur regalia were exclusively royal, and their reintroduction by Yangdi marked a major departure from his father's dress code. They were reserved for a select number of rites for the Lord on High (at the Round Mound) and Ganshengdi, among others.[34]

In addition, based on Yu Shiji's suggestions, changes were introduced in the dragon regalia design. Yu criticized Wendi's dragon regalia for continuing a Northern Zhou convention, whereby the three quintessential symbols of imperial power—the sun, the moon, and the stars—were missing. The practice, according to Yu, was attributable to the Northern Zhou assumption of modesty and violated the legitimate regalia standards. Thus, a new set of dragon regalia with appropriate patterns were created for Yangdi for a variety of occasions, including ancestral worship, She and Ji services, and sacred fields rites, as well as ceremonies associated with capping, imperial matrimony, and winter solstice audiences and investiture.[35]

For the dress code of court officials in his retinue, Yangdi, out of practical concern, introduced a major ritual innovation. Originally, attending officials on an imperial tour were required by ritual to wear the cumbersome outfit known as *kuzhe* 袴褶 (a kind of baggy trousers with a loose fitting cloak). Yangdi in 610 ordered that the *kuzhe* be replaced with a kind of battle outfit known as *rongyi* 戎衣 (battle fatigues), which, although ritually less appropriate, offered much more convenience.[36]

Next to the carriage system and regalia, the most talked about ritual paraphernalia in Yangdi's time were various kinds of ritual headgear. Yangdi played a major role in reforming their appearance. As emperor, he was required to wear the imperial headgear with its top board, tassels, and ornaments. He then rediscovered a much lighter headpiece with a simpler design, *wubian* 武弁 (warrior's cap), traditionally worn by army officers. It derived from a type of ancient cap known as *bian* worn by court officials. The *wubian* became Yangdi's favorite cap for the road. He wore it on hunting trips, military expeditions, and at related ceremonies. He also made it available to ministers and other government officials, both military and civil. On his own *bian* cap, imperial authority was distinguished by a gold *boshan* 博山 (mountain symbol).

Another kind of cap favored by the Sui sovereigns for less formal occasions was *mao* 帽 in black or white gauze. The white gauze (*baisha* 白紗) cap with its matching outfit was worn by Liu-Song and Southern Qi sovereigns on occasions of informal banquets. The black gauze (*wusha* 烏紗) cap was worn by people of various descriptions, ranging from court officials to commoners. Sui Wendi had chosen the black gauze cap for himself and court officials. Yangdi, however, switched to the white gauze cap, after the fashion of the Southern sovereigns, on occasions of entertaining imperial guests.[37]

A special kind of cap, known as *jinxian guan* 進賢冠 (the cap that presents the worthy), was worn by civil officials at court. It originally was matched to a complicated outfit with ostentatious ornaments—*pannang* 鞶囊 (ribbons with openwork designs in gold, silver, or other colors), *pei* 佩 (jade ornament sets) and *shou* 綬 (decorative brocade with hanging ribbons).[38] In Wendi's time, all these ornaments were abandoned probably for the sake of simplicity.[39] But in his memorial about the cap, He Chou, one of Yangdi's court officials, made references to *shou* brocades, *pannang* ribbons, and *pei* jades. Obviously, under Yangdi, these ornaments were once again in fashion.[40] Thus in revamping the old convention of the *jinxian guan*, complex ornamentation was favored over simplicity of design.

During Wendi's reign, the official headgear for the court censors (*yushi* 御史) was the standard justice cap (*quefei guan* 卻非冠, or the cap that rejects the wrong), which was also the cap of the gatekeeper. Yangdi replaced it with another ancient cap, the *xiezhi* 獬豸,[41] with a complicated design. Depending on his rank, a censor would wear a *xiezhi* cap in gold or made of rhino or antelope horn.[42]

Under Yangdi, a debate took place concerning the proper headgear for the crown prince on the occasion of the winter solstice audience. A convention that went as far back as the Jin period required that the crown prince wear the excursion cap (*yuanyou guan* 遠遊冠) and its matching outfit. It was the Liu-Song dynasty that replaced it with the dragon design regalia (*gunmian* 袞冕). The Liang Emperor Jianwendi reverted to the earlier excursion cap convention, which continued till the end of the Chen dynasty. Meanwhile, the Northern Dynasties had favored the dragon design regalia. When Wendi became emperor, he followed the Southern Dynasties convention whereby the excursion cap was the headwear for the crown prince. During Yangdi's reign, a suggestion was made to readopt the dragon design regalia, which Yangdi did not accept, thus preserving his father's convention. Yangdi made this decision not necessarily out of filial piety, but rather out of a fear that the crown prince might pose a symbolic challenge to the supreme authority of the emperor.[43] Furthermore, Wendi's *yuanyou guan* convention had been influenced by the Southern culture of the Liang and Chen, to which Yangdi was known to be partial.

Yangdi's reforms in regalia, although by no means drastic, did testify to his penchant for the ostentatious. In one of the grandest displays of Sui ritual paraphernalia on record, Yangdi showed off his magnificent regalia to officials and foreign dignitaries on the Chinese New Year's day in 607. Impressed by the display, Qimin qaghan of Eastern Tujue and his envoys asked for a replica, which Yangdi declined. Obviously pleased with the powerful effect of the new ritual items, he said:

> In the old days, [Liu Bang] did not really know the nobility of the Son of Heaven until the completion of the Han [ritual] system. Today the regalia are so abundantly prepared that they cause the *chanyu* 單于 (Xiongnu chieftain) to untie his plaits.

Thereupon he amply rewarded court officials responsible for the ritual reform—Niu Hong, Yuwen Kai, Yu Shiji, He Chou, and Yan Pi.[44]

## LAW

Both Wendi and Yangdi introduced major, substantive changes to the medieval legal system that impacted both theory and practice. Yangdi in particular showed a much greater interest in law than in state ritual, of which he was neither a significant reformer nor an enthusiastic practitioner. To understand Yangdi's contributions, it is necessary to place them within the changing framework of the Sui legal system.[45]

### Wendi

Upon founding the Sui in 581, Wendi appointed a group of leading bureaucrats, and legal and ritual scholars to reform the legal system. The new corpus of laws had two essential components: the legal code (*lü* 律) and the statutes (*ling* 令). In addition, there were two minor components: the regulations (*ge* 格) and the ordinances (*shi* 式), of which we know very little. Not much information survives on the Sui statutes except for the thirty section names of the Kaihuang statutes promulgated under Wendi, covering official ranks, palace security, costume, ritual, land tenure, corvée, prison, and funeral, among others.[46]

By comparison, we have far more data on the legal code, which is basically a penal code. Wendi's code stipulated five categories of punishments for offenders:

1. two types of death: strangulation and decapitation (*jiao* 絞 and *zhan* 斬);
2. three types of exile (*liu* 流): 1,000, 1,500, and 2,000 *li*;
3. five types of penal servitude (*tu* 徒): one, one and a half, two, two and a half, and three years;
4. five types of heavy stick punishment (*zhang* 杖): from fifty[47] to one hundred strokes; and
5. five types of light stick punishment (*chi* 笞): from ten to fifty strokes.[48]

Recipients of punishments were sometimes pardoned by imperial amnesties. However, following a Northern Qi model, ten most heinous crimes, grouped together as the Ten Abominations (*shi'e* 十惡), were considered unpardonable:

1. plotting rebellion (*moufan* 謀反);
2. plotting great sedition (*mou dani* 謀大逆);
3. plotting treason (*moupan* 謀叛);
4. contumacy (*e'ni* 惡逆);
5. depravity (*budao* 不道);
6. great irreverence (*da bujing* 大不敬);
7. lack of filial piety (*buxiao* 不孝);
8. discord (*bumu* 不睦);
9. unrighteousness (*buyi* 不義); and
10. incest (*neiluan* 內亂).[49]

Some of the more barbaric practices—display of the decapitated head of the criminal (*xiaoshou* 梟首), quartering (*huanlie* 轘裂), and flagellation (*bian* 鞭)—were abolished. Some conventional punishments were reduced. To avoid government cruelty and abuse of power, Wendi set up a grievance system from the grassroots level all the way up to the court where the complainant was permitted to beat the remonstrator's drum (*dengwen gu* 登聞鼓) outside the south entrance of the palace in Daxingcheng to voice his grievances.[50]

Despite these efforts at reduction of severe punishment, the early Sui laws remained excessively harsh. With proper legal procedure and leniency in mind, Wendi ordered Su Wei, Niu Hong, and others in 583 to create a new body of laws. The resultant *Kaihuang Code* 開皇律 is a milestone in Chinese legal history, and served as the basis for the classic legal work, the *Tang Code* 唐律, compiled in the Early Tang period. As was the case with other state institutions, Wendi intended to set up a new system that differentiated the Sui from the Northern Zhou. Wendi and his advisers were able to draw on a centuries-old, rich legal tradition. Although codification of law can be traced as far back as the Warring States period, the legal system the *Kaihuang Code* was most indebted to was that of the Northern Qi, the Northern Zhou's rival in the east.[51]

The *Kaihuang Code* eliminated eighty-one capital offenses, one hundred fifty-four offenses punishable by exile, and more than one thousand offenses punishable by penal servitude or flogging. The new code contained a total of five hundred articles, grouped into twelve sections:

1. general principles (*mingli* 名例);
2. imperial guard and prohibitions (*weijin* 衛禁);
3. administrative regulations (*zhizhi* 職制);
4. the household and marriage (*huhun* 戶婚);
5. the public stables and warehouses (*jiuku* 廄庫);
6. unauthorized levies (*shanxing* 擅興);
7. violence and robbery (*zeidao* 賊盜);
8. assaults and accusations (*dousong* 鬥訟);
9. fraud and counterfeit (*zhawei* 詐偽);
10. miscellaneous articles (*zalü* 雜律);
11. arrest and flight (*buwang* 捕亡); and
12. judgment and prison (*duanyu* 斷獄).[52]

Although the *Kaihuang Code* won much praise for offering simplicity, clarity, and leniency without being negligent,[53] Wendi preferred to take matters into his own hands. He himself often flogged people within the palace grounds. Once, angry with an flogger for failure to apply sufficient force, Wendi had him beheaded. The stick Wendi used was thick as a finger, and people who were flogged often died.[54] The discovery of the loss of a significant amount of millet in the Hechuan 合川 Granary (west of Têwo, Gansu) prompted Wendi to impose capital punishment on anyone caught stealing more than one *sheng* 升 (594.4 ml) of grain reserves in a frontier area. The offender's family were then enslaved at court. It is obvious that Wendi did not wish to see corrupt officials prosecuted in accordance with the law for fear they should receive light punishment. Law enforcement officers tended to regard this as a license to execute offenders regardless of legal procedure. Faced with growing crime, Wendi imposed public execution in the market on those who stole more than one copper coin. Later, he extended the putative single coin law to the officialdom. Those in office who heard of or witnessed a case of misappropriation involving more than one coin but failed to report it were given varying degrees of punishment, up to death. Similarly, four men caught stealing a rafter or a beam,[55] and three men caught pilfering a melon were all summarily executed. Only public outcry against the Single Coin Death Law prompted Wendi to repeal it.[56]

Underlying the unduly severe punishments Wendi meted out to petty offenders and officials accused of wrongdoing was a resolve to intimidate his subjects into submission by extreme measures. In the process, he overrode the new legal system he had painstakingly helped set up.

## Yangdi

Keenly aware of the oppressive nature of Wendi's rule, Yangdi set out to rewrite the legal code as soon as he ascended the throne, vowing to "rule humbly, aspire to the code of old, deal with matters from his heart, and on each and every occasion favor benevolence in government."[57]

The *Daye Code* 大業律 by Yangdi was promulgated in the fourth month of 607.[58] Extant sources record only Niu Hong and Liu Xuan 劉炫 as its compilers. But it is almost certain that other scholars of lower rank also contributed to it. At any rate, it is very likely that in the absence of key players like Yang Su and Gao Jiong, Yangdi had a free hand to reshape the Sui legal system, which at least in part accounts for the major differences with the *Kaihuang Code*.[59] The five hundred articles of the *Daye Code* were grouped in eighteen, instead of twelve, sections:

1. general principles;
2. imperial guard and the palace (*weigong* 衛宮);
3. violations of standards (*weizhi* 違制);
4. bribery (*qingqiu* 請求);[60]
5. the household (*hu* 戶);
6. marriage (*hun* 婚);
7. unauthorized levies;
8. accusation and impeachment (*gaohe* 告劾);
9. violence (*zei* 賊);
10. robbery (*dao* 盜);
11. assaults (*dou* 鬥);
12. arrest and flight;
13. warehouses (*cangku* 倉庫);
14. stables and grazing (*jiumu* 廄牧);
15. passes and markets (*guanshi* 關市);
16. miscellanies;
17. fraud and counterfeit; and
18. judgment and prison.[61]

Of these eighteen sections, four—(3) violations of standards, (4) bribery, (8) accusation and impeachment, and (15) passes and markets—were new additions. The remaining sections were either identical with their counterparts in the *Kaihuang Code* or were spinoffs from its relevant sections. Judging from the titles of these section names, the *Daye Code* was very likely based on the *Northern Wei Code*, an obvious departure from the *Kaihuang Code*, which was clearly indebted to the more recent Northern Qi tradition.[62]

Another major departure from the *Kaihuang Code* is in the area of the Ten Abominations. According to the *Sui shu*, they disappeared in the *Daye Code*; but according to the *Tanglü shuyi* (*Tang Code*), eight of the original ten abominations survived in the *Daye Code*. It is possible that the remaining eight abominations were scattered in different parts, following a Northern Zhou convention.[63] The *Yōrō ritsu* 養老律 (*Yōrō Code*; early eighth century) in Japan contains a section called Eight Abuses (*hachigyaku* 八虐), apparently based on the Eight Abominations.[64] From the Eight Abuses, two items of the original Ten Abominations—discord (*bumu*) and incest (*neiluan*)—are missing.[65] Some scholars speculate, not without reason, that these were the two items Yangdi struck out. According to the *Tang Code*, the word, "discord" means "to plot to kill or also to sell relatives who are of the fifth or closer degree of mourning." Acts of patricide and fratricide like those committed by Yangdi were crimes against one's close relatives, not unlike those of discord. But they more closely matched the crimes of contumacy (*e'ni*), another abomination in the *Kaihuang Code*, which covers such acts as "beating or plotting to kill one's paternal grandparents or parents," and the killing of "one's paternal uncles or their wives, or one's elder brothers or sisters," and so on.[66] Yangdi was probably not pleased with the continued existence of the terms discord and contumacy in the legal code. The rationale for removing discord while retaining contumacy is not quite clear, probably because contumacy was grounded in some of the most fundamental Confucian tenets—filial piety and ancestral worship—which Yangdi still accepted.

As for the removal of incest from the code, if that happened at all, there is hardly any satisfactory explanation other than its evocation of Yangdi's own incestuous behavior involving two of his father's concubines. The word "incest" is defined in the *Tang Code* as "having illicit sexual intercourse with relatives who are of the fourth degree of mourning or closer." The subcommentary of the same source further stipulates that incestuous relations include sexual relations with the concubine of one's father.[67] Yangdi, as an offender guilty of incest, surely had no reason to like its association with the Ten Abominations.

Whatever Yangdi's motivation, these changes were in line with the overriding theme of the new code: lightening punishments. Penalties for more than two hundred crimes, which fell within the range of the Five Punishments, were lessened. The use of cangueing, flogging, execution, interrogation, and imprisonment was reduced. His subjects welcomed these changes, having long grown sick of Wendi's harsh rule. But before very long, the social order the new code was intended to maintain was in serious trouble. The *Sui shu* identifies two main causes—external and internal. Externally, Yangdi conducted expeditions against neighboring countries; internally, Yangdi indulged in excessive extravagances. In consequence, the burden of taxes and levies became heavier with each passing year. In their effort to fulfill their quotas, government officials drove the poor to desperation, who gathered together to form bands of robbers and thieves. In reaction, Yangdi imposed increasingly severe punishments. Anyone caught stealing, robbing, or committing a more serious offense was executed without due process. As the number of rebels grew, Yangdi implemented even harsher measures, not only against the rebels themselves but also their families. In the case of the Yang Xuangan rebellion of 613, Yangdi criminalized even distant relatives of the accused, who were within the ninth degree of mourning. In extreme instances, some of the defunct, ancient cruel punishments—display of the decapitated head of the criminal, and quartering, among others—were revived to terrorize the rebels. To the very end of Yangdi's reign, the situation never improved.[68]

To varying degrees, Yang's reforms impacted Sui society and posterity in the areas of education, ritual, and law. In education, Yangdi's reign was characterized by the revival of Confucian learning and the restoration of a school system damaged by his father, and, more importantly, the introduction of the *jinshi* category to the examination system, which was the equivalent of a doctorate in Tang times. Continuation of Sui academic degrees and their qualification exams under the Tang set the stage for the maturation of a meritocratic civil service examination system that dominated Chinese education until the end of the Qing dynasty.

Yangdi's tangible ritual reforms focused more on form than substance, with much of the attention devoted to elaborate and expensive presentation of ritual paraphernalia—the imperial carriage system and regalia. Occasionally, they dealt with the issue of practicality, as, for example, in the case of certain headgear. But overall, Yangdi did not make much of an effort to substantively transform the existing ritual system and essentially left his father's ritual legacy in key state sacrifices untouched, with the notable exception of the rite of the Ancestral Temple.

Moreover, his participation in ritual activities often displayed a disregard for both conventional spatiotemporal requirements of ritual practice and strict adherence to ritual procedure. Surviving evidence on his ritual practice—his casual reversals of attitude concerning ancestral services devoted to his father, his perfunctory handling of ritual at Mount Heng and Mount Hua, his omission of the purification rite, and his decision to conduct ancestral rites at his father's surrogate temple in Luoyang for his own convenience—often points to his lack of serious interest in state ritual. Instead, his energies were consumed by his relentless reform of the bureaucratic structure, his endless projects to build palace complexes and public works on a grand scale, his ambitious plans to establish hegemony in East Asia, and his quest for immortality.

Yangdi's legal reform was exemplified by his *Daye Code*, which, driven by his idea of a benevolent government, was a major improvement over the *Kaihuang Code* in terms of rationalizing the legal system. However, he came to ignore this more lenient body of law. In his attempt to arrest the disintegration of established order, he imposed harsher and harsher penalties on his subjects. After his fall, the Tang deliberately avoided the *Daye Code* in setting up its own legal system and went directly to the *Kaihuang Code* for inspiration and precedent. Although the *Daye Code* may have been more lenient, impartial, and rational than its predecessor, the reckless behavior of Yangdi and his subsequent loss of the dynasty seriously damaged the reputation of the code itself. While the *Kaihuang Code* has essentially survived through its reincarnation in the *Tang Code*, the *Daye Code* faded into oblivion.[69]

# 8

---

# Religions

In Sui times, Buddhism, Daoism, and Confucianism, collectively known as the Three Teachings (*sanjiao* 三教), were regarded as three competitive yet complementary systems of thought. The Sui scholar Li Shiqian 李士謙 expressed the prevailing sentiment about them when he declared, "Buddhism is the sun, Daoism the moon, and Confucianism the five planets."[1] By comparing the Three Teachings to the seven celestial bodies, known as the Seven Luminaries (*qiyao* 七曜) in astrology,[2] Li ranked Buddhism the highest, followed by Daoism and Confucianism. As the last of the Three Teachings, Confucianism played an important religious role in society, particularly in ancestral worship, Heaven worship, and a host of ritual sacrifices. However, having neither priesthood nor church organization, Confucianism by Sui times had been essentially an ethnical tradition.[3] Furthermore, policy decisions of the Sui court regarding Confucianism were primarily concerned with its secular aspects.[4] So despite its involvement in contention for supremacy as a thought system against Buddhism and Daoism, Confucianism was by no means a major religious force under the Sui.

The focus of this chapter is on the first two of the Three Teachings, Buddhism and Daoism. As institutional religions with distinct theologies, ordination practices, clergies, and church organizations, both Buddhism and Daoism underwent a crucial period of transition during the Sui dynasty.

## DAOISM

Throughout his reign, Wendi, judging from the sporadic surviving records, had remained a strong patron of Daoism and consistently regarded it with respect despite the contempt he showed for certain Daoist adepts. The immediate revival of the religion after it had just survived a persecution under the Northern Zhou would not have been possible without royal support.

In his early days as sovereign, Wendi rewarded three Daoist adepts, Zhang Bin 張賓, Jiao Zishun 焦子順, and Dong Zihua 董子華, who had predicted Wendi's rise to royal power. He even invited the famed Daoist medical doctor Sun Simiao 孫思邈 to serve as erudite of the National Academy (*guozi boshi* 國子博士), an offer Sun declined. It is no coincidence that his first reign title, Kaihuang, was from the reign title of Tianzun 天尊, the supreme deity of Daoism.[5]

When Wendi's initial effort to suppress the rebellion by the Northern Zhou loyalist Wang Qian 王謙 in Shu 蜀 (Sichuan)[6] was stymied, with many of his troops allegedly killed or sickened by a miasma, he came to Daoism for help, and set up a Yellow Register Tract of the Way (*huanglu daochang* 黃籙道場) inside his palace. The Yellow Register was a key Daoist rite of salvation that took place at an altar set up for the occasion.[7] After praying to Heaven for three days and nights for protection, Wendi met a divine person in his dream, who took forbidden water from the altar, and spurt it towards the southwest, while saying, "As soon as rain falls they shall heal. There is no need for His Majesty to worry. If an attack is launched on the day of $zi$ 子, Shu shall be conquered." The prophesy was soon fulfilled: Wang Qian and his followers were indeed crushed on a day of $zi$.[8] This record clearly testifies to Wendi's belief in Daoism, even though the de facto state religion was Buddhism. In a 600 edict, he declared, "The law of the Buddha is profound and miraculous, and the teachings of the Dao are empty and harmonious. Both bring great blessings to creatures of all kinds. All those with feelings receive protection from them."[9] For Wendi, Daoism was not a rival to Buddhism, but a complementary faith.

The high esteem Wendi held for Daoism is reflected both by the stiff penalty he imposed for acts of vandalism against Daoist icons and by his patronage of Daoist structures. Under him, theft or destruction of Tianzun statues by lay people was a crime of depravity; destruction of Tianzun statues by clerics was a crime of contumacy. Both are among the unpardonable Ten Abominations. Meanwhile, he also extensively sponsored the building of Daoist abbeys. According to the Late Tang Daoist adept Du Guangting 杜光庭 (850–933), Wendi built thirty-six Daoist abbeys (*guan* 觀), known then as mysterious altars (*xuantan* 玄壇), in the metropolitan area of Daxingcheng.[10]

A major beneficiary of Wendi's pro-Daoist policy was the Louguan 樓觀 (Lou Abbey) school, with its main abbey about 60 kilometers southwest of Xi'an in the Zhongnan Mountains 終南山. It was characterized by the worship of the Eastern Zhou official Yin Xi 尹喜 as its first patriarch. Legend has it that, upon receiving the *Daode jing* 道德經 from Laozi 老子, Yin Xi set up a multistoried structure (*louguan*) to watch stars and auras; this marked the beginning of the school. Hundreds of years later, Yin Gui 尹軌, a transcendent who was allegedly Yin Xi's cousin, descended on Louguan to pass on Daoist commandments and scriptures to the Daoist adept Liang Chen 梁諶 (late third and early fourth centuries). Revered as a major patriarch of the school, Liang was probably its true founder. The Louguan school rose steadily in importance over the next two to three hundred years.[11]

During the Northern Dynasties, the most influential Louguan master, Wang Yan 王延 of Fufeng (b. 520), took up residence at the Lou Abbey at the age of eighteen (seventeen) in 537 in Western Wei times. In the wake of the 574 proscription campaign against both Buddhism and Daoism, Wudi 武帝 of the Northern Zhou ordered the Tongdao Abbey 通道觀 built in Chang'an. Although it gathered learned clerics of both Buddhism and Daoism, Tongdao unmistakably focused on Daoism and functioned much like the state monastery of Daoism, with a clergy dominated by Louguan Daoists.[12] Wang Yan was appointed the chief editor of the Daoist scriptures of the Three Caverns housed at the abbey, where he wrote the *Sandong zhunang* 三洞珠囊 (Pouch of pearls of the Three Caverns) in seven *juan*, which records more than eight thousand *juan* of Daoist scriptures and scriptural commentaries. The completion of this work signified the revival of Daoism under the Northern Zhou. A new era termed Daxiang 大象 was declared to mark the occasion (table 8.1).

Upon founding the Sui dynasty, Wendi built a new capital Daxingcheng southeast of old Chang'an in 583, where he set up two religious institutions, the Daxingshan Monastery 大興善寺 and the Xuandu Abbey 玄都觀, as the national religious centers for Buddhism and Daoism, respectively. In the case of Xuandu Abbey, Wendi transferred its paraphernalia and clergy from Tongdao, the celebrated Louguan master Wang Yan among them. Appointed by Wendi, Wang served as abbot of Xuandu. In 586, Wendi sent a jeweled carriage to bring Wang Yan into the Daxing Basilica 大興殿, the central structure of the Palace City, where he presided over the ritual to pass on the *Grand Commandments of Wisdom* (*Zhihui dajie* 智慧大戒) to Wendi, who had gone to all the trouble of purification and abstinence to prepare himself for the sacred occasion. What Wendi experienced here was actually an ordination ceremony, not unlike the *pusa jie* rite Yangdi was to receive a number of years later from the Buddhist monk Zhiyi. In so doing, Wendi virtually elevated Wang Yan to the highest religious position in the country. At that moment, vermilion phoenixes were observed descending on the altar and the basilica. Leading officials like Su Wei and Yang Su all faced north to perform the disciple's ritual. Wendi thereupon ordered Wang Yan to set up rules on Daoist ritual ceremonies and to set standards for future practice.

TABLE 8.1 Louguan patriarchs, to Early Tang

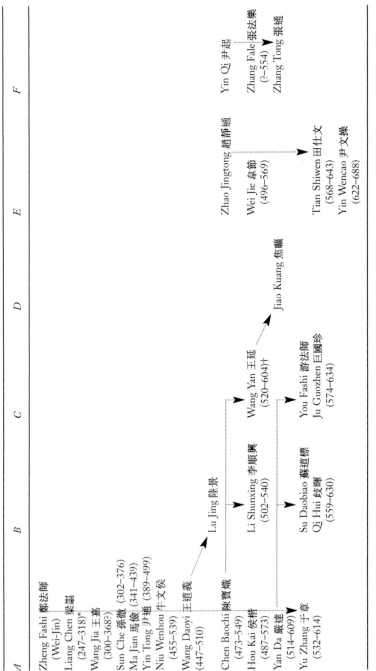

| A | B | C | D | E | F |
|---|---|---|---|---|---|
| Zheng Fashi 鄭法師 (Wei-Jin) | | | | | |
| Liang Chen 梁諶 (247–318)* | | | | | |
| Wang Jia 王嘉 (300–368?) | | | | | |
| Sun Che 孫徹 (302–376) | | | | | |
| Ma Jian 馬儉 (341–439) | | | | | |
| Yin Tong 尹通 (389–499) | | | | | |
| Niu Wenhou 牛文侯 (455–539) | | | | | |
| Wang Daoyi 王道義 (447–510) | | | | | |
| Chen Baochi 陳寶熾 (473–549) | Lu Jing 陸景 | | | | |
| Hou Kai 侯楷 (487–573) | Li Shunxing 李順興 (502–540) | Wang Yan 王延 (520–604)† | Jiao Kuang 焦曠 | Zhao Jingtong 趙靜通 | Yin Qi 尹起 |
| | | | | Wei Jie 韋節 (496–569) | Zhang Fale 張法樂 (?–554) |
| | | | | | Zhang Tong 張通 |
| Yan Da 嚴達 (514–609) | Su Daobiao 蘇道標 Qi Hui 歧暉 (559–630) | You Fashi 游法師 Ju Guozhen 巨國珍 (574–634) | | Tian Shiwen 田仕文 (568–643) | |
| Yu Zhang 于章 (532–614) | | | | Yin Wencao 尹文操 (622–688) | |

Sources:  Ren Jiyu 1990, 230; Sunayama 1990, 181.
*Ren reads Liang Kan 堪 for Liang Chen 諶.
†Based on YJQQ 85.602–603. Ren reads 519 for 520.

Meanwhile, the Lou Abbey itself continued to thrive after Wang Yan's departure. In early Sui times, the Daoist adept Yan Da 嚴達 renovated the abbey's imposing structures. At one point, it hosted as many as one hundred and twenty ordained clerics. Throughout the first reign, the Louguan school enjoyed sustained popularity with both the royal and nonroyal.[13]

Like his father, Yangdi never wavered in his patronage of the Daoist religion. He built twenty-four Daoist abbeys in and around the Eastern Capital Luoyang and ordained one hundred and ten Daoist adepts. Two of Yangdi's Daoist abbeys—Yuqing 玉清 and Tongzhen 通真—were located within the palace grounds. Together with their Buddhist counterparts Huiri and Fayun, they constituted his Four Places of Enlightenment (*si daochang* 四道場).[14] Yangdi also differed from his father in his approach to the religion. While Yangdi endeavored to have Daoist scriptures collected and cataloged in Luoyang, Wendi showed little interest in them.[15] And unlike his father, Yangdi never disparaged the Daoist clergy on record.

Yangdi's support of the Daoist tradition had been consistent since his days in Jiangdu, as is witnessed by his letter to the eminent Daoist recluse of the South, Xu Ze 徐則, who then was living in a hermitage in the Tiantai 天台 Mountains in east Zhejiang:

Alas, the Dao achieves various miracles and the [Daoist] law embodies nature. [The Dao] embraces the Two Forces, and creates by amalgamating all things. If man can aggrandize the Dao, the Dao will not exist in vain. Sir, you follow virtue and cultivate emptiness, base your work on the concept of mysteries and equate things. You show a profound appreciation for their meanings and a clear understanding of the path to the [Daoist] law. Agreeable by nature but mysterious, and delightful in spirit but empty, [you] live on pine water, take thistles as medicine, and perch on smoke and colored clouds. Relying on wind and cloud, [you arrive] to view Mount Chicheng 赤城 (in Tiantai), and riding on dragons and phoenixes, [you] travel through the jade hall (where the transcendents reside). Although you have once again hidden your name in Taiyue 台岳 (Tiantai Mountains), it still spreads to the Yangzi and Huai valleys. [You] labor night and day to [keep] your excellent reputation and [give] great advice. Having personally taken the road of simplicity and long cultivated the spirit of emptiness, [you] sit next to the mysterious men (transcendents) and dream of the rock caves. When it becomes chilly with frost and wind, the pneuma of the sea will turn cold. Reposing quietly in the lush forest, your Daoist body lies at rest. Of old, the Four White-headed Elders at the Shang Mountains 商山 performed levitation at the Han court, and the Eight Lords of Huainan descended graciously upon the princely mansion.[16]

Past and present are indeed different, but hills and vales remain the same. Concerning reclusion from the court and market, and other received ideas of past worthies, who is better to guide the laity and expound their sagely teachings than you, Sir? Therefore, [I have] dispatched a messenger to invite you. It is my wish that [your reverence] would arrive spectacularly without bothering to wear formal attire, and leave your valley of emptiness without riding on a welcoming carriage. Hoping that you will oblige me with a visit, I am looking forward to your arrival.

Here, Yangdi shows a familiarity with the fundamental concepts of Daoism—the Dao, emptiness, the equality of things, riding on wind and cloud, and living on pine water and thistles—as well as Daoist allegories—the Four White-headed Elders and the Eight Lords. Upon receiving this letter, Xu Ze proceeded to Yangzhou (Jiangdu). Yangdi then sought to learn the law of the Dao with Xu. But Xu died that night. Yangdi deeply lamented his passing and ordered that his remains be transferred to the Tiantai Mountains for proper burial.[17]

Unlike his father who favored the Louguan school, Yangdi preferred the Shangqing 上清 (Highest Clarity) or Maoshan 茅山 school.[18] The influence of this Southern school was strong enough to allow it to spread to the North. During his sojourn at Mount Hua, the Shangqing master Jiao Kuang 焦曠 had a mentoring relationship with Wang Yan.[19] This valuable learning experience allowed Wang Yan to acquire a deep knowledge of "the mysteries of the Three Caverns, the scriptures of the Perfected, and jade books," laying the foundation for his later editorship of the Three Caverns scriptures.[20]

Shangqing's impact on Daoism was also embodied in the prevailing Daoist cosmology. In Sui times, it was widely accepted that Yuanshi Tianzun 元始天尊, a timeless cosmic deity that predated the beginning of the universe, ordained the highest celestial transcendents, among whom was Taishang Laojun 太上老君. This claim was clearly a reflection of the influence of the Shangqing school, with its typical worship of Tianzun as its supreme deity, and a departure from the cosmological tradition of earlier times which regarded Taishang Laojun as the highest Daoist god.[21] The ascendancy of the Shangqing school was further indicated by the order in which Daoist registers were transmitted: The Shangqing register was given the most prominent place.[22]

Yangdi's association with Shangqing dates back to his long sojourn in the South as the Prince of Jin. Once, he summoned the Shangqing patriarch Wang Yuanzhi 王遠之, allegedly trained by the great Shangqing master Tao Hongjing 陶弘景,[23] only to witness the sudden whitening of his beard and hair. A frightened Yangdi sent him away. After his enthronement, Yangdi brought him to the Linshuo Palace where Yangdi personally conducted the disciple's ritual and set up an abbey in the capital to house him. Becoming Wang Yuanzhi's nominal disciple, Yangdi held the celebrated Shangqing master in high esteem. After Yangdi decided to move his base south at the end of his reign, he would kill almost anyone who stood in his way; Yuanzhi was among the very few who attempted to dissuade him without having to face punishment. Yangdi's favoritism to Yuanzhi was clearly reminiscent of his father's practice of revering the top Louguan leader of the North, Wang Yan. One other cleric who was honored by Yangdi in a similar manner was Zhiyi, the eminent Buddhist monk of the South. In view of this, at least in a symbolic sense, Yangdi respected Shangqing Daoism as much as Tiantai Buddhism.[24]

When Wang Yuanzhi returned south to Maoshan, his best known student, Pan Shizheng 潘師正, accompanied him. At Wang's request, Pan returned north to reside at Mount Song 嵩山. Pan's presence in the North clearly favored the continued transmission of Shangqing teachings. One of Pan's students, Sima Chengzhen 司馬承禎, was to become the leading Shangqing Daoist in Early Tang times.[25]

One of the main reasons Yangdi admired the Daoist Wang Yuanzhi so much was the latter's renowned occultist practices, such as the avoidance of grains and living on pine water, both associated with the pursuit of longevity. This points to Yangdi's enormous interest in the occult aspects of Daoism. He patronized the Daoists Song Yuquan 宋玉泉 of Jian'an 建安 and Kong Daomao 孔道茂 of Guiji 會稽. Both practiced similar longevity-seeking techniques. He ordered the occultist-cum-Daoist Xue Yi 薛頤 into the palace monastery to perform the astroalchemical *jiao* 醮 rite (cosmodrama), which

TABLE 8.2   Patriarchs of the Shangqing school, from inception to Tang

| A | B |
|---|---|
| 9 | Tao Hongjing 陶弘景 (456–536) |
| 10 | Wang Yuanzhi 王遠知 (510–635)[26] |
| 11 | Pan Shizheng 潘師正 (585–682) |
| 12 | Sima Chengzhen 司馬承禎 (647–735) |
| 13 | Li Hanguang 李含光 (683–769) |
| 14 | Wei Jingzhao 韋景昭 (694–785) |
| 15 | Huang Dongyuan 黃洞元 (697–791) |
| 16 | Sun Zhiqing 孫智清 (fl. 832–833) |
| 17 | Wu Fatong 吳法通 (825–) |
| 18 | Liu Dechang 劉得常 |
| 19 | Wang Qixia 王棲霞 (882–943) |

Source: *MSZ* 10–11.600–603. A = Patriarchal sequence in the *Maoshan zhi*. B = Patriarchs.

involved making offerings to celestial deities to bring about the apparition of transcendents. Yangdi was also a believer in the occult Daoist transformation known as corpse deliverance (*shijie* 尸解), which allowed an adept to cheat death and achieve transcendence. When the abbot of the Xuandu Abbey, Wang Yan, allegedly achieved transfiguration, an amazed Yangdi gave generously to sponsor a large-scale vegetarian feast in his honor. Wang Yan's remains were sent to his final resting place in the Western Marchmount (*xiyue* 西嶽; Mount Hua). He achieved corpse deliverance on the day of his entombment: His casket was found empty of its contents. Another Daoist named Zhou Yinyao 周隱遙 of the Dongting Mountain 洞庭山 was believed to have achieved transfiguration three times through corpse deliverance; when he was almost eighty years old, he looked as if he were in his thirties. Yangdi summoned him to the Eastern Capital (Luoyang), rewarded him handsomely, and kept him in his entourage.[27]

During the Daye reign, a large number of Daoist adepts were presented to the court on account of their Daoist techniques. In Luoyang, a residential ward immediately south of the Luo River was named Daoshu 道術 (Daoist techniques) Ward, on which a revealing description survives: "Yangdi had many taboos and avoidances. Five-phases experts, diviners, and medicine men were gathered in this ward in the Eastern Capital. Commissioners were sent over to oversee them. People were not allowed to exit or enter [the ward]." This ward played host to masters of esoterica (*fangshi* 方士) of various descriptions, who were Daoists, Buddho-Daoist synthesists, or occultists with no particular religious affiliations, while the Huiri Monastery, Yangdi's favorite, housed the *yiseng* 藝僧 (or *daoyi* 道藝), the Buddhist practitioners of the occult arts.[28]

Not only did Yangdi keep the *fangshi* in close quarters, he also made use of their services. For example, after Crown Prince Yuande 元德 (Yang Zhao 楊昭) came down with a serious disease, Yangdi consulted a ghost-seer by the name of Cui Shanying 崔善影 to detect ghostly influence. In another instance, reacting to the claim of an aeromancer that the aura of a Son of Heaven was detected northwest of the Eastern Capital that extended as far north as Taiyuan and beyond, Yangdi ordered the construction of the [Fenyang 汾陽] Palace (southwest of Ningwu, north Shanxi) in Loufan Commandery 樓繁郡 (seat: Jingle, in north Shanxi) to suppress that potential; he also paid several trips to Fenyang to enhance the effect.[29]

His association with the Daoist alchemist Pan Dan 潘誕 of Mount Song 嵩山 (in Henan) exemplifies his quest for longevity or immortality within the Daoist framework. Yangdi not only built the luxurious Songyang Abbey 嵩陽觀 to house him and provided him with the services of one hundred and twenty boys and one hundred and twenty girls, but promoted him to a rank three position. In return, Pan Dan promised to produce gold cinnabar, a longevity elixir. But for six years, Pan had nothing to show for it. When Pan requested human gall and marrow as substitute raw material, an enraged Yangdi had him delivered in chains to Zhuo Commandery where he was executed.[30] Apparently, Yangdi, in his quest for eternal life, had lavished a fortune on Pan Dan and his alchemical project.

In spite of his patronage of the Shangqing school, his high respect for the Daoist religion in general, and his abiding fascination with the supernatural powers of the Daoists, Yangdi targeted Daoist communities as part of his plan to rein in religious institutions. He ordered that supervisors and assistant supervisors be installed at Daoist abbeys, and repeatedly requested Daoists to reverence the sovereign in 607 and 609, according to the Buddhist source *Guang hongming ji*. The Daoists, referred to as gentlemen and ladies in yellow turban (*huangjin shinü* 黃巾士女), cravenly complied with the imperial demand and made obeisances incessantly.[31] However, for lack of collaborative evidence in Daoist and other types of sources, it is difficult to establish with certainty what the Daoist reaction to Yangdi's request was. Since it was the Buddhist, not the Daoist, church that consistently claimed immunity from reverencing the sovereign, Yangdi's request may not have been so objectionable to Daoists after all.

The intrusive approach Yangdi occasionally adopted towards the Daoist clergy did not, in the end, seem to damage Yangdi's relationship with the Daoist community, which on the whole remained harmonious throughout his reign.

## BUDDHISM

By the time the Sui dynasty was founded, Daoism had matured into a powerful, organized religion, wielding significant influence at court. But the truly ecumenical religion at that time was its rival, Buddhism. All sectors of the population came under its spell. Large numbers of Buddhist monasteries were set up and Buddhist imagery—statues, paintings, and murals—dominated religious iconography. A vast corpus of Buddhist literature was written and multitudes of believers left their families behind to join the clergy. Yet, Buddhism traveled a tortuous path in the decades before the rise of the Sui. Untoward events that had taken place in the pre-Sui age tested Wendi's religious conviction and destined him to play a historic role in the annals of Chinese Buddhism.[32]

Despite the increasing popularity of Buddhism, during the Six Dynasties period, there were occasionally undercurrents that moved in the opposite direction. Under the Southern regime of Liang, Fan Zhen 范縝 attacked the fundamental values of Mahāyāna Buddhism on life, death, karma, and soul. Fan's contemporary, Xun Ji 荀濟, even faulted Buddhism for shortening the life-span of both the Liu-Song and Southern Qi dynasties.[33] But the main threat to the spread of Buddhism came from the North. The first state sanctioned anti-Buddhist campaign took place as early as the mid-fifth century, during the reign of Taiwudi 太武帝 (Tuoba Tao 拓跋燾, r. 423–452) of the North-ern Wei. More than a century later, the second anti-Buddhist campaign was launched during Yangdi's childhood in 574. The Northern Zhou sovereign, Wudi 武帝 (Yuwen Yong 宇文邕, r. 560–578), persuaded by the renegade monk Wei Yuansong 衞元嵩 and the Daoist Zhang Bin 張賓, instituted a number of prohibitive measures against the Buddhist church, destroying both sūtras and icons.[34]

Although Wudi was inclined to single out Buddhism for proscription, the Daoist Zhang Bin failed to make a convincing argument for the action. Prob-ably to show his impartiality, Wudi also included Daoism as the target of his proscription. The impact on the Buddhist church was devastating:

When the Buddhist and Daoist religions were first proscribed, both *shamen* 沙門 (*śramaṇa*) and Daoist adepts were ordered to laicize. The assets of the Three Jewels (*sanbao* 三寶) were scattered among ministers and other subordinates, and Buddhist monasteries, Daoist abbeys, stūpas, and temples were bestowed upon princes and dukes.[35]

In spite of their severity, these initial anti-Buddhist measures had only a limited impact thanks to the relatively small size of the Northern Zhou terri-tory. But after Wudi annexed the vast territory of the Northern Qi in the lower Yellow River valley, he brought the proscription campaign to the newly van-quished land with far more ruinous results for the religion.

These repressive measures, however, did not reverse the long-term trend of growth for Buddhism in North China. The prohibitive religious policy began to unravel not long after Wudi's death in 578. His successor Xuandi 宣帝 (Yuwen Yun 宇文贇, r. 578–579), who obviously resented the austere manner in which he had been brought up, moved to relax the ban on making Buddhist and Daoist statues in 579. In the sixth month of 580, the newly enthroned child-emperor Jingdi 靜帝 (r. 579–581) authorized the official rehabilitation of both Buddhism and Daoism. An imperial edict was issued in his name in the first month of 581 ". . . to restore both the Buddhist and Daoist religions, and to reestablish statues of the Buddha and Tianzun. Chief Min-ister Yang Jian, and Zhizang 智藏, Linggan 靈幹, and others of the Zhihu Monastery 陟岵寺 retonsured two hundred and twenty monks." Of symbolic significance was the presence at the ceremony of a layperson—Yang Jian, the de facto ruler of North China, and the future Wendi. The restoration of

Buddhism under the Northern Zhou in the name of Jingdi was without doubt the work of Wendi.[36]

Wendi's public endorsement of Buddhism may have been a strategic move—he wanted to rally support from the Buddhist clergy. But behind this move was his firm belief in the tenets of the religion. Not surprisingly, both his birth and childhood were closely associated with Buddhism. A Buddhist source records:

> A nun from the Bore 般若 (*prajñā*) Convent in Tong Prefecture 同州 (seat: in Dali, Shaanxi) known as Zhixian 智仙 excelled in *dhyāna*-meditation, and accurately divined people's fortunes and mishaps on every occasion. When Wendi (Yang Jian) was born in the convent, [Zhixian] said to Taizu (Yang Zhong, Wendi's father), "This son is protected by the Buddha Heaven (*fotian* 佛天)," and consequently gave him the name Naluoyan 那羅延 (*nārāyaṇ*; hero of divine power). Taizu [then donated his house for the establishment of a convent and] entrusted her with the raising [of Wendi]. One day Wendi's mother came to carry him, and was startled to see him transformed into a dragon, and dropped him onto the ground. The nun could not help saying, "You have startled my son, and that would delay his conquest of all under Heaven." When [Wendi] grew older [at age seven (six)], [the nun] secretly informed him, "The religion of the image (*xiangjiao* 像教) will be destroyed. All ghosts and gods will face west. You will acquire a status of extremely high nobility. The Buddhist dharma will be temporarily extinguished, and will depend on you for revival." When Wudi of Zhou abolished the religion, the nun (Zhixian) ended up hiding herself in the emperor's (Wendi) home.[37]

This passage is based on an account from Wendi's court diary written by Editorial Director (*zhuzuo lang* 著作郎) Wang Shao 王劭, whose job it was to chronicle court events and decisions. Apart from the standard dragon myth associated with the early childhood of a dynastic founder, the passage should be considered reliable. It is obvious that Wendi's parents were devout Buddhists themselves. The fact that Wendi spent his crucial formative years under the care of a Buddhist nun (his surrogate mother) in a religious environment must have had a profound impact on the formation of his character and religious belief. When the proscription started in 574, Wendi took Zhixian under his wing. This act, if exposed, could have jeopardized Wendi's career in spite of his powerful position. So it can only be explained in terms of his profound sense of gratitude and his dedication to the religion.[38]

Throughout his reign, Wendi remained a vigorous supporter of the Buddhist cause. One of the widespread problems facing the Buddhist community early in his reign was the iconoclastic impact of the anti-Buddhist proscription of the previous age that had left a large number of Buddhist icons defaced or fragmented. Wendi made it a responsibility of local officials to collect and deliver broken pieces of Buddhist statues to monasteries for appropriate treatment.[39] Not satisfied with the traditional role of patronage, he went out of his way to expand it. Thus, he stated in an edict:

> The various dharmas are expansive and are in essence inseparable, yet in charitable deeds there are still [differences between] public and private. From this day forward, wherever meritorious works are to be set up, let them be built with combined [public and private] support under Heaven. [We should] grant their (the builders') wishes without trying to make a distinction [between them and us]. Let us pray that all doors to enlightenment lead to the same goal.[40]

In addition to his unreserved sponsorship of Buddhist building projects Wendi pledged to lend a supporting hand to private endeavors.

Of the monastic projects Wendi sponsored, the case of the Daxingshan Monastery especially deserves close examination. As the only national monastery (*guosi* 國寺) then under the Sui, it was named after the capital and the ward where it was located. Wendi modeled its layout on that of the Ancestral Temple, and located the monastery east of the central north-south axis on the same side as the Ancestral Temple. The symbolic association with ancestral worship not only suggests Wendi's profound reverence for the religion, but also the transference of his filial sentiments to the Buddha Heaven that had blessed him at birth.[41]

In addition to being an unparalleled sponsor of monasteries and statues, Wendi played a major part in aggressively swelling the ranks of the clergy. To him, the secular power of the Sui court and the religious authority of the Buddhist church were equal in status. This provided him with the rationale for supporting expanded ordinations. He declared to the Vinaya master (*lüshi* 律師) Lingzang 靈藏, a leading Buddhist figure in the North, "Your disciple (Wendi) is the lay Son of Heaven, and the Vinaya master is the religious Son of Heaven. You are free to ordain anyone who wants to quit the mundane world." As the number of the ordained grew into tens of thousands, he assuaged his doubters by elevating his argument to higher moral grounds, "The Vinaya master transforms people into doing good. This emperor stops people from doing evil. The goal is the same." Meanwhile Wendi waived all the etiquette requirements for Lingzang in his contact with the emperor. Later, even Buddhist scholars faulted Wendi for going too far.[42]

In his dealings with the Southern clergy, we encounter similar themes. In early 590, immediately after the conquest of the Chen, Wendi issued an edict in which he pledged his support for the religion, and exalted the virtues of Zhiyi, the most prominent Southern monk:

> When Wudi of the Northern Zhou was destroying the religion, this emperor vowed to himself to uphold it. Upon receiving the Mandate of Heaven, [he] immediately revived the religion. The master (Zhiyi) has quit the mundane world to cultivate himself and transform others. It is the hope [of this emperor] that the master should promote saṅgha ethics to illuminate the Great Way.[43]

As Wendi sought to extend his pro-Buddhist policy to the South and pacify its Buddhist community, he appealed to the leader of the church to lend his support.

In terms of accumulating meritorious works and successfully supporting and promoting ordinations, Wendi was second to none. Even the reigns of Liang Wudi 梁武帝 (a most devoted Buddhist sovereign) and his two successors paled by comparison. Under these sovereigns, a total of 2,846 monasteries were built, and a total of 82,700 monks and nuns ordained. The reign of Wendi, however, witnessed the construction of 3,792 monasteries, and the compilation of 132,086 *juan* of sūtras, in addition to the ordination of the largest number of monks ever (two hundred and thirty thousand) under a single sovereign (see table 8.3).[44]

The unparalleled support Wendi showed Buddhism does not necessarily mean the church operated completely independent of the state. A case in point is the creation of the *datong* 大統 (controller-in-chief), the leading government official in charge of the Buddhist clergy and monasteries. Appointing an official national leader of the Buddhist church had been a long-standing tradition in the Six Dynasties period. Under the Northern Dynasties, it was known as *shamen tong*, *daoren* 道人 *tong* or *zhaoxuan* 昭玄 *tong*; under the Southern Dynasties, as *sengzheng* 僧正 or *sengzhu* 僧主. In the Tianbao period (550–559) of the Northern Qi, a system of *shitong* (ten controllers) was set up with the top-ranking controller as *datong*.[45] Not long after the 574 proscription, the Sui under Wendi established its own *shitong* system, which was a revival of the Northern Qi system. Wendi appointed the Vinaya master Sengmeng 僧猛 as the first *datong* of the Sui in 581. For symbolic reasons, Wendi located the *datong* in the first monastery of the nation, Daxingshan in Daxingcheng. Without doubt, the presence of the *datong* there does suggest some kind of official connection. But Sengmeng's appointment, according to his biography, "was not sufficient to boost his authority."[46] The appointed religious officials, always prominent monks themselves, could also decline the offer.[47] In appointing Sengmeng to the post of *datong*, Wendi was primarily concerned with how to propagate and protect the Law of the Buddha, not how to let Sengmeng take control of the religion on behalf of the state.[48] The precise purpose of the office of *datong* is not clear. Judging from extant evidence, it seemed to function like a court-appointed self-regulating body.[49]

Another instance cited as evidence of the political manipulation of religion is an edict issued in 583 in which Wendi stipulated specific dates for recurrent religious events at state-sponsored monasteries. This seems to indicate Wendi's intention to take advantage of existing Buddhist institutions to advance his own agenda. However, the agenda in question was primarily a religious one—to periodically ban the killing of sentient beings when ritual circumambulations were taking place at government-sponsored Buddhist monasteries.[50]

In spite of Wendi's consistent support of Buddhism, the Buddhist community in the South was adversely impacted at the time of the Northern conquest, albeit the Sui overall religious policy there was favorable. The leveling of Jiankang on Wendi's orders meant the destruction of numerous Buddhist structures in and around that great city. Official efforts were made even to reduce the holdings of the church. As a record in the *Xu gaoseng zhuan* (*XGSZ*) indicates:

> After the Sui conquest and pacification of the South, government orders aimed at reform were issued: "Within a prefecture, only two Buddhist monasteries are allowed. All other Saṅghārāmas should be abolished." [The monk] Huijue 慧覺 feared that many places of Vajra (monasteries) would get destroyed. He traveled hundreds of *she* 舍 (1 *she* = 30 *li*) nonstop to report to His Majesty and call attention to [this decision]. An edict was then issued which magnanimously granted his request [to stop the implementation of the decision].[51]

It may well be that Sui officials directly in charge of the occupation issued orders in the name of the government to restrain the Southern Buddhist clergy. However, it should not be regarded as having come directly from Wendi, whose directives would be issued as edicts (*zhao* 詔) or rescripts (*chi* 敕). It is impossible to know who was behind this potentially destructive decision. But thanks to Wendi's timely intervention it was reversed.[52]

One notable exception to Wendi's otherwise favorable policy towards Buddhism was his handling of the Three Stages school (*sanjie jiao* 三階教) founded by Xinxing 信行. In 600, Wendi issued an edict to ban two Three Stages sūtras authored by Xinxing, probably because of its alleged doctrinal heterodoxy and subversive potentials. In view of the fact that the key Three Stages doctrine was considered heretical even by mainstream

Buddhism,[53] Wendi's attempt to ban these sūtras should not be construed as a deviation.

So far, our findings demonstrate that while Wendi may have harbored political intentions in his dealings with the clergy in general, to see these and other anecdotal records as evidence of Wendi's long-term scheme to unify his empire with the help of the religion is an exaggeration.[54] In fact, Wendi acted more like the Indian king Aśoka, an overzealous sovereign intent on protecting and expanding Buddhism, than a calculating emperor bent on bringing the clergy under state control. The main characteristic of his Buddhist policy was the eclectic concept of combining church and state and fusing divine power and temporal authority instead of subjecting church to secular authority.[55]

To better understand Wendi's attitude toward Buddhism, it is illuminating to compare his approach with that of an earlier sovereign, Liang Wudi (r. 502–549), arguably the most fervent imperial supporter of Buddhism in Chinese history. Both gave generous support to the Buddhist cause and both had a life-long passion for the religion that was translated into the concrete deeds of generous patronage. Yet in religious terms, Wendi's reign was markedly different from Wudi's in that, while Wendi maintained his temporal power as the lay Son of Heaven, Wudi blurred the boundary between laity and clergy. However, even though Wendi did not share Liang Wudi's religious fanaticism, his edicts to prohibit slaughter on certain sacred dates, pardon minor criminals, and commute death sentences were evidence of his efforts to rule in accord with the Buddhist concept of law.[56]

Yangdi began to play a significant role in Sui Buddhism after 590 when, as the prince of Jin, he was ordered by his father to take office as the top Sui administrator of the South.[57] During his tenure, Yangdi was a major patron of Buddhist institutions. The Huiri Monastery 慧日寺 he set up in Jiangdu became the Southern center of Buddhist learning, and gathered many prominent monks. The close connections Huiri had with Yangdi are well documented. A Buddhist record refers to it as *Jinfu Huiri daochang* 晉府慧日道場 (Huiri Monastery of the Residence of [the Prince of] Jin). In an epitaph, the name of the monastery is prefixed with *Jinwang* 晉王 (Prince of Jin).[58] Not only was Huiri located within the grounds of his princely residence, it was also regarded, appropriately, as his personal monastery.

One of the monks Yangdi patronized was Huiyun 惠雲, whom Yangdi brought to Huiri because of his erudition and eloquence. Thoroughly enjoying his company and friendship, Yangdi would take him on his trips north. When Huiyun died in Daxingcheng at age fifty (forty-nine), a grief-stricken Yangdi commissioned an epitaph for him in 594.[59] After he became crown prince, Yangdi moved to Daxingcheng, where he set up the Riyan Monastery 日嚴寺 in the southwest corner of Qinglong 青龍 Ward (12I). But he still

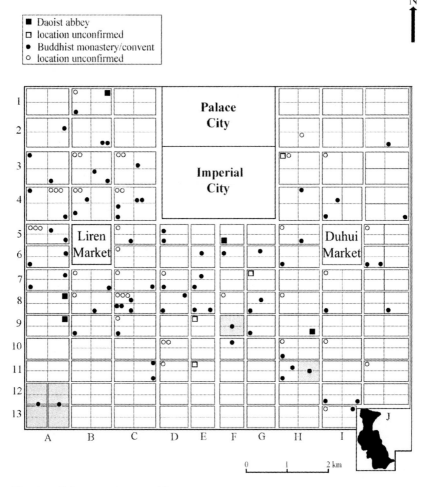

MAP 8.1   Religious institutions of Daxingcheng

maintained close contact with the Southern Buddhist clergy, staffing Riyan with a number of monks from Jiangdu's Huiri[60] (map 8.1).

As emperor, Yangdi continued to support Buddhism, sponsoring monastic projects in the capital. In 605, he built one of the largest monasteries in Daxingcheng, West Chanding 西禪定, together with its wooden pagoda, in memory of his father. In addition, he set up ten government-supported monasteries.[61] Located in the southwest corner of the capital, West Chanding (Dachanding 大禪定, Dazongchi 大總持, or Zongchi) extended across two

Key to Map 8.1

Daoist institutions (*guan* 觀)
Chengxu 澄虛 (11E)
Huisheng 會聖 (9A) NE
Linggan 靈感 (7G)
Lingying 靈應 (9H) SE
Qingdu 清都 (3H)
Qingxu 清虛 (8A) NE
Wutong 五通 (1B)
Xuandu 玄都 (9E)
Zhide 至德 (5F)

Buddhist institutions (*si* 寺)
Bao'an 寶岸 (4A)
Baocha 寶刹 (4H) NE
Baochang 寶昌 (4A) SE
Baoji 寶積 (10D)
Baosheng 寶勝 (8G)
Baowang 寶王 (5A)
Baoyi 襃義 (9B) SW
Biancai 辨才 (5A)
Chanding 禪定 (12A) E
   and (13A) E
Changfa 常法 (6C)
Chanlin 禪林 (4J) SE
Chengdao 成道 (7D)
Chengjue 澄覺 (3C)
Chongjing 崇敬 (9G) SW
Cihe 慈和 (2B) SE
Cimen 慈門 (5C) SW
Ciren 慈仁 (8C) SW
Dachanding 大禪定 (12A) W
   and (13A) W
Daci 大慈 (6J) SW
Dajue 大覺 (8C) NW
Daojue 道覺 (4C)
Dingshui 定水 (5D) NW
East Chanding 東禪定.
   *See* Chanding.
Fabao 法寶 (7B)
Fahai 法海 (4C) SW
Fajie 法界 (7E) SW
Fajue 法覺 (11C) SE
Falun 法輪 (8I) SW

Faming 法明 (8C) SW
Fashen 法身 (5A)
Fashou 法壽 (6F) NW
Fazhong 法眾 (3B)
Ganlu 甘露 (4I)
Gongde 功德 (1B)
Guangbao 光寶 (4B)
Guangming 光明 (7B) SE
Haijue 海覺 (8C) SW
Honghua 宏(弘)化 (11J)
Hongji 宏濟 (4I) NW
Hongshan 宏善 (6J) SW
Hongye 宏(弘)業 (7E) SW;
   post-607: (8C) SE
Huchi 護持 (5J)
Huijue 惠覺 (5C)
Huiri 慧日 (6A) NE
Huiyun 惠雲 (3C)
Jianfa 建法 (3C) NE
Jidu 濟度 (8D)
Jifa 濟法 (4C) NE
Jiguo 紀國 (9C) SW
Jingfa 靜法 (7C) SE
Jingjue 靜覺 (13I)
Jingle 靜樂 (7A) SW
Jingxing 經行 (7A) NE
Jingying 淨影 (6E)
Jingyu 淨域 (6H) SW
Jingzhu 淨住 (11H) NW
Jishan 積善 (3A) NW
Jiudu 救度 (4B)
Kaishan 開善 (3B) SE
Kongguan 空觀 (7D) SW
Linggan靈感 (8J) SE
Linghua 靈化 (2A) NE
Lingjue 靈覺 (11C) NE
Liquan 醴泉 (4B) NW
Luohan 羅漢 (Arhat) (6A) SW
Lüzang 律藏 (1B) SW
Miaosheng 妙勝 (4B) SW
Mingfa 明法 (4C)
Mingjue明覺 (8H)
Minglun 明輪 (7C)
Ningguan 凝觀 (4A)

Puji 普集 (4A) NW
Puti 菩提 (Bodhi) (5H) SE
Puyao 普耀 (12I) SE
Qingchan 清禪 (2J) SE
Renfa 仁法 (2H)
Riyan 日嚴 (12I) SW
Rongjue 融覺 (8C)
Shanguo 善果 (3H)
Shengguang 勝光 (7E) N;
   post-605: (6C) SW
Shengjing 聖敬(經) (8F)
Shentong 神通 (9C)
Shewei 舍衛 (3B) SE
Shifan 釋梵 (3B)
Shiji 實際 (5D) SW
Tianbao 天寶 (13I) NE
Tongfa 通法 (10I)
Wanshan 萬善 (2B) SE
West Chanding 西禪定.
   *See* Dachanding.
Wulou 無漏 (11H) E
Xianghai 香海 (10H)
Xianjue 賢覺 (8C)
Xianjue 顯覺 (4C) NE
Xingdao 興道 (11H) SW
Xiuci 修慈 (10H) SW
Xiushan 修善 (8E) SE
Xuanfa 玄法 (7I) N
Xuanhua 宣化 (11D)
Yanghua 陽化 (5H) N
Yanxing 延興 (8B) SE
Yifa 依法 (4A)
Yingfa 應法 (10D)
Yuanjue 緣覺 (8C)
Yuanli 願力 (8B)
Yueai 月愛 (8D) NE
Zhengjue 正覺 (6G) N
Zhenhua 真化 (5A) NE
Zhenji 真寂 (3A) SE
Zhenxin 真心 (5A) SE
Zijing 資敬 (8G) N
Zishan 資善 (8E) SW
Zonghua 總化 (3I)
Zunshan 遵善 (9F)

MAP 8.1   Continued

wards—Heping 和平 and Yongyang 永陽. Building this large Buddhist structure so soon after Yangdi's usurpation and dedicating it to the victim of the usurpation testify to Yangdi's faith in the religion and his ambivalent feelings towards his father.

TABLE 8.3    Meritorious works for Buddhism under Wendi (W) and Yangdi (Y)

|   | monks & nuns ordained | sūtras in juan | | B + C | statues | | monasteries built |
|---|---|---|---|---|---|---|---|
|   |   | copied | repaired |   | erected | repaired |   |
| W | 230,000 | 132,086 | 115,590* | 247,676 | 106,580 | 1,508,940 | 3,792 |
| Y | 6,200† |   |   | 903,580 | 3,850 | 101,000 | 193‡ |
|   | A | B | C | D | E | F | G |

Source: *BZL* 3:509b–c. *Converted from 3,853 *bu* (1 *bu* = 30 *juan*). † *FYZL* 100.26. *BZL* 3.509c records 16,200. ‡ Derived from deducting 3,792 (total under Wendi) from 3,985 (Sui total).

After he finished the construction of Luoyang, Yangdi established four Places of Enlightenment (*daochang*) located on the west side of the street that led from the Jingyun 景運 Gate north into the palace.[62] Two of these *daochang* were Buddhist monasteries, Huiri and Fayun, which probably used their namesakes in Jiangdu as prototypes, also built by Yangdi. The Luoyang Huiri, identified as a *nei daochang* 內道場 (palace monastery), was of special, personal importance to Yangdi, just like the Jiangdu Huiri and Riyan in Daxingcheng. It was there, on Yangdi's orders, the monk Zhiguo 智果 started a massive project to classify and catalog Buddhist sūtras extant at the time.[63]

To put Yangdi's patronage of Buddhism in proper perspective, table 8.3 tabulates some statistics based on records in the Tang source *Bianzheng lun* of Yangdi's and Wendi's good works for the cause of Buddhism.

A close examination of table 8.3 provides revealing insight into the imperial patronage of Buddhism under the two Sui sovereigns. The comparison is appropriate in view of the fact that both Wendi and Yangdi lived in the same dynasty and ruled over populations and territories of similar sizes. The only major variable is the differential in their reign periods, with Wendi's twenty-three years versus Yangdi's nearly fourteen years. However, this differential is not that meaningful because Yangdi's merits also include those achieved before his enthronement.

As column A indicates, the number of ordained monks and nuns under Yangdi reached sixty-two hundred, but it only represented about 2.7 percent of Wendi's total. Obviously, for Wendi, to increase the size of the Buddhist clergy was one of his highest priorities, whereas for Yangdi, it was not. Yangdi's efforts to create new and repair old Buddhist statues (columns E and F) and build monasteries were very impressive indeed. Yet, they were dwarfed by Wendi's efforts in the same area. In the area of sūtra translation, which is not covered by the table, Yangdi made a significant contribution. By 606, he had set up the Institute for Sūtra Translation (*fanjing guan* 翻經館) south of the

Luo in the Shanglin Garden 上林園 (Western Park). The Indian monk Dharmagupta (Damojiduo 達摩笈多) served as the main translator, with a group of eminent Buddhist scholars working under him.[64] But here again, Yangdi paled beside his father.[65] The only category in which Yangdi led Wendi in quantitative terms was that of sūtras copied and sūtras repaired in column D. Those attributable to Yangdi were about 3.65 times as many as those completed under Wendi. It should be pointed out that the duplication and restoration of sūtras under Yangdi took place when he was still a prince resident in the South.[66] Since Wendi was then the reigning emperor, these should probably be considered his achievements as well.[67]

Based on the comparative data, in almost every measurable area of Buddhist patronage, Yangdi trailed far behind Wendi, who had demonstrated a level of dynamism in supporting his chosen religion rarely matched by other sovereigns. Nevertheless, although Yangdi's support for the Buddhist cause was much less vigorous, it can still be considered normative by medieval standards. Moreover, the extraordinarily successful effort of Wendi at promoting Buddhism made it impossible to surpass him in expanding church property and clergy; nor was it necessary.

One area of Buddhism in which Yangdi demonstrated a much stronger passion than his father is occultism. As Buddhism spread in early medieval China, some of its missionaries displayed their power to accomplish miracles. In the meantime, the occult elements of the religion became intermingled with indigenous religious practices, especially those of spirit mediums, who could allegedly contact the world of the supernatural to effect changes in the human world. This occult component of Buddhism held Yangdi spellbound. His contact with Buddhist practitioners of occultism dates back to his days as an imperial prince resident in Jiangdu, where he came to know an occultist monk by the name of Fa'an 法安. Upon accession to the throne, Yangdi showered favors upon him and built the Baoyang Monastery 寶楊寺 to house him. Known for his ability to conjure water from stone, and his connections with the transcendents, Fa'an was treated by like a living god.[68]

When informed of the supernatural powers of the Southern monk Faxi 法喜, Yangdi brought him into his Jiangdu Palace so as to have long-term access to his service. After Faxi's death and burial, his apparition was reported to the court. Yangdi ordered his tomb to be opened, only to find an empty casket. Faxi seems to have escaped death through corpse deliverance, a common Daoist practice.[69]

Upon building the city of Luoyang, Yangdi gathered and supported in its Huiri Monastery more than two thousand *daoyi* 道藝 or *yiseng* 藝僧—monks who specialized in the occult arts. Among those *yiseng* Yangdi befriended was one known as Faji 法濟, who:

could see through the tenuous and knew the anomalous. His rise had started under the Chen. In Sui times, the two sovereigns both settled him within the palace. Living among the concubines and consorts, he was well focused and abstentious in a way rarely surpassed by others. Wendi built a Xiangtai Monastery 香臺寺 for him in Chang'an. Later on he arrived in the Eastern Capital where [Yangdi] built the Longtian Monastery 龍天道場 [for him]. The emperor (Yangdi) gave him a white horse, which he often rode within the palace grounds. If anyone suffering from measles [came to see him], he would cast a spell by incantation over some water, and let the patient drink it. The disease would always be cured. [He] could also see ghosts, and predict the future.[70]

Yangdi's reverence for the supernatural and prescient powers of Buddhism transferred to objects as well. He began to show a special interest in inspirational imagery after he first took up residence in the South and long before his enthronement. He was then informed of the existence of a precious Buddhist statue with a height of 1 *chi* 尺 and a diameter of 6 *cun* 寸. Purple in color, this translucent icon had been presented to the court of Liang Wudi as a gift by an Indian monk. Yangdi had the statue brought to his residence, where he housed it permanently for veneration. Whenever he went on a trip, the statue would accompany him as a guardian. After he was appointed heir apparent, he relocated it to the capital where he placed it in the Riyan Monastery. All the while, he kept it hidden from outsiders, obviously for the purpose of having exclusive access to its supernatural power and divine protection.[71]

After his enthronement, Yangdi continued to show a strong passion for inspirational objects, as is clearly illustrated by his association with a monastery in Liang Prefecture 涼州 (with its seat in Wuwei, Gansu). Known as the Ruixiang (Propitious Statue) Monastery 瑞像寺, it housed a statue of legendary prophetic power. According to tradition, the statue had been set up following a prediction made by the Northern Wei monk Huida 慧達 in 435. It was believed that when the statue was intact, peace and prosperity would prevail, and when it was broken, chaos and suffering would follow. More than one hundred years later, when Yangdi went on an extensive tour of inspection in the Longyou 隴右 (Gansu) area in 609, he made a special side trip to this monastery to pay homage to the miraculous statue in person, and renamed the monastery Gantong 感通 (Thaumaturgy).[72]

His abiding obsession with the occultist powers of *yiseng* and religious icons did not necessarily have an adverse impact on his relations with the church establishment. In fact, he was in frequent contact with prominent members of the Buddhist community. Particularly well-known was his close association with Zhiyi 智顗 of the Tiantai school during his residency in the

South.[73] In the eleventh month of 591, in a most dramatic religious event symbolic of his devotion to Buddhism, Yangdi received from Zhiyi the bodhisattvasīla (*pusa jie* 菩薩戒), an ordination ritual in which Buddhist commandments based on the *Fanwang jing* 梵網經 (*Brahmajāla-sūtra* [Sūtra of the Brahma-net]) were passed on to their recipients.[74] In his acceptance letter, a grateful Yangdi first paid tribute to family influence as a decisive factor in helping him shape his religious belief:

> As a result of the charitable deeds of his past life, your disciple was born into the imperial family. In his early years, he was given family instructions, and at a young age, he was gradually edified by the teaching [of Buddhism] he received.[75]

He proceeded to elucidate his rationale for embracing Mahāyāna Buddhism, on which the Tiantai school was based:

> Without deigning to follow the twists and turns of the narrow path (i.e., Hīnayāna Buddhism), I aspire to travel leisurely on the Great Vehicle. Laughing at the idea of entering the transformed city,[76] I pledge myself to sail by boat to the other shore. Of the myriad deeds accomplished by the enlightened,[77] the good practice of keeping the commandments comes first. Concerning these ten commandments of Bodhisattva, the most important is to focus single-mindedly on them.[78]

This passage not only demonstrates his fundamental belief in Buddhism for obvious, soteriological and transcendental reasons, but also his preference for the Mahāyāna over the Theravāda. This is followed by an allusion to the powers of the founders of the three dominant "religions," namely, Confucianism, Daoism, and Buddhism:

> To give advice on building a palace, one must rely on the foundation. If merely the empty frame is set up, eventually [the structure] will not be erected. Do not give consideration to the mediocre and the obtuse, and you may learn thus: "Confucius, Laozi and Śakyamuni can all help in molding [one's spirit]. [But] without proper ritual, what can I rely upon?"

At the close of the ritual, Zhiyi conferred upon Yangdi the clerical title *zongchi* 總持 (*dhāraṇī*) bodhisattva (Protector General Bodhisattva).[79] In return, Yangdi granted Zhiyi the title Zhizhe 智者 (the Wise One).[80] The ritual ceremony served to reaffirm Yangdi's faith in the Buddha.

The fact that Yangdi displayed such a strong religious conviction is not surprising, considering that all his close family members—his father, mother, and four brothers—were Buddhist believers.[81] The Buddhist master of the ceremony, Zhiyi, who had been a most favored Buddhist priest of the Chen court, was no stranger to the Yang family. Yangdi's father had written a respectful letter to him in the wake of the Sui conquest of Chen in 589, in which he pledged to advance the cause of Buddhism in the South, and appealed to Zhiyi for cooperation.[82] But before long the Sui policy of pacification was in grave danger as a consequence of widespread rebellions in the South under its inept administrator, Yang Jun, Yangdi's brother.[83]

Yangdi's participation in the *pusa jie* ritual so soon after his appointment as the Sui governor of the South can be viewed as an attempt to reinstate Sui religious policy; it would not have been possible without Wendi's permission. Despite his overall support for Buddhism, Wendi did not grant major religious requests of his offspring easily. Previously he had flatly rejected a proposal submitted by Yang Jun to become a monk.[84]

In contrast to his father, who had attempted to cajole Zhiyi to rally religious forces to support the Sui cause, Yangdi acted out the role of a faithful disciple of Zhiyi, and symbolically subjected himself to the religious authority of the most respected clergyman of the Buddhist community in the newly conquered territory of the former Chen.

In view of Yangdi's later transgressions against the established moral norms of Buddhism, it is not unreasonable to look for ulterior motives behind his participation in this Buddhist ritual. Arthur Wright calls attention to a visit Yangdi paid to his mother in the capital. Allegedly, this visit took place before he departed for his post in the South.[85] During the visit, Yangdi became aware of his mother's displeasure with Yang Yong. Wright also hints at a possible connection between Yangdi's ambition to replace the sitting crown prince and his active involvement in Buddhism in the South. Yangdi's true intention was to ingratiate himself to his parents under the disguise of religious piety. However, extant evidence suggests Yangdi may have made the visit to his mother after he had settled in the South. If that was the case, much of his pro-Buddhist activity, including his participation in the *pusa jie* ceremony, may have already taken place before he realized the rift between his mother and elder brother. Thus, his visit should not be linked to a hidden agenda to unseat his brother.[86]

Regardless of Yangdi's political motivation, his association with Zhiyi blossomed into a lasting friendship that was strengthened by a common religious bond. In the tenth month of 597, Zhiyi, on a summons from Yangdi, started his journey for Jiangdu, but he fell seriously ill en route in the eleventh month. He wrote his will addressed to Yangdi, and died soon after. When Zhiyi's disciple Guanding 灌頂 delivered the will and a few mementos, a tearful Yangdi, overcome by sorrow, prostrated himself in front of these precious objects. On Yangdi's orders, his lieutenant Wang Hong escorted Guanding back to the Tiantai Mountains, where a Thousand Monk Vegetarian Feast was held in honor of Zhiyi and a Tiantai (Guoqing 國清) Monastery was set up in accord with Zhiyi's last wishes.[87] Lamenting Zhiyi's passing, Yangdi wrote a long letter, in which he says, "I bow to his spirit image from afar with a heartfelt sorrow."[88]

Three years after Zhiyi's death, upon appointment as heir apparent in the eleventh month of 600, Yangdi left the South to take up residence in the capital. But he continued to maintain close relations with the Tiantai school. As crown prince, he visited the former Chen territory and was met by Guanding, who joined others in congratulating him. Later, as envoy of the Tiantai school, Guanding visited Yangdi again in Daxingcheng to personally thank him for the establishment of the Tiantai Monastery. Thanks to Zhiyi's dominant influence at the Jiangdu Huiri, Yangdi's favorite, Guanding, who had been Zhiyi's best student, was eventually invited to reside in Daxingcheng in 602.[89]

After his enthronement, Yangdi visited Jiangdu in the South in the ninth month of 605, and granted an audience there to Zhizao 智璪, another Tiantai envoy. At Zhizao's suggestion, the Tiantai Monastery was rechristened Guoqing 國清 (country pacified), inspired by a prophesy revealed by the meditation master Dingguang 定光 to Zhizao in his dream. Yangdi sent his men to deliver and set up the monastery's new nameplate, and requested the high official Liu Guyan 柳顧言 to erect a stone tablet at the entrance of the monastery in memory of Zhiyi. The twenty-fourth of the eleventh month, the date of Zhiyi's passing, was then declared his memorial day. A Thousand Monk Vegetarian Feast was held for the occasion. In 611, while Yangdi was resident in Zhuo Commandery, preparing for his military campaign against the Koguryŏ, he summoned Guanding to his residence where they reminisced about the old days when they were fellow students under their common master Zhiyi.[90]

These records attest to the continued harmonious relations between Yangdi and Tiantai after Zhiyi's death and Yangdi's enthronement. Later, when scholars condemned Yangdi as an evil ruler and faulted him for the fall of the Sui dynasty, followers of Tiantai felt obligated to defend its founder Zhiyi, whom Yangdi had befriended:

It is said that although Yangdi by learning the Buddhist commandments became wise, he committed patricide to usurp power. How come the Wise One (Zhiyi) had no premonition of it? But if we compare it with the case of King Ajātaśatru (Shewang 闍王 or Asheshi 阿闍世),[91] our doubt simply disappears by itself. Therefore, we can identify two points from the sūtra and its commentary:[92] First, [Wendi and his son Yangdi] were destined by the enmity in their prior lives to become father and son. That is why Ajātaśatru was known as the "enemy that has yet to be born (*weisheng yuan* 未生怨)."[93] Second, contumacy involving royal power cannot be compared with vicious contumacy at the popular level. Thus speaks the Buddha, "Thanks to the awakening of his mind in the past while in search of bodhi (enlightenment) in front of the Vipaśyin (Piposhi 毘婆尸) Buddha,[94] [Ajātaśatru] did not go to hell."[95]

This passage, written by Zhipan 志磐, a leading Tiantai scholar of the Song dynasty, treats Yangdi the sovereign more kindly than most traditional accounts. It inspires Chen Yinke to conclude that Yangdi occupied an elevated place in Buddhist circles, which stands in sharp contrast with the Confucian assessment of him.[96] There is no question about the gratitude the Southern clergy felt towards Yangdi's patronage of Buddhism. However, by making the Ajātaśatru analogy and stressing the complexity of the situation when royal power was involved, Zhipan was more interested in protecting Zhiyi's reputation than exonerating Yangdi. To Zhipan, the fact that in death, Yangdi received the censorious posthumous title *yang*, the same one that he had given the Chen ex-emperor Houzhu 後主 (Chen Shubao 陳叔寶), was an indication of karmic retribution.[97]

The Tang *śramaṇa* Shenqing 神清 offers a typical Buddhist judgment in the post-Sui era when he says, "Considering the great stability under Heaven during the reigns of Renshou (601–604) and Kaihuang (581–600), [Wendi] can also be said to have succeeded with the greatest virtue. However, his wisdom did not see far into the future. His beloved son [Yangdi] was unvirtuous, and consequently the dynastic line did not last for long."[98] Although milder than the traditionalist verdict on Yangdi, this view still holds Yangdi's moral turpitude responsible for the fall of the Sui dynasty.

Whatever the verdict by the Buddhist community on Yangdi as a patron of Buddhism, all evidence points to his close ties with the clergy during his tenure as the top Sui leader of the South. But those ties were soon put to the test after his enthronement. In the first major crisis of his reign, the Yang Liang rebellion in the Bing area, the rebels used the Xingguo Monastery 興國寺 as their armory. After General Yang Su crushed the rebellion, he wanted to prosecute the monks of that monastery as accomplices to the rebels, but Yangdi intervened to pardon them. Since the rebellion was up to that time the most serious challenge to Yangdi's usurpation of power, he was unlikely to treat it lightly. The fact that he was lenient with the monks probably indicates a reluctance to alienate the Buddhist community.[99] However, despite his continued support for Buddhism, over time he grew assertive of his temporal power in dealing with the clergy. Apart from suppressing a number of Buddhism-inspired rebellions, particularly those based on the popular belief in Maitreya the future Buddha, Yangdi took the initiative to challenge the clerical authority of the church repeatedly.[100] On one important winter ritual occasion in 606, Yangdi issued an edict that Buddhist monks and Daoist adepts should both reverence lay [authority]. Buddhist sources record the reaction of the religious communities:

> None of the Daoist adepts dared raise their voice. The Buddhist monks as usual declined to act upon the edict. The emperor questioned them, "The edict was issued a long time ago. Why do you refuse to obey it?" Then the dharma master Mingzhan 明瞻 answered, "If Your Majesty abolishes the Way (Buddhism) according to law, how dare yours truly not comply with it? If it is known that the Great Law [of the Buddha] should be revered, the monks in dharma garments have no ritual obligation to worship lay deities." The emperor said, "Why did you reverence Northern Zhou Wudi?" Mingzhan said, "Northern Zhou Wudi indulged in intimidation and violence, and did not act in accord with benevolence and virtue. His example is not worth following by a sovereign. Your Majesty exercises sacred government with a focus on benevolence, and never wrongs the innocent. That is why this poor monk can unreservedly speak out his loyal advice." The emperor gave up without a word. Officials wanted to press charges against Mingzhan for his confrontational stand. Mingzhan replied, "The only person who has committed the offense is myself. Hopefully, my disciples will not be charged with unlawfulness." The emperor admired his courage, and chose to ignore the case. From this point on, debates about venerating the sovereign died out.[101]

The issue of subjecting the clergy to temporal authority was an extremely sensitive one. The reason it had not surfaced during the previous reign was probably that Wendi, out of his respect for the religion, may have granted the clergy the privilege not to bow to the sovereign.[102] At any rate, by Yangdi's time, it had become an established convention. Yangdi wanted to revert to an old pre-Sui practice. However, forcing the clergy to venerate laypersons was considered a serious infringement on religious independence, and Yangdi eventually had to give in to the clergy's opposition.[103]

In 609, Yangdi made another attempt to rein in the Buddhist church. In an edict, "[He] ordered that, of all Buddhist monks under Heaven, those without virtuous achievements be laicized. Monasteries are to be preserved based on the number of their monks. The others are to be demolished."[104] This edict prompted one of Zhiyi's disciples, the Chan master Dazhi 大志 of Lushan, to take action:

> [Dazhi], dressed in white mourning attire, cried in front of the Buddha [statue] for three days, vowing to sacrifice his life to illuminate the Way [of the Buddha]. Arriving in the Eastern Capital, he sent in a *biao* 表-memorial: "[I] implore His Majesty to greatly promote the Three Jewels. This poor monk would burn his arm to express his gratitude to the state." The emperor respectfully granted his wish. [Dazhi] wrapped up one arm with a piece of cloth, covered it with wax, and then ascended to a large shed where he took up a ritual sitting position. Thereupon, [he] set his arm on fire. After the burning was over, [he] entered into a state of tranquility, and died in seven days in the cross-legged lotus position. From then on, in spite of its promulgation, the edict was not enforced.[105]

In reality, the 609 edict was the reinstatement of a similar policy introduced in the South during the previous reign. Not only was Wendi not the formulator of the policy, but he also stopped it in its tracks after Huijue voiced his opposition. In contrast, Yangdi, as author of the 609 edict, refused to revoke it even when Dazhi threatened self-immolation. Yangdi eventually gave in only after the martyrdom of the Chan master. However, that did not stop Yangdi from encroaching on church authority.

Two years later in 611, Yangdi carried out a major campaign to abolish Buddhist monasteries in the capital area.[106] Table 8.4 shows that in that year alone at least twenty-two monasteries were shut down.[107] In addition, the closure of twelve more monasteries can be dated to Yangdi's reign. These thirty-four monasteries constituted about 28 percent of the one hundred and twenty Buddhist monasteries that had existed in the capital at the beginning of his reign (maps 4.2, 8.1) (table 8.4).[108]

What did Yangdi hope to gain by closing Buddhist cloisters? Was this attempt linked with an early attempt in 609? Should they be viewed in the context of a larger scheme, particularly, Yangdi's war preparedness against Koguryŏ?[109] Indeed, Yangdi may have targeted the church as a potential labor force of tens of thousands, even though he was notorious for his indifference to cost, human and otherwise. By the year 609, not only had Yangdi been preparing for war for quite some time, he had also undertaken a series of costly projects (table 9.1 in chapter 9). A record in the *Sui shu* illustrates the situation well: By the time the Yongji Canal project was underway in 608, male laborers were in such short supply that female substitutes had to be used.[110] Yangdi's ambitious military campaign to conquer Koguryŏ had yet to begin, and labor shortages had already become a serious problem. Under these

TABLE 8.4    Buddhist monasteries in Daxingcheng abolished by Yangdi

| No. | Name | Location (fang 坊) in Daxingcheng | Time of abolition | |
|---|---|---|---|---|
| | | | 611 | 605–618 |
| 1. | Bao'an 寶岸 | Jude 居德 (4A) | | x |
| 2. | Baowang 寶王 | Qunxian 群賢 (5A) | x | |
| 3. | Changfa 常法 | Guangde 光德 (6C) | x | |
| 4. | Chengdao 成道 | Xinghua 興化 (7D) | x | |
| 5. | Chengjue 澄覺 | Banzheng 頒政 (3C) | x | |
| 6. | Chongjing 崇敬 | Jing'an 靖安 (9G) | | x |
| 7. | Daojue 道覺* | Longheng 隆政 (4C) | | x |
| 8. | Fabao 法寶 | Huaiyuan 懷遠 (7B) | x | |
| 9. | Fashen 法身 | Qunxian 群賢 (5A) | x | |
| 10. | Fazhong 法眾 | Jincheng 金城 (3B) | x | |
| 11. | Guangbao 法眾 | Liquan 醴泉 (4B) | | x |
| 12. | Honghua 宏化 | Lizheng 立政 (11J) | x | |
| 13. | Huchi 護持 | Daozheng 道政 (5J) | x | |
| 14. | Huijue 惠覺 | Yanshou 延壽 (5C) | x | |
| 15. | Huiyun 惠雲 | Banzheng 頒政 (3C) | x | |
| 16. | Jiudu 救度 | Liquan 醴泉 (4B) | | x |
| 17. | Mingfa 明法* | Longzheng 隆政 (4C) | | x |
| 18. | Mingjue 明覺 | Yongning 永寧 (8H) | x | |
| 19. | Minglun 明輪 | Yankang 延康 (7C) | x | |
| 20. | Ningguan 凝觀 | Jude 居德 (4A) | | x |
| 21. | Renfa 仁法 | Yongchang 永昌 (2H) | x | |
| 22. | Rongjue 融覺* | Chongxian 崇賢 (8C) | | x |
| 23. | Shanguo 善果 | Yongxing 永興 (3H) | | x |
| 24. | Shengjing 聖敬 | Guangfu 光福 (8F) | x | |
| 25. | Shentong 神通 | Yanfu 延福 (9C) | x | |
| 26. | Shifan 釋梵 | Jincheng 金城 (3B) | x | |
| 27. | Tongfa 通法 | Xiuhua 修華 (10I) | x | |
| 28. | Xianghai 香海 | Xianguo 顯國 (10H) | x | |
| 29. | Xianjue 賢覺* | Chongxian 崇賢 (8C) | | x |
| 30. | Xingdao 興道 | Jinchang 進昌 (11H) | x | |
| 31. | Yifa 依法 | Jude 居德 (4A) | | x |
| 32. | Yuanjue 緣覺* | Chongxian 崇賢 (8C) | | x |
| 33. | Yuanli 願力 | Guang'en 廣恩 (8B) | x | |
| 34. | Zonghua 總化 | Anxing 安興 (3I) | x | |

Source: Ono 1989, *Shiryō hen*: 453–70.

*CAZ (10.2–3) places the abolition of Daojue, Mingfa, Rongjue, Xianjue, and Yuanjue in the Daye and Wude (618–626) reigns.

circumstances, even Yangdi may have been tempted to tap into the Buddhist community. But to meaningfully alleviate the labor problem required massive laicization, and that did not take place under Yangdi. Obviously, the measure he took against the Buddhist community was unlikely to have much of an impact on the economy.[111]

Whatever its practical implications, Yangdi's move to reduce the number of monasteries, like his attempt to force the clergy to reverence the throne, served the fundamental purpose of subjecting church authority to temporal power. Prior to 611, on every occasion Yangdi was forced to soften his position due to the clergy's opposition and his unwillingness to antagonize the Buddhist community. However, the abolition of monasteries in 611, and other monastic closures thereafter in the capital, testify to Yangdi's major success in controlling the clergy. Judging from the scale of this effort in the affected area, it may also have been part of a larger nationwide campaign.

The age of the Sui was dominated by the powerful religious forces of Daoism and Buddhism. Although Wendi was responsible for the revival of both, he expressly regarded Daoism as a lesser religion. Yet convinced of its spiritual powers, he showed due reverence to Daoism, patronizing such famed Daoists as the Louguan master Wang Yan of the North. Yangdi continued with his father's pro-Daoist policy, but was more closely associated with the Shangqing school of the South. It is his patronage that laid the groundwork for its continued ascendancy in Early Tang times.[112]

Both Wendi and Yangdi believed in the potency of certain occult elements of Daoism. On the whole, Yangdi seemed to have a much greater involvement in occultism, as was evidenced by his numerous attempts to seek divine protection and immortality with the assistance of spirit mediums of Daoist and other religious affiliations, and by his intense interest in certain supernatural elements of Buddhism.

For all the attraction Daoism held for father and son, without doubt Buddhism was their primary religion. Having just survived the second major proscription campaign in Chinese history under the Northern Zhou, Buddhism, under the auspices of Wendi, entered the initial phase of a prolonged renaissance. A devout follower of Buddhism, Wendi gave expression to his faith by action, passionately sponsoring monastic institutions and icons and vigorously lending support to the clergy.

Brought up in a Buddhist family, Yangdi was a believer in the religion all his life. While an imperial prince, he participated in the *pusa jie* ritual and cultivated a personal relationship with the most famous monk in the South. Although these developments would certainly enhance his image as an exemplary son of the Yang family and strengthen his position in his bid for the post of the crown prince,[113] existing evidence suggests that religious piety rather than personal ambition was the prime reason for Yangdi's close association with the Buddhist community.

Like his father, Yangdi pursued a pro-Buddhist policy. But he also chose to be different from his father in dealing with the clergy. In addressing the sensitive issue of court-clergy relations, Wendi, in spite of his penchant for political manipulation, primarily adopted an accommodationist approach. Yangdi, on the other hand, was more willing to impose political oversight on church authority than his predecessor, and was more likely to strain his relationship with the Buddhist clergy.

While extant sources have not registered major confrontations between Wendi and the clergy, anecdotal records and circumstantial evidence indicate that Yangdi clashed with the church on the issues of forcing the clerics to pay homage to the lay sovereign, reducing the size of the clergy, and closing monasteries. These conflicts inevitably tarnished his reputation as follower and patron of Buddhism. Still, in the overall judgment of some traditional Buddhist scholars, Yangdi was "reverential and consistent, and from beginning to end without lapses" in his treatment of Buddhism.[114]

# 9

---

# Economic Order

A complex economic system was developed under Wendi to store and transport grain reserves, distribute land resources, collect taxes, levy corvée duty, and monitor the population. It worked relatively well throughout the first reign. The treasury coffer was full when Yangdi took over. Although Yangdi essentially did not overhaul his father's economic system, the economy deteriorated on his watch, spelling the doom of the dynasty. What set Yangdi apart from his father in economic policy? What were the fatal steps that triggered the downward economic spiral? Why did Yangdi fail so miserably to reverse the situation? With these questions in mind, we will examine the Sui economic system—from inception to maturation, to its final collapse—and its legacy.

## MONEY, WEIGHTS, AND MEASURES

We begin with a brief introduction to various standard instruments for measuring the performance of the economy: coinage, units of weight, and mass and length measurements.

### Money

The monetary system of the Sui was underdeveloped, in large part, because of the long-term impact of the collapse of the money economy following the fall of the Han dynasty. During the pre-495 period under the Northern Wei, for quite some time coinage was completely withdrawn from circulation. Even though the minting of coins was resumed under Xiaowendi 孝文帝 in 495, money only accounted for a miniscule part of the economy of the North. In the South, the monetary situation was much better. Still, commodities such as silk and cotton cloth, rather than coin money, were the preferred medium of business transactions.[1] The situation persisted throughout the Sui when grain and textile instead of money were received as main government revenues.

At the beginning of the Sui, lack of uniform standards was the most conspicuous problem of the monetary system. Three types of Northern Zhou coins—*yongtong wanguo* 永通萬國, *wuxing dabu* 五行大布 (large spade), and *wuzhu* 五銖—and coins of Northern Qi mintage were in circulation.[2] Wendi then created his own standard currency, which, lettered with the characters *wuzhu* on its face, is referred to in history as the Sui *wuzhu*. This was followed by a series of edicts aimed at phasing out coinages of pre-Sui vintage. By 585, these efforts began to pay off and the monetary system was standardized. As the top Sui leader in the South, Yangdi was ordered by his father to set up five furnaces to manufacture coins in Yangzhou. Aware of the inadequate money supply in the South, he requested that furnaces be set up at copper mines in E Prefecture 鄂州 (with its seat in Wuchang, Hubei). At that time, Yangdi was familiar with the process of coin production, and understood its significance to the economy. But as emperor, he soon lost control of the government's monopoly on mintage. As private minting became rampant, the weight of the coin deteriorated noticeably. The standard weight of 1,000 cash declined under Yangdi from 4 *jin* 斤 2 *liang* 兩 (pre-607) or 2,756 grams,[3] first to 2 *jin* (post-607) or 445 grams, then to 1 *jin* (post-607) or 223 grams—less than one twelfth of the standard. Coins made of sheet iron, leather, and paper were in circulation.[4] The deterioration of numismatic standards in weight and metal content is a telltale sign of a weakened economy and this was clearly the case in Yangdi's reign. The debasement of coins that started in late-Sui times, compounded by the rise in commodity values, resulted in runaway inflation that continued well into Early Tang times.[5]

## Weights and Measures

Standardized weights and measures were essential for the formulation and implementation of land and tax statutes. On the basis of the system of the South, Wendi tripled the sizes of the capacity measure *sheng* 升 and the weight measure *jin* to 594.4 ml and 668.19 g, respectively, while keeping the length measure *chi* unchanged at 29.51 cm.

Not long after accession, Yangdi announced sweeping changes to his father's system in 607. The capacity and weight measures reverted to the pre-

Sui standards of the South and were reduced by two thirds to 198.1 ml and 222.73 g, respectively, while the length measure shrank to 23.55 cm. It is not known how widely Yangdi's new, shorter length measure was accepted. There is evidence that Wendi's measure continued to be in private use. At any rate, the adoption of the shorter length measure also translated into a smaller *mu* 畝, the standard area measure. It was reduced by more than one-third from approximately 752 m² to 479 m².[6]

If no adjustments were made to existing tax statutes, these changes seemed to benefit the populace more than the government. While a smaller *mu* could mean smaller future land allotments to taxpayers, it did not matter to land grants already made unless they were reassessed nationwide according to new standards, which does not seem to have happened. On the other hand, a smaller capacity measure would translate into smaller tax payments in grain. What were Yangdi's reasons for introducing these changes if profit was not one of them? The answer may be sought in one of his edicts in the fourth month of 607, which ordained that weights and measures be reformed, both according to ancient rules. So a desire to restore previous standards was the apparent reason for the reform in weights and measures, which was obviously part of Yangdi's overall endeavor to create his own identity.[7] The fact that the so-called ancient rules were essentially those of the Liang and Chen suggests his deliberate attempt to follow the Southern conventions in altering his father's system.

## GRANARIES

Immeasurably more significant for the Sui economy than coinage and measurement standards was grain. For purposes of storage and distribution, an extensive granary network took shape under the first Sui sovereign that continued to grow and mature under the following Tang dynasty. Much better documented than its Sui predecessor, the Tang grain storage system was composed of a variety of granaries: transportation granaries (*zhuanyun cang*), capital granaries, price-regulating granaries (*changping cang*), charitable granaries (*yicang*), regular granaries (*zhengcang*), and army granaries (*juncang*). It is believed that all six types of granaries were in operation under the Sui.[8]

### Transportation Granaries (*zhuanyun cang* 轉運倉)

This term was concocted by modern historians who combined the expression *zhuanyun* (transportation) with *cang* (granaries) to refer to a particular type of riparian storage facility in premodern times where grains were temporarily held before shipped out to various destinations. The first Sui network of transportation granaries was built in 583 by Wendi. As is recorded in the *Sui shu*, Wendi

> set up the Liyang Granary 黎陽倉 (southeast of Xun County, Henan) in Wei Prefecture 衛州, the Heyang Granary 河陽倉 in Luo Prefecture 洛州 (seat: Luoyang, Henan), the Changping Granary 常平倉 (west of Sanmenxia, Henan) in Shan Prefecture 陜州, and the Guangtong Granary 廣通倉 (northeast of Tongguan, Shaanxi) in Hua Prefecture 華州. [Grains] were shipped from one granary to another. Millet was transported from Guandong 關東 (Henan), Fen 汾, and Jin 晉 (Shanxi) to support the capital.[9]

The establishment of this network of granaries was part of a larger strategy to reform economic policy following the building and settlement of the new capital. The main purpose was to guarantee a constant supply of grains to meet the needs of its population.[10]

To expedite transportation of grain from the East, Wendi offered a special arrangement for grain transporters, whereby if an adult laborer transported forty *shi* 石 (*hu* 斛; 1 pre-607 *shi* is 59.44 lit.) of rice from Luoyang to the Changping Granary in Shan Prefecture (near present-day Sanmenxia), he would be exempt from garrison duties. But the buildup of silt in the section of the Wei River that connected the capital to the Yellow River made navigation extremely difficult. Consequently, Wendi ordered the construction of a new east-west waterway, the Guangtong Canal, as an alternate route to the Wei River.[11] The canal would greatly facilitate grain delivery from the East to the capital.

Yangdi added two super-size granaries in the Luoyang area in 606 to the grain transportation system: Luokou 洛口 (Xingluo 興洛) and Huiluo 迴洛. Located east of present-day Gong County, Henan, Luokou was composed of three thousand silos, each with a capacity of over eight thousand *shi*. The total capacity was twenty-four million *shi*. The storage area was enclosed by a ring of granary wall more than twenty *li* long (10.6 km). About one thousand personnel served as supervising officers and security troops.

Much smaller in capacity but still gigantic was the Huiluo Granary, set up by the end of the same year immediately north of Luoyang. Composed of three hundred silos, Huiluo was enclosed with a ring of wall about ten *li* (5.3 km) in length.[12] Assuming that each silo had a capacity of eight thousand *shi*, the total capacity of Huiluo would be 2.4 million *shi*, or one tenth of that of Luokou.

These super-size granaries began to play an increasingly significant role in the economy, as Yangdi shifted political and economic foci to the East and the South with the construction of the Eastern Capital at Luoyang and the digging of the Grand Canal.

## Capital Granaries

The first capital granary was the Grand Granary (*taicang* 太倉)[13] located in Daxingcheng, the main supplier of grains to the capital. Each month it delivered a set amount of grain as emolument to the court, central government agencies, the capital administration in Daxingcheng, and various personnel working and studying under contract with the government, as well as their dependents. It was governed by the Court of the National Granaries (*sinong si* 司農寺) through the bureaucratic office known as the *taicang shu* 太倉署 (Grand Granary Administration), which had two directors (*ling* 令) who ranked the same as the magistrate of a lower county (rank 8a). Under the directors were two rice storage supervisors (*milin du* 米廩督), four grain storage supervisors (*gucang du* 穀倉督), and two salt storage supervisors (*yancang du* 鹽倉督).[14] The granary's capacity was in the range of millions to ten millions of *shi*.[15]

With the creation of the Eastern Capital, Yangdi ordered the construction there of the Hanjia Granary 含嘉倉, northeast of the palace area and north of the Eastern City (map 5.1).[16] As the main grain storage facility of Luoyang and one of the few super-size granaries, Hanjia can be regarded as the second capital granary. Textual or archaeological evidence of Hanjia in Sui times is scanty. By comparison, there is much more information on the Tang period. Recent archaeological research discovered over four hundred subterranean silos of Tang vintage at the site. Epigraphic information unearthed from the silos reveals a complicated administrative system at work during the Tang with at least sixteen bureaucratic posts, both civil and military.[17] Like the Grand Granary, Hanjia in Tang times was under the jurisdiction of the Grand Granary Administration, one of whose functions was to provide grains, through the capital granaries, to central government agencies and the two capital administrations in Daxingcheng and Luoyang.[18] The administration and functions of Hanjia under Yangdi were probably similar.

## Price-regulating Granaries (*changping cang* 常平倉)

Establishment of government controlled price-stabilizing granaries was an ancient concept, traceable to the work of Guanzi 管子. The idea was to buy grains at a higher price when the market was down and to sell them at a lower price when the market was up.

During Wendi's reign, a central government agency called the "Inspectorate of Price-regulating Granaries" (*changping jian* 常平監) was set up in 583. In the same year, in Shan Prefecture 陝州, a super size granary known as Changping Granary (price-regulating granary) was built. Without doubt, it was so named because of its primary function of stabilizing grain prices. However, it also functioned as a transportation granary in Wendi's strategic network of grain shipment.[19]

## Charitable Granaries

In Sui times, the term "charitable granary" (*yicang* 義倉) was interchangeable with the term "community granary" (*shecang* 社倉). Both types of granaries served the purpose of supporting local populations in times of need and both made their debut during the Sui dynasty.

In 585, in response to the request of President of the Board of Work Zhangsun Ping 長孫平 for building up grain reserves for famine relief:

a decree was issued to civilians and military personnel in various prefectures, whereby they were urged to contribute to their local communities in a common effort to set up charitable granaries. At the time of harvest, they were encouraged to contribute as their share either millet or wheat, depending on what they harvested, for storage in granaries to be constructed in the local communities. Granary administrators were responsible for their book-keeping and inspection, accumulating grains annually, and making sure they would not rot. At the time of a poor harvest or famine in the community, the grain would be used to provide relief.[20]

Because they were scattered at the grassroots level, the charitable granaries were probably not well-managed. In 595, Wendi issued an edict requesting that grains of charitable granaries in a number of Northwestern prefectures be transferred to the local prefectural authorities. A 596 edict emphatically demanded that in some other Northwestern prefectures, community (charitable) granaries should be located at the county level. This was followed by a mandatory community granary tax levied on various households based on assets.[21] By this time, the charitable granary had lost its meaning as a community-based granary supported by grains contributed by local residents. The administration of these granaries was taken over by higher level governments, and a mandatory poll tax replaced loosely regulated donations as the source of grain supply.

Sui Yangdi continued the charitable (community) granary system developed under his father. But when the financial situation deteriorated, the government started appropriating grain reserves in these granaries for official purposes until the system collapsed.[22]

## Other Types of Granaries

Other types that may have existed in Sui times include regular granaries (*zhengcang* 正倉) and army granaries (*juncang* 軍倉). Regular granaries were county and prefectural government granaries responsible for receiving and storing tax grains, and for providing grains for famine relief and official salaries. The use of the term can be traced as far back as the Early Tang. Its prototype must have existed much earlier although it cannot be positively identified during the Sui period in extant sources.[23]

The term *juncang* was used in the Turfan documents of the Tang dynasty. Its usage under the Sui is unclear. However, one extant source records that in Yulin 榆林 County (seat: southwest of Togtoh, Inner Mongolia), Wendi dug the Pinghe River 平河 which allowed *tuncang* 屯倉 (garrison granaries) access to the Yellow River. Since garrison granaries were storage facilities for military units, they may be regarded as the forerunners of Tang army granaries.[24]

## Strategic Importance

Despite government abuse of the charitable granary system towards the end of the second reign, official granaries on the whole were relatively untouched. The Liyang Granary, for example, contained a plentiful supply of grains when the Henan and Shandong areas were hit by floods and famines.[25] Thanks to the strict laws regulating the use of official grain reserves, officials in charge did not want to open the granaries without proper authorization to feed the starving masses, who, huddled in fortified villages, were reduced to cannibalism.[26] When the two great granaries near Luoyang—Huiluo and Luokou—were lost to the rebel leader Li Mi, they were still relatively intact. Their seemingly inexhaustible grain supply not only enabled Li to feed his rebel army of a million but also allowed him to attract the poor and needy to his anti-Sui cause with free grain.[27] The loss of these two granaries was a devastating blow to the Sui. In consequence, Yangdi lost any hope of recovering the North, and Luoyang, cut off from these granaries, soon exhausted its food supply.[28] The city of Daxingcheng faced a similar situation; only relief grains from the nearby Yongfeng 永豐 (Guangtong) Granary (northeast of Tongguan, Shaanxi) in

Huayin 華陰 County provided by another rebel leader, Li Yuan, saved the city
from the fate of Luoyang.[29]

As a key component of the economic infrastructure of the Sui, the granary
system played a decisive role in provisioning large metropolitan centers such
as Daxingcheng and Luoyang, and in providing famine relief in times of war
and natural disaster. During the late-Sui civil war, major granaries became foci
of contention precisely because they held the key to economic survival and
military victory in strategic areas such as the Central Plain and Guanzhong.

## The Equal-field System

The existence of an extensive complex granary network in Sui China brought
into focus the most important commodity of the economy—grains. Needless
to say, for an agrarian society with an inadequately developed monetary system
like Sui China, grain production was the essential economic activity and land
ownership was a crucial aspect of the economic system. The prevailing land
tenure system of the Sui was the *juntian zhi* 均田制 or equal-field system,
aimed at equitable distribution of arable lands.[30] First introduced in North
China under the Northern Wei in 485, the system continued under the Northern Qi and Northern Zhou.

Essential for the implementation of the equal-field system was a legally
defined, precise population classification system. Wendi, upon founding the
Sui dynasty, promulgated statutes to set new standards for it in 582:

> Both males and females under the age of three (two) are termed
> "infants" (*huang* 黃); under ten (nine), "children" (*xiao* 小); under sev-
> enteen (sixteen), "adolescents" (*zhong* 中); over eighteen (seventeen),
> "adults" (*ding* 丁). The adults are subject to tax levies and corvée. At
> sixty (fifty-nine), one becomes "elderly" (*lao* 老), and will be exempt.[31]

The 582 statutes also governed the equal-field system itself:

> From various princes down to area commanders (*dudu* 都督), all are
> granted inheritable (*yongye* 永業) lands in sizes ranging from 100
> *qing* 頃 to 40 *mu*. As for adult males (*dingnan* 丁男) and adolescent
> males (*zhongnan* 丁男), their inheritable lands and open (*lu* 露) fields
> are both based on the practice of the Northern Qi. In addition, a tax
> is imposed on mulberry, elm, and date trees. As for lands for gardens
> and housing, for every three household members, 1 *mu* will be
> granted. As for [lands for gardens and housing for] bondservants
> (*nubi* 奴婢), for every five of them, 1 *mu* will be granted.[32]

Here, the key elements in the Sui equal-field system were the two population categories—adults and adolescents (whose upper age limit was extended to 20 in 583, and to 21 under Yangdi). They received the largest share of the land grants among those with no official rank or title. The 582 statutes contain the earliest records of land entitlements granted to adolescent males in extant sources. But since the Northern Qi statutes, which are regarded as the prototype for the 582 statutes, do not record this rule, some scholars suspect that the 582 rule is an interpolation. In fact, the recorded Qi minimum age for receiving land grants was eighteen (seventeen), which was also the lower age limit for an adult. And that would disqualify all adolescents.[33] An opposing view argues that even though the extant Northern Qi statutes make no mention of the rule, it may still have been added within the same dynasty later, since the statutes were often subject to amendment.[34]

To properly understand the 582 statutes, let us examine the Northern Qi statutes of 564:

Each married man is granted 80 *mu* of open fields, and each married woman 40 *mu*. Bondservants' land grants are based on those of free persons. The maximum of [eligible] bondservants [per nonofficial household] is the same as that allowed for a [low-ranking] official household in the capital. . . . In addition, each adult is granted 20 *mu* of inheritable lands as mulberry fields.[35]

Further, a Sui record of 592 indicates that land grants were made to the elderly and children as well, albeit in smaller sizes.[36]

From these and other pieces of evidence we may infer that the following standards for land allocation in Sui times were set:

1. a married man is granted 80 *mu* of open fields;
2. a married woman is granted 40 *mu* of open fields;
3. a [married] adult male is granted 20 *mu* of inheritable lands as mulberry fields;[37]
4. an adolescent male receives land grants;
5. a bondservant receives the same land grants as a free person (except for lands for gardens and housing);
6. the elderly and children also received land grants.

Inadequate textual information makes it difficult to work out the precise Sui land allocation standards for unmarried adult males and adolescent males. The Tang land statutes in the Wude period (618–626) prescribe the same land quotas for adult males regardless of marital status and adolescent males. However, since the Sui statutes reduced taxes for unmarried adult males (*danding* 單丁) by half, it is reasonable to expect that they were entitled to only one half of the land quotas for married adult males.[38]

Taking into account variations in availability of land, a convention had been adopted from Northern Wei times to distinguish between restricted (*xiaxiang* 狹鄉) and unrestricted (*kuanxiang* 寬鄉) localities. The Tang land statutes of the Wude reign specified that those residing in a restricted locality should receive one half of the land they would have received in an unrestricted locality. Specifically, an adult male was entitled to 50 *mu* instead of 100 *mu* of land.[39] Sui standards for *xiaxiang* land grants were probably similar.

Because of the prescriptive nature of the statutes, the quotas they stipulated were, for most, always those of the best-case scenario, a scenario that rarely became reality, if at all. A 592 record actually testifies to a serious scarcity of land in restricted localities with a higher population density. Here an adult on average was granted 20 *mu*, which, even by *xiaxiang* standards, was still 30 *mu* short of his prescribed quota. The elderly and children received even less.[40]

The way these quotas were implemented are better understood if placed in the context of availability of lands for allocation at the national level. Unfortunately, that information is not reliably provided by the sources. It is true that the *Tong dian* does contain two figures for the total acreage of Sui China in two different periods. But these figures are misleading. The first figure is 19,404,267 *qing* for the year 589, and that is indicated as the figure of land allocations (*renken tian* 任墾田). The commentary says, "Based on the acreage allocated for cultivation (*dingken zhi shu* 定墾之數), every household on average possessed more than two *qing*." This figure, however, should not be accepted at face value. By comparison, for the year 740, the sources record a total acreage of 14,403,862 *qing*, which is not only smaller than the 589 figure (one pre-607 Sui *qing* was much larger than a Tang *qing*), but is also clearly labeled as "lands that ought to be granted."[41] The fact that the total acreage under cultivation in Republican China was much smaller than the 589 figure makes it even less credible.[42] In view of this, the 589 figure should refer to the hypothetical acreage needed to fill the equal-field quotas of the whole country rather than the actual national acreage.

The second figure of 55,854,040 *qing* for the Daye period (605–618) allegedly covered all cultivated lands. But the commentary to the *Tong dian* hastens to add, "Note that at that time, there were 8,907,536 households. On average, one household possessed more than 5 [*sic*] *qing* of cultivated lands. This is probably historically untrue."[43] Obviously, the Daye figure, which is much higher than the grossly exaggerated figure of 589, is erroneous, even though the size of a *mu* under Yangdi in the post-607 period was reduced to less than two-third of a pre-607 *mu*. At any rate, the statutory standards for the equal-field system in Sui times constituted the upper limits of land quotas, and judging by available data on Sui land ownership, the overwhelming majority of Sui households never came close to receiving the full amounts of their quotas.

# The Tax System

## Direct Taxes

Hand in hand with the Sui equal-field system was the tax system, the main purpose of which was to derive state revenues from taxpayers, primarily in the form of grains and textile. The 582 statutes stipulate the basic rules concerning taxes under the Sui:

> An adult male with full tax responsibility (*yichuang* 一牀) (married adult male) pays 3 *shi* of *su* 粟 -millet as a grain tax (*zu* 租). A cloth tax (*diao* 調) is levied in terms of fine or coarse silk in mulberry-growing areas, or in terms of hempen or silk cloth (*bujuan* 布絹) in hemp-growing areas. In the case of coarse silk cloth, 1 *pi* [per couple] should be paid in addition to 3 *liang* of silk floss. In the case of hempen cloth, 1 *duan* should be paid in addition to 3 *jin* of hemp.[44] Single adults, servants and bondservants pay only half the taxes. Nonrecipients of land grants are tax-exempt. In the case of bearers of official ranks or noble titles, filial sons, obedient grandsons, righteous husbands, and virtuous wives, both taxes and corvée are exempt.[45]

In the third month of 583, the annual payment of cloth tax was reduced from 1 *pi* to 2 *zhang*.[46]

Here, two kinds of direct taxes were levied—a grain tax and a cloth tax— which may be considered the primary taxes of Sui China. These statutes were issued at a time when the Sui was only in control of North China where millet was the staple food. As the Sui empire grew in size, with the annexation of the Later Liang and the Chen in the South, amendments must have been made to the 582 statutes to accommodate the rice growing areas. Under the Tang, in the southernmost area, Lingnan 嶺南, the taxation statutes levied the grain tax in terms of the local staple—rice. Since the provision regarding taxes in rice in the Tang statutes was written at the very beginning of the Tang dynasty in the Wude period (618–626), it was probably a carryover directly from the Sui.[47]

To figure out the impact of direct taxes in grain and in cloth on a married adult male, it is necessary to estimate his annual income. Sui economic data in this regard are almost nonexistent. I have to use the data of the Tang dynasty as the basis for my estimates, while assuming no major technological breakthroughs had significantly raised productivity.

A study by Han Guopan reveals that in Tang times, 1 *mu* of land of medium quality yielded 1 *shi* (*hu*) of grain (millet) a year. Since 1 pre-607 Sui *mu* was about 1.3 Tang *mu* (1 Tang *mu* = 580 m²), and 1 pre-607 Sui *hu* was the same as a Tang *hu*, the annual millet yield of 1 pre-607 *mu* was approximately 1.3 *hu*.

The full quotas of a married adult male were 80 *mu* of farm land (open fields) and 20 *mu* of mulberry fields. The income from sericulture supported by the mulberry fields is not yet quantifiable, based on extant literature. But the per unit yield of the mulberry fields should be worth at least twice that of the open fields. The 20 *mu* mulberry fields can be converted into 40 *mu* of farm land, and the total land grants in terms of farm land should be 120 *mu*. The annual grain production would be 156 *hu* (120 × 1.3). The amount of grain tax for the married adult male—3 *shi* (*hu*)—constituted only 1/52 of his annual grain production.

To estimate cloth taxes in terms of silk or hemp, I have made use of data recorded in the Turfan documents of the Tang dynasty. In the Tianbao period (742–756), 1 *pi* of raw silk was worth 450–470 cash, and 1 *liang* of silk floss was worth 40–60 cash. The cloth tax per couple under the Sui—1 *pi* of silk cloth plus 3 *liang* of silk floss—would be worth 610 cash (460 + 150). After the tax reduction act of 583, 230 cash worth of silk cloth (0.5 *pi*) plus 150 cash worth of silk floss, or 380 cash, was the value of the standard cloth tax payment.

At the time, the price for a *dou* of millet ranged from 27 to 32 cash or 270 to 320 cash per *hu* (with a medium price of 295 cash per *hu*) in Dunhuang. In other words, the Sui cloth tax of 380 cash was approximately equal to 1.29 *hu* of millet. Adding that to the grain tax of 3 *hu*, in all, the adult male had to pay out 4.29 *hu* of millet for his annual direct taxes, or a little more than 1/36 of his annual income under the most ideal situation. This figure, however, should probably be adjusted for temporal and geographical differences. First of all, from the beginning of the Sui to the end of the Tianbao period more than one hundred and fifty years elapsed. Second, the two areas in question—Turfan and Dunhuang—were in a remote northwestern frontier region, where prices may have differed somewhat from China proper. Still, the Tianbao period was one of economic prosperity and low inflation, comparable to the Kaihuang period of Sui. So the estimates here may be justifiable so long as they are used to approximate the tax burden of a Sui family as a portion of its annual income, and not to establish its precise market value.[48]

Apart from the married adult male, a typical household usually had other types of land recipients, including his wife as married adult female, and unmarried adult males. Their land taxes should be based on their land grants and their tax rates should be similar to that of the married adult male. So their presence should not significantly change the tax rate of the entire household.

The *Sui shu* also records adolescent males (*zhongnan* 中男) as recipients of government land grants including *yongye tian* (inheritable lands) for permanent holding and *lutian* (open fields), following a Northern Qi convention.

Unlike in the case of adult males, the same record does not include them as providers of grain taxes and corvée labor at all. In view of this, adolescent males must have been either exempt from them or granted much lower tax and corvée obligations. Otherwise, the adolescent male category would be unnecessary.[49] Under the Northern Qi the age range for adolescents was sixteen to seventeen (fifteen to sixteen),[50] and under the Tang it was sixteen to twenty (fifteen to nineteen).[51] The Sui had the longest duration of the adolescent age range— nine years under Wendi, from eleven to twenty (ten to nineteen), and ten years under Yangdi, from eleven to twenty-one (ten to twenty)—of any dynasty that practiced the equal-field system.[52] Given the possibility that adolescent males paid low or zero taxes under the Sui equal-field system, the adolescent category may have constituted a major tax break offered by the state to taxpaying households. A longer adolescent period translated into greater benefits to the households, and higher cost to the government.

Our calculation of the Sui tax burden so far is based on the maximum amount of land a married adult male would receive under the law. To reflect the average land grant he was likely to receive, that amount has to be adjusted considerably downward. Furthermore, other fiscal impositions such as mandatory labor services have to be taken into consideration.

## Adjustments

In addition to the two direct taxes, annual corvée service was the third component of the Sui taxation system. Following a Northern Zhou convention, adult males were required to perform corvée service for a duration of one month each year at the beginning of the Sui. This practice was necessitated by the heavy use of labor during the construction of Daxingcheng. In 583, after Wendi moved into the newly completed capital, he reduced the mandatory corvée period to 20 days.[53] The same practice was later inherited by the Tang. But under the Tang statutes, corvée service and the grain and cloth taxes were also convertible. Fifteen days of corvée service was equal to the annual cloth tax for an adult while thirty days of corvée service was worth the grain and cloth taxes combined.[54] Based on the Tang conversion rates, and assuming that a Sui married adult male was obliged to pay about 4.29 *hu* of millet in direct taxes, the Sui corvée service of twenty days would be worth an additional 2.86 *hu* of millet (about two third of the grain and cloth taxes). The combination of the two amounted to 7.15 *hu* of millet.

In an edict issued in the second month of 596, Wendi endorsed a community granary (*shecang*) tax, which was virtually a household tax. It was levied at three different rates on three classes of households based on family assets— upper, middle, and lower.[55] Specifically, an upper household would pay up to

1 *shi* of grain, a middle household up to 0.7 *shi*, and a lower household up to 0.3 *shi*.[56] Assuming a married adult male was on average responsible for 50 percent of the land grants and taxes of his household, his share of the household tax would be 0.35 *shi* (50 percent of 0.7 *shi*, the additional tax on a middle household). Adding that to the existing tax payment of 7.15 *hu*, we get approximately 7.45 *hu* as the estimated overall tax payment per married adult male, or about 4.8 percent of his total annual income (156 *hu*).

A number of variables could change to significantly impact the tax situation of a married adult male and his household. Having a tax-exempt adolescent would certainly boost the household income. Land quality, productivity improvement, and climate could greatly affect annual outputs. However, the least predictable variable was the actual land grant size per person or household. The figures we have worked on were for the optimal situation in which the key member of the household was granted his full shares of land. The reality for an average adult male was quite different. As we have cited above, in 592, the average possession of lands per adult male was 20 *mu* in restricted localities. Assuming that 20 percent (4 *mu*) of the lands were mulberry fields with a double production value, the adjusted land size per adult would be 24 *mu* with an annual output of 31.2 *hu* (24 × 1.3). With a tax payment equal to 7.45 *hu*, the tax rate of the married adult male in a restricted locality was slightly less than 24 percent. Although this was five times the tax rate of someone who received his land grants in full, it was still tolerable.

Moreover, in prosperous years, the Sui sovereigns reduced taxes. In 597, for example, Wendi suspended regular taxes to pass on surplus in the treasury to his subjects.[57] Further, Wendi often remitted tax levies in areas affected by droughts or floods, in addition to providing government relief.[58]

After Yangdi ascended the throne, the Sui empire continued to enjoy population growth and economic prosperity. He too started instituting measures to reduce financial burdens, abolishing taxes (*ke* 課) for adult females and bondservants, and raising the age limit for adults from twenty-one (twenty) to twenty-two (twenty-one). Since only adults were required to pay direct taxes and perform corvée service, by raising the age limit for adults even by one year, Yangdi significantly eased the tax and corvée burdens of his subjects. Like his father, Yangdi also exempted taxpayers' tax obligations on an ad hoc basis. A case in point was his 606 edict, which, on the occasion of issuing a nationwide pardon of inmates from the Eastern Capital, declared a year-long tax exemption.[59]

## Corvée and Impressment

The state-levied recurrent taxes, based on extant sources, cannot be said to be excessive under normal circumstances. Indeed, anecdotal records indicate that as the economy improved steadily, the taxation system based on the equal-field system seems to have functioned smoothly under Wendi.[60] What eventually went wrong was not the direct taxes, but the institution of corvée labor, which was most susceptible to abuse by government.

From time to time, Wendi resorted to excessive use of corvée labor. After completing Daxingcheng on an unprecedented scale, he proceeded to build the Renshou Palace 仁壽 to its west in 593, an extremely costly project, where "the officers in charge of corvée labor were harsh and impatient; and many of the adult males (dingfu 丁夫) commandeered died." In 598, in the face of extensive flooding in the North, Wendi mobilized local adults (jinding 近丁) to dredge rivers.[61] For major public works projects like these, the standard corvée period of twenty days was obviously insufficient.

Wendi's use of corvée labor paled in comparison with his successor, Yangdi, who is notorious for his extensive construction projects. He began to abuse corvée labor almost immediately after he ascended the throne. In the eleventh month of 604, he mobilized tens of thousands of adult males around the Luoyang area to dig strategic trenches, which was followed by the use of two million adults every month in the building of Luoyang in 605. Simultaneously, Yangdi began to build the Tongji Canal section of the Grand Canal with a labor force of more than one million. In the first Liaodong campaign in 612, Yangdi employed a work force in excess of two million for logistical support, in addition to an invading force of more than 1.1 million. On the second Liaodong campaign in 613, adults in various commanderies were commandeered to gather for work in state farms in Liaoxi in four rotational groups, which would probably require a corvée laborer to work for the government on that project alone for a duration of three months per year.[62]

One important source of labor for Yangdi was women, who seemed to have been initially exempt from corvée duties. Yangdi even waived all taxes (ke) for them.[63] But shortly thereafter, Yangdi started to tap into the female labor force. He used women first on his Tongji Canal project in 605, then on

TABLE 9.1   Laborers used for major public works projects under Yangdi, 604–608

| Y/M launched | Project | Laborers used | Sources |
|---|---|---|---|
| 604/11 | Strategic trenches near Luoyang | 200,000+* | SuS 3.60 |
| 605/3 | Luoyang | 2,000,000 per mo. | SuS 24.686 |
| 605/3 | Tongji Canal | 1,000,000+ | SuS 3.63 |
| 607/7 | Great Wall | 1,000,000+ | SuS 3.70 |
| 608/1 | Yongji Canal | 1,000,000+ | SuS 3.70 |
| 608/7 | Great Wall | 200,000+ | SuS 3.71 |

*Estimate. Recorded as "several hundred thousands."

his Yongji Canal project in 608. If the case of Tongji shows Yangdi's willingness to deviate from a past convention, the case of Yongji indicates a serious
economic crisis as a result of male labor shortage. From 608 onward, as the
crisis continued, the use of female laborers became commonplace.[64]

Yangdi was also known for his ad hoc fiscal impositions. In 610, to prepare
for his first Liaodong campaign against Koguryŏ, Yangdi imposed a horse tax
on the rich. The imperial acquisition of horses on a grand scale led to much
higher horse prices. In 613, Yangdi imposed a donkey tax on the rich in the
Guanzhong area—some of them had to contribute as many as hundreds of
donkeys. Consequently, donkey prices soared.[65]

In 611, as Yangdi stepped up war preparations against Koguryŏ, the
Northern population had to disproportionately shoulder the heavy task of supporting the Sui expeditionary army, regardless of the fact that early in the same
year, in the vast Shandong (east of the Taihang Mountains) and Henan areas,
more than forty commanderies had suffered serious droughts. The subsequent
defeat of the Sui army in Liaodong added to the misery of the local population.[66] The situation was worsened by corrupt officials in charge of government levies. They profited from hoarding at lower prices commodities
requisitioned by the state and selling them at higher prices to the people after
the requisition was announced.

Lastly, the significant military buildup largely through impressment under
the Sui, especially during Yangdi's reign, added a crushing financial burden to
the economy. More than a decade before the founding of the Sui, at the time
of the war against the Northern Qi, the Northern Zhou mobilized an army
of one hundred seventy thousand to one hundred eighty thousand. By the time
Wendi launched the invasion against the Chen, he dispatched an armed force
in excess of half a million. Under Yangdi, the *fubing* garrisons, as the main
force of the Sui military, had a standing army of six hundred thousand. For
the first Liaodong campaign against Koguryŏ alone, an army of 1.13 million
was raised.[67] The Late Tang scholar Sun Qiao 孫樵 estimated that the production of "five middle households (*zhonghu* 中戶) can only support a single
soldier."[68] The situation in Sui times was probably similar. That would suggest
that the maintenance of the expeditionary army alone would require the combined productive work of 5.5 million households, more than half of the 8.9
million registered households in 609.[69] In addition, there were garrison forces
stationed in border areas elsewhere and in China proper, as well as non-*fubing*
palace guard units. Since only legally defined adult males, the main taxpayers
of the country, were eligible for conscription, the extraordinarily large military
force under Yangdi could not be maintained without significantly reducing the
rural labor force in the field. Consequently, as Yangdi "increased the number
of garrisons, and searched everywhere for new recruits . . . revenues from taxes
and levies shrank progressively."[70]

There is virtually no primary information extant on the sociological impact of excessive corvée and impressment on the public. But one contemporary poem entitled "Xixi yan" 昔昔鹽 affords us a glimpse of the prevailing sentiments of the families left behind. In this poem the leading Sui poet Xue Daoheng, through the voice of a woman whose husband had been summoned away on extended conscription duty, conveys a sense of sorrow and melancholy:

Drooping willows screen the golden dyke,
The foliage of sweet herbs grows again to the same height.
Water overflows the pond of lotus blossoms,
Flowers float across the path of peach and plum trees.
Picking mulberry leaves was the daughter of the Qins 秦,[71]
Weaving silk embroidery was Dou Tao's 竇滔 wife.[72]
Since bidding farewell to my wandering man at the mountain pass,
I have stayed in the empty boudoir accompanied by the wind and
    moon.
No longer smiling my smile worth one thousand pieces of gold,
I constantly wear two traces of translucent tears on my face.
The hand mirror has disappeared with its coiled dragon,
The curtain hangs low with its colorful phoenix.
My soul takes off like a nocturnal magpie,
In my tired sleep, I am awakened by a rooster at dawn.
Spider's webs are hanging from dark windows,
From bare rafters fall crumbs of the swallow's nest.
Last year, he passed through northern Dai 代,
This year, he has left for Liaoxi.
There has been no news since his departure,
How can one spare the hooves of the [relay] horse?[73]


## POPULATION

The dramatic demographic changes that accompanied the political and economic transformation in the late sixth and early seventh centuries may serve as a major barometer of social stability and the economy. In Sui demography, three relatively well-documented key aspects deserve close attention: the method of visual inspection for the purpose of improving population data gathering; population registration; and lastly, population fluctuations.

## Visual Inspection

The accuracy of censuses often relied on effective calculation methods employed in the field. In this aspect the Sui made a major contribution with its invention of an inspection mechanism known as *maoyue* 貌閱 (visual inspection) or *tuanmao* 團貌 (group inspection).[74] In Sui times, two cases of *maoyue* are recorded. The first one was completed under Wendi in 583. It resulted in a significant gain in population by more than 1.6 million.[75]

The second one took place in 609. The driving force behind it was Pei Yun. Having served as prefect under Wendi, Pei was promoted to vice president of the Court of Imperial Sacrifices (*taichang shaoqing* 太常少卿) by Yangdi, thanks to his excellent administrative performances.[76] As such, he launched a nationwide *maoyue* campaign, which resulted in a population gain of 641,500.[77] Pei's success was in no small part due to his detailed knowledge of various schemes being used to mislead government censuses and escape taxes, a knowledge he had acquired in his previous experience as prefect. The main rationale behind this campaign was to stop the many loopholes in the population registration system of the previous reign, which unwittingly allowed young adults to claim child status, and middle-aged adults to claim elderly status. In either case, the claimant would be exempt from taxation and corvée. Pei Yun targeted the grassroots officials at the township (*xiang* 鄉) and village (*li* 里) levels, who would be punished by exile to a remote area if a single case of incorrect identification among residents under their jurisdiction was discovered. For more efficient population registration, Pei introduced the practice of mutual surveillance, encouraging people to inform against one another. If an adult claiming child or elderly status was exposed, he would be held responsible for all the taxes and corvée of the informant. Commenting on the situation, Yangdi said, "The reason why deception and fraud was so rampant was because there were no worthy and talented people under the previous reign. Thanks to Pei Yun, household registration is now all accurate."[78] It was obvious that Yangdi, while voicing his resentment against his father's reign, was satisfied with Pei Yun's campaign.

The mechanism of visual inspection à la Pei Yun, probably traceable to the early years of the Sui dynasty, contributed in an important way to enhancing the accuracy of censuses, thereby producing a larger population base for taxation. Its implementation under the Sui must have had a significant impact on the economy. Surviving the Sui, visual inspection was to become a lasting legacy—an important component of the Tang household statutes.[79]

## Household Registration

The records on Pei Yun's *maoyue* campaign also mention a particular kind of mechanism, through which the state kept track of the population—*jizhang* 計帳 (tax registers). *Jizhang* made their debut at least as early as the Western Wei dynasty. At that time Yuwen Tai's close adviser Su Chuo "started creating official document forms with outgoing items in red and incoming items in black, as well as rules for *jizhang* and *huji* 戶籍 (household registers)."[80] The famous Western Wei document of Datong 大統 13 (547) discovered in Dunhuang is identified by modern scholars as *jizhang* or tax registers.[81] The so-called *jizhang* were a component part of the household registration system (*ji*ᵃ*zhang* 籍帳), which attained maturity around Sui times.

A most effective way to study the Sui household registration system is to start with its regulatory rules, which should fall under the *ling* (statutes) division of Sui written law. Unfortunately, in that area, little has survived. However, an examination of the successor Tang system that came into being immediately after the fall of Sui may provide some clues to the household registration of its Sui predecessor.

Concerning tax registers, *Tōryō shūi* (*Tang Statutes Reassembled*) by Niida Noboru records a number of Tang statutes initially issued in the Wude period (618–626) in the early years of the dynasty:

> 9. *art.* 21. The tax registers (*jizhang*) should be compiled annually. The village headman (*lizheng* 里正) should scrutinize the declarations (*shoushi* 手實) from the people under his jurisdiction and enter in them the ages of household members.[82]
>
> 9. *art.* 22. Household registers (*huji* 戶籍) are compiled every three years between the first month and the third month.[83]
>
> 9. *art.* 23. Concerning all households under Heaven, their assets should be assessed and categorized into nine ranks. In every third year, the county authorities determine the ranks. Upon verification by the prefectural authorities, the household registers are recorded and submitted to the Department of State Affairs. Household ranking takes place in the middle year [of each triennium] (the years of *zi*, *mao*, *wu*, and *you*), while household registers are compiled in the last year [of each triennium] (the years of *chou*, *chen*, *wei*, and *xu*).[84]

These statutes indicate that the household registration system of the Early Tang processed three types of basic data: *shoushi* (declarations), *jizhang* (tax registers), and *huji* (household registers). Every household was required to compile a new declaration annually, with information on household members, land holdings, housing, and other assets. Annual tax registers were then compiled, based on declarations. Household registers, compiled once every three years, were based on both declarations and tax registers. Copies of both tax registers and household registers were sent to the central government.[85]

Documents of *shoushi* (declarations)—the basic building blocks of the Tang system—recently came to light in Turfan, Xinjiang, where the arid climate has allowed thousands of pieces of paper documents of the Tang and earlier periods to survive underground.[86]

The 640 declaration by Li Shizhu 李石住
[Missing]

| | |
|---|---|
| ☐ ]47 years of age adult male (*dingnan* 丁男) | 1 |
| ☐ ] 40 years of age wife of an adult male (*dingqi* 丁妻) | 2 |
| ☐An]hai 安海, 15 years of age adolescent male (*zhongnan* 中男) | 3 |
| ☐ four] male infant (*huangnan* 黃男) | 4 |
| ☐ ☐ female(*nü* 女) | 5 |
| ☐ 80 *mu*, not yet granted | 6 |

Document pertains to the declaration of the household concerned.

Everything has been [truthfully] entered above, with no insertion or deletion. If any fraudulent claims were discovered, 7
[the undersigned] would like to be penalized. Respectfully submitted. 8
Zhenguan 14, 9th month, ___ day. Submitted by the head of the household, Li Shizhu[87] 9

This earliest surviving *shoushi* document was completed in the ninth month of 640. One month earlier, Turfan had been annexed to Tang China as Xi Prefecture 西州 after having remained independent of Chinese suzerainty for centuries. The Tang government immediately brought its population registration system to this newly annexed territory. Because of the relatively early date of this bona fide *shoushi* (declaration) document, it was probably compliant with the Wude Statutes and was still close to the Sui prototype. Lines 7–8 indicate that the document contains a pro forma punitive clause, which, clearly reminiscent of the punitive measures adopted by Pei Yun under Yangdi, was very likely a direct carryover from the previous dynasty.

A related Tang record in the *Tang huiyao* states, "Those who have fraudulently concealed their true identities in an attempt to avoid taxes and corvée are subjected to all taxes and corvée regardless of the times of their household registration."[88] This record aimed to discourage frauds by threatening to take away levy and corvée exemptions granted to newly registered adults. This practice is labeled "old ruling" (*jiuzhi* 舊制), which suggests its link to the Sui dynasty.

Obviously, the hypothetical approach employed here to the reconstruction of the Sui household registration system has its serious limitations. But enough evidence points to the key functions it played in the economy: to monitor changes in population and provide demographic bases for the enforcement of the land tenure system and taxation.

## Population Trends

A major consequence of the Sui household registration system is the preservation of precious demographic data. From these data, we can work out the population trends of the period in question, which are oftentimes effective indicators of the general health of a premodern economy. From his birth under the Northern Zhou to the height of his reign, Yangdi lived through a period of sustained economic growth and relative prosperity. Not coincidentally, it was accompanied by a general uptrend in population as a result of natural growth and territorial acquisition.

Prior to the conquest of the Northern Qi in 577, the population of the Northern Zhou is tentatively estimated at 11,680,000. The conquest added an additional 20,000,000. At the time of the Sui's founding in 581, the population approached 33 million. With the conquest of the South in 589 and continued growth, the population reached 38 million.[89] As emperor, Yangdi ruled over a population of 46,019,956 in 8,907,546 households in 609 (Daye 5).[90] In the words of Du You 杜佑, that year was "the peak of the Sui."[91] This Sui peak figure still trailed behind the Western Han census figure for AD 2 more than six centuries before, which records a registered population of close to 60 million. As the earliest extant reliable data of a national census, the AD 2 figure represents the highest point in population for early imperial China. The 609 figure was an interim high between the disintegration of the Eastern Han and the 734 High Tang census which recorded a population of 46,285,161.[92] The Tang population continued to grow before it topped out in 755 at 52,919,309.[93]

Most significantly for Yangdi's reign, the Sui population after 609 began to decline precipitously.[94] Precise demographic information on the post-609 period is not available. Still we can get a sense of the speed of the decline by comparing existing aggregate numbers of households. The number of Sui households stood at 8.9 million in 609 and shrank to less than three million in the Zhenguan 貞觀 reign (627–649) at the beginning of the Tang.[95] In other words, the number of households probably decreased by more than 60 percent in about a decade. By inference, the population may have declined from more than 46 million in 609 to around 15 million in Early Tang times.

Because of statistical complexities, such calculations cannot be simply taken at face value. Typically, end-of-dynasty chaos would greatly reduce the government's ability to gather demographic information and cause significant territorial and population losses to neighboring powers and independent forces. A large number·of the registered residents simply disappeared from government statistics. This is, of course, the case with the Sui-Tang transitional period as well. But in 652, after thirty-four years of uninterrupted growth and expansion, when the Tang empire was in control of a territory probably larger than the Sui empire at its height, the number of Tang households was only 3.8 million, or less than 43 percent of the 609 figure.[96] This fact suggests that the factor of hidden population in Early Tang China was not enough to alter the conclusion that from its zenith in 609 to its nadir in 618, the population of Sui China was severely decimated, with a significant portion, if not most, of the population losses attributable to unnatural causes such as war, famine, and corvée.

To sum up the economic conditions of Wendi's reign, the "Shihuo" chapter (Treatise on food and money) of the *Sui shu* offers the following overview:

> After Sui Wendi had pacified the lower Yangzi area, all under Heaven was united. He set a personal example of simple living, so as to help fill up the state storehouse. In Kaihuang 17 (597), the population was booming, and storehouses both in the capital and the provinces were overflowing with goods. All grants and supplies were within budget. Capital storehouses were so full that goods had to be piled up in the corridors. So Gaozu (Wendi) waived that year's official taxes, in order to reward the ordinary people.

This rosy portrayal stands in stark contrast with the chapter's judgment on the economy of Yangdi's reign:

> Because of defeats in the battlefield and fatalities caused by overwork, more than half [of the people commandeered] failed to return home. Yet the impressment continued year in and year out. The boys of law-abiding households were sent to the border areas in large numbers. The sound of endless sobbing and crying at departure was heard in prefectures and counties. The old and weak tilled the land, but could not produce enough to save the hungry; women wove and spun, but could not produce enough to keep up with the demands for work clothes.[97]

The writers of these remarks clearly intended to characterize the economies of father and son in antipodal terms. But considering the corroborative evidence, it is impossible to dismiss the dismal picture they paint of the second reign. As shown in this chapter, in spite of the stable and workable economic system set up by Wendi and the huge fortune amassed during the first reign, the Sui empire sank into a vicious economic cycle under Yangdi. His endless building projects and ambitious military campaigns had a cumulative impact on the economy. His egregious abuse and maltreatment of corvée labor, natural disasters, and wars combined to bring about a drastic decline in population, which in turn resulted in a long-term, severe shortage of manpower. The situation was further aggravated by massive desertion of laborers and conscripts, who fled, on pain of death, from senseless external expeditions or, worse still, joined the fast growing ranks of rebels. The economic order broke down as the dynasty was collapsing.

# 10

# Foreign Policy

By the time Wendi usurped power and founded his Sui dynasty, his Northern Zhou predecessor Wudi 武帝 (Yuwen Yong 宇文邕, r. 560–578) had set in motion the trend of unification. It was Wudi who conquered the Northern Qi in 577, thus bringing North China once again under the control of one government for the first time since 534. Wendi determined to follow that trend by striking beyond the North. Not long after accession in 581, he embarked on the road to expansion. In the wake of the bloodless annexation of the Later Liang in the middle Yangzi valley, the Sui army under the general command of Yangdi swept victoriously to the South in 589 and subjugated the rival regime of Chen. These newly added territories, conquered in a short span of twelve years, shared common cultural, linguistic, and ethnic traditions with the Sui, and historically had been under the direct jurisdiction of united Chinese empires. These factors were conducive to the official efforts at assimilation. But the extraordinary growth of the Sui territory in a relatively short period of time often brought it into contact and conflict with neighbors with different cultural traditions.

Faced with such a complex international environment, Wendi's advisers formulated a foreign policy that purported both to facilitate the long-term strategy of territorial expansion and consolidation of power in areas dominated by Chinese cultural influence, and to protect agricultural communities in the Northern and Northwestern frontier regions and trade routes in the Northwest. Focusing on Tujue and Koguryŏ, Wendi strove to reestablish the Chinese world order in East Asia, a concept rooted in the ancient Sinocentric idea of universal overlordship, and in the Middle Kingdom's centuries-old self-perception of superiority in reference to its neighbors.

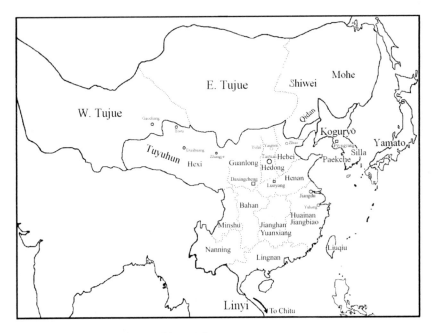

MAP 10.1    Sui China and its neighbors, 612

While seeking to maintain the Chinese world order he inherited from his father, Yangdi pursued a much more expansionist foreign policy, sending expeditionary and explorative missions overseas, and launching full-fledged wars against neighboring states. Under Yangdi, the Sui empire projected its power far beyond China proper: Linyi and Chitu in the Far South; Liuqiu 流球 and Yamato 倭 in the East; Tiele 鐵勒 (Tölös), Tuyuhun 吐谷渾, Dangxiang 黨項 (Tangut), and the Western Regions in the Northwest; Tujue in the North and Northwest; Koguryŏ, Mohe 靺鞨 (Malgal), and Qidan 契丹 (Khitan) in the Northeast (map 10.1).

## THE FAR SOUTH

The faraway kingdoms beyond the Southern frontier received little attention from the Sui court during the first reign. After Yangdi ascended the throne, the focus of foreign policy remained overwhelmingly on the North, but with Tujue posing no immediate threat, he also set his sights on the Southern barbarians (*nanman* 南蠻). The *Sui shu* contains information on more than ten

Southern tributary states during the Sui period. Of these, detailed records about four have survived: Linyi (Champa), Chitu (in the Malay Peninsula), Zhenla 真臘 (Cambodia),[1] and Poli (Bali) 婆利. Although all four sent tributary missions to China, only two, Linyi and Chitu, received missions from the Sui court. And they warrant further attention.

## Linyi 林邑

Located in present-day central Vietnam, the kingdom of Linyi[2] was a recipient of both Chinese and Indian influences. Towards the end of the Han dynasty, part of its Jiaozhi Commandery 交阯/趾郡 broke away to become an independent kingdom, which evolved into Linyi. The produce of Linyi was similar to that of Jiaozhi. Its musical instruments resembled those of China while its mortuary customs, for example, cremation on a pyral fire, were clearly reminiscent of those prevalent in the subcontinent. Buddhism was the universal religion. The written language was believed to be similar to Sanskrit. This land of several thousand *li* across was inhabited by a people, in the words of the *Sui shu*, "with deep-set eyes and tall noses."[3] Following the Sui conquest of the Chen, Linyi sent one tributary mission to Wendi, but did not attract much court attention. At the end of the Renshou period (600–604), General Liu Fang 劉方, who had just crushed a rebellion in Jiao Prefecture 交州 (north Vietnam) led by Li Fozi 李佛子, was ordered to subjugate Linyi. Given that since the beginning of the 604 Yangdi had been trusted with court affairs by his father, who soon fell sick and died, it is likely that Liu's mission was sent by Yangdi, even though it is not recorded in the sources. Commanding a cavalry force of ten thousand strong and several thousand convicts, Liu battled King Fanzhi's 梵志 elephant-mounted army and eventually, in the fourth month of 605, defeated it by using pitfalls to entrap the elephants. The Sui army captured the capital and eighteen gold statues from the state temple. Before his return, Liu ordered an inscribed stone tablet to be set up in honor of his victory. Three prefectures—Dang 蕩, Nong 農, and Chong 沖—were created, which were then converted to Bijing 比景, Haiyin 海陰, and Linyi Commanderies, respectively. King Fanzhi thenceforth recovered his lost territory and dispatched an envoy to offer an official apology. From then on, Linyi began to send tributary missions frequently to pay homage to the Sui court.[4]

Obviously Liu Fang's expedition was a predatory treasure hunt carried out within the framework of universal overlordship. The exotic treasures Linyi reputedly possessed made military conquest desirable. With superior force, the hegemonic power of the Sui reduced Linyi to the status of a vassal state that could supply exotica to the Sui court on a continual basis.

# Chitu 赤土

On accession, Yangdi began to recruit adventurers who could explore inaccessible regions, distant areas where no Chinese had gone before. Chitu, a tropical kingdom in the Malay Peninsula hardly noticed by Wendi, was one of the exotic regions Yangdi explored.[5] The Chitu are considered cognate with the Funan 扶南 (Bnam, on the Gulf of Siam, Cambodia). According to a *Sui shu* record:

> [The king] lives in the city of Sengzhi 僧祇 with a series of three gates about 100 *bu* from each other. Gold embroidered feather cloths decorated with bells are suspended from the gates, each of which is painted with the figures of flying transcendents (asparas), transcendents, and bodhisattvas. There are dozens of women, playing music, or holding gold flowers. In addition, four more women are displayed standing on either side of the gates, with facial features and costumes similar to those of vajra-guardians at the side of a pagoda. . . . Among their customs are ear-piercing and hair-cutting. They do not perform the kneeling ritual. Their bodies are anointed with fragrant oil. It is their custom to worship the Buddha, and particularly Brahman. Women tie their hair in a bun behind the neck. Men and women all wear clothes with colored patterns of sunrise glows and morning clouds. The powerful and rich can indulge in extravagances unchecked. One exception are gold chains. One cannot wear them unless they are given by the king.[6]

In the third month of 608, Chitu sent its first tributary mission on record to China. Yangdi reciprocated by sending a Sui mission headed by the low-ranking official Chang Jun 常駿. Chang brought with him 5,000 *duan*[a7] of silk as an imperial gift to the local sovereign. The Chitu king sent out a fleet of thirty ships to greet the Sui delegation. Upon receiving the edict from Yangdi, the king declared, "From now on, [we] are the people of the great power (i.e., the Sui), and are no longer the state of Chitu." The host showered the Chinese guests with lavish gifts, and treated them to sumptuous banquets and musical entertainment. During Chang's visit, Chitu dispatched another tributary mission to the Sui court, which arrived in the second month of 609. On his return journey, Chang Jun brought with him Prince Nayejia 那邪迦, leading the third tributary mission. When they appeared in the Sui court in the sixth month of 610, an overjoyed Yangdi lavished gifts and official titles on the prince and the officials accompanying him.[8]

## The East

The *Sui shu* lists six states as those of the eastern barbarians: Liuqiu, Yamato, the three states of Korea, and Mohe. Of these, the first two are of particular interest because of their remote locations and Yangdi's personal involvement in dealing with them.[9]

### Liuqiu 流求

The identification of Liuqiu, located in the East China Sea, is still controversial. In the late nineteenth and early twentieth centuries, some Western scholars began to identify it with Taiwan. Japanese scholars echoed this view. But there has been a strong opposing view, particularly among Chinese scholars.[10] Like Chitu, the island state of Liuqiu had its initial official contact with the Sui during the reign of Yangdi. The *Sui shu* attributes certain Caucasian facial features such as deep-set eyes and tall nose to the Liuqiu, who lived in a preliterate community, where the distance between sovereign and subject was never emphasized. Their produce including rice was believed to be similar to that of the Far South in China. Living in what seemed like a primitive monarchical society, they cultivated their fields with a technique akin to swidden, using tools made of stone.[11] Located to the east of Jian'an Commandery 建安 (seat: Fuzhou, Fujian), Liuqiu could be reached after five days' travel by sea. In the third month of 607, Yangdi sent Zhu Kuan 朱寬, a minor officer, on the first Chinese mission to Liuqiu ever recorded. Upon arrival, Zhu and his followers could not communicate with the local people. After capturing one native, they returned. Zhu then went on his second mission, which also failed. The third mission was headed by Chen Leng 陳稜 and Zhang Zhenzhou 張鎮州 with an army of more than ten thousand from Dongyang 東陽 (seat: Jinhua, Zhejiang). Chen and Zhang also brought along natives of Southeast Asia who spoke the local language. The ensuing Sui-Liuqiu conflict resulted in the death of the Liuqiu king Keladou 渴剌兜 and the burning of the palace at the capital. Upon their return, Chen and Zhang presented to the court 17,000 captured natives, both men and women, in early 610, and were rewarded with promotion. But the main objective of these missions—to impose tributary relations on Liuqiu—was a failure. No Liuqiu mission came calling in the remainder of the Sui dynasty.[12]

### Yamato 倭

In Sui times, the Yamato in Japan were regarded as a borderline civilized people in the process of transformation. Having imported Buddhist sūtras from Paekche and accepted Buddhism, they were beginning to have their own written language. During the reign of Suiko Tennō 推古天皇 (r. 592–628), the first female emperor in Japanese history, Yamato sent missions to Sui China. The Chinese sources record four of them. The first mission arrived in Wendi's court in 600;[13] the remaining three missions took place in Yangdi's reign: in 607, the third month of 608, and the first/third month of 610, respectively.[14] The Japanese sources record three missions, all under Yangdi: (1) the seventh month of 607–the fourth month of 608; (2) the ninth month of 608–the ninth month of 609; (3) the sixth month of 614–ninth month of 615. Due to discrepancies between the Chinese and Japanese records, scholars are divided on the number of Yamato missions sent during Sui times, with the focus of their debate on the accuracy of the Japanese records.[15]

On the 600 mission, the only one sent to Wendi's court, the Yamato envoy informed Wendi that the Yamato sovereign regarded Heaven as her elder brother, and the sun as her younger brother; and that she held court before dawn, and quit court at sunrise to entrust government to the sun. These outlandish claims did not please Wendi.[16]

As the first Yamato official visit to Yangdi's court on record, the 607 mission is also the best documented Yamato mission to the Sui. It was headed by the famous Ono no Imoko 小野妹子 (or Su Yingao 蘇因高 in Chinese), generally believed to have been dispatched by Regent Shōtoku Taishi 聖德太子. In his mission statement, Ono informed Yangdi, "[The Yamato sovereign] heard that the Bodhisattva Son of Heaven west of the sea vigorously promotes the law of the Buddha, therefore [she] sent us to pay homage, with several dozens of śramaṇa to learn the law of the Buddha." Ono's information was probably based on the fact that Yangdi as prince had received the clerical title "zongchi pusa" 總持菩薩 (Protector General Bodhisattva).[17] But Yangdi was displeased with the official letter of state addressed to him, which claimed, "Sunrise Son of Heaven wishes Sunset Son of Heaven well."[18] His negative reaction notwithstanding, Yangdi was interested in continuing the relationship with Japan. On his orders, Pei Shiqing 裴世清 as Sui envoy accompanied Ono back to Japan via Paekche in the fourth month of 608.[19]

The Chinese and Japanese records differ on what happened next. The *Sui shu* records the warm welcome Pei Shiqing received from the Yamato sovereign, who said, "I heard that the Great Sui, located west of the sea, was a country of ritual and justice. That is why I sent a mission to pay tribute. We, as barbarians living in a corner of the sea, did not know ritual and justice. Consequently, [I] did not immediately meet you even if you had stayed within our borders. Therefore, today we have cleared the road and decorated the hotel, hoping to receive the great envoy and to hear about the transforming power of reform." Pei replied, "The virtue of our emperor matches that of the Two Forces (yin and yang), and his radiance shines over the four seas, so much so that [he] extends his sovereign rule over those transformed through adoration [of Chinese culture]. Therefore he sent an envoy here to announce the imperial rescript." On the occasion of Pei's return, the Yamato sovereign sent Ono to accompany Pei and to pay tribute with local produce.[20]

In the Japanese source *Nihon shoki* 日本書記, both Ono and Pei Shiqing carried with them a letter of state from Yangdi on their way to Japan. However, Ono claimed to have lost the letter in a robbery incident in Paekche. Pei, who had traveled with Ono, managed to deliver his letter to the Yamato court, which started with, "The emperor sends his greetings to the sovereign of Yamato. Head Envoy and Great Ritualist (*tairei* 大禮; rank five in Japan's twelve ranks system) Su Yingao (Ono) and others arrived. Thanks for the letter. . . ." In the response, the Yamato sovereign wrote, "The celestial sovereign of the east respectfully addresses the emperor of the west. . . ."[21]

That the *Sui shu* and *Nihon shoki* stress different aspects of the mission gave rise to some discrepancies in both accounts. The fundamental difference lies in the dissimilar perceptions each held of the other. The Sui source conveys a strong sense that, in spite of their hubris, the Yamato acknowledged their inferior status and that the Sui sovereign dealt with Yamato as a peripheral state attracted to the great civilization of China. But the *Nihon shoki* clearly indicates that the sovereigns of Sui China and Yamato Japan treated each other as equals.

The different circumstances under which these two sources were written may also help explain their different perspectives of the event. The *Sui shu* was completed in the early seventh century, immediately after the fall of the Sui. The *Nihon shoki* was compiled in the early eighth century, almost a hundred years later. The *Sui shu* is a standard history based on official documents, chronicling historical events in the tradition of Sima Qian. The *Nihon shoki* is the first Japanese effort to create their own comprehensive history, aimed at countering China's dominant cultural influence. As such, it is a mixture of history and myth. It is thus possible that the authors of the *Nihon shoki* embellished their account to make Yamato look like Sui China's equal. Some scholars even argue, not without reason, that the *Nihon shoki* record of Yangdi's letter of state in 608 to Yamato was a fabrication.[22] In any event, the information in the *Sui shu* clearly conveys the view Wendi and Yangdi held of Yamato as a subordinate state in the Chinese world order.

Why did the Yamato brave the rough seas to visit China? It is widely accepted that the 600 mission to Sui China was a diplomatic move aimed at Silla, which was then under attack by a Japanese expeditionary army, although there is no supporting evidence in the Chinese sources. The 607 mission undoubtedly had a predominantly religious focus, with a singular aim of acquiring more knowledge about Buddhism. Yangdi's reciprocal mission, on the other hand, purported to spread continental civilization.

# The West

## Xiyu 西域

Perhaps the most elucidating example of a Sui exercise in universal overlordship is found in its relations with its neighbors to the northwest, in Central Asia, particularly those active in a loosely defined area known as the Western Regions (Xiyu 西域).[23] Ever since its appearance in Han times, Xiyu has been configured differently. The narrow definition of the area refers to the land east of the Pamirs and west of Yumen Pass near Dunhuang, which encompasses mainly the present-day Xinjiang region. The broad definition, however, extends west beyond the Pamirs to include Russian Turkistan, West Asia, the subcontinent, and even the Roman Orient.

The *Sui shu* records that more than thirty Xiyu states sent tributary missions to the Sui court under Yangdi; from the Tuyuhun and the Dangxiang 黨項 (Tangut) on the borders of Northwestern Chinese communities, to Sasanian Persia in West Asia, and Bokhara (Anguo 安國) in Transoxiana. Of these, Persia and Bokhara were merely symbolically affiliated with the imagined geopolitical space of the Sui empire with occasional diplomatic missions.[24]

The paramount interest Yangdi had in the Western Regions was control of the trade routes extending from Dunhuang to the west, now known as the Silk Road. The leading Sui official in charge of diplomacy, Pei Ju, in his *Xiyu tuji* 西域圖記 (An illustrated account of the Western Regions) identified three trade routes.[25] The first one, the north route, went through Yiwu 伊吾 (Hami), Tiele and Tujue territories, to the Roman Orient (Fulin 拂菻); the second one, the middle route, originated from Gaochang 高昌 (Turfan), and proceeded through Yanqi 焉耆 (Karashahr), Qiuci 龜茲 (Kucha), Shule 疏勒 (Kashgar), the Pamirs, and a number of Central Asian states, such as Samarkand (Sogdiana or Kangguo 康國) and Bokhara, to reach Persia; the third one, the south route, went through Shanshan 鄯善, Yutian 于闐 (Khotan), the Pamirs and Tukhara, to North India (Beipolomen 北婆羅門). All three routes ended in the Western Sea (Xihai 西海), which means the Mediterranean, the Persian Gulf, or the north Indian Ocean (map 10.2).[26]

Pei Ju envisioned an effortless incorporation of the various states in the narrowly defined Xiyu area into the geopolitical space of the Sui empire by establishing tributary and trade relations. However, two main obstacles—Tujue and Tuyuhun—stood in the way of Sui dominance. Pei thus proposed, "After various barbarian states are subjugated, Tujue and Tuyuhun can be destroyed. This will lead to the amalgamation of the Western 'barbarians' and the Chinese." Acting on Pei's vision of a dominant China projecting its power

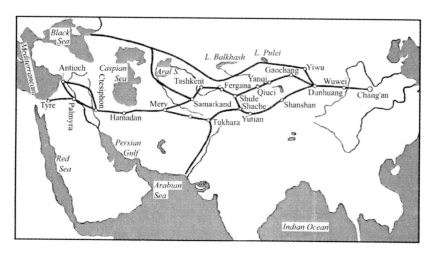

MAP 10.2    Sui China and the Western Regions

into the Northwest, Central Asia and beyond, the Sui used divisive tactics to weaken the Tujue.

Meanwhile, during the early years of Yangdi's reign, the Tuyuhun 吐谷渾 were the people Sui Central Asia policy focused on. They had a hierarchical system with princes, dukes, vice presidents of the Department of State Affairs, board presidents, bureau directors, and generals. Their weapons and clothes were similar to those used in China. Although they had their walled cities, they were primarily nomadic. Their ethnic origins can be traced to the Liaoxi Xianbei 遼西鮮卑. During the time of the Western Wei-Northern Zhou transition, their leader declared himself qaghan.[27] To the Sui, culturally and economically, the Tuyuhun were similar to the Tujue. But militarily they were much inferior. That probably explains why the strategy Pei pursued against Tuyuhun was much more aggressive. In 608, under the sway of his persuasive power, another powerful northern nomadic state, Tiele 鐵勒, mounted an attack on Tuyuhun and won a decisive victory. When the Tuyuhun leader Fuyun 伏允 qaghan, who was still in the dark about Pei's involvement, sought assistance from the Sui court, Yangdi dispatched General Yuwen Shu 宇文述 to launch a series of onslaughts against him. Subsequently, the Tuyuhun were dislodged from the vast area they called home and the Tuyuhun territory, measuring 4,000 *li* east-west and 2,000 *li* north-south, was annexed by the Sui.

About the same time, General Xue Shixiong 薛世雄 was ordered to coordinate a joint attack with Qimin qaghan of Eastern Tujue against Yiwu 伊吾, one of the easternmost oasis cities in the Western Regions. Although

Qimin did not launch his attack as expected, Xue single-handedly crossed the desert, and his show of force caused the Yiwu to surrender.

In the wake of Sui victories, Yangdi went on an inspection tour that took him as far as Zhangye 張掖 (in central Gansu) in the sixth month of 609, the westernmost point he reached in his career. Enticed by the great incentives offered by Pei Ju, the Gaochang king Qu Boya 麴伯雅 arrived to pay homage to Yangdi, accompanied by missions from dozens of Western barbarian states. Yangdi was especially pleased with the visit of the tutun she 土屯設 (chieftain) of Yiwu, who ceded a large stretch of land, reportedly several thousand *li* across.[28]

The new territories from Tuyuhun and Yiwu allowed the Sui to set up four commanderies—Heyuan 河源, Xihai 西海, Jumo 且末, and Shanshan—in an area from east Qinghai to south Xinjiang. Crime offenders were dispatched to colonize these sparsely populated areas. General Liu Quan 劉權 was stationed in a garrison in Heyuan, where he vigorously developed state farms (*tuntian* 屯田). The strategic objective of incorporating such a vast expanse of land was to protect the Hexi Corridor in Gansu, and the Silk Road trade.

As for the Tuyuhun leader Fuyun, he was denied access to this area until the end of the Sui dynasty when he took advantage of the domestic turmoil that engulfed China to repossess his territory.[29]


## Gaochang 高昌

Of all the oasis states along the Silk Road, Gaochang (Turfan) had the closest ties with the Sui court, as is testified by King Qu Boya's presence on Yangdi's first Liaodong campaign.[30] With its early residents originally coming from the Middle Kingdom, it is no coincidence that Gaochang was the most Chinese or Sinicized of any oasis state in Central Asia.[31] Despite Tujue's dominance in the area, it sent a tributary mission to the Sui court in 608, and Qu Boya went on a long journey to pay homage to Yangdi in 609. In a strategic move aimed at further strengthening that relationship, Yangdi married Sui princess Huarong 華容 to the king. Behind this friendly gesture was a desire to bring Gaochang into the orbit of the Sui empire. On his return in 612, Qu voluntarily discarded the Tujue customs, a move that won an accolade from Yangdi, who had called Gaochang a country of caps and sashes.

But Gaochang simultaneously maintained tributary relations with a closer power, Tiele, to which it had to transfer the commercial taxes it levied on passing merchants. This fact gives testimony to the limitation of Sui expansion in the Western Regions. For all its cultural and linguistic affinities it had with Sui China, Gaochang remained a client state of a non-Sinitic, nomadic power, even though it continued to send tributary missions to the Sui court.[32]

## TUJUE

In strategic terms, the most important neighboring regimes for the Sui were the empires established by the Tujue 突厥 (Turks) in the North and the North-west.[33] The Sui-Tujue relationship, alternately punctuated by contention and rapprochement, dominated the politics of Mongolia and the Western Regions.

The Tujue emerged from obscure origins in the mid-sixth century in the Altai region when the Eurasian steppes were dominated by two nomadic powers: the Rouran 柔然 and the Yeda 嚈噠 (Ephthalites). The Rouran, based in Mongolia, ruled over a vast area, from the Turfan basin in the west to Manchuria in the east, and from the Orkhon in the north to the Great Wall in the south. To the west of the Rouran were the Ephthalites, whose control extended from Lake Balkhash and the Aral Sea, west to Merv, dominating Russian Turkistan, Afghanistan, and the Punjab.[34]

The Chinese sources began to provide detailed information about the Tujue in the early seventh century:

They make a living out of herding and grazing cattle, chasing after water and grass, and not staying long in a single place. Their dwellings are domed huts and felt tents. They wear their hair loose, and fasten their garments on the left. They consume meat and drink horse milk wine. They are clad in clothes of fur and coarse cloth. They despise the old and value the young. Their officialdom is composed of 28 ranks, from *yehu* 葉護 (*yabghu*), *she* 設 (*shad*), *teqin* 特勤 (*tegin*), *silifa* 俟利發, and *tutunfa* 吐屯發 (*tudun*), all the way down to minor posts.[35] All of them are hereditary. They have [as their weapons] horned bows, whistling arrows, armors, lances, scimitars, and swords. They are good equestrians and archers, but cruel by nature. They do not have a written language, and carve their contracts on wood.[36] They wait until the moon is almost full to conduct their raids.

Those who conspire to rebel and those who have taken a human life are punished by death. Sex offenders are punished by the severing of the torso after castration. A person damaging another person's eye in an affray shall compensate the victim with his own daughter. In case he does not have a daughter, he shall pay with his wife's dowry. Those who have broken an extremity shall pay with a horse. Those who steal shall pay ten times the value of the stolen goods. The deceased is kept in a tent. His family and other relatives oftentimes slaughter oxen and horses as offerings. They circle the tent while wailing.[37] They gash their faces with knifes so that blood and tears stream down together. They will do so seven times before they stop. Thereafter, they will select a date to have the corpse placed on the back of a horse and cremated. The ashes are collected for burial. The burial plot is marked with wood tablets. Inside, a hut is set up [wherein are hung] the portrait of the deceased and paintings of him in combat. For every person he slew, a stone is set up. There are cases where hundreds or thousands of stones are set up.

When the father or the elder brother dies, the son marries the mother of the family, or the younger brother marries his sister-in-law (wife of his deceased brother). In the fifth month, they usually slaughter sheep and horses to make offerings to Heaven. Men love dice-throwing (*chupu* 樗蒲), and women, football (*taju* 踏鞠). They drink horse milk wine (*malao* 馬酪) to get drunk, singing and shouting while facing each other. They worship ghosts and spirits and believe in shamanism; respect dying in battle and are ashamed of dying of illness. [Their customs] are more or less the same as those of the Xiongnu.[38]

As a people of the steppe, the Tujue had unique customs that distinguished them from neighboring ethnic groups, especially their official system of twenty-eight ranks and their mourning and burial rituals. History has conflicting records about their written language at this early stage. While both the *Sui shu* and *Bei shi* claim they did not have their own written language, the *Zhou shu* refers to a Tujue script, akin to the Sogdian script. Epigraphical evidence suggests that early Tujue records were written in the Sogdian language. Their own Runic script, in which such famous epigraphs as the *Kül Tegin Monument* and the *Bilgä Qaghan Monument* were inscribed, was invented later under the Eastern Tujue.[39]

The Chinese sources are consistent in their records about the similarity between the customs of the Tujue and those of the Xiongnu, who had controlled a similar territorial range during the Han dynasty. Essentially, the Tujue shared with various early nomadic peoples north of China proper such characteristics as nomadism, respecting the young and despising the old, levirate, living in domed huts and felt tents, loose hairstyle, fastening their garments on the left, wearing fur clothes,[40] and the worship of the Celestial God.[41] The accounts of Tujue in the *Sui shu* and other standard histories, written by court historians schooled in traditional historiography, apart from their less than flattering view of nomadic groups in general, portray Tujue as the very antithesis of China in terms of economy, culture, customs, and values. This perception may well have contributed to the formation of the Sui's Tujue policy.

The Chinese became increasingly aware of the presence of the Tujue after the middle of the sixth century when they shook off the yoke of Rouran oppression in 552 and became overlords of Mongolia. After the death of the founding father of the Tujue empire—Tumen 土門 (Bumïn) qaghan, the empire was divided de facto into two separate territories, the Eastern (Northern) Tujue and the Western Tujue.[42] It was the Western Tujue, in alliance with Sasanian Persia, who exterminated the erstwhile rival of the Rouran—the Ephthalites.[43]

In spite of the east-west division, the nominal central court of the Tujue empire remained in the east. South of the Eastern Tujue was a North China split between two rival regimes: the Northern Zhou and the Northern Qi. Capitalizing on the hostility between the two, the Eastern Tujue exacted lavish tribute from both and conducted sporadic raids into their settled communities. Tuo(Ta)bo 佗/他鉢 (Taspar) qaghan boasted, "So long as my two sons to the south remain filial and submissive, why worry about lack of stuff?"[44] The two sons were the sovereigns of the Northern Zhou and the Northern Qi. Both were anxious to conclude a marriage alliance with the Tujue.[45]

With the rise of a united North China in 577 and the emergence of the Sui in 581, the balance of power in the North began to shift in favor of the Han Chinese. Still, the Tujue issue continued to be the most challenging foreign policy issue. In the initial years of his reign, Wendi found himself subjected to incessant raids by the Tujue from the north.[46]

Just as Wendi began to consolidate his power, an internecine strife in Tujue fragmented it into five contending powers, each under its own qaghan.[47] This development gave Wendi the opportunity to reassess the traditional Tujue strategy. The lack of a unified central leadership among the Tujue prompted Zhangsun Sheng 長孫晟, a major policymaker at the Sui court, to propose adoption of the ancient strategy of "befriending distant states and attacking those nearby."[48] Wendi was very much aware of the futility of the appeasement policy embraced by earlier Northern regimes:

> In the past, the Zhou-Qi rivalry fragmented China proper, and the Tujue barbarians were in contact with both states. The Zhou was worried about its east side, frightened of the Qi's firm friendship [with the Tujue], while the Qi was concerned about its west side, horrified by the Zhou's close relationship [with the Tujue].

In light of these considerations, Wendi shifted to a much for defiant and aggressive strategy in dealing with the Tujue.[49]

The most serious challenge came from Shabolue 沙鉢略 (Ishbara) qaghan (r. 581–587), the nominal leader of all Tujue tribes. In response to Shabolue's attacks, Wendi repaired the Great Wall, set up barriers and reinforced

garrisons in Northern frontier areas. One of the underlying causes of this
mutual hostility was the founding of the Sui itself. In the process of usurping
dynastic power, Wendi exterminated the royal Yuwen family of the Northern
Zhou. There was no love lost between Shabolue's wife Princess Qianjin
千金公主, a Yuwen herself, and the Sui sovereign.[50]

After an internecine war broke out between Shabolue and his challenger
Abo 阿波 (Apa) qaghan (Daluobian 大邏便) (r. 581–587) in 583, a much
weakened Shabolue, as leader of Eastern Tujue, had no choice but to make
peace with the Sui court.[51] In 585, he accepted the overlordship of
Wendi. The Sui sovereign invested Shabolue's wife, Princess Qianjin, with the
title "Princess Dayi 大義公主", after bestowing upon her the royal surname
of Yang, which marked the beginning of a symbolic marriage alliance. As
part of the agreement, Shabolue sent his son as hostage to the Sui court, and
started paying annual tribute.[52] Shabolue's submission was a consequence
of the success of Sui power politics and the internal strife among Tujue
contenders.

During the reign of Dulan 都藍 qaghan (Yongyulü 雍虞閭, son of
Shabolue; r. 588–599), Eastern Tujue continued to honor the tributary relationship, which eventually dissolved because of two developments. First,
Wendi felt increasingly uneasy about the presence of Princess Qianjin at
Dulan's court, who had urged Shabolue to overthrow the Sui.[53] Second, to the
north of Dulan, Tuli 突利 (Tölish) qaghan (Rangan 染干, son of Shabolue's
brother Chuluohou 處羅侯)[54] rose to rival Dulan's authority.

Wendi's hatred for Qianjin intensified after his subjugation of the Chen
in 589. He resented the fact that she expressed empathy with the ousted Chen
sovereign Chen Shubao in a poem, and was concerned about her contact with
Nili qaghan 泥利可汗 (r. 587–603).[55] After Qianjin was caught having illicit
relations with a Sogdian, Dulan had her killed and thenceforth submitted a
request for a marriage alliance.[56] Dulan made the decision on his own but pres-
sure from the Sui court may have had some impact.[57] On Zhangsun Sheng's
advice, Wendi rejected Dulan's request. But he granted a marriage alliance with
Tuli, Dulan's challenger, whereby in 597, Princess Anyi 安義公主 of Sui
became his new bride. Subsequently, communications between the Sui and
Tuli became increasingly frequent. Tuli, thanks to his marriage alliance with
the Sui, moved south, and Wendi heaped favors upon him. All this was
intended to foster rivalry between Tuli and Dulan, who regarded himself as
the great qaghan of all Tujue tribes. Feeling deeply offended by the Sui's par-
tiality towards Tuli, Dulan cut off his tributary ties and began to harass frontier areas bordering on Sui territory. Allying himself with his former enemy
Datou (Tardu) qaghan 達頭可汗 (Dianjue 玷厥) of Western Tujue, Dulan
declared war on Tuli. Having suffered major losses, Tuli took shelter at the Sui
court. Datou's troops advanced on the frontier area, but were repelled by

General Shi Wansui 史萬歲 in the fourth month of 599,[58] then put to rout by Gao Jiong and Yang Su in the sixth month.[59]

Tuli was handsomely rewarded for his loyalty to the Sui court. In the tenth month of 599, he was invested by the Sui sovereign with the title of "Yilizhendou qimin kehan" 意利珍豆啟民可汗, or "Qimin qaghan" (r. 599–611) for short, meaning "the qaghan of will power, wisdom and health."[60] The title Qimin was clearly intended as that of the great qaghan, the supreme leader of all Tujue territories. A town was set up as Dalicheng 大利城 to accommodate him and his entourage in Shuo Prefecture 朔州 (seat: Shuozhou, Shanxi). By that time, Qimin's Chinese wife, Princess Anyi, had died. The Sui court sent Princess Yicheng 義成 as his new wife.[61]

Despite Sui endorsement, Qimin's supreme leadership was not acknowledged by other Tujue groups who conducted raids against people in his new home territory. The Sui court then resettled Qimin in Xia 夏 and Sheng Prefectures 勝州 (west of Shuo Prefecture) in the Ordos area. It also set up a special garrison with twenty thousand troops under the command of General Zhao Zhongqing 趙仲卿, in an attempt to protect Qimin from attacks by Datou qaghan.[62] Still, Qimin remained vulnerable. In a 602 raid, a hostile Tujue army abducted six thousand people and two hundred thousand cattle from Qimin. Qimin did not get them back until the Sui forces attacked and defeated the invading army.[63]

Despite the military protection the Sui offered Qimin, it rarely involved itself in direct military intervention deep into Tujue territory, because the overriding aim of Wendi's policy was to support a friendly Tujue power as a buffer zone against other hostile Tujue forces. To that end, the Sui also encouraged continued settlement of subjugated Tujue population in the frontier area.[64]

The long-term investment in Qimin qaghan yielded its greatest payoff in 603 when the Tujue empire under Datou (Bujia 步迦) suddenly found itself in disarray. By then Datou had claimed leadership over all Tujue territories, with more than ten ethnic or tribal groups under his control, including the formidable Tiele, a nomadic Turkic people whose wide range of activity extended from Transoxiana to Gaochang. Having risen against him, they submitted themselves to Qimin's leadership.[65] As for Datou himself, he escaped west to Tuyuhun in present-day Qinghai.[66]

Yangdi inherited a cordial relationship with Eastern Tujue from his father. Its ruler Qimin, now a Sui protégé, had owed everything to the Sui—the grazing lands in the Ordos, his Chinese wives, the defense of his territory, the defeat of his challengers, and his dominance among the Tujue, among others. Like Wendi, Yangdi continued to shower favors on Qimin. When Qimin visited Luoyang in 606, to entertain him, Yangdi revived an artistic tradition at court, that of *sanyue* 散樂 (incidental music for acrobatic performance), which had been discontinued by Wendi. A *sanyue* troupe was gathered on the bank of Jicui 積翠 (Jadeite Green) Pond in the Park of Fragrant Flowers (Fanghua 芳華)[67] to put on a spectacular acrobatic show. It began with the appearance of a *sheli* 舍利 (dragon fish), cavorting, jumping, and splashing water, accompanied by large turtles, humans, and lesser animals.[68] A huge whale spurting out mist suddenly turned into a yellow dragon. Two entertainers danced facing each other on a tightrope, while a strong man performed acrobatic stunts, sometimes lifting a tripod, sometimes playing a cartwheel, a stone mortar, or a large urn on his palms. Two men balanced poles on their heads, on which acrobats showed off their gymnastic feats. There was also a divine turtle carrying a mountain on its back, and a magician spitting fire.[69]

While Qimin was reportedly startled by some of the performances, he seemed quite impressed with the show in general. However, a number of Sui high officials were highly critical of this ostentatious return to a decadent art form. But Yangdi was not to be deterred by criticism. Obviously Yangdi's style of displaying imperial generosity was quite different from that of his frugal father. He spent an enormous fortune on extravagant gifts to Qimin, and as expected, Qimin continued to show unswerving allegiance to the Sui throne. In a poem Yangdi wrote on the occasion of his 607 meeting with Qimin, he expressed a sense of great joy in bringing Qimin and his associates into submission:[70]

In [Ji]lusai were stationed [soldiers with their] giant flags,[71]
Around the Dragon Court the carriage with green plumage wound its way.[72]
[The curtain of] the felt tent[73] was raised when they saw which way the wind was,
The domed hut[74] was opened towards the sun.
Huhan[ye] 呼韓邪 came kowtowing,[75]
Tuqi 屠耆 followed in his footsteps.[76]
The braided-hair presented mutton,
The leather arm covers offered a cup of wine.[77]
What kind of Han Son of Heaven was [Wudi],
Who mounted the Platform of the Chanyu[78] in vain?[79]

Not only did Yangdi demonstrate a hegemonic view towards his northern nomadic neighbors in general, he also took great pride in having achieved more in pacifying the Tujue than what the Han emperors had done in subduing the Xiongnu.

As Yangdi was still on his inspection tour, an unexpected interlude further confirmed Qimin's loyalty. A Koguryŏ envoy went on an unannounced mission to see Qimin in 607, obviously seeking to form an alliance with Eastern Tujue.

Qimin had the envoy delivered to Yangdi, who would be suspicious of any secret Tujue-Koguryŏ liaison.[80]

In the last years of his life, Qimin requested Sinification of his Tujue tribes through the adoption of Chinese costumes. Yangdi declined Qimin's proposal and revealed his true intent in keeping the status quo, "The area north of the desert is not yet pacified. Expeditions and battles are still necessary. So long as you show your respect and submissiveness, why do you need to change your costumes?"[81]

Qimin and his people were to serve as a protective shield against potential threats lurking in Mongolia.[82] Qimin remained loyal to the Sui court until his death in 611. Yangdi absented himself from court for three days in mourning, the highest honor a foreign sovereign would receive in death. When Qimin's son, who had succeeded as Shibi qaghan 始畢可汗 (Duojishi 咄吉世, Duoji, or Tuji 吐吉; r. 611–619), requested to marry the Sui princess at his court, the wife of his deceased father, Yangdi gave his approval out of respect for a Tujue custom.[83]

In the wake of the disintegration of the tribal confederation under Datou qaghan in 603, a new dominant Tujue leader emerged—Chuluo qaghan 處羅可汗 (Daman 達漫, r. 603–611). The son of Nili and his Chinese wife Xiang 向, Chuluo, although identified in the sources as a Western Tujue leader, should probably be regarded as the third leader of the Abo branch of Eastern Tujue.[84] Yangdi and his advisers soon began to devise plans to deal with the perceived threat of Chuluo. Following Nili's death, Xiang married his brother Poshi 婆實, in compliance with a leviratic tradition. While the couple were paying a visit to Wendi's court Datou qaghan rebelled against the Sui in 599. The couple thereafter had stayed on in Daxingcheng. It is not known whether Xiang and her husband were held against their will, but the Sui used Xiang as a hostage against her son Chuluo. Like Datou before him, Chuluo was challenged by various groups nominally under his control. For example, his efforts to rein in the Tiele rebels failed miserably. At Yangdi's request, Chuluo became a nominal Sui vassal. After Chuluo turned down Yangdi's summons in 610 because of opposition from his own people, Pei Ju, who had devised a long-term stratagem of divide and rule towards China's northern neighbors, came up with a scheme to bring him to submission. By then Datou's grandson Shegui 射匱 (r. 605–617), now Western Tujue qaghan, had presented a marriage proposal. On Pei Ju's advice, the proposal was accepted, in an attempt to undercut Chuluo's authority. Yangdi and Pei Ju promised not only to support Shegui as the great qaghan, but also to allow him to marry a Sui princess on condition he should attack Chuluo. Shegui immediately struck and routed Chuluo, who had to abandon his wife and sons in order to escape to the oasis state of Gaochang in Turfan. On the intelligence provided by the Gaochang king Qu Boya, Pei Ju sent Chuluo's mother to persuade Chuluo to submit himself. As a Sui vassal, he was received by Yangdi in the Linshuo Palace in the twelfth month of 611.[85]

After Chuluo had been brought to submission, Yangdi lost no time in partitioning what was left of Chuluo's territory into three parts.[86] Paradoxically, with his wings clipped, Chuluo now began to receive more and more imperial favors. Yangdi entertained him lavishly with music performances and sumptuous banquets, and heaped generous rewards upon him. With five hundred cavalrymen under his command, Chuluo accompanied Yangdi on his expeditions, including those against Koguryŏ. Crowning all, Yangdi married Princess Xinyi 信義 to Chuluo in the first month of 614, and made an attempt to recover his lost territory, an attempt that was eventually abandoned because of the turmoil in China proper.

Completely deprived of any political and military power, Chuluo became a common fixture at the Sui court. As for his rival Shegui of Western Tujue, he owed his rise to the Sui, and did not intrude into Sui territory.[87] Yangdi's long-term strategy to subjugate the Abo branch of Eastern Tujue and keeping Western Tujue at bay was a success.

The relationship with Eastern Tujue itself, however, had deteriorated in the wake of the death of Qimin qaghan thanks largely to the intrigues carried out by Pei Ju, who attempted to duplicate the success of his divide and rule stratagem. Noticing that the population under Shibi's control had increased significantly, Pei Ju formulated a plan to create a rival against him. On his advice, a Sui princess was offered to Eji She 叱吉設, Shibi's younger brother. The idea was to set him up as the qaghan of the south. Eji turned down the offer and Shibi was soon informed about it. To add insult to injury, Pei Ju lured Shishu Huxi 史蜀胡悉, a trusted Tujue strategist, into the frontier area for trade and had him killed. Pei Ju then reported to Shibi that Shishu Huxi was killed because he attempted to defect to the Sui. Yangdi was well informed of Pei Ju's scheme and attempted to cover it up in an edict to the Tujue qaghan, "Since the Tujue are my subjects, if he (Shishu Huxi) defected, we both should eliminate him."[88] When Shibi realized what had really transpired, he was instantly transformed from a tribute-paying vassal into a most dangerous foe. Pei Ju's diplomacy of manipulation and deception in dealing with the Eastern Tujue not only ended in fiasco, but also placed the security of the Northern frontier in jeopardy.[89]

## Koguryŏ

Located to the east of Tujue, Koguryŏ was a lesser power with its southern frontier bordering on Sui China. As the most powerful of the three kingdoms

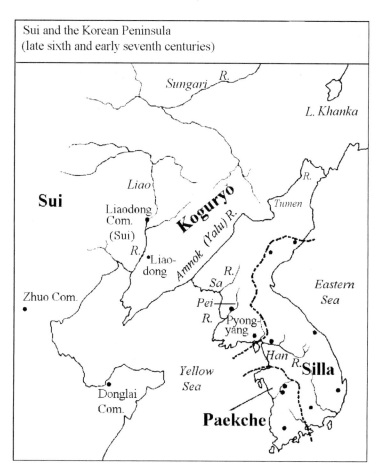

Map 10.3    Sui China and the Korean Peninsula

that occupied the Korean Peninsula (the other two being Paekche and Silla), Koguryŏ controlled north Korea and part of Manchuria (map 10.3).

Chinese sovereigns often regarded as a matter of course their claim to overlordship over Koguryŏ, a claim based on cultural and economic affinities and on historical precedents.[90] King Wu 武王 of the Western Zhou was believed to have enfeoffed Jizi 箕子, a Shang loyalist, in ancient Chosŏn in Korea.[91] Later, in the Western Han dynasty, Wudi 武帝 (r. 141–87 BC) conquered and colonized the area in 108 BC.[92]

After its emergence in the late first century BC, Koguryŏ as a state increasingly challenged the dominance of the Han Chinese in the centuries that followed.[93] With the weakening and fall of the Western Jin, Koguryŏ ended four centuries of Chinese rule in Korea. By the early fifth century, Koguryŏ, under King Kwanggaet'o 廣開土, took over the vast stretch of fertile land in southern Manchuria known as Liaodong.[94] Although its sovereigns thereafter received investiture from the Northern Wei and its two successor states, Northern Zhou and Northern Qi, Koguryŏ remained an independent state.[95]

In Sui times, Koguryŏ was a monarchy with a territory of about 2,000 *li* east-west and more than 1,000 *li* north-south. It had a triple capital system with Pyongyang as its main capital. The officialdom was divided into twelve ranks. The government derived its revenues from two kinds of tax: cloth and grain. Its military was armed with various kinds of weaponry similar to those of the Sui forces. For ritual and entertainment, the Koguryŏ had a complex array of musical instruments. Their funeral rites required those bereft of a parent or a husband to observe a mourning period of three years. At the funeral, a crying ceremony was followed by a drum dance accompanied by music to send off the deceased. Ghosts and spirits were worshipped, and their temples abounded.[96] Apparently, their economy, like that of China proper, was predominantly agrarian, and many of their customs were similar to those practiced by the Chinese. All this set them apart from the nomadic powers of Tujue, Rouran, Tiele, or Tuyuhun.[97]

At the founding of the Sui dynasty, King P'yŏngwŏn 平原 of Koguryŏ (r. 559–590), sent his embassy to Daxingcheng to receive the title of "king of Koryŏ" 高麗.[98] This was followed by a string of tributary missions. Although the tributary status of Koguryŏ had existed for centuries, it was only nominal. And the Sinitic or semi-Sinitic regimes to the south were not able to exert much influence on Koguryŏ. With the rise of the Sui as a united empire, in the judgment of the Sui leadership, that situation had to change, particularly in view of the fact that the Liaodong area under the suzerainty of Koguryŏ was traditionally a strategic area of paramount importance for North China.[99]

Wendi then sent an official letter to P'yŏngwŏn, which carried a strong sense of universal overlordship: "This emperor, having received the Mandate of Heaven, loves and nurtures all lands, and entrusts His Majesty with a corner of the sea to disseminate the civilizing influence of the court."[100] Indeed, the same concept governed Wendi's relations with other neighboring powers, including the mighty Tujue. However, Wendi's approaches to Tujue and Koguryŏ were quite different. While the Tujue were the dominant nomadic people with a formidable cavalry and vast territories, the Koguryŏ were a sedentary people like the Chinese, but with a much smaller population and territory. For Wendi, there was always the hope that Koguryŏ could be subjugated with a show of force.

After his easy victory over South China, Wendi became the undisputed ruler of China proper. The unexpected foray of the Mohe (Malgal) warriors led by the newly enthroned Koguryŏ king Yŏngyang 嬰陽 (r. 590–618) into Liaoxi enraged Wendi. Self-confident and contemptuous of the little kingdom in the Northeast, Wendi reacted with overwhelming force to the provocation. However, due to logistical problems, diseases, and inclement weather, Wendi's Koguryŏ campaign of 598 came to an ignominious end with the destruction of the mighty invading army.[101]

Fearing further reprisals from the Sui, King Yŏngyang hastened to deliver a self-deprecating letter to the Sui court in which he addressed himself as "Won 元 (Yŏngyang)—your vassal of night soil from Liaodong." Exhausted by the expedition, Wendi saw no point in attempting to punish a repentant Yŏngyang. Consequently, he was allowed to resume tributary relations.[102]

After Wendi was frustrated in his attempt at invasion, he was wise enough to keep a face-saving tributary relationship with Koguryŏ. Yangdi, however, was not content with the arrangement. By the time Chuluo was brought to submission, Yangdi was well on his way to initiate the first of his three aggressive military operations against Koguryŏ.[103]

The 607 incident in which King Yŏngyang's secret envoy was sighted at Qimin qaghan's tent provided Yangdi with an excuse for resuming punitive action against Koguryŏ. In response, Pei Ju presented a memorial in which he talked of Koguryŏ as "a land of caps and sashes," an expression often used to distinguish the Middle Kingdom from its barbarian neighbors. Koguryŏ as a civilized state should be incorporated on historical and cultural grounds. To conquer Koguryŏ was to lay claim to what rightfully belonged to China.[104] Wendi had failed in his attempt to subdue the small state because of the mediocre performance of Yang Liang. Pei urged Yangdi to make another attempt. Otherwise, Pei warned, a civilized country would be reduced to a land of barbarians. Using the co-option of Qimin as an example, Pei argued that the Sui court could easily subjugate Won (Yŏngyang).[105] Based on this advice, Yangdi delivered an edict to King Yŏngyang, which read like an ultimatum: "If you fail to come to the court, we will lead Qimin on a tour of inspection in your country."[106]

Commanding an army in excess of 1.1 million, Yangdi launched the first campaign against Koguryŏ in 612. After the invaders stormed the Koguryŏ outpost of Wuliluo, the captured town and its surrounding territory were incorporated into the Sui system of local administration as Liaodong Commandery 遼東郡. This clearly attests to Yangdi's intention to completely assimilate rather than just pacify this land of caps and sashes.[107] But this tiny territory turned out to be the only tangible gain of the campaign. The crushing defeats the Sui forces suffered, despite their vast superiority in number and equipment, at the hands of the Koguryŏ, humiliated Yangdi, and seriously challenged his aggressive frontier policy. In 613 and 614, the revengeful Yangdi mounted his second and third Liaodong campaigns. Instead of helping Yangdi achieve the ultimate goal of subjugating Koguryŏ, they deepened the domestic crisis already brewing in consequence of the first campaign. In that sense, the military actions against Koguryŏ marked a turning point in the history of the second reign.

Underscoring the foreign policy of the Sui was a centuries-old yet unarticulated concept, which can be described as that of universal overlordship. The earliest evidence of its existence is found in the "Yugong" 禹貢 (Tribute of Yu) chapter of the *Shang shu* (Book of documents), which devises a schematized government system of five domains (*wufu* 五服). Rulership emanated from the capital area to the rest of China and neighboring areas: *dianfu* 甸服 (royal domain), *houfu* 侯服 (domain of the nobles), *suifu* 綏服 (pacified domain), *yaofu* 要服 (domain of restraint), and *huangfu* 荒服 (wild domain).[108] From *dianfu* to *huangfu* central control mitigated as the distance of a given area from the capital increased.[109] While this idealized system had never been strictly followed, its basic idea remained the foundation for governing the geographical space of the Middle Kingdom. In times of political fragmentation, this system was reduced to little more than a utopia. But with the rise of a reunified empire under Wendi, serious efforts were made to actualize the fundamental concept of the five domains to restore the Chinese world order.[110]

Over the years, this concept had been further refined to reflect the reality of the frontier areas with proper consideration given to cultural and power elements. Countries permeated with Chinese culture like Koguryŏ and Gaochang were considered pan-Sinitic countries of caps and sashes. Yamato, which had been transformed thanks to the admiration it had for Chinese culture, could be included in the same category. Other neighbors like Tujue, Tuyuhun, Tiele, Qidan, and Mohe were barbarian powers with little cultural affinity with China. All of them participated in the Chinese world order by paying tribute to the Sui court.

The diplomatic maneuverings of the Sui á la Pei Ju to consolidate the Chinese world order were marked by a touch of realpolitik. In dealing with Tujue, the mightiest power on China's borders, the Sui army avoided costly strategic offensives to completely dislocate them from their home territory.[111] Instead, the Sui sovereigns preferred to marry off their imperial princesses to Tujue qaghans in exchange for peace, and did not hesitate to use the promise for marriage to play off one Tujue leader against another and to keep Tujue divided and weak. Although the Sui sovereigns were incensed by the impertinence of the sovereign of Yamato, a peripheral power, they chose not to take punitive military action. That would have been impractical, in light of the great land and sea distances that separated Sui China from Yamato and the latter's strategic insignificance.[112]

Sometimes in lieu of diplomacy, the Sui sovereigns carried out military operations beyond China proper to stabilize frontier situations or to impose Chinese dominance abroad. Occasionally these operations resulted in permanent territorial expansion. Two major annexations of non-Chinese territories occurred in Sui times, both during Yangdi's reign—the Qinghai-east Xinjiang area acquired from Tuyuhun and Yiwu in 609, and the Liaodong Commandery area seized from Koguryŏ in 612. Following the 609 invasion that resulted in the displacement of the Tuyuhun, the nomadic inhabitants whom the Sui court had no intention to assimilate, Yangdi set up a number of Chinese-style commanderies in the Qinghai-east Xinjiang area. Since the main objective of annexing this sparsely populated area was to protect the trade routes in Gansu, these new commanderies functioned more like military outposts colonized by convicts than fully incorporated local administrative units.[113] Along similar lines, Yangdi rejected the repeated requests Qimin qaghan made on behalf of his people to adopt the Chinese way of life, nor did he attempt to administratively absorb Tujue territory, even though the Sui court built settlements to accommodate Qimin and his Tujue subjects.[114]

On the other hand, the complete incorporation of the Liaodong area, inhabited by settled agricultural communities of the Koguryŏ, into the Sui system of local administration in 612 indicates the Sui's much greater willingness to assimilate a civilized pan-Sinitic people.[115] Gaochang, an oasis state with the closest cultural ties with China proper in the Western Regions, would have been treated in the same way had it not been for the collapse of the Sui itself. The incorporation of Gaochang was eventually carried out in 640 by Taizong (r. 626–649), the second emperor of the Tang dynasty.[116]

The predominant factor in determining whether a neighboring state had achieved a civilized status or not hinged on the degree of success it had in absorbing the complex Chinese institutions through adoption of Chinese-style legal codes and statutes. In the judgment of the Sui policymakers, the greater the success, the more civilized the state became. Agrarian societies, like the three states on the Korean peninsula and Japan, were successful and enthusiastic borrowers of the Chinese institutions. Nomadic powers, like Tujue, were not susceptible to the influence of the institutions of China, especially its legal codes and statutes.[117] Accordingly, the Sui court formulated two different types of strategy in its foreign policy: assimilation in the case of pan-Sinitic states and pacification in the case of nomadic powers.

Without doubt there was a strong sense of continuity in Sui foreign policy, but Wendi and Yangdi showed marked differences in its implementation. For an ambitious founder of an expansionist empire, Wendi was rather cautious in his approach to his neighbors. His style in external affairs can be described as one of limited engagement. His activity mainly concentrated on the Northern and Northeastern frontiers, with the subjugation of Tujue through diplomacy as his greatest achievement and the ill-fated Liaodong campaign as his worst fiasco.

Yangdi, on the other hand, with his ambitious vision for a dominant Chinese empire in East Asia, pursued a much more ambitious goal with greater tenacity. While he strove to keep the peace with Tujue on China's Northern frontier, he sent his generals on missions of conquest beyond the borders of the Sui empire in every direction, and enlarged Sui territory at the expense of Tuyuhun and Koguryŏ. Eventually, obsessed with his own great vision and completely blind to the odds stacked against him, Yangdi launched three military campaigns against Koguryŏ, which not only exhausted manpower and paralyzed the economy, but also caused his mighty empire to crumble.

# 11

# Epilogue

The reign of Yangdi was epitomized by the pursuit of grandeur as is evidenced by a series of overambitious enterprises, from the building of the most luxurious city to the undertaking of the greatest inland waterway project, to the launching of the largest military operation in known history. It is precisely this quest for grandeur and its apparent corollary, the loss of empire, that have invited so much passionate censure in traditional scholarship, censure that has clouded the prevailing view of Yangdi and his reign. Thus, it is proper at the conclusion of this study to attempt an impartial historical analysis of the dynamics of the age Yangdi lived in and a dispassionate reassessment of his place in history.

The significance of the age of Yangdi lies not only in its close association and reciprocal interaction with Yangdi, but also in the fact that it was one of the few pivotal periods where centuries of historical development were telescoped into the span of a generation.

In part thanks to its ephemeral character, the age of the Sui is hardly a favorite subject of hermeneutic analysis. Nonetheless, the issues of the Sui are unavoidable in any of the major macrohistorical theories on medieval China. Consequently, the most influential of those—the theses advanced by the twentieth century scholars Naitō Konan and Chen Yinke—give it serious consideration, even though their foci are not on the Sui era itself.

In a grand historiographical framework clearly reminiscent of the *Lebensalter* theory in the West that goes as far back as St. Augustine,[1] Naitō analogizes the history of a nation to that of a human being, from infancy to adulthood, to old age.[2] Within this framework, Naitō formulated his unique thesis on the periodization of Chinese history. In that thesis, Naitō argues that

221

the Sui and the early phases of the Tang were still rooted in a quintessentially medieval age, where court politics was dominated by an aristocracy of which the sovereign was simply the first among equals. A momentous transformation that took place in the later phases of the Tang and the ensuing Wudai and Northern Song periods brought about the collapse of the old aristocracy, while a meritocracy-based bureaucracy replaced the aristocracy-dominated officialdom. By promoting to leadership posts individuals of lower social stations, who depended more on imperial favors than pedigree and family prestige for prominence, the sovereign found himself in a position to rule in an increasingly absolutist fashion.[3]

The Naitō thesis purports to reveal some of the most dynamic historical trends in early imperial and medieval China, and does not intend to distinguish the short cycle of the Sui from the following Tang dynasty or one reign from another. It is not surprising that on closer examination, the Sui period does not fit squarely into the pattern. Its first sovereign, Wendi, had been a member of a powerful bloc within the Northern aristocracy. Whether it was geographically identified with Wuchuan or Guanlong, this elite group had been behind the creation of the Western Wei and Northern Zhou and provided dynastic founders for both the Sui and the Tang. During the initial phase of his rule, Wendi, with few exceptions, staffed key leadership posts with members of the aristocracy who belonged to the choronym-defined Guanzhong bloc and Shandong bloc. Imperial power was somewhat limited by decision-making court advisers from these blocs and by powerful personages like the Four Nobles. However, Wendi was able to significantly augment imperial authority at the expense of the aristocracy-dominated officialdom through centralizing civil and military powers both at the central and local levels.

During the second reign, while officialdom continued to be dominated by individuals of aristocratic background (particularly those of the Guanlong bloc), Yangdi made a greater effort at governmental and military centralization. The power of the aristocracy, as a counterweight against imperial despotism, was seriously weakened when Yangdi moved to stifle court dissent and circumvent the officially appointed chief ministers, the most powerful elements of the aristocratic officialdom. In their place, Yangdi appointed de facto chief ministers, who were in most cases personally indebted to the emperor for their career advancement and were thus less able or willing to confront the sovereign on issues of principle. Powerful personages did exist as in the case of the Seven Nobles and Five Nobles. But, in terms of prestige and power, they were in no way comparable to the Four Nobles under Wendi. The overall, diminished influence of the aristocracy contributed significantly to the extreme form of absolute sovereignty Yangdi exercised during his reign.

These observations are not intended to refute the Natiō thesis as a whole. Instead, they underscore the perennial potential for absolutism in a medieval society, which was actualized and magnified by the Sui experience, especially during its second reign. Still, the kind of absolutism practiced under the Sui did not continue after the founding of the Tang, due to a variety of reasons:

- First, the institution of chief ministership (*zaixiang* 宰相), although damaged on Yangdi's watch, was not officially abolished, and would be vigorously revived by the early Tang sovereigns.

- Second, although the mechanism of de facto chief ministership remained an option for the Tang sovereigns, its use was limited until much later.

- Third, although the power of the aristocracy was eclipsed during the Sui, the aristocracy itself continued to exist as a viable political force. With the rise of the Tang, the aristocracy reassumed its significant role in court politics.

- Fourth, the practice of meritocracy-based recruiting, which de-emphasized pedigree and could serve as a counterweight to aristocratic dominance, was still in its initial stages of development.

- Fifth, perhaps most important, the founding sovereigns of the Tang did not have the despotic temperament of either of the Sui sovereigns.

Chen Yinke approaches the political history of the Sui-Tang periods from the perspective of his primacy of Guanzhong thesis, which posits as the focus of political struggle the factional tension between essentially two choronym-based power groups, namely, the Guanlong bloc and the Shandong bloc. The Guanlong bloc had come into being in Western Wei times as is indicated by a *Sui shu* passage:

After Taizu 太祖 of Northern Zhou (Yuwen Tai) entered the pass (i.e., Guanzhong), he ordered the meritorious male offspring [of the Tuoba aristocracy] to become chiefs of their clans. Genealogical records were made to trace their ancestral lines. He then assigned various prefectures within the pass (i.e., Guanzhong) as places of their choronyms.

From the time of its formation, the Guanlong bloc, Chen argues, had attempted to perpetuate its dominance of court politics through the primacy of Guanzhong policy, a policy resisted by non-Guanlong groups, especially the Shandong bloc. Gradual displacement of the Guanlong bloc ensued which paralleled the decline of the old aristocracy, and the ascendancy of professional bureaucrats.[4]

Some scholars view the existence of the Guanlong bloc in a different light, arguing that Guanlong as the home territory of the former Western Wei and Northern Zhou was the only viable geographical area from which the court could draw trustworthy talents. Consequently, the central officialdom could not help but be dominated by that bloc.[5] There is prima facie evidence of the continued dominance of the bloc at the founding of the Sui dynasty. Apart from this, however, there is little evidence that the Sui sovereigns consistently pursued the pro-Guanlong policy. Neither did Sui officials and scholars form factions along the lines of bloc interests and identity in favor of or against Guanlong.

During the second reign, an overwhelming majority of high ranking officials were still of Guanlong choronym. However, most of the appointees to de facto chief ministership were from non-Guanlong blocs. This does not necessarily indicate a deliberate effort on the part of Yangdi to bypass the primacy of Guanzhong policy. Instead, it may well have been the result of an enlarged talent pool as the process of integration deepened in the East and South.

While the theses by Naitō and Chen illuminate the dynamics of court-elite relations and inter-elite relations in medieval China, which may have provided the driving force behind certain historical developments, the pertinence of these theses to the Sui is an issue of academic debate and will continue to be so. There is, however, a much greater academic consensus on the significance and nature of the Sui institutions, political, legal, and educational, which came into being as a result of wide-ranging reforms introduced during the first reign. The reformist trend continued unabated during the second reign. In certain areas there was clear consistency in reform objectives throughout the Sui. The administrative reforms established a governmental synthesis that was to exert a dominant influence on the bureaucratic system for hundreds of years to come and paved the way for more effective centralization. The legal reforms strove for greater legal clarity and leniency. The education reforms laid to rest the obsolete, recommendation-based recruitment system, and laid the groundwork for the formation of a much more effective new system with a greater focus on merit.

Despite apparent consistency in reform themes throughout the Sui period, Yangdi, not infrequently, adopted measures that were diametrically opposed to those of his father. Take, for example, the school system. Towards the end of the first reign, a minimalist approach was adopted to close a large number of state-run schools thanks to Wendi's disillusionment with Confucian learning. During the second reign, this trend was deliberately reversed. The school system was vigorously revitalized in order to underscore the imperial commitment to kingly rule.

Outside the realm of institutional reform, few issues were of greater significance for royalty and commoner alike than religion. Wendi played a crucial role in reviving both Daoism and Buddhism as China emerged from one of the darkest periods in the history of organized religion. Consequently, the Sui saw the sustained growth of Daoism and the vigorous renaissance of Buddhism. During the first reign, the Louguan school of Daoism became a court favorite, while Buddhism with aggressive royal support reassumed its position as a truly ecumenical religion. During the second reign, while there was little deviation from the official pro-Daoist policy of the first reign, the greatest Daoist beneficiary was not the Louguan school of the North but the Shangqing school of the South, which may testify to the greater integration of the South and Yangdi's personal preference for Southern culture.

Meanwhile, Buddhism (especially the Tiantai school) continued to receive court favors. The court was involved in the patronage of such diverse religious activities as monastery construction, ordinations, and icon productions, although royal patronage of the second reign paled besides that of the first reign in terms of quantities. A most striking difference in religious policy between the first and second reigns lay in their treatments of the Buddhist clergy. During the first reign, Buddhism may have occasionally been used for certain political purposes, but there are no records of serious sovereign-clergy conflict on such major issues as immunity from reverencing the sovereign, ordination, and the expansion of monastic property. The second reign, however, saw Yangdi, out of a desire for heightened temporal power, clash time and again with the clergy on these issues with damaging consequences for the church and court-clergy relations. Nevertheless, even in confrontations with the clergy, Yangdi displayed an amazingly high degree of tolerance. Thus to the end of his life he remained on favorable terms with the clergy. What is more important, organized religion, despite a few impetuous demands by the second Sui sovereign, did not sustain major setbacks. In the last analysis, the Sui, on the whole, was an age of imperially sponsored religious prosperity, which paved the way for the vigorous embrace and promotion of Daoism by the Tang court and the doctrinal diversity and scholastic sophistication of Tang Buddhism.

In the more mundane area of the economy, the Sui constructed an interlocking web of institutions to guarantee timely receipt of revenues on the basis of long-term economic stability, ranging from the monetary system to the granary network, to demographic monitoring, to the equal-field land tenure system, and, above all, the taxation system, which provided a reliable source of income for the government without overburdening the taxpaying population. Thanks to the proper functioning of the economic institutions, at its peak in 609, the Sui boasted a registered population in excess of forty-six million, the largest ever recorded since the fall of the Han empire. The economic equilibrium was eventually thrown off balance because of excessive demands on the labor force for public works, defense projects, and external war. Ironically, the same economic institutions, reconstituted by the much more prudent sovereigns of the Tang and under their careful management, provided the foundation for a prolonged period of economic growth and expansion.

As Sui China evolved into an expanding, united empire, a foreign policy was formulated during the first reign to enhance the prestige of the empire and to safeguard the settled communities from nomadic raids. And this profoundly transformed China's relations with the outside world. In the second reign, Yangdi pursued a much more expansionist foreign policy with vigor and dynamism. Consequently, the empire, buttressed by its economic power and military might, took on the role of a hegemonic power, extending its influence far beyond neighboring areas and occasionally engaging in territorial aggrandizement. Diplomatic missions arrived from as far afield as Persia in West Asia, Tujue in the North, the Korean states in the Northeast, Japan in the East, and Linyi, Zhenla and Chitu in Southeast Asia. Court missions of exploration or conquest traveled to faraway lands in all four directions. Convoluted schemes were engineered to weaken the most powerful nomadic empire of the North, Tujue, and large-scale military operations were launched to bring Koguryŏ, a semi-Sinified state with close historical and cultural connections with China proper, into the orbit of the empire. These international actions bespoke a grand vision in which China assumed the dominant position in the world, a vision infused into the Sui foreign policy.

Fostered by this environment of proactive international engagement, the Sui, particularly during the second reign, refreshed and greatly expanded knowledge about its neighbors, a knowledge epitomized by Pei Ju's famous work on the Western Regions,[6] and became a most dynamic age for political, economic, and cultural exchanges across the borders.

## YANGDI AS MAN AND SOVEREIGN

No matter how significant the various social, political, cultural, economic, and diplomatic forces of the Sui may have been, it was Yangdi, by virtue of his personality and power, who played the dominant part in shaping the last phase of the Sui empire before destroying it. Against these historical contexts, Yangdi's life and actions merit further examination.

Any attempt at assessing Yangdi's accomplishments and failures will inevitably involve addressing the numerous judgments Yangdi has received in the past. One of the earliest and most influential examples of these judgments was his posthumous title "Yangdi" or "Emperor Yang" itself. Traditionally, posthumous titles were conferred on royalty and famous personages to encapsulate the essence of their lives in a succinct manner. Yangdi's was issued not long after his death in the ninth month of 618 by the successor Tang court.

According to the *Rules of Posthumous Titles* (*Shifa* 諡法), the key character *yang* 煬 means (1) to lust after beautiful women and distance oneself from ritual; (2) to abandon ritual and stay away from the masses; and (3) to defy Heaven and abuse the people. Although as a disparaging posthumous epithet *yang* had been available since antiquity, it was rarely used for dynasts. In fact, the only one who shared this title before Sui Yangdi was Chen Shubao, the last emperor of the Chen dynasty, who lost his country through incompetence, neglect of government, and overindulgence.[7] Ironically, Chen received the title in death from none other than Sui Yangdi himself. In conferring the same title on Sui Yangdi, the Tang court not only conveyed its condemnatory view on the recipient, but also set the tone for the negative discourse on him in traditional historiography and popular literature.[8]

This negative discourse is rooted in the widespread anti-Yangdi sentiment that began to surface in the period of Sui-Tang transition as evidenced by some of the public denunciations that have survived in the sources. As early as 613, Yang Xuangan issued one of the first vituperative statements against Yangdi, almost five years before his death.[9] When Yuwen Huaji and his fellow conspirators captured Yangdi in the third month of 618, they announced to his face the ten heinous crimes he had allegedly committed as emperor.[10] The most influential early critique of Yangdi, however, is found in the commentary appended to Yangdi's basic annals in the *Sui shu*, a work penned not long after Yangdi's death by a group of Tang scholars headed by Wei Zheng, an ex-Sui official who became Taizong's confidant and close adviser during the Tang dynasty:

> Relying on his wealth and might, he sought to satisfy his insatiable desires. Considering the institutions of the Yin and the Zhou inadequate, he emulated the Qin and Han [institutions] in terms of scale and magnitude. Conceited about his talent and full of himself, he despised apparent virtue. Restless at heart, he assumed an appearance of uprightness. He put on magnificent hats and costumes to conceal his treachery and exterminated remonstrators to cover up his errors. He was excessively lascivious, [and created] an increasing number of [harsh] laws and statutes. [Under him], the teaching of the Four Standards (*siwei* 四維) was abolished and legal punishments were [as cruel] as the Five Disfigurements (*wunue* 五虐). He destroyed his own flesh and blood, and butchered his loyal subjects. Those who received rewards had done no meritorious deeds, and those who were executed were unaware of their crimes.
>
> He waged war frequently as a result of his arrogance and anger, and pursued endlessly his building projects. On many occasions, he toured Shuofang 朔方 and descended on Liaodong three times. The

banners [of his procession] trailed ten thousand *li* long. Taxes were levied on one hundred items. Cunning bureaucrats oppressed and squeezed [the subjects], making their life unbearable. Thus on his urgent orders, despotic rules were laid down to harass them, harsh penalties and severe laws were created to subdue them, and armored warriors with their military might were dispatched to watch them. From then on, all was in turmoil within the seas, and [the people] could no longer go on living.[11]

These late Sui and early Tang records portrayed Yangdi as a hedonistic philanderer, a prodigal spendthrift, an oppressive ruler, a cold-blooded murderer, an impulsive aggressor, a hater of remonstrance, a lover of sycophancy, and, above all, a tyrant who had concentrated in himself the worst possible attributes for a sovereign. No doubt, this kind of judgment contributed significantly to the formation of the unanimously negative view traditional scholars held of Yangdi, a view that has persisted into our time.[12]

While it is impossible to ignore these statements, since all of them contain some elements of truth, beneath the generic accusations lie the ill-concealed attempts by the accusers to advance their own agendas. Yang Xuangan hoped to win over Sui government officials to his anti-Sui cause. Yuwen Huaji and his associates wanted to rationalize their regicidal decision. Wei Zheng provided a moral justification for the dynastic change. Apparently, the self-serving intent of these animadversions undercut their own veracity.

This persistent, accusatory bias among traditional scholars makes all the more necessary a reevaluation of Yangdi, one which, based on rigorous textual research and recent scholarship, examines him as man and sovereign in his totality, focusing on those crucial factors that played, individually and in combination with one another, determining roles in his life and reign.

First and foremost, Yangdi was a man of extraordinary achievement, different from other stereotypical, evil last rulers. Notable among his personal accomplishments was his mastery of poetry and prose, generally acknowledged by later literati in spite of their prejudice against his personality.

He was a competent administrator, at least during his preaccession years, a fact attested by his peaceful tenure as the imperial prince stationed in the Bingzhou area, albeit under the tutelage of his mentors; by his successful administrative coordination of the conquest of the South; and especially by his exemplary service as the highest Sui governing official of the South. His Southern experience in no small way contributed to Wendi's decision to appoint him as crown prince in place of his brother Yang Yong.

He was a great visionary like the First Emperor and Han Wudi, two of his most admired heroes in history. The strategic structures he created no doubt stood as testimony to his extraordinary foresight and brilliant strategic sense, which was also manifest in his thoroughgoing preparations for war against Koguryŏ. Sui Luoyang, the vital political and economic center of the East, was one of the greatest legacies he left to the Tang dynasty. The Grand Canal system, of which Luoyang functioned as a pivot of communication, closely integrated the Guanzhong area, the North, and the South, for the first time in history. Both Luoyang and the Grand Canal yielded enormous benefits to posterity for generations to come. The Great Wall, although possibly of questionable effectiveness, served as a physical bulwark to deter raids from the steppe. Pursuing a foreign policy of expansionism, Yangdi, for better or worse, enlarged Sui China's territory to its largest extent.[13]

He was a highly energetic and innovative reformer. Yangdi's reforms are grossly underrated by scholars past and present. This academic neglect may be partially explained by the fact that Yangdi was overshadowed by his predecessor Wendi, one of the great reformers of all times. Moreover, thanks to the ill repute of Yangdi, later governments strove to dissociate themselves from him and were reluctant to acknowledge their debt to his reform legacy. Nevertheless, through reform, Yangdi significantly strengthened the power of the court while reducing local administrative and military authority. He restored the Confucian education system demoted by his father to its full glory and then developed it to levels never seen under the first reign. The *jinshi* degree introduced during his reign was to become the most prized academic degree in the Tang civil service examination system. He overhauled the overly harsh legal system of the previous reign, and recodified the laws with an emphasis on clemency, a welcome relief for his subjects.

For all his accomplishments, Yangdi had his share of blunders, scandals, and vices, and his reign was plagued with serious political, economic, and foreign policy problems. The process of his succession was tainted by palace intrigues. In his pursuit of the throne, he was criminally implicated in the death of the ailing sovereign, contrary to the view held by certain revisionists who attempt to absolve him. The tragic event was rooted in the inherently flawed institution of hereditary succession by imperial fiat. Theoretically, this system would allow the sovereign the flexibility to select the very best scion in terms of moral integrity and political competence, and to remove him in case he proved to be unworthy of the task. The post of heir apparent itself offered so much hope and promise of power that it was the most sought after prize among imperial princes. But to the disadvantage of the heir apparent, under normal circumstances, his fate was entirely at the whim of the emperor. To make things still worse, the system provided no exit mechanism at all. The holder of the post could not possibly return to an ordinary princely life even if he desired it. He either had to succeed his father on the throne or be deposed in humiliation. To avoid the fate of a deposed crown prince, Yangdi, against great odds, secretly took control of the emperor's security unit. When Wendi made the sudden move to replace him, Yangdi was prompted into action out of an instinct for self-preservation and a thirst for the ultimate power. While successful usurpers of the throne in Chinese history routinely exterminated the sovereign either on the throne or after deposition, what made Yangdi's case unique was the fact that the victim, Wendi, was the sovereign and the father of the regicide. Viewed in this context, Yangdi's was the ultimate act of lèse majesté and a flagrant violation of the fundamental tenet of filial piety. Suspicion of usurpation weakened his claim to legitimacy, and touched off a rebellion. The speedy suppression of the rebellion helped consolidate his grip on power but the seeds of mistrust had already been sown.

Closely related to the murder scandal was a sex scandal that unfolded prior to the accession and continued thereafter. The sexual advances Yangdi made on Lady Chen triggered a violent response from a dying Wendi, whose order to have him removed from the post of crown prince became the prime reason for his own murder. Immediately after Wendi's death, Yangdi moved recklessly to consummate his incestuous relations with Ladies Chen and Cai, two of his father's favorite concubines. Since his behavior flouted established mores, Yangdi was perennially stigmatized as an immoral sex pervert and a philanderer.[14]

Far more damaging than sexual excesses to Yangdi's reputation was his heavy-handed handling of criticism at court. When it became obvious that Yangdi's rule was headed for disaster, some high officials attempted by way of remonstration to guide the newly enthroned sovereign away from his policy of overspending and overbuilding while others voiced their unofficial criticisms. But Yangdi, who claimed that "I by nature dislike remonstration,"[15] went out of his way to destroy the mechanism of remonstratoin and silence criticism: He ousted Su Wei, a key decision-maker at both Wendi's and Yangdi's courts, for his unpalatable suggestions, and executed the officials who dared to criticize him. Suppression of court critics allowed Yangdi to rule with virtual immunity. But the same immunity blinded him to his own errors and excesses, which in turn jeopardized his rule.

The situation was further exacerbated by his lack of good interpersonal communications skills, so essential for the success of exemplary sovereigns like Han Gaozu and Tang Taizong. Cut off from rational advice, Yangdi moved to override the new and more lenient legal system he had helped to create, and, when faced with a deteriorating social order, introduced severe penalties to keep the populace in check.

Harsh laws themselves probably would not have brought about the collapse of the dynasty, but they were symptomatic of the serious malaise of society and, particularly, of the economy. Obviously, the destruction of the Sui economic system intensified in the last few years of the second reign, but it was a gradual process that took years to complete. When Yangdi inherited the

Sui empire from his father, the economy was in excellent condition. The economic base of the empire began to erode as Yangdi implemented an irresponsible fiscal policy and pursued extravagances. To bring his public works projects, which entailed enormous economic and human costs, to timely completion, Yangdi resorted to excessive fiscal impositions, notably the abusive use of corvée labor. In addition to national super-projects such as Luoyang and the Grand Canal, he dotted the landscape of North and South China with numerous, lavishly built secondary and touring palaces. He frequently undertook grandiose tours by river and land, stretching an already overstrained economy to the limit. Eventually the economic system meticulously constructed by Wendi unraveled under the crushing weight of an oppressive government.

Compounding the economic problems were a series of misjudgments in foreign policy which would result in the débâcle of the empire. The Tujue strategy of containment and pacification (as devised by Pei Ju), in spite of its initial success, led to estranged Sui-Eastern Tujue relations. With Shibi qaghan turning hostile, Yangdi lost a powerful ally, whose formidable cavalry might have served as a deterrent against other Northern neighbors, including Koguryŏ. Instead, Yangdi himself narrowly escaped Shibi's assault at the Northern outpost of Yanmen. His subsequent failure to appease his disgruntled officers, who had risked their lives to defend Yanmen, gravely compromised their loyalty, sowing the seeds of defection and mutiny.

Despite the prominent place Tujue occupied in Sui foreign policy, Yangdi devoted the lion's share of his attention to Koguryŏ, with a strategy of conquest and total assimilation that adversely affected the domestic situation. As early as 611, as his war preparations against the tiny Northeastern state were underway, the North China plain, the granary of the Sui, was devastated by a severe flood followed by a widespread famine. The economy, seriously impacted by the loss of labor and crop failures, was brought to the brink of collapse with continued impressment and war requisitions. Consequently, insurgencies organized by destitute commoners in the flood-stricken area broke out. In the three ensuing expeditionary campaigns, Yangdi foolhardily threw the main force of his army into the conflict on unfamiliar terrain, impervious to ruinously heavy casualties. All three campaigns failed to break the resistance of the Koguryŏ and bring them to submission.

There are specific factors accounting for the failure of each campaign. The routing of the Sui army on the first campaign can be attributed, among other things, to the devastating defeats inflicted on the Sui army on the Sa River by a mobile and well-prepared enemy force and to Yangdi's own unwilling to delegate sufficient power to the field commanders; the retreat from the second campaign was caused by the rebellion organized by the high-ranking Sui official Yang Xuangan; and the calling off of the third campaign, in spite of initial victories, was probably a result of massive desertion of conscripts. Other problems were shared by all three: an economy weakened by the flood and worsened by the war efforts, hastily conscripted and poorly trained troops, lack of tactical coordination, and failure to build international alliances. Above all, despite his astuteness, Yangdi did not possess the military talent of a great general to execute a large-scale operation.

The impact of these external campaigns was catastrophic enough by itself. When accompanied by the severe economic depression that resulted from extraordinarily costly public works projects and other extravagances, they generated a synergetic effect that led to massive dislocation, disruption of livelihood, and loss of life. The populace, pushed beyond their threshold of tolerance, joined the tide of rebellion in increasing numbers, which seriously undermined the already tenuous fabric of the empire.

Yangdi's response to popular rebellion—the most menacing domestic crisis—was conspicuously slow and ill-informed. This was symptomatic of his rigidly established military priorities. He regarded insurgencies led by royal members or high officials such as Yang Liang and Yang Xuangan as serious threats to the throne, and would spare no effort to crush them. However, he would assign low priority to the suppression of those local rebellions led by disaffected commoners. This problem of misplaced military priorities, which came about from grossly underestimating the disruptive power of popular rebellion, was aggravated by Yangdi's inability to adapt to new developments. When rebellion was crying out for attention, he took no initiative in dealing with it militarily, nor did he attempt to adopt any socioeconomic measures to eradicate its root causes.

Just as fatal as his flawed military priorities was his hierarchical ordering of geographical regions in China proper in terms of strategic importance. To him, the Central Plain area with Luoyang at its core was the center of activity. Next came the South, which held considerable cultural and sentimental value for him. The Guanzhong area with Daxingcheng at its center ranked the lowest of the three key areas. This ranking system made some strategic sense in the formative years of the second reign when the recalcitrant East was being fully incorporated into his sphere of influence, and when effective communication with the South was being gradually established. It continued to serve certain strategic purpose during his Liaodong campaigns. But when the entire country was embroiled in turmoil towards the end of the second reign, his only option was to shift his strategic focus to Guanzhong, a place known for its defensibility, vast riches, and easy access to the North China plain, because neither the Central Plain nor the South was ideal for the remaining Sui forces to regroup, entrench, and rejuvenate.[16]

Nonetheless, Yangdi strenuously refused to acknowledge the strategic importance of Guanzhong—he would execute almost anyone who attempted to persuade him to move west. In consequence of his obdurate opposition to making Guanzhong his base of operations, when the time came for him to abandon the East, Yangdi made the fatal decision to move his power center to the South, and forfeited his last chance to reverse the deteriorating situation.

Ultimately, Yangdi's inordinate number of errors and missteps set in motion the process of rapid decline. The subsequent degeneration of the socioeconomic, military, and political structures of the Sui brought about its precipitous fall, which neither the glorious institutional, architectural and infrastructural achievements of the empire nor the intellect, brilliance and vision of its sovereign could prevent.

By the time of Yangdi's death, Li Yuan, a powerful Sui court official and one of the many claimants to imperial power, had been well-entrenched in Guanzhong, an area whose strategic importance he clearly understood. After forcing the puppet Sui emperor Gongdi 恭帝 (r. 617–618) into retirement, Li Yuan, in the fifth month of 618, held his own coronation ceremony at the Taiji 太極 (Daxing) Basilica in Chang'an (Daxingcheng) to declare the establishment of the Tang dynasty (618–907).[17] Deriving much of its strength from the Sui legacy left by Yangdi and his predecessor, this Guanzhong-based new dynasty blossomed into a brilliant empire.

# Appendix 1

Central Government Appointments

TABLE 1   Key central government offices under the Sui and Early Tang

| | Wendi | Yangdi | Early Tang |
|---|---|---|---|
| **Three Preceptors (sanshi 三師)** | | | |
| Grand Preceptor (taishi 太師) | Ditto | Ditto | Ditto |
| Grand Mentor (taifu 太傅) | Ditto | Ditto | Ditto |
| Grand Guardian (taibao 太保) | Ditto | Ditto | Ditto |
| **Three Dukes (sangong 三公)** | | | |
| Defender-in-chief (taiwei 太尉) | Ditto | Ditto | Ditto |
| Minister of Education (situ 司徒) | Ditto | Ditto | Ditto |
| Minister of Works (sikong 司空) | Ditto | Ditto | Ditto |
| **Departments (sheng 省)** | | | |
| State Affairs (shangshu 尚書) | Ditto | Ditto | Ditto |
| Chancellery (menxia 門下) | Ditto | Ditto | Ditto |
| Secretariat (neishi 內史) | Ditto | Ditto | zhongshu 中書 |
| Palace Library (mishu 秘書) | Ditto | Ditto | Ditto |
| Palace Domestic Service (neishi[a] 內侍) | Palace Administration (dianmei 殿內) | Ditto | neishi[a] |
| **Boards (bu 部)** | | | |
| **under the Department** | | | |
| **of State Affairs** | | | |
| Board of Personnel (li 吏) | Ditto | Ditto | Ditto |
| Board of Rites (li[a] 禮) | Ditto | Ditto | Ditto |
| Board of War (bing 兵) | Ditto | Ditto | Ditto |
| Board of Justice (duguan 都官/after 583: xing 刑) | xing | Ditto | Ditto |
| Board of Revenue (duzhi 度支 /after 583: min 民) | min | hu 戶 | hu 戶 |
| Board of Works (gong 工) | Ditto | Ditto | Ditto |

| Category | | | |
|---|---|---|---|
| Terraces (*tai* 臺) | Terrace of Censors; Censorate (*yushi* 御史) | Ditto | Ditto |
| | Terrace of Waterways (*dushui* 都水) | Became a directorate | Ditto |
| | | Terrace of Receptions (*yezhe* 謁者) | Abolished |
| | | Terrace of Inspectors (*sili* 司隸) | Abolished |
| Directorates (*jian* 監) | None | Palace Domestic Service (*changqiu* 長秋) | *neishi³ sheng* |
| | After 600: Palace Buildings (*jiangzuo* 將作) | Education (*guozi* 國子) | *guozi xue* 學 |
| | | Ditto | Ditto |
| | After 601: Waterways (*dushui* 都水) | Imperial Manufactories (*shaofu* 少府) | Ditto |
| | | Ditto | Ditto |
| Courts (*si* 寺) | Court of Imperial Sacrifices (*taichang* 太常) | Ditto | Ditto |
| | Court of Imperial Entertainments (*guanglu* 光祿) | Ditto | Ditto |
| | Court of the Palace Garrison (*weiwei* 衛尉) | Ditto | Ditto |
| | Court of the Imperial Clan (*zongzheng* 宗正) | Ditto | Ditto |
| | Court of the Imperial Stud (*taipu* 太僕) | Ditto | Ditto |
| | Court of Judicial Review (*dali* 大理) | Ditto | Ditto |
| | Court for Dependencies (*honglu* 鴻臚) | Ditto | Ditto |
| | Court of the National Granaries (*sinong* 司農) | Ditto | Ditto |
| | Court for the Palace Revenues (*taifu* 太府) | Ditto | Ditto |
| | Court for Education (*guozi* 國子) | Became a directorate | Ditto |
| | Court of Palace Buildings (*jiangzuo* 將作) | Became a directorate | Ditto |

TABLE 2　Garrison commands and guards under the Sui

| A Wendi | B Yangdi |
|---|---|
| 1. Left and Right Guard Garrison Commands (weifu 衛府) | Left and Right Guards/Standby Guards (wei/yiwei 翊衛) |
| 2. Left and Right Armed Guard Garrison Commands (wuwei fu 武衛府) | Left and Right Militant Guards (wuwei 武衛) |
| 3. Left and Right Armed Reserve Garrison Commands (wubou fu 武候府) | Left and Right Reserve Guards (bowei 候衛) |
| 4. | Left and Right Cavalry Guards (qiwei 騎衛) |
| 5. | Left and Right Protective Guards (yuwei 御衛) |
| 6. Left and Right Metropolitan Garrison Commands (lingjun fu 領軍府) | Left and Right Encampment Guards (tunwei 屯衛) |
| 7. Left and Right Commanding Left and Right Garrison Commands (ling zuoyou fu 領左右府) | **Left and Right Imperial Bodyguard Garrison Commands** (beishen fu 備身府) |
| 8. Left and Right Palace Gate Garrison Commands (jianmen fu 監門府) | **Left and Right Gate Palace Garrison Commands** (jianmen fu) |

Sources: *SuS* 28.778–79, 28.793–94, 28.800–801; Gu Jiguang 1978, 107–108, 116–118.
A1–A3, A6–A8 were also known as the Twelve Garrison Commands; **B7 and B8 in boldface** = non-*fubing* units; B1–B6 were also known as the Twelve Guards; B1–B8 were also known as the Sixteen Garrison Commands.

TABLE 3 Chief ministers under Wendi (581–604)*
Total (posts): 21 (100%); Guanlong: 17 (81%); Shandong: 4 (19%). Total (appointees): 14

A. Vice presidents of the left and right of the Department of State Affairs (shangshu zuo you puye 尚書左右僕射)
Subtotal: 6

| Name | Choronym in | Bloc | yr/m–yr/m | Father/Note | Sources |
|---|---|---|---|---|---|
| Gao Jiong 高潁 | Bohai 渤海 | Shandong | 581/1–581/8; 582/6–599/8 | NZ prefect/Left | ZS 37; SuS 41; BS 72 |
| Zhao Jiong 趙煚十 | Tianshui 天水 | Guanlong | 581/2–584/? | NW assist. dir. of SSS/Right | SuS 46; BS 75 |
| Zhao Fen 趙芬 | Tianshui | Guanlong | 581/8–582/6 | NZ prefect/Left | SuS 46; BS 75; Jinshi cuibian 38 |
| Yu Qingze 虞慶則 | Jingzhao 京兆 | Guanlong | 584/4–589/1 | NZ comm. governor/Right | SuS 40; BS 73 |
| Su Wei 蘇威 | Jingzhao | Guanlong | 589/4–592/7 601/1–607/7 | WW board president/Right | SuS 41; BS 63 |
| Yang Su 楊素 | Huayin 華陰 | Guanlong | 592/12–601/1 601/1–605/2 | NZ prefect/Right /Left | SuS 48; BS 41 |

B. President (nayan 納言) of the Chancellery (menxia sheng 門下省)
Subtotal: 6

| Name | Choronym in | Bloc | yr/m–yr/m | Father/Note | Sources |
|---|---|---|---|---|---|
| **Gao Jiong 高潁** | Bohai | Shandong | 581/2–? | NZ prefect | ZS 37; SuS 41; BS 72 |
| Liu Ji 柳機 | Hedong 河東 | Shandong | Early KH | NW VP of SSS | ZS 22; SuS 47; BS 64 |
| **Su Wei 蘇威** | Jingzhao | Guanlong | 581/3–590/7; 594/7–601/1 | WW board president | SuS 41; BS 63 |
| **Yang Su 楊素** | Huayin | Guanlong | 589/6–590/7 | NZ prefect | SuS 48; BS 41 |
| Yang Shuang 楊爽 | Huayin | Guanlong | ?–587 | Yang Zhong/Wendi's stepbrother | SuS 44 |
| Yang Da 楊達 | Huayin | Guanlong | 602/10–612/5 | NZ prefect/Wendi's nephew | SuS 43 |

TABLE 3   Continued

C. President of the Secretariat (*neishi ling/jian* 內史令/監)
Subtotal: 9

| Name | Choronym in | Bloc | yr/m–yr/m | Father/Note | Sources |
|---|---|---|---|---|---|
| **Yu Qingze** | Jingzhao | Guanlong | 581/2–584/4 | NZ comm. governor | *SuS* 40; *BS* 73 |
| Li Delin 李德林 | Boling 博陵 | Shandong | 581/2–590/4 | NW erudite | *SuS* 42; *BS* 72 |
| **Zhao Fen** | Tianshui | Guanlong | Early KH | NZ prefect | *SuS* 46; *BS* 75 |
| **Zhao Jiong** | Tianshui | Guanlong | 583/4–? | NW assist. dir. of SSS | *SuS* 46; *BS* 75 |
| Yang Guang 楊廣 | Huayin | Guanlong | 586–588 | Wendi/Yangdi | *SuS* 3 |
| **Yang Su** 楊素 | Huayin | Guanlong | 590/7–592/7 | Wendi | *SuS* 48; *BS* 41 |
| Yang Xiu 楊秀 | Huayin | Guanlong | 592/2–593/6 | Wendi | *SuS* 45 |
| Yang Jian⁺ 楊暕 | Huayin | Guanlong | 599/6–601 | Yangdi | *SuS* 59; *BS* 71 |
| Yang Zhao 楊昭 | Huayin | Guanlong | 601/1–604 | Yangdi | *SuS* 59; *BS* 71 |

comm. = commandery (*jun* 郡); KH = Kaihuang 開皇 reign (581–600); prefect = *zhou cishi* 州刺史; SSS = *shangshu sheng* (Department of State Affairs); **boldface** = subsequent appointments

* The tabulations in this and later tables are in part based on the research of Yamazaki 1956. Similar tables for the first reign are also found in Han Sheng 1998, 259–67. We regard as aristocratic all those whose father and/or grandfather ranked 5 and above. Of the paternal positions listed in these tables, only that held by Li Delin's father was lower than rank 5. Cf. Mao Hanguang's (1988, 140–46) grouping of Six Dynasties aristocrats into three categories: *shizu* 士族 (genteel clans), *xiaoxing* 小姓 (minor lineages) and *hansu* 寒素 (humble origins).

⁺ Zhao Jiong must have been dismissed from this position in 584 or earlier because by that time Yu Qingze had been appointed to the same position, apparently to replace him.

TABLE 4 Chief ministerial appointments under Wendi

A. Vice presidents of the left of the Department of State Affairs (*shangshu zuo puye*)

| Name | yr/m–yr/m |
| --- | --- |
| Gao Jiong | 581/1–581/8 |
| Zhao Fen | 581/8–582/6 |
| Gao Jiong | 582/6–599/8 |
| Yang Su | 601/1–605/2 |

B. Vice presidents of the right of the Department of State Affairs (*shangshu you puye*)

| Name | yr/m–yr/m |
| --- | --- |
| Zhao Jiong | 581/2–584/? |
| Yu Qingze | 584/4–589/1 |
| Su Wei | 589/4–592/7 |
| Yang Su | 592/12–601/1 |
| Su Wei | 601/1–607/7 |

C. President (*nayan*) of the Chancellery (*menxia sheng*)

| Name | yr/m–yr/m | Group |
| --- | --- | --- |
| Su Wei | 581/3–590/7 | A |
| Su Wei | 594/7–601/1 | A |
| Yang Da | 602/10–612/5 | A |
| Gao Jiong | 581/2–? | B |
| Liu Ji | Early KH | B |
| Yang Shuang | ?–587 | B |
| Yang Su | 589/6–590/7 | B |

D. President of the Secretariat (*neishi ling/jian*)

| Name | yr/m–yr/m | Group |
| --- | --- | --- |
| Li Delin | 581/2–590/4 | A |
| Yang Su | 590/7–592/7 | A |
| Yang Jian | 599/6–601 | A |
| Yang Zhao | 601/1–604 | A |
| Yu Qingze | 581/2–584/4 | B |
| Yang Guang | 586–588 | B |
| Yang Xiu | 592/2–593/6 | B |
| Zhao Jiong | 583/4–? | C |
| Zhao Fen | Early KH | C |

TABLE 5   De facto chief ministerial appointments under Wendi

| Name | Choronym in | Bloc | yr/m–yr/m | Father/Note | Sources |
|---|---|---|---|---|---|
| Yang Yong 楊勇 | Huayin | Guanlong | 581–600/10 | Wendi/crown prince | SuS 45; BS 71 |
| Yang Xiong 楊雄 | Huayin | Guanlong | 581*–589 | NZ prefect/Nephew of Wendi | SuS 43; BS 68; ZS 29 |
| Chen Mao 陳茂 | Hedong | Shandong | 581–590s | Commoner/dian jimi 典機密 | SuS 64.1508 |
| Linghu Xi 令狐熙 | Dunhuang | Guanlong | 581–? | NZ prefect; general-in-chief/acting president of the Chancellery | SuS 56.1385 |
| Xue Daoheng 薛道衡 | Hedong | Shandong | RS | NW comm. governor/zhi jimi 知機密 | SuS 57.1408 |
| Liu Shu | Hedong | Shnadong | RS | President of Chancellery/canzhang jimi 參掌機密 | SuS 47; BS 64 |

RS = Renshou 仁壽 reign (601–604).
*Estimate.

TABLE 6  Presidents of the Six Boards under Wendi (581–604)
Total: 33 (100%); Guanlong: 16 (48.5%); Shandong: 16 (48.5%); Unknown: 1 (3%)

| Name | Choronym in | Bloc | yr/m–yr/m | Father/Note | Sources |
|---|---|---|---|---|---|
| Yuan Hui 元暉 | Luoyang | Shandong | 581/2–582?; Early KH | NW VP of SSS | SuS 46; BS 15 |
| Yuan Yan 元巖 | Luoyang | Shandong | 581/2–582 | NW prefect | SuS 62; BS 11, 75 |
| Zhangsun Pi 長孫毗 | Luoyang? | Shandong? | 581/2–582 | NW? | SuS 1 |
| Yang Shangxi 楊尚希 | Hongnong | Guanlong | 581/2–582/5; 584/4–589 | NW comm. governor | SuS 46; BS 75 |
| Yu Qingze | Jingzhao | Guanlong | 581/2–584/4 | NZ comm. governor | SuS 40; BS 73 |
| Su Wei | Jingzhao | Guanlong | 581/3–581/12; ?–583/12; 583/12–589/4 | WW board president | SuS 41; BS 63 |
| Du Gao 杜杲 | Duling 杜陵? | Guanlong | ?–582 | NW comm. governor | ZS 39; BS 70 |
| Helou Zigan 賀婁子幹 | Dai | Shandong | 582/10–583 | NW general-in-chief | SuS 53; BS 73 |
| Wei Shikang 韋世康 | Jingzhao | Guanlong | 582/1–587/4; 593/1–595/10 | /G father: NW prefect | SuS 47; BS 64 |
| Huangfu Ji 皇甫績 | Anding | Guanlong | 582/5 | NZ prefect | SuS 38; BS 74 |
| Zhangsun Ping 長孫平 | Luoyang | Shandong | 582/5–583/12; Early KH–? | NZ zhuguo 柱國 | SuS 46; BS 22 |
| Su Xiaoci 蘇孝慈 | Fufeng 扶風 | Guanlong | 582/6–584/4; Early KH; 591/2–595 | NZ prefect | SuS 46; BS 75; Cen Zhongmian 1974, 363; Zhao Wanli 1956, plate 409 |
| Niu Hong 牛弘 | Anding | Guanlong | 583–586; 599/9–610/11 | NW board president | SuS 49; BS 72 |
| Liu Ren'en 劉仁恩 | ? | ? | 584/4 | ? | SuS 46.1262; BS 75 |
| Zhang Jiong 張奨 | Hejian 河間 | Shandong | 587/4–590 | NZ prefect | SuS 46; BS 75 |
| Yuwen Bi 宇文㢸 | Luoyang | Shandong | 589/4– | NZ prefect | SuS 56; BS 75; YHXZ 6.902 |
| Yang Yi 楊异 | Hongnong | Guanlong | 589/4–592/9 | NW pres. of Chancellery | SuS 46; BS 41 |

TABLE 6 Continued

| Name | Choronym in | Bloc | yr/m–yr/m | Father/Note | Sources |
|---|---|---|---|---|---|
| Lu Kai 盧愷 | Zhuojun 涿郡 | Shandong | 589–?<br>589/6–592/7 | NW pres. of Secretariat | SuS 56; BS 30 |
| Yang Da | | Guanlong | 595/4–602/10 | NZ prefect | SuS 43 |
| Hulü Xiaoqing 斛律孝卿 | Hongnong | Shandong | 598–599 | NQ prefect | BQS 20; BS 53; YHXZ 10 |
| Wei Xuan 衛玄 | Tai'an 太安 | Shandong | 602/7–604/1 | NW pres. of Chancellery | SuS 63; BS 76 |
| Wei Chong 韋沖 | Luoyang | Guanlong | 603/9–605/5 | Shikang's brother | SuS 47; BS 64 |
| Xin Yanzhi 辛彥之 | Jingzhao | Guanlong | Early KH | NZ prefect | SuS 75; BS 82; YHXZ 3 |
| Li Yuantong 李圓通<br>(Li Tong) | Longxi 隴西 | Guanlong | Early KH–599–604 | /Commoner | SuS 64; BS 75 |
| Yuan Yuxiu 袁聿修 | Jingzhao | Shandong | Early KH | NW pres. of Secretariat | BQS 42; WS 85 |
| Linghu Xi 令狐熙 | Chenjun | Guanlong | KH | NZ prefect | SuS 56; BS 67; ZS 36 |
| Feng Shiji 馮世基<br>(Feng Ye 馮業) | Dunhuang | Shandong | KH? | ? | SuS 46.1262; BS 75; YHXZ 1 |
| Kudi Qin 庫狄嶔 | Shangdang 上黨 | Shandong | KH | ? | SuS 46.1263 |
| Zhangsun Chi 長孫熾 | Dai 代 | Shandong | KH | NZ prefect | Zhou Shaoliang and<br>Zhao Chao 1992,47 |
| Guo Jun 郭均 | Luoyang | Guanlong | KH? | ? | SuS 46.1262; BS 75 |
| Liu Shu 柳逑 | Pingyi 馮翊 | Shandong | Late KH–RS–604/8 | Sui pres. of Chancellery | SuS 47; BS 64 |
| Xue Zhou 薛冑 | Hedong | Shandong | Late KH | NZ prefect | SuS 56; ZS 35 |
| Yang Wenji 楊文紀 | Hedong | Guanlong | Mid-KH–602 | NZ vice min. of state | SuS 48; BS 41. |

president of Chancellery (NW) = shizhong 侍中.
president of Secretariat = zhongshu ling 中書令.
vice min. (minister) of state = xiao zhongzai 小冢宰 (vice chief minister).

TABLE 7 Chief ministers under Yangdi (604–618)

Total (posts): 9 (100%); Guanlong 7 (78%); Shandong; 1 (11%); South: 1 (11%). Total (appointees): 7.

A. President of the Department of State Affairs (shangshu ling 尚書令)

| Name | Choronym in | Bloc | yr/m–yr/m | Father/Note | Sources |
|---|---|---|---|---|---|
| Yang Su | Huayin | Guanlong | 605/2–606/6 | NZ prefect | SuS 48; BS 41 |

B. Vice presidents of the left and right of the Department of State Affairs (shangshu zuo you puye)

| Name | Choronym in | Bloc | yr/m–yr/m | Father/Note | Sources |
|---|---|---|---|---|---|
| Yang Su | Huayin | Guanlong | 601/1–605/2 | NZ prefect/Left | SuS 48; BS 41 |
| Su Wei | Jingzhao | Guanlong | 601/1–605/2* | WW board president/ Right | SuS 41; BS 63 |
|  |  |  | 605/2–607/7* | /Left |  |

C. President (nayan) of the Chancellery (menxia sheng; in 616, nayan was renamed shinei 侍内)+

| Name | Choronym in | Bloc | yr/m–yr/m | Father/Note | Sources |
|---|---|---|---|---|---|
| Su Wei | Jingzhao | Guanlong | 610–616/5 | see above | SuS 41; BS 63; Zhao Wanli 1956, "Jishi" 9.106 |
| Yang Da | Huayin | Guanlong | 602/10–612/5 | NZ prefect/Wendi's nephew | SuS 43; ZZTJ 181.562 |
| Yang Wensi 楊文思 | Huayin | Guanlong | 607/9–610* | NZ vice min. of state/ Yang Su's uncle | SuS 48; BS 41; ZZTJ 180.5634 |

TABLE 7 Continued

D. President of the Secretariat (neishi ling 內史令; in 616 neishi sheng was renamed neishu sheng 內書省)†

| Name | Choronym in | Bloc | yr/m–yr/m | Father/Note | Sources |
|---|---|---|---|---|---|
| Yang Yue 楊約‡ | Huayin | Guanlong | 604–608* | NZ prefect/Yang Su's stepbrother | SuS 48; BS 41 |
| Xiao Cong 蕭琮 | Nanlanling 南蘭陵 | South | 605/1–607/7 | L. Liang Mingdi | SuS 79; ZS 48 |
| Yuan Shou 元壽 | Luoyang | Shandong | 608/1–612/1 | NZ prefect | SuS 63; ZS 38; ZZTJ 181.5660; Cen Zhongmian 1974, 368 |

* Estimates.
† SuS 28.795.
‡ Yamazaki places his date of disenrollment at 605. However, according to his biographies, it happened at a time when his nephew Yang Xuangan was president of the Board of Rites. Xuangan was appointed to that position in 608. Cf. Yamazaki 1956, 16.

TABLE 8 De facto chief ministerial appointments under Yangdi

| Name | Choronym in | Bloc | yr/m–yr/m | Father/Note | Sources |
|---|---|---|---|---|---|
| Xiao Yu 蕭瑀 | Nanlanling | South | DY | L Liang Mingdi/weizhi jiwu 委之機務 | JTS 63.2399 |
| Su Wei | Jingzhao | Guanlong | 608–616/5 | WW board president | SuS 41; BS 63 |
| Yuwen Shu 宇文述 | Wuchuan | Guanlong | 608–616/10 | NZ shang zhuguo 上柱國 | SuS 61; BS 79; ZS 29 |
| Yu Shiji 虞世基 | Yuyao 餘姚 | South | 608*–618 | Chen palace cadet | SuS 67; BS 83 |
| Pei Yun 裴蘊 | Wenxi 聞喜 | South | 609*–618 | Chen board president/ Shandong choronym | SuS 67; BS 74 |
| Pei Ju 裴矩 | Wenxi | Shandong | 609–618 | NQ secretary of crown prince/G father: NW board president | SuS 67; BS 38; ZZTJ 181.5647 |

*Estimates.

DY = Daye 大業 reign (605–618).

palace cadet = taizi zhongshu zi 太子中庶子.

secretary of crown prince = taizi sheren 太子舍人.

TABLE 9   Presidents of the Six Boards under Yangdi (604–618)
Total: 18 (100%);* Guanlong: 10 (55.5%); Shandong: 7 (39%); South: 1 (5.5%)

| Name | Choronym in | Bloc | yr/m–yr/m | Father/Note | Sources |
|---|---|---|---|---|---|
| Niu Hong 牛弘 | Anding 安定 | Guanlong | 599/9–610/11 | NW board president | SuS 49; BS 72 |
| Wei Chong 韋沖 | Jingzhao | Guanlong | 603/9–605/5 | /G father: NW prefect | SuS 47; BS 64 |
| Zhao Zhongqing 趙仲卿 | Tianshui 天水 | Guanlong | Early DY | NZ general-in-chief | SuS 74 |
| Li Yuantong 李圓通 (Li Tong) | Jingzhao | Guanlong | Early DY–606/5 | /Commoner | SuS 64; BS 75 |
| Cui Zhongfang 崔仲方 | Boling 博陵 | Shandong | 605–607/4 | NZ vice min. of education | SuS 60; BS 32 |
| Yuwen Bi 宇文弼 | Luoyang | Shandong | 605/1–607/7 | NZ prefect | SuS 56; BS 75 |
| Li Zixiong 李子雄 | Bohai 渤海 | Shandong | 605–606 | NZ prefect | SuS 70 |
| Liang Pi 梁毗 | Anding | Guanlong | 606/1–612/6 | NZ prefect | SuS 62; BS 77 |
| Yuwen Kai 宇文愷 | Jingzhao | Guanlong | 606/2–612/10 | NZ min. of war | SuS 68; BS 60 |
| Yang Wensi 楊文思 | Hongnong | Guanlong | 606/4–607/9 | NZ vice min. of state | SuS 48; BS 41 |
|  |  |  | 610?/10–611? |  |  |
| Duan Wenzhen 段文振 | Beihai 北海 | Shandong | 606/10–612/1 | NZ prefect | SuS 60; BS 76 |
| Zhangsun Chi 長孫熾 | Luoyang | Shandong | 608/1–610/10 | NZ prefect | SuS 51; BS 22 |
| Yang Xuangan 楊玄感 | Hongnong | Guanlong | 608/1–613/6 | Sui pres. of SSS | SuS 70; BS 41 |
| Fan Zigai 樊子蓋 | Lujiang 廬江 | South | 611/5–616/7 | NQ prefect | SuS 63; BS 76 |
| Wei Xuan 葡玄 | Luoyang | Shandong | 612/1–617? | NW pres.of Chancellery | SuS 63; BS 76 |
| Yang Yichen 楊義臣 | Dai 代 | Shandong | 615–? | NZ general-in-chief | SuS 63; BS 73 |
| Wei Jin 韋津 | Jingzhao | Guanlong | 616/7 | NZ area commander | SuS 47; BS 64 |
| Li Zhe 李哲 | Longxi | Guanlong | DY | NZ prefect | BS 75; SuS 50 |

area commander = zongguan 總管.
general-in-chief = da jiangjun 大將軍.
minister of war = da sima 大司馬.
president of Chancellery = shizhong 侍中.
vice minister of education = xiao situ 小司徒.
vice minister of state = xiao zhongzai 小冢宰 (vice chief minister).

*Yamazaki lists 19 board presidents including one Fang Ze 房則 of Qinghe choronym, based on Mangluo zhongmu yiwen 芒洛冢墓遺文 3 (MLZMYW). But the MLZMYW and its sequels I have access to do not contain Fang's epitaph, nor does Cen Zhongmian 1974, 348ff, "Suidai shike mulu (zhuanfu chuji" 隋代石刻 (磚附)目錄初集). ZZTJ (183.5721) and SuS (4.92) record Fang as a court vice chamberlain (guanglu shaoqing 光祿少卿).

# Appendix 2

## Maoyue (Visual Inspection)

From comparative studies of the two *maoyue* 貌閱 figures, Shida Fudōmaro and Tonami Mamoru determined that the record of the 583 campaign was an interpolation. They have discovered that although on the surface markedly different results were recorded for the two campaigns, when compared digit by digit they show inexplicable similarities (table 1). In column A, only the first digits are different (4 versus 2), the rest are identical (43,000). In column B, the 583 figure has an extra first digit (1), the rest are the same for both 583 and 609. It is thus possible that the 609 figure was slightly altered and interpolated into the 583 record.

While admitting that the eerie similarity between the two sets of figures may be attributable to some clerical mistakes, Kanai Yukitada, who disagrees with this conclusion, calls attention to the following section of the 583 record, which is absent in the 609 record, "Those [adult male household members] whose relations [with the head of the household] are below the third-degree of mourning are all required to set up their own households and serve as their heads."[1] Furthermore, the 583 *maoyue* campaign was only part of an ongoing effort to increase administrative efficiency and population control. In view of this, the 583 campaign must have taken place even though the numbers it produced were somewhat suspect.[2]

## Northern Zhou, Chen, and Sui Populations

The Sui, with improved population censuses, and sophisticated population registration and classification, were in better control of population informa-

TABLE 1   The two *Maoyue* campaigns under the Sui

|  | A | B |  |
|---|---|---|---|
| *year* | *increase of adult males* | *increase of population* | *sources* |
| 583 | 443,000 | 1,641,500 | *SuS* 24.681; *ZZTJ* 176.5481 |
| 609 | 243,000 | 641,500 | *SuS* 67.1575; *ZZTJ* 181.5646 |

tion than previous dynasties. Even though the surviving population data are still far from being sufficient for a satisfactory statistical study, they nonetheless offer the basis for examining major population trends in this era. To put these data in historical perspective, we will begin our demographic survey with the Northern Zhou, at a time when this local power of the Northwest significantly expanded its territory and population by annexing the Northern Qi to its east. Traditional sources have preserved some key population figures (table 2), which are indispensable for the demographic study of the period in question.

However, before we can begin to make sense of these figures, we must first reconcile some of the contradictions between them. The main problem is the Northern Zhou population number—9,009,604—in 579–580 at C1. The *Tong dian*, the only source that records that number, regards it as the entire population of the Northern Zhou after its annexation of the Northern Qi. But this claim is unreliable for a number of reasons. First, with the total household number of 3,590,000, the average number of individuals per household would be 2.5 (E1), too low by any standard. Second, the newly acquired territory of the Northern Qi had added 20,006,880 people (C3). It is inconceivable that this population alone was more than twice the size of the combined population of the Northern Qi and Northern Zhou. Third, the last four digits of the population number 9,009,604 (C1) are identical with those of the household number—3,599,604—for the late Northern Zhou and early Sui at D2 and D8. Clearly the number 9,009,604 was entered in error.[3] Ikeda On suggests that a 1 should be prefixed to the C1 number to make it 19,009,604. But even this revised number was less than the Northern Qi population.[4]

To tentatively estimate the population of the Northern Zhou at the time of its conquest of the Northern Qi in 577, the following formula for calculating population growth is used:

$$A(1 + X)^r = B$$

TABLE 2 Populations: late sixth to early seventh centuries

| A | B | C | D | E | F |
|---|---|---|---|---|---|
| period | dates | population | no. of households | average household size | sources |
| 1 N. Zhou | 579–80 | 9,009,604 | 3,590,000 | 2.5 | TD 7.14748 |
| 2 N. Zhou | 579–80 | | 3,599,604 | | CFYG 486.5808b |
| 3 N. Qi | 577 | 20,006,880 | 3,032,528 | 6.06 | TD 7.147 |
| 4 | | | 3,030,000 | | SuS 29. 807 |
| 5 | 577 | | 3,032,500 | | ZZTJ 173.5375 |
| 6 | 577 | 20,006,886 | 3,302,528 | | ZS 6.101 |
| 7 | 577 | 20,006,880 | 2,032,528 | | CFYG 486.5808a |
| 8 Sui | 581 | | 3,999,604 | | TD 7.147–48 |
| | | | (3,599,604)* | | |
| 9 | 582 | | 3,600,000 | | CFYG 486.5808b |
| 10 Chen | 589 | 2,000,000 | 500,000 | 4 | TD 7.146 |
| 11 | 582–89 | 2,000,000 | 500,000 | 4 | CFYG 486.5807b |
| 12 Sui | 589 | | 4,807,932 | | TD 7.148 |
| 13 | 609 | 46,019,956 | 8,907,546 | 5.17 | SuS 29.808 |
| 14 | 609 | 46,019,956 | 8,907,536 | | TD 7.147 |
| 15 | 606 | 46,019,056 | 8,907,536 | | CFYG 486.5809a |

*The original population figure in the *Tong dian* for the Sui at 581 is 3,599,604, which is the same as the *Cefu yuangui* figure for the late Northern Zhou (D2). The editors of the punctuated edition of the *Tong dian* changed the figure to 3,999,604 based on other *Tong dian* editions. See *TD* 7.161, note 28.

(A is the population before growth; X is the known growth rate; $^t$ is the number of years; B is the population after growth).
To bring known quantities into the formula, we get:

$$[(20,000,000 + A) \times 1.01^{12} + 2,000,000] \times 1.01^{20} = 46,000,000$$

12 yrs. (577–589) over Qi pop., Zhou pop.; 20 yrs. (589–609) over Chen pop., Sui 609 pop.

According to Kang Chao (Zhao Gang), an annual rate of 1% is acceptable for population growth in premodern China.[5] Here I have applied it to late sixth century and early seventh century China. I have also modified A to make it the population of the Northern Zhou at 577 before the conquest of the Northern Qi. The combined population of the Northern Qi and Northern

Zhou should be approximately (20,000,000 + A). Multiply it by $1.01^{12}$ to calculate the population of the Sui twelve years later, that is, in 589 before it acquired an additional two million people from the South. The sum of the numbers in brackets is the population of the Sui after its unification of China in 589. The product of the sum and the growth index $1.01^{20}$ is the Sui population twenty years later (in 609), which we know to have been around forty-six million. And the result of the calculation is approximately 11,680,000 for the Northern Zhou population at 577.[6]

Add 20,000,000 to the Northern Zhou population in 577 and we get 31,680,000 as the approximate population of North China after the Northern Zhou conquest of the Northern Qi. To calculate the Sui population in 581, multiply 31,680,000 by $1.01^4$ (approximately 1.0406), and we get 32,966,208. To work out the Sui population at 589 on the eve of the annexation of the Chen, multiply that number by $1.01^8$ (approximately 1.0937) to arrive at 36,055,141 or around 36,000,000. Add 2,000,000 to get 38,000,000 as the combined population of Sui and Chen at 589.[7]

There were a number of other variables affecting the growth rate. The official population could be increased through annexation of territories, especially in the Northwest and the Far South, and through more efficient censuses. Natural disasters, war, and public works projects could decrease the official population. All these factors occurred in the period covered (577–609). I have not included them in my study because they are normally unquantifiable and thus of little statistical significance.

# Chronology of Sui Yangdi (569–618)

| Year | Age* | Events |
|------|------|--------|
| 569 | | Born as Yang Guang. |
| *580*† | 11 | Enfeoffed as commandery duke of Yanmen. |
| 580 | 11 | Posted to Bingzhou near Taiyuan, Shanxi. |
| 581 | 12 | Second month: Sui founded. Yang Yong appointed crown prince. Yangdi enfeoffed as prince of Jin; appointed commander of Bingzhou Area Command. |

\* \* \*

| Year | Age* | Events |
|------|------|--------|
| | | Received the title pillar of state.‡ |
| 582 | 13 | Promoted to superior pillar of state and president of the Branch Department of State of Hebei Circuit while residing in Bingzhou. |
| 585 | 16 | Eleventh month: Visited the court in Daxingcheng (Xi'an, Shaanxi). |
| 586 | 17 | Intercalary eighth month: Visited the court in Daxingcheng. Tenth month: Appointed concurrently governor of Yongzhou (seat: Xi'an, Shaanxi). |
| 587 | 18 | Fourth month: Wendi visited Yangdi's mansion in Daxingcheng[?]. Ninth month: Annexation of Later Liang by Sui. |
| 588 | 19 | Tenth month: Appointed president of the Branch Department of State of Huainan Circuit and field marshal of the Southern expedition army with the power of commander-in-chief; the Southern expedition launched. |
| 589 | 20 | First month: Entered Jiankang (Nanjing) as conqueror of Chen. Second month: Chen resistance crushed. Fourth month: Returned in triumph to Daxingcheng and promoted defender-in-chief (*taiwei*). |

\* \* \*

| Year | Age* | Events |
|------|------|--------|
| 590 | 21 | Returned to Bingzhou as its area commander.<br>Eleventh month: Popular rebellion broke out in former Chen territory.<br>Late 590: Posted to Jiangdu (Yangzhou, Jiangsu) in the South to replace his brother Yang Jun as commander of Yangzhou Superior Area Command; from then on until 600, would pay annual visits to the court in Daxingcheng. Yang Jun became leader of Bingzhou. |
| 591 | 22 | Eleventh month: Received Buddhist commandments from Zhiyi, founder of the Tiantai school. |
| 595 | 26 | First month: Wendi visited Mount Tai. Yangdi served as acting general-in-chief of Armed Reserve Garrison Command (*wuhou da jiangjun*) in Daxingcheng, and returned to Jiangdu not long after. |
| 597 | 28 | Eleventh month: Zhiyi died while on his way to Jiangdu. |
| 598 | 29 | Sixth–ninth months: Wendi launched a failed invasion of Koguryŏ led by Gao Jiong and Yang Liang.<br>Ninth month: Paekche sent a mission to offer assistance to the Sui against Koguryŏ. |
| 599 | 30 | Second month: Visited the court in Daxingcheng.<br>Eighth month: Gao Jiong removed from office.<br>Tenth month: Wendi conferred the title Qimin upon Tuli qaghan, and married Princess Yicheng to him. |
| 600 | 32 | Fourth month: Led a Sui army to rout Tujue forces on the Northern front.<br>Tenth month: Yang Yong deposed as crown prince.<br>Eleventh month: Designated crown prince. |
| | | * * * |
| 601 | 32 | Yamato (in Japan) sent its first mission to the Sui court.<br>Sixth month: Wendi issued an edict to curtail enrollment of students at the national level and abolish provincial schools. |
| 602 | 33 | Eighth month: Empress Dugu (Wenxian) died. |
| 604 | 35 | First month: Trusted with the running of the court when Wendi was away in the Renshou Palace.<br>Seventh month: Wendi died in Renshou under suspicious circumstances; Yangdi succeeded as emperor.<br>Eighth month: Yang Liang suspected foul play and started a rebellion in Bingzhou, which was later suppressed by Yang Su. |

| Year | Age* | Events |
|------|------|--------|
| | | Eleventh month: Visited Luoyang; employed several hundreds of thousands of laborers to dig strategic trenches east, south, and west of Luoyang, which went as far west as east Shaanxi. Issued the edict on the Luoyang project, which employed a labor force of 2,000,000. |
| 605 | 36 | First month: Appointed his wife Xiao empress, and his son Yang Zhao crown prince. |
| | | Third month: Appointed Yang Su, Yang Da, and Yuwen Kai to take charge of the Luoyang project; ordered tens of thousands of rich merchant households to relocate to Luoyang. Started digging the Tongji section of the Grand Canal (which linked Luoyang with the Huai area to the south), using a labor force of more than 1,000,000 (the project was not completed until 611). Started digging the Han Conduit section of the Grand Canal (which connected the Huai with the Yangzi) with more than 100,000 laborers (the project was probably completed not long after). |
| | | Fourth month: Liu Fang captured the capital of Linyi in central Vietnam. |
| | | Eighth month: Embarked on his first Southern tour by water. |
| | | * * * |
| 605– | | Silla sent tributary missions annually in the Daye reign (605–618). |
| 606 | 37 | First month: The building of Luoyang completed. Yangdi sent ten commissioners to abolish and merge a number of prefectures and counties. |
| | | Third month: Started on his return journey from Jiangdu by water. |
| | | Fourth month: Arrived in Luoyang. |
| | | Seventh month: Crown Prince Yang Zhao died; Yang Su died. |
| 607 | 38 | Third month: Arrived in Daxingcheng; sent Zhu Kuan as envoy to Liuqiu (Taiwan[?]) in the East China Sea. |
| | | Fourth month: Promulgated the *Daye Code* and new statutes to introduce sweeping reforms to the bureaucracy; converted prefectures (*zhou*) to commanderies (*jun*); |

| Year | Age* | Events |
|------|------|--------|

reformed weights and measures based on previous systems of the South. Embarked on an overland journey to inspect the Northern frontier.

Fifth month: Qimin qaghan sent his son to the court. Yangdi employed male laborers from more than ten commanderies to build a road from the Taihang Mountains to Bingzhou.

Sixth month: Received Qimin qaghan in Yulin Commandery (seat: southwest of Togtoh, Inner Mongolia).

Seven month: Entertained Qimin and his people lavishly. Executed Heruo Bi, Yuwen Bi, and Gao Jiong, and dismissed Su Wei from office. Employed more than 1 million male laborers to build a section of the Great Wall to the east of Yulin.

Eighth month: Issued a warning to the Koguryŏ king through his envoy who had attempted to form a secret alliance with Qimin. Ordered the construction of the Jinyang Palace while in Taiyuan.

Ninth month: Arrived in Luoyang.

* * *

Yamato sent its first mission to Yangdi's court, headed by Ono no Imoko.

Paekche sent a mission to request an expedition against Koguryŏ.

608   39   First month: Began digging the Yongji section of the Grand Canal north of the Yellow River (it would extend the reach of the Grand Canal as far north as Zhuo Commandery in present-day north Hebei), employing more than 1 million male and female laborers.

Third month: Visited Wuyuan (south of Wuyuan, central Inner Mongolia) and went on a tour to inspect the Great Wall. Paekche, Yamato, and Chitu sent tributary missions. Yangdi sent Chang Jun as envoy to visit Chitu (in Malaysia).

Fourth month: Began building the Fenyang Palace in north Shaanxi. Pei Shiqing as Sui envoy accompanied Ono no Imoko back to Yamato.

Seventh month: Employed more than 200,000 male laborers to construct a section of the Great Wall east of Yulin. General Yuwen Shu defeated the Tuyuhun.

| Year | Age* | Events |
|------|------|--------|
|      |      | Eighth month: Visited Mount Heng 恒岳. |
|      |      | * * * |
|      |      | Sent Zhu Kuan on his second mission to Liuqiu. |
| 608  |      | Conquest of Yiwu (Hami, Xinjiang) by General Xue Shixiong. |
| 609  | 40   | First month: Returned from Luoyang to Daxingcheng. |
|      |      | Second month: Visited Min Township (east of Tongguan) and returned to Daxingcheng. |
|      |      | Third month: Went on a tour of the Northwest. |
|      |      | Fifth month: Tuyuhun forces defeated; more than 100,000 of its people submitted themselves. |
|      |      | Sixth month: Arrived in Zhangye (in Gansu); welcomed and entertained Qu Boya of Gaochang and the tutun she of Yiwu (the latter ceded a large area to Sui). Set up four commanderies in former Tuyuhun territory. |
|      |      | Ninth month: Returned to Daxingcheng (Chang'an). |
|      |      | Eleventh month: Went to Luoyang. |
| 610  | 41   | First month: An acrobatic extravaganza staged south of the Duan Gate in Luoyang. Yamato sent a tributary mission. |
|      |      | Second month: Chen Leng and Zhang Zhenzhou conquered Liuqiu. |
|      |      | Third month: Went to Jiangdu. |
|      |      | Sixth month: Shiwei 室韋 (a power in northwest Manchuria and east Mongolia and the area to their north) and Chitu sent tributary missions. |
|      |      | * * * |
|      |      | Ordered the digging of the Jiangnan Canal, which extended the Grand Canal south of the Yangzi. |
| 611  | 42   | Second month: Paekche sent a tributary mission. Yangdi took the Grand Canal north to Zhuo Commandery to prepare for war against Koguryŏ. |
|      |      | Fourth month: Arrived in the Linshuo Palace. |
|      |      | Fall: More than 40 prefectures in Henan and Shandong flooded, and the local population devastated. |
|      |      | Twelfth month: Received Chuluo qaghan in the Linshuo Palace, which marked his submission. Wang Bo started a rebellion in Mount Changbai, which was the first large-scale anti-Sui rebellion on record. |
|      |      | * * * |
|      |      | Paekche sent an envoy to offer help to Yangdi's Liaodong campaign. |

| Year | Age* | Events |
|------|------|--------|
| *611* | | Qimin qaghan died. |
| 612 | 43 | First month: Launched the first Liaodong campaign with a force of more than 1.13 million. |
| | | Third month: The Sui army crossed the Liao River after suffering staggering losses. |
| | | Sixth month: Yangdi arrived in Liaodong to chastise the generals. General Lai Huer charged into Pyongyang, only to be routed. |
| | | Seventh month: Generals Yu Zhongwen and Yuwen Shu suffered a major defeat at the Sa River; only 2,700 men returned out of an expeditionary force of 305,000. |
| | | Eleventh month: Married Princess Huarong to King Qu Boya of Gaochang. |

* * *

Set up Liaodong Commandery with territory captured from Koguryŏ in Wuliluo (southwest of Shenyang, Liaoning) and surrounding areas.

A major drought hit the North (especially the Shandong area), resulting in epidemics and a loss of lives on a large scale.

| Year | Age* | Events |
|------|------|--------|
| 613 | 44 | First month: Issued a general mobilization, obviously in preparation for the second Liaodong campaign. |
| | | Third month: Employed 100,000 male laborers to wall Daxingcheng; arrived in Liaodong. |
| | | Fourth month: Crossed the Liao River as the second Liaodong campaign was underway. |
| | | Six month: Yang Xuangan rebelled in Liyang 黎陽 (Xun County, Henan), posing a threat to Luoyang. Husi Zheng, a friend of Xuangan's, defected to Koguryŏ. Yangdi called off the second campaign to deal with the Yang Xuangan rebellion. |
| | | Eighth month: Yang Xuangan defeated in Min Township. |
| | | Ninth month: Visited Shanggu Commandery (seat: Yi County, Hebei). |
| | | Intercalary ninth month: Passed through Boling Commandery (seat: Dingzhou, Hebei), which was renamed Gaoyang 高陽. |
| | | Tenth month: The rebel army under Wang Bo and Meng Rang in the Mount Changbai area now grew to more than 100,000. |

| Year | Age* | Events |
|------|------|--------|
| 614 | 45 | First month: Married Princess Xinyi to Chuluo qaghan. |
| | | Second month: Issued the edict for the third Liaodong campaign. |
| | | Third month: Arrived in the Linyu Palace (near Funing, Hebei). |
| | | Fourth month: Passed by Beiping 北平 (Lulong, Hebei). |
| | | Seventh month: Arrived in Huaiyuanzhen 懷遠鎮 (northwest of Liaoyang, Liaoning). Koguryŏ returned the Sui defector Husi Zheng in exchange for truce; the third campaign ended. |
| | | Eighth month: Started on the return journey from the Liaodong front. |
| | | Tenth month: Arrived first in Luoyang, and then in Daxingcheng. |
| | | Twelfth month: Returned to Luoyang. Rebel leader Meng Rang led his 100,000-plus army to occupy the Duliang Palace; he was later defeated by Wang Shichong. |
| | | * * * |
| | | Paekche sent a tributary mission. |
| 615 | 46 | First month: More than twenty states from East, North, and Central Asia, including Tujue, Qidan, Mohe, and Silla, sent tributary missions. |
| | | Fifth month: Arrived in Taiyuan, and then went to the Fenyang Palace for the summer. |
| | | Eighth month: Inspected the Northern frontier; forced to retreat to Yanmen (Dai County, north Shanxi) when tipped off by Princess Yicheng about an imminent attack by Shibi qaghan of Tujue; the siege of Yanmen began. |
| | | Ninth month: Tujue lifted the siege when rescue forces arrived. |
| | | Tenth month: Arrived in Luoyang. |
| 616 | 47 | First month: Built the Piling Palace (near Wuxi, Jiangsu), using tens of thousands of soldiers. |
| | | Fifth month: Ordered underlings to catch fireflies in the Jinghua Palace within the Western Park for lighting purposes. |
| | | Seventh month: Embarked on a journey to move south; remonstrators who attempted to persuade Yangdi to stay in Luoyang or move to Guanzhong were killed. |

| Year | Age* | Events |
|------|------|--------|
| | | Tenth month: Yuwen Shu died; by that time, Yangdi had arrived in Jiangdu. |
| | | * * * |
| | | Officer Luo Yi rebelled in Zhuo Commandery and declared himself commander of Youzhou Area Command (in north Hebei). |
| 617 | 48 | First month: Rebel leader Du Fuwei moved south across the Huai River. Rebel leader Dou Jiande declared himself prince of Changle 長樂王 in Leshou 樂壽 (Xian County, Hebei). |
| | | Second month: Officer Liang Shidu rebelled in Shuofang Commandery (seat: near Baichengzi, north Shaanxi). Officer Liu Wuzhou rebelled in Mayi Commandery (seat: Shuozhou, north Shanxi), and supported by Tujue, declared himself Dingyang qaghan; Liang and Liu set off a new trend of rebellion by Sui officers. Rebel leader Li Mi captured the Xingluo and Huiluo Granaries. |
| | | Fourth month: Officer Xue Ju rebelled in Jincheng Commandery (seat: Lanzhou, Gansu) and declared himself "hegemonic prince of Western Qin" 西秦霸王. Rebel leader Meng Rang stormed into Luoyang and torched its Fengdu Market. Rebel leader Li Mi sacked the Huiluo East Granary. |
| | | Fifth month: Duke of Tang Li Yuan rebelled in Taiyuan. |
| | | Seventh month: Officer Li Gui 李軌 rebelled in Wuwei, and declared himself prince of Liang 涼王. |
| | | Ninth month: Gathered Jiangdu women including widows to match them up with soldiers so as to prevent the latter from defecting. The Liyang Granary fell to rebel leader Li Wenxiang 李文相. |
| | | Tenth month: Later Liang royal Xiao Xian set up his rival government and named himself prince of Liang 梁王. |
| | | Eleventh month: Li Yuan entered Daxingcheng, set up Yang You 楊侑 as emperor (Gongdi) with Yining 義寧 as the new reign period, and designated Yangdi honorary emperor. Yangdi began building a palace in Danyang. |

| Year | Age* | Events |
|------|------|--------|
| 618 | 49 | Third month: Yuwen Huaji and associates started the Jiangdu incident in which Yangdi was captured and killed; Empress Xiao had Yangdi and his son Yang Gao buried nearby (in Early Tang, Yangdi's remains were moved to Leitang for reburial). |
| | | Fifth month: Li Yuan founded the Tang dynasty in Chang'an after Gongdi abdicated. Prince of Zhao Yang Tong ascended the throne in Luoyang, and gave Yangdi the posthumous title Minghuangdi 明皇帝. |
| | | Ninth month: Given the posthumous title "Yangdi" by the Tang court. |

* Modern way of calculation.
† Estimated dates are in italics.
‡ When the month of an event is unknown, it is placed under three asterisks (∗ ∗ ∗).

# Notes

## Introduction

1. This book treats the Qin-Han periods as early imperial; the Six Dynasties, Sui-Tang and Five Dynasties periods as medieval; and the Song, Yuan, Ming and Qing periods as late imperial.

2. For a discussion of Sui contributions to the Tang with a focus on the first reign, see Somers 1978. In addition to the prefecture-county local administrations, there was a higher level of government, *da zongguan* 大總管 (superior area command) or *dao* 道 (circuit), under Wendi, to take charge of the military and civil affairs of dozens of prefectures. It was abolished under Yangdi (see chapters 1 and 6) and revived later as circuit under Taizong of the Tang dynasty.

3. For example, *ZGZY* 1.5–6; 8.248; 2.17; 5.57.

4. On traditional Chinese biographical writing, see Twitchett 1961, 95–114.

5. See Han Sheng 1998, 533. For Wright's works, see Wright 1978, 1979.

6. Han Guopan 1957. On the modern debate on the merit or demerit of Yangdi, see Yuan Gang 2001, 336.

7. Hu Ji 1995, esp. 242–43.

8. Yuan Gang 2001.

9. Miyazaki 1965.

10. Nunome 1980.

11. For a discussion on the *Sui shu*, see Wright 1978, 14–15.

12. *JTS* 73.2597.

13. *JTS* 73.2598. Gardner 1961, 88 poignantly points out, "It must be admitted that at least the later standard histories have a valid claim on grounds of authenticity as well as form to recognition as standard. Their peculiarly authentic character is derived from the official manuscript sources upon which they are based."

14. *ST* 24.192–93; Gardner 1961, 16–17.

15. *ST* 12.371–73; *SuS* "Chuban Shuoming," 1–2.

16. On the issue of inclusion and exclusion, see Twitchett 1979b, 42. On numbers in the sources, see Graff 2002, 9–10.

17. On the genesis of the *Sui shu*, see Balazs 1953, 114–120. For an authoritative assessment of the *Sui shu*, see *SKTY* 45.408c–409a. A discussion of the significance of the *Sui shu* is found in Gardiner 1975, 49–50.

18. Kenneth Gardiner sums up the value of such early standard histories as *Sui shu* and *Bei shi* well, "Nevertheless, with all their faults, the standard histories before T'ang provide an unrivalled source of information; it is hard to imagine the shape which Chinese history would assume were it not for them." See Gardiner 1975, 50.

19. For a typical traditional assessment of *ZZTJ*, see *SKTY* 47.420c–421a. For a critical study of *ZZTJ*, see Franke 1930, 103–44. In the words of Denis Twitchett (1979a, 38–39), the *Zizhi tongjian* "is one of the finest achievements of traditional Chinese historiography."

20. The court historian Wang Zhou 王冑 and his associates did compile *The Court Diary of the Daye Reign*, but it was lost in the great turmoil at the end of the dynasty. See *ST* 12.370–71.

21. Some of these sources are treated briefly in Wright 1978, 15–16.

22. Commenting on the textual sources for the study of Tang history, Twitchett (1979b, 39) laments that "the T'ang remains the last major period of Chinese history for the study of which the modern historian is almost wholly dependent upon officially compiled histories and works deriving from them." Needless to say, it is much more so for students of the Sui, a period earlier than the Tang. This fact helps explain the dependence of the present study on official or semi-official historiography.

23. See, for example, Zhou Shaoliang and Zhao Chao 1992; Wu Gang 1991; Cen Zhongmian 1974, 348–78. The most complete collection of rubbings of Sui epitaphs is in Zhao Wanli 1956.

24. Key economic documents from Turfan and Dunhuang are those of Tang not Sui vintage. They can only be used retroactively to study the Sui economy.

25. On the limitations of epigraphic evidence, see Twitchett 1979b, 46.

## CHAPTER 1

1. Sovereigns are normally referred to in traditional sources by posthumous title or temple name even before enthronement. I follow this practice as well and consistently refer to Yang Guang as Yangdi.

2. For critical assessments of the Yangs' ancestral history, see Chen Yinke 1995, 323–24; Yuan Gang 2001, 26–32. Note: Huayin was part of Hongnong Commandery in Eastern Han times, and was under Yong Prefecture 雍州 or Jingzhao Commandery 京兆郡 in Sui times.

3. On Yangdi, see *SuS* 3.59; *BS* 12.439; Han Guopan 1957, 3–21; Wright 1978, 157–71; Wright 1979, 115–20; Wright 1975, 158–68; Wright 1957 (ideology);

Miyazaki 1965, 36–100 (family background); Liu Shufen 1978 (Southern connections).

4. On Liu Fang and Zheng Yi, see *SuS* 38.1131–32, 1135–37. On the rise of Yang Jian, see *SuS* 1.2–5, 13; *ZS* 7.124; Lü Chunsheng 2000, 167–96. On the rise and fall of the Yang house, see Boodberg 1939b, 253–70.

5. On Wendi's instruction, see *SuS* 47.1276. On Yangdi's appointment, see *SuS* 3.59. Notes: Unless otherwise indicated, ages are based on the traditional way of counting; their modern equivalents are given in parentheses.

6. On Wang Shao, see *SuS* 62.1473–74. On Yang Jun, see *SuS* 45.1240–41. On Yang Xiu, see below; *SuS* 45.1241–42.

7. On Xiao Yang, see Zhao Wanli 1956 "Jishi" 9.98, plate 450; Li Chunmin 1996. On Jiangling, see *SuS* 79.1792. On Later Liang, see *ZZTJ* 175.5459. On the ritual, see *ZZTJ* 176.5472.

8. On Jiangling, see *ZZTJ* 175.5459; 176.5484. Note: *SuS* 31.888 records 587 as the year the area command was revived. On the fall of Liang, see *SuS* 79.1793; *ZZTJ* 176.5491.

9. On Wendi's policies on the South, see He Dezhang 1993. On the death of Xuandi, see *ZZTJ* 175.5455–56. On Wendi's concerns about Chen, see *SuS* 79.1793 (borders); *ZZTJ* 176.5492 (invasion).

10. On *shang zhuguo*, see Balazs 1953, 274. On *zongguan*, see Kakehata 1986, 93–107; Yan Gengwang 1972, 23–54. On *da zongguan*, see *SuS* 47.1267; *ZS* 21.351. Note: As an official title, *da zongguan* had been adopted during Northern Zhou times by Yuchi Jiong 尉遲迥, a challenger to Wendi's (Yang Jian) dominance.

On Luozhou/Henan, see *SuS* 30.843. On Bingzhou/Hebei, see *SuS* 30.854, 1.14. On Yizhou/Xinan, see *SuS* 29.826, 1.15; *BS* 62.2209–13. On Jiangling-Jingzhou, see *SuS* 31.888. On Huainan, see *SuS* 2.31–32. On Yangzhou, see *SuS* 31.873. See also *TD* 32 894; *SuS* 47.1266–67; *BS* 64.2272. On *xingtai*, see *ZZTJ* 175.5454.

11. On Yangdi's Yongzhou office, see *SuS* 24.680. On Yangdi's Huainan appointment in 588, see *SuS* 2.31. *SuS* 3.60 records a different date (586) in error. On the abolition of the post in 589, see *SuS* 2.32. On Han Qinhu's original name as Han Qin, see Cen Zhongmian 1974, 5. On the conquest of Chen, see *ZZTJ* 177.5503–14. On Yan Rong, see *SuS* 74.1695.

12. On Wendi's unification, see Gao Mingshi 1995, 89–128. For Wendi's words to Gao Jiong, see *NS* 10.307. For Wendi's denunciation of the Chen ruler, see *SuS* 2.30.

13. *Quan Sui wen* 6.3–4 in *QSQHSL*; *WYYH* 645.17–19. Yuan Gang (2001, 96) speculates that the letter was penned by Xue Daoheng.

14. On Jiang Zong, see *CS* 27.343–46. On the Six Sages, see *TD* 12.295. On Wuchuan, see *SuS* 1.1; Nunome 1980, 32–34; Miyazaki 1965, 21–37. On Dugu Xin, see *BS* 61.2167–70; Dien 1990, 331–32. On Wenxian, see *SuS* 41.1179. On Wendi and Gao Jiong, see *BS* 61.2167–70; *SuS* 41.1180.

15. On Wendi's order, see *ZZTJ* 176.5492–93. On Gao Jiong's actual power, see *SuS* 41.1181; *ZZTJ* 176.5498. There are conflicting records of Zhang Lihua's death. I

follow the account in *SuS* 41.1181; *BS* 72.2489; *ZZTJ* 177.5510. A different account in *CS* (7.131) and *NS* (12.348) suggests that Lihua was killed by Yangdi. A recent attempt to justify the second account is found in Yuan Gang 2001, 114.

16. On Pei Ju, see *ZZTJ* 177.5510–12. On Yangdi's return, see *SuS* 2.32; *ZZTJ* 177.5516.

17. On Yangdi's posting to Bingzhou, see *SuS* 1.60. On Yang Jun's posting to Yangzhou, see *ZZTJ* 177.5518. On Jun's refusal to attack, see *SuS* 45.1239. On the suppression of rebellion, see *ZZTJ* 177.5529–32; *SuS* 2.35; Han Sheng 1998, 338–46. Some scholars fault the imposition of a Northern variety of Confucian morality for causing the rebellion. See Yuan Gang 2001, 119–27.

18. On Yangdi's posting to the South, see *ZZTJ* 177.5532; *SuS* 3.60. On Lady Xiao, see *SuS* 36.1111–13; *BS* 14.535–37. On second-month newborns, see *SJ* 75.2352, especially note 1. On Zhang Ke, see Zhao Wanli 1956 "Jishi" 9.102, plate 483. On the Xiaos of Lanling, see Chen Yinke 1995, 207; Mao Hanguang 1988, 56–59, 408–412. On intermarriage between the Yangs and the Southern aristocrats, see Yamazaki 1956, 5, 8. On Wendi's respect for her, see *SuS* 36.1111. On her religious piety, see *TPGJ* 102.688. On Wendi's discussion with Gao Jiong, see *SuS* 41.1182.

19. On Yangdi's divinatory skills and proficiency in the Wu dialect, see *ZZTJ* 185.5775. On Xiao Cha, see *BS* 93.3086. On Southern culture, see *TD* 182.4850. On Yangdi's Southern style poetry, see Liu Shufen 1978, 64–68. On palace style, see Marney 1986, 516–17. On Lady Xiao's writing, see *SuS* 36.1111–12.

20. On Luoyang's indebtedness to the South, see *SuS* 24.672; Balazs 1953, 20. For Yangdi's remarks on the South and on Dou and Cui, see *Quan Sui wen* 5.4043b in *QSQHSL*.

21. On Wendi's letter, see *SuS* 81.1815–16; *CFYG* 996.11695b–96a. On the Mohe, see *BS* 94.3123–26; *SuS* 81.1821–22. On the Qidan, see *BS* 94.3127–29; *SuS* 84.1881–82. On Sui's relations with Koguryŏ, Qidan, and Mohe at that time, see Wong 1980, 122–58. Note: King P'yŏngwŏn is known in *SuS* as Gao Yang 高陽 (1.16), or Tang 湯 (81.1814). *SuS* 81 dates his death and Wendi's letter to 597 in error. See Han Sheng 1998, 353.

22. Nishijima 1983, 423–35; *SuS* 41.1182; *BS* 72.2490; *ZZTJ* 182.5692. Note: Wendi declared war in the second month, but launched the attack in the sixth month. See *ZZTJ* 178.5560–61; *SuS* 2.43.

23. *SuS* 45.1229–30; *BS* 71.2458.

24. On Yang Yong's conduct, see *SuS* 45.1230–31. On the Eastern Palace, see *SuS* 45.1231. On prejudice against concubines, see *YSJX* 4.47; Teng 1968, 12–13.

25. On Yangdi giving away his children, see *SuS* 4.94; 45.1231. On Yangdi's confession to his mother, see *SuS* 45.1231–32; *BS* 71.2460. On Yuwen Shu's key role, see *SuS* 61.1465.

26. On Yang Su, see Wu Gang 1991, vol. 3, 8; Yao Shuangnian 1991, 88–90; Liu Jianmin 1999, 219–45. On Gao Jiong's opposition to Yong's removal, see *SuS* 41.1182. On Wendi's fear of the Gao Jiong-Yang Yong alliance, see Lü Simian 1980, 7. On Gao

Jiong's removal, see *SuS* 41.1179–83; *ZZTJ* 178.5565–68. On Yang Liang, see *SuS* 45.1244–45.

27. On Yong's commoners' village, see *SuS* 45.1232–33. Liu Jushi was a gang leader and the son of a high-ranking official. See *ZZTJ* 178.5556–57. On Yang Su's report, see *BS* 71.2642–63. Cf. *SuS* 45.1233–34; *ZZTJ* 179.5578–79.

28. On the divination, see *SuS* 45.1235; cf. *SuS* 41.1183. On Yang Yong, see *SuS* 45.1229–39; *ZZTJ* 179.5573–83. On Yun Dingxing, see *SuS* 61.1467–68; on Yuan Xiaoju and Wendi's motive in marrying his son to Yuan's daughter, see *SuS* 50.1317. On Yang Yong's confinement, see *SuS* 45.1236–38.

29. On Yangdi's request, see *ZZTJ* 179.5585; *SuS* 2.45. On Yang Yong, see *SuS* 9.188.

30. On the death of Wenxian, see *BS* 14.533; Boodberg 1939a, 271–72. Cf. *SuS* 36.1109.

31. For Sima Guang's portrayal of Yangdi, see *ZZTJ* 179.5592. On Yangdi's histrionic behavior, see *SuS* 3.59. On Wenxian and Wendi, see *SuS* 36.1108–109.

32. On the death of Yang Jun, see *SuS* 45.1240. Yangdi wrote a eulogy for the occasion. See *Quan Sui wen* 6.14–16 in *QSQHSL*.

33. For Yang Su's remark on Yang Yong, see *SuS* 45.1238. On Yang Xiu, see *SuS* 45.1241–42.

34. By that time, of Wendi's five sons, apart from Yangdi himself, only Yang Liang was still at large. So here the princes should include members of other branches of the Yang lineage.

35. *SuS* 15.1242 and *ZZTJ* 179.5594.

36. Yang Xiu would outlive Yangdi and perish at the hands of Yuwen Huaji. See *SuS* 45.1242–44; *ZZTJ* 179.5593–94. For Wendi's denunciation of Yang Xiu, see Cen Zhongmian 1974, 86–88.

37. *ZZTJ* 180.5605.

38. *ZZTJ* 179.5583–84.

## Chapter 2

1. *SuS* 3.60; *ZZTJ* 180.5601; *BS* 12.440. On Renshou, see Xiong 2000, 55, 76. On Zhangqiu/Yu Taiyi, see *SuS* 78.1769. Yuan Gang (2001, 236) claims that Liu Shu was behind Zhangqiu's warning.

2. On the incident, see *ZZTJ* 180.5601–604; *SuS* 34.1110–11; *TPYL* 106.509b. On the edict, see *SuS* 2.53.

3. Lü Simian 1980, 26–27. Cf. Han Sheng 1998, 488–90. Miyazaki (1965, 109–111) initially accepted the traditional account, only to change his mind later (1978, 79–91; 1989, 311–12). On Lady Chen, see *SuS* 36.1110.

4. On Wendi's passing, see *SuS* 2.52. On Yangdi's death, see *SuS* 4.93. On the convention of using *beng* to describe Yangdi's death, see Liu Jianming 1999, 82–83, note 6. On Zhang Heng and Wendi's death, see *SuS* 48.1288. On Zhang's posthumous title, see *SuS* 56.1393.

5. On Wang Shao, see *SuS* 69.1609–10. On Zhang Dasu, see *JTS* 68.2506–7. For *Taiping yulan*'s record, see *TPYL* 106.509b. For Taizong's remark, see *ZGZY* 6.200. For the epigraphic evidence, see Zhou Shaoliang and Zhao Chao 1992, 33, Guo Ti's epitaph.

6. On Lanling, see *SuS* 80.1798. On Liu Shu, see *SuS* 47.1272. On Yuan Yan, see *SuS* 80.1800. On efforts to conceal Wendi's death, see Liu Jianming 1999, 68.

7. For an excellent study of the incident, see Liu Jianming 1999, 82–83, note 6.

8. *SuS* 36.1110; *BS* 14.534. Hu Ji (1995, 52–53), Han Sheng (1998, 489), and Wang Guangzhao (1993, 98–107) also cast doubts on the record. For a rebuttal, see Liu Jianming 1999, 64–65. Yuan Gang (2001, 242–46) suggests unconvincingly that Chen took part in an anti-Yangdi conspiracy led by Liu Shu.

9. *SuS* 36.1111; *BS* 14.535; *ZZTJ* 180.5602–604.

10. *SuS* 36.1110–11; *ZZTJ* 180.5604, text and commentary; *SSD*.3. For a definition of *zheng*, see *YWLJ* 35.618, commentary; *HS* 20.862, note 13. The very fact that *zheng* is used to characterize Yangdi's action even after his father's death suggests that death does not dissolve relations governed by the incest taboo.

11. For example, *BS* 12.475; *SSD*.3.

12. On Yong's death, see *ZZTJ* 180.5604; *SuS* 45.1238. On Liang, see *ZZTJ* 180.5605ff.

13. *SuS* 45.1244–46. The quote on brothers is from the *Shi jing* 詩經. See *MSZY* 4.4.345c.

14. *BS* 79.2653; *ZZTJ* 180.5628, 180.5604, commentary. *SuS* (45.1238) records a total of ten sons. Apparently the two that survived were not considered Yang Yong's legitimate heirs.

15. *SuS* 3.60; *ZZTJ* 180.5614–15. Another edict on Luoyang was issued later in the third month of 605. It seems that the project was launched by the first edict. See *SuS* 3.63; Xiong 1993, 67. Cf. *YHJXTZ* 5.129.

16. Based on a figure provided by *SuS* 24.686 and *ZZTJ* 180.5617. This is a very rough estimate. We do not know whether it means two million people working on the job continuously for the whole month or two million man-days of labor. I am more inclined towards the latter. We need only to be reminded that entire Henan Commandery—the metropolitan area of Luoyang—after completion of the Eastern Capital, had a total of 202,230 registered households in its eighteen counties, or a population of approximately slightly more than one million. See *SuS* 30.834.

17. *SuS* 24.686; *ZZTJ* 193.6079; Xiong 1993, 78–79; Balazs 1953, 166; Bingham 1941, 13–14.

18. *KHJ*.5094b.

19. Regrettably, Needham (1954, 123–24) accepts these figures without criticism.

20. Based on Liang Fangzhong 1980, 69, 74–76. See also *SuS* 30.834–36, 31.870, 872. The population figures in the sources refer to registered population. Counting the unregistered population may boost the total population by as much as one fifth to one third. However, there is no way to quantify the unregistered population in this period.

21. *SuS* 3.63; *TD* 10.220. The number seven million, as provided by *BS* 12.443, is even less credible. See also *BS* 12.477, note 5. A similar project, that of the Yongji Canal, was completed with a labor force of more than one million, and this further supports my rejection of the claim that more than five million people were employed in building the Tongji.

22. *SGSZ* 18.823b. Serious depopulation occurred in the drainage area of the Tongji Canal, which is attributed to the excessive harshness of the project. See Tao Wenniu 1993, 51.

23. *ZZTJ* 181.5652, *DYZJ*.5b; *DYZJ* 180.5618.

24. His two other Southern journeys by water took place in 610 and 616.

25. *SuS* 3.65; *ZZTJ* 180.5620.

26. *FZTJ* 39.361b.

27. Weng Junxiong 1995, 533–34. It has been taken for granted that Yangdi took the Tongji Canal on his first Southern journey. See, for example, *YHJXTZ* 5.137; Bingham 1941, 17.

28. *ZZTJ* 180.5620–2; *SuS* 3.65. For a shorter account, see *SuS* 24.686–87; Balazs 1953, 166–67; Wright 1978, 180; 1979, 137.

29. The figure in parentheses is based on post-607 standards.

30. *ZZTJ* 180.5618. There were 6 *chi* (1 *chi* = 0.2951 meter before 607) in 1 *bu*.

31. *SuS* 3.65–66.

32. *SuS* 59.1435–37, 3.62; *BS* 71.2473–74.

33. *SuS* 59.1442–44. For Yang Jian[a]'s letters to these three people, see *Quan Sui wen* 8.7–9 in *QSQHSL*. On Cui Ze, see *SuS* 77.1755–58; on Wang Zhen, see *SuS* 76.1736–38; on Zhizhong, see *XGSZ* 10.502c–503a.

34. *SuS* 59.1442–44.

35. On his third son, see his obituary inscription in *XGSZ* 19.581c. On his other sons, see *SuS* 4.95.

36. *SuS* 3.68. *ZZTJ* 180.5629 records the day of *bingyin* 丙寅 of the fourth month as the date of Yangdi's departure, which is an error for *bingshen*.

37. There is a gap in this otherwise detailed itinerary. The sources, instead of identifying Yangdi's next stop, record that he ordered laborers to build a road from the Taihang Mountains to Bing Prefecture in the fifth month. Judging from this, Yangdi probably went to Bing Prefecture in central Shanxi before he reached northern Shanxi.

38. One *duan*[a] = one half of a *pi* 疋/匹 (bolt).

39. *CFYG* 974.8.

40. Cen Zhongmian (1964, 15) points out the absurdity of this figure.

41. According to the post-607 standard, 1 *bu* = 1.41 m.

42. *ZZTJ* 180.5629–34; *SuS* 3.68–70.

43. *SuS* 41.1179–84; *BS* 72.2487–92.

44. *SuS* 41.1186–87; Yamazaki 1956, 21–23. Su Wei held the post of vice president of the left at the time of his dismissal in 607.

45. On Heruo Bi, see *SuS* 52.1344–46; *BS* 68.2380–83. On Yuwen Bi, see *SuS* 56.1389–93; *BS* 75.2569–71.

46. On the duration of the project, see *ZZTJ* 180.5632. *SuS* 3.70 records ten days.

47. On Qimin's visit, see *SuS* 15.381. On the performance, see *SuS* 15.380–81; *ZZTJ* 180.5626 places this event in 607.

48. On Su Wei, see *SuS* 41.1187–88; on Gao Jiong, see *SuS* 41.1184; on Heruo Bi, see *SuS* 52.1343–46; on Yuwen Bi, see *SuS* 56.1389–91. See also *ZZTJ* 180.5632–33. In Sui-Tang times, it was generally considered ineffective to rely on the Great Wall to ward off nomadic raids. See *ZGZY* 3.43, comment by Tang Taizong.

49. *SuS* 67.1576.

50. On the use of female labor, see *SuS* 24.687. On the Great Wall, see *SuS* 3.71; *ZZTJ* 181.5641; Waldron 1990, 46–47; Needham 1971, 54.

51. *ZZTJ* 181.5648 places Xue's death in 609. See also Jiang Liangfu 1965.111.

52. On Xue Daoheng, see *SuS* 57.1405–13; *BS* 36.1337–40. For Yangdi's remark, see *STJH* shang.2; also *ZZTJ* 182.5684.

53. *SuS* 84.1288–92; *BS* 41.1516; *ZZTJ* 180.5625. Boodberg (1939a, 269) suggests that Yang Su died by Yangdi's orders. But there is little direct evidence to support his argument.

54. *SuS* 56.1392–93; *BS* 74.2548–50. *ZZTJ* 181.5667 places the year of Zhang Heng's death in 612. See also Jiang Liangfu 1965.131.

55. *ZZTJ* 180.5624. During the reign of Yang Tong in Luoyang after the death of Yangdi, seven powerful figures were put in charge of state affairs at court, known also as the Seven Nobles, which apparently followed this precedent. See *SuS* 59.1438.

56. For Yang Su's remark on Niu Hong, see *SuS* 49.1297–1310; *BS* 72.2492–504. On Zhang Jin, see *SuS* 61.1465. On the Five Nobles, see *SuS* 41.1188. On Yuwen Shu, see *BS* 62.2211–13 (against Yuchi Jiong); *SuS* 61.1463–67; *BS* 78.2649–53 (death).

57. *SuS* 28.785. Note: The title *huangmen shilang* under the Sui is rendered as "director of the Chancellery" by Hucker (1985, 262), which is inaccurate.

58. On Pei Ju, see *SuS* 67.1577–84. On Pei Yun, see *SuS* 67.1574–77. On Yu Shiji, see *SuS* 67.1569–74; *BS* 83.2797–99. On Su Wei, see *SuS* 41.1184–90.

59. On Yangdi's foreign policy, see chapter 10.

## CHAPTER 3

1. Traditional figures on foreign troops and rebels are often rough estimates and prone to inaccuracy. Efforts are made to verify them where possible. The figures cited are based on my best judgment and in the absence of counterevidence. On population figures, see *TD* 7.147. On insurgencies, see Kegasawa 1978, 155. On the estimated number of rebels, see Wang Zhongluo 1988–90, 76. My periodization follows that of Qi Xia (1958, 97–118) except for Phase Two, which for him, starts in 614. See also Kegasawa 1978, 159–60; Tanigawa 1995, 55–81.

2. On Wang Bo et al., see *ZZTJ* 181.5656–57; Qi Xia 1958, 97–100. On the flood, see *SuS* 24.688; Balazs 1953, 170. On the bandits, see *ZZTJ* 181.5656. See also *SuS* 24.687–88; Balazs 1953, 170–71.

3. Based on *JTS* 54.2235; Kegasawa 1978, 170. The *XTS* (85.3696) account is different but less reliable. See *ZZTJ* 181.5655–57; Nunome 1980, 118–19.

4. Cf. Wright 1979, 143–44; Jin Baoxiang et al. 1989, 3–4. On Mohe and Qidan, see *SuS* 81.1821–22; 84.1881–82. On Qidan's defeat, see *ZZTJ* 180.5621–22.

5. On the Great Wall, see *SuS* 3.71; *ZZTJ* 181.5641. On military supplies, see *ZZTJ* 181.5653. On the mobilization, see *ZZTJ* 181.5654; *SuS* 4.79ff. On the corvée laborers, see *SuS* 74.1701.

6. *SuS* 4.79–80; *ZZTJ* 181.5659.

7. *SuS* 4.81; *ZZTJ* 181.5660. Some scholars regard this number as overinflated, based on estimated troop strengths (Asami 1985, 24–29; Graff 2002, 148). A total of twenty-four armies were dispatched plus a naval force and Yangdi's Son of Heaven's Six Armies, with each army about twenty thousand in strength. But troop strengths did not stay constant. They could be much higher (see Gu Jiguang 1978, 119). For example, the nine armies under Yu Zhongwen's command were about 305,000 men or 33,900 per army.

Li Zefen (1989, 225) bases his skepticism of the number on geopolitical factors. But the geopolitical argument is hard to support without specific textual evidence.

8. On the campaign, see *SuS* 4.82; *ZZTJ* 181.5662. On the Liao River, see *SuS* 81.1817. On General Mai, see *SuS* 64.1512. Probably, Yangdi launched this campaign well before the rain season to avoid his father's mistake. See Chen Yinke 1982, 140; Graff 2002, 149.

9. On the commissioners, see *SuS* 8.161; 60.1455. On Lai, see *ZZTJ* 181.5663; *SuS* 64.1516. On Yangdi's direction of the campaign, see *SuS* 81.1817; *ZZTJ* 181.5662.

10. *ZZTJ* 181.5659–67; *SuS* 81.1817. See also *SuS* 4.79–83. On Yu Zhongwen, see *SuS* 60.1455. On Yuwen Shu, see *SuS* 61.1466. On Ülchi's role, see Han Woo-keun 1970, 76–77. The *SuS* cites twenty-seven hundred as the number of Sui troops that returned. It probably refers to survivors of Yuwen Shu's army only, not the entire expeditionary force. See Li Zefen 1989, 226.

11. On the *fubing* system, see Han Sheng 1995, 367. On the various factors that led to the failure of the Liaodong campaigns based on John Jamieson's dissertation, see Wright 1978, 194–95.

12. On Silla, see Liu Jianming 1999, 308–310. On Paekche, see *ZZTJ* 181. 5666; Pan Yihong 1997, 125. On Mohe, see *SuS* 81.1821–22.

13. The size of Koguryŏ's army, at its height, was around three hundred thousand in Tang times. Its size in Sui times should not exceed that figure. See Liu Jianming 1999, 321.

14. The so-called old city of Liaodong (Liaoyang) was probably the old site that was either adjacent or close to the city under Koguryŏ's control. See *ZZTJ* 182.5668.

15. On Lai Huer, see *ZZTJ* 182.5672. On Liaodong, see *ZZTJ* 182.5668–69, 5671; *SuS* 4.83–84. On Yangdi's withdrawal, see *SuS* 70.1622–23; *BS* 94.1790; *ZZTJ* 182.5677. On the failure of the campaign, see *ZZTJ* 182.5677–78; *SuS* 4.84.

16. On Yang Xuangan, see *ZZTJ* 182.5672; Liu Jianming 1999, 122–27; Nunome 1968b, 19–52. On Yang Shen, see *SuS* 70.1615–16.

17. *SuS* 70.1615–16; *BS* 41.1517–18. On the first Liaodong campaign, see *SuS* 24.687–88; Balazs 1953, 170–73.

18. On Lai Huer, see *SuS* 70.1616. On Xuangan's strategy, see *ZZTJ* 182.5674. On Li Mi's advice to Yang Xuangan, see Nunome 1968c, 63–65.

19. *SuS* 35.1617; *BS* 41.1518.

20. *SuS* 70.1616; *BS* 41.1519; *ZZTJ* 182.5675. On the Shangdong Gate, see *TLJCFK* 5.146.

21. *ZZTJ* 182.5676. Note that the name, Yang Xiong, is probably a corruption for Yang Shixiong 楊士雄. See Cen Zhongmian 1974, 84.

22. On these structures, see *TLJCFK* 5.131–41.

23. On Wei Xuan, see *SuS* 70.1618; *BS* 41.1519. On Yangdi's withdrawal, see *ZZTJ* 182.5677. On Hongnong, see *ZZTJ* 182.5680–81. On Yang Xuangan's death, see *ZZTJ* 182.5682; on Yang Jishan's death, see *ZZTJ* 182.5686.

24. *SuS* 4.84; Nunome 1968b, 19–52; Nunome 1980, 113–15. Bingham 1941, 44.

25. On Sui rebellions, see Wang Zhongluo 1988–90, 76. On the reign of terror, see *ZZTJ* 182.5683–84; Zhou Shaoliang and Zhao Chao 1992, 47, Zhangsun Ren's epitaph.

26. On Liu Yuanjin, Zhu Xie, Guan Chong, Wu Hailiu, and Peng Xiaocai, see *SuS* 4.84–85. On Ge Qian and Sun Xuanya, see *ZZTJ* 182.5669; *SuS* 4.85. On Wang Bo and Meng Rang, see *ZZTJ* 182.5669–70; *SuS* 4.85. On Xiang Minghai, see *SuS* 4.86; *ZZTJ* 182.5687.

27. *ZZTJ* 182.5689–92; *SuS* 4.81, 4.86–88; Bingham 1941, 46.

28. *SuS* 78.1767–68.

29. *ZZTJ* 182.5692.

30. See, for example, *SuS* 39.1149; *SuS* I43.1214.

31. Liu Jianming 1999, 242–44.

32. Zhao Wanli 1956 "Jishi" 9.105, plate 502. *SuS* (84.1874, 4.84) reads Fan Gui for Fan Angui. See Cen Zhongmian 1974, 109.

33. *ZZTJ* 182.5697–5700; *SuS* 4.89; 84.1876; *BS* 87.3299. Note, Lü Simian (1982, 991) doubts Yicheng's involvement. But his view is not widely accepted.

34. Cen Zhongmian 1958, 97–102; Bingham 1941, 46–48; Franke 1961, II. Band, 337–38; Wright 1978, 195; Liu Jianming 1999, 238–47; Wang Sanbei and Zhao Hongbo 1996.

35. On the reward problem, see *ZZTJ* 182.5698–700.

36. *SuS* 24.688–89; Balazs 1953, 172–73. The granary system failed to provide relief grains thanks to the strict Sui law against unauthorized appropriation of grain reverses.

37. For example, the Li Hong 李弘-Tang Bi 唐弼 group in Fufeng 扶風 (614) in south Shaanxi; Zuo Xiaoyou 左孝友 in Shandong (614); the Wang Xuba 王須拔 group (615) and the Wei Diaoer 魏刁兒 (615) group in Shanggu 上谷 (Yi County, Hebei); the Lu Mingyue 盧明月 group in the Chen 陳 and Ru 汝 areas (Huaiyang and Ruzhou, Henan) (615); the Zhen Zhaier 甄翟兒 group (616) in Taiyuan 太原. See *SuS* 4.87–91; *ZZTJ* 182.5689–183.5705; Kegasawa 1978, 281–84.

38. *SuS* 4.90–91.

39. On Yuwen Shu, see *ZZTJ* 182.5699. On bandits, see Tanigawa 1995, 55–58. On Su Wei, see *ZZTJ* 183.5703–704; *SuS* 41.1189.

40. On Yangdi's edict, see *SuS* 4.88–89; *BS* 12.466; *ZZTJ* 182.5695. On Yangdi's discomfort in Luoyang, see *ZZTJ* 183.5702–703.

41. On Lai Huer, see *BS* 76.2593. On the other remonstrators, see *ZZTJ* 183.5705–706.

42. *ZZTJ* 183.5706; *SuS* 4.91. On the rebels, see *SuS* 64.1519; Kegasawa 1978, 276–81, 263–69.

43. On Luo Yi, see *ZZTJ* 183.5716–17; *JTS* 56.2278; *XTS* 92.3806. On Liang Shidu, *XTS* 78.3730–31; *JTS* 56.2280; *SuS* 4.92; Kegasawa 1978, 246–51.

44. On Liu Wuzhou, see *XTS* 86.3711–12; *JTS* 55.2252–53; *SuS* 4.92. On Xue Ju, see *SuS* 4.92; *JTS* 55.2245–47; *XTS* 86.3705–3707; Kegasawa 1978, 200–209.

45. On the military might of Tujue at that time, see *ZZTJ* 185.5792.

46. A rebellious ex-officer by the name of Guo Zihe 郭子和 in Yulin was given a Son of Heaven title, which he declined. Liang Shidu was given a qaghan title. Other rebel leaders/warlords that submitted themselves to Tujue overlordship included Xue Ju, Dou Jiande, Wang Shichong, Li Gui 李軌, and Gao Kaidao. See *SuS* 84.1876; *ZZTJ* 183.5724; *JTS* 56.2280, 55.2253; *XTS* 87.3730, 86.3712.

47. On Li Yuan's rebellion, see Wechsler 1979, 153–160; Nunome 1968d, 101–149.

48. For Tang and later definitions of *liushou*, see Hucker 1985, 320; Qu Tuiyuan 1965, "Lidai zhiguan jianshi" 114.

49. *CFYG* 7.74b–75b; *JTS* 1.2–3; *XTS* 1.2–3; *ZZTJ* 183.5730–35. Cf. Bingham 1941, 83–90.

50. Li Shutong 1985; Wang Jian 1981, 77–79; Wechsler 1979, 154–56.

51. Nunome (1968d, 136–46) emphasizes the aristocratic nature of this rebellion by pointing out that the main supporters and followers of Li Yuan were from great (genteel) families.

52. On Xiao Xian, see *SuS* 4.93; *ZZTJ* 184.5760–61; *JTS* 56.2263–66; *XTS* 87.3721–24; Kegasawa 1978, 252–56. On Yangdi's depression, see *ZZTJ* 183.5703; 185.5775–76.

53. On Yang Yichen, see *SuS* 63.1500–51. For Yu Shiji's remark, see *ZZTJ* 183.5715.

54. On Li Mi, see *JTS* 53.2210–11; *ZZTJ* 183.5719–20; *XTS* 84.3679–80; Nunome 1968c, 53–100.

55. On the rebels, see *ZZTJ* 183.5713–15 (Dou Jiande), 5716 (Gao Kaidao), 5717–18 (Du Fuwei); Kegasawa 1978, 230–32. On Li Yuan's advance, see *ZZTJ* 184.5748, 5757, 5761, 5768.

56. *SuS* 99–102. The news of Yangdi's death reached Daxingcheng in the fourth month. Li Yuan immediately orchestrated Gongdi's abdication in favor of himself. See *ZZTJ* 185.5791.

57. On *xiaoguo*, see Liu Jianming 1996, 273–76; *SuS* 24.688; Balazs 1953, 172; *SuS* 85.1888. Among the *xiaoguo* troops Yuwen Huaji led north after the murder of Yangdi, more than ten thousand from Lingnan (Far South) and several thousands from Jiangdong 江東 (South) surrendered to Li Mi, leaving Huaji with about twenty thousand troops. From this we know that the claim that the mutiny was attributable to Guanzhong *xiaoguo*'s nostalgia is not entirely accurate. See Liu Jianming 1999, 148–49, 177–78.

58. Li Mi sacked both the Luokou (Xingluo 興洛) and Huiluo 迴洛 Granaries near Luoyang. See *JTS* 53.2211–12.

59. On Dou Xian, see *ZZTJ* 185.5776. On Sima Dekan et al., see *SuS* 85.1888–89. For Dekan's remark, see *ZZTJ* 185.5776–77. On Yuwen Huaji, see *SuS* 36.1113; *ZZTJ* 185.5777. On royal guardsmen becoming conspirators, see *SuS* 85.1889–90; *ZZTJ* 185.5778–79.

60. On Yangdi's capture, see *SuS* 85.1889–90; *ZZTJ* 185.5780. On Yangdi's crimes, see *ZZTJ* 185.5781. On Yangdi's death, see *ZZTJ* 185.5779–81; *SuS* 85.1890; Nunome 1980, 134–37; Bingham 1941, 111–12; Liu Jianming 1996.

61. On Yangdi's burial, see *ZZTJ* 185.5782; *SuS* 4.93–94; on Leitang, see *TPHYJ* 123.165b.

62. The site was recently investigated. See Kaochadui 1985, 77–78.

63. *ZZTJ* 185.5781.

CHAPTER 4

1. *CXJ* 3.48. See also *WYYH* 157.740.

2. On Luoyang, see Xiong 1993. On Yuwen Kai, see *SuS* 3.63; 68.1588. On the Sui-Tang perception of the city, see *ZGZY* 2.5.57.

3. On the authorship, see *SuS* 76.1730. For the edict, see *SuS* 3.60–62; *ZZTJ* 180.5615. Translation by Xiong 1993, 82–83, with modifications. For the first two quotes from the *Book of Changes*, see *ZYZY* 8.74c. For the last quote, see *ZYZY* 7.64b. Note: The last quote in the current edition of the *Book of Changes* reads *qin* 親 (attachment or affinity) for *de* 德 (virtue).

4. *ZS* 7.117–18; Xiong 1993, 83–84.

5. *TDZLJ* 79.407; Xiong 1993, 70–71.

6. For Wendi's edict on building Daxingcheng, see *SuS* 1.17–18; Xiong 2000, 35–36.

7. Wright 1975, 167.

8. *SuS* 68.1588; Xiong 1993.

9. According to *SuS* 3.63, nonmerchant urban households were from Yuzhou 豫州. *SuS* 24.686 and *ZZTJ* 180.5617 read "Luozhou" 洛州 for "Yuzhou." According to *SuS* 30.834 and *DYZJ*.1a, Luozhou was renamed Yuzhou by Yangdi.

10. Chen Yinke 1977, 79.

11. On Yuwen Kai, see Tanaka Tan 1978, 224–25; *SuS* 68.1588. Cf. Chen Yinke 1977, 74–75. 48.1291, 43.1218.

12. See, for example, Gao Min 1983, 268

13. Symbolically named, these structures embodied imperial power.

14. *SuS* 24.672; Balazs 1953, 132.

15. On dwelling geomancy, see Yu Haomin 1991, 156–57. On Luoyang, see *TLJCFK* "Dongdu waiguocheng tu." On Luoyang's inferior status, see Su Bai 1978, 421. On Daxingcheng, see Xiong 2000, 76.

16. *Jian* (bay) is a traditional floor space in Chinese architecture, similar to the Japanese *tsubo* 坪. Oblong in shape, it varies in length and width. Normally, the central *jian* is significantly wider than the side *jian*. An average *jian* is about 3–4 m wide. A floor plan is generally comprised of *jian* in odd number. The depth of the floor plan is decided by the number of *jia* (spaces between purlins, and between purlins and ridgepoles). *DYZJ* (2b) records thirteen bays for the Qianyang Basilica. However, the Tang Hanyuan Basilica (different from its namesake in Chang'an), as the replacement of Qianyang, is reported to have had an east-west length of 345 Tang *chi* or 107 m, which is within the possible range of 30 *jian* (90–120 m). In view of this, I follow the record of 30 *jian* in *YHNZ* 3.15b (*HNZ*.102). See Xiong 1996, 267–68; Zhang Yuhuan 1990, 553–54. On the Hanyuan Basilica in Luoyang, see *TLJCFK* 5.133.

17. *DYZJ*.2b. The *YHNZ* (3.15b) record of 270 *chi* (63.6 m) seems less credible.

18. An Jiayao and Li Chunli 1997, 352.

19. *ZGZY* 2.5.57. See also *TLJCFK* 5.133.

20. The existence of the penetrating axis was confirmed by archaeology, although the Qing scholar Xu Song places Dingdingmen Street slightly out of alignment with the central axis. See Chen Jiuheng 1978, 373. Cf. *TLJCFK* "Dongdu waiguocheng tu."

21. *SuS* 30.834.

22. Luoyang's ward system underwent a number of changes in the Tang and Song periods, resulting in different total numbers of wards recorded in various sources. See Xin Deyong 1991, 156–60.

23. *YHNZ* 1.2a; Mori Shikazō 1970, 248–49; Xiong 1993, 80. On Northern Wei Luoyang wards, see *HNZ*.84. On Daxingcheng ward sizes, see *TLJCFK* 2.34–35.

24. The exact location of the Tongyuan Market has been evasive. A study by Xin Deyong (1991, 160–62, and fig. 23) locates it between the Luo River to the south and Jingxing 景行 Ward and Shiyong 時邕 Ward to the north.

25. *YHNZ* 1.18b; *TLJCFK* 5.169.

26. On the location of the three markets under the Sui, see Xin Deyong 1991, fig. 23. On local influences over the triple market system, see Xiong 1993, 80. On early triple-market systems in the Luoyang area, see *YHNZ* 2.11a.

27 *SuS* 30.834. The figure is the result of 202,230 times 5.17 (Sui average household size).

28. Yangdi transferred several tens of thousands of rich merchants to the city. See *SuS* 3.63; *ZZTJ* 180.5617. There must have been numerous other types of urban residents, including officials and their servants, petty peddlers, craftsmen, entertainers, and even farmers.

29. The most populous city was Daxingcheng. See Xiong 2000, 196–97.

30. Chen Jiuheng 1978, 369.

31. *ZZTJ* 181.5649.

32. Cen Zhongmian 1958, 88, commentary.

33. Elsewhere *SuS* (3.74) gives "Duanmen Street," which should be the same as Tianjin Street, as the locale of the 610 event.

*SuS* (15.381) gives several accounts of acrobatic performances under Yangdi. The first one was about a performance in 606 on the bank of Jicui Pond in the Western Park. The second one describes a performance that took place recurrently on the 15th of the first month: It involved about 30,000 elaborately decorated dancers in a contiguous area 8 *li* in length extending from the Duan Gate south to the Jianguo 建國 Gate (Tang Dingding Gate). The third one is about the 610 event.

34. On the Sui Grand Canal, see Zhang Kunhe 1937, 201–11. See also Aoyama 1931, 1–49; Cen Zhongmian 1957, 295–311; Twitchett 1970, 182–89; Ma Zhenglin 1986, 1–28.

35. The Tong Pass of Sui times at present-day Fenglingdu is northeast of Tongguan. Note: Based on field research, Ma Zhenglin (1986, 2–5) points out that the resultant canal route was somewhat different at its eastern terminus from the textual record. Instead of joining the Tong Pass as claimed by the *Sui shu*, it emptied into the Wei River at present-day Sanhekou. Cf. Tan Qixiang 1982–1987 vol. 5, 7–8. *SuS* 24.683–84; Balazs 1953, 159–60; *ZZTJ* 176.5474; Zhang Kunhe 1937, 203–204; Wright 1978, 177–78; Xiong 1993, 67–68.

36. One pre-607 *li* is approximately 0.637 km. One post-607 *li* is approximately 0.509 km. One Tang *li* is approximately 0.56 km.

37. Pan Yong 1987, 29; Quan Hansheng 1976b, 269.

38. Needham gives a most accessible account of the canal in English, yet it is marred by its uncritical acceptance of the *Kai he ji*, a work of fiction. For example, Needham accepts the *Kai he ji*'s claim that a certain Ma Shumou 麻叔謀 was charged with building the Tongji Canal. But Ma is never recorded in the historical sources. Ma is mentioned, however, in the *Daye shiyi ji*, another work of fiction (*DYSYJ*.1). In fact, both the *Kai he ji* and *Daye shiyi ji* are apocryphal. See Deng Ruiquan and Wang Guanying 1998, 571–76. Also Needham's reference to Yuwen Kai as the chief engineer of the Tongji Canal seems to have no textual basis. See *SuS* 68.1587; Tanaka 1978, 245. Cf. Needham 1971, 306–308. See also Twitchett 1970, 187.

39. *QTS* 427.4708, Bai Juyi, "Sui di liu"; Tan Qixiang 1982–1987, vol. 5, 5–6.

40. Huaiyi was later renamed Tongji after the canal. See Gao Min 1980, 175–80. Cf. *TLJCFK* 5.179. See also *SuS* 3.63; *SuS* 24.686.

41. *LNL*.3000a; Pan Yong 1987, 31–34; Quan Hansheng 1976b, 281, note 1.

42. The shortcut route utilized the existing course of the Sui 睢 River, and the old route of the Qi 蕲 River. There are also different opinions as to the exact course of the route. But they are essentially minor variations from the main argument. See Ma Zhenglin 1986, 11–12; Pan Yong 1987, 33; Twitchett 1970, 186–87.

43. *YHJXTZ* 5.137 (Li Jifu's record); *ZZTJ* 180.5618.

44. A strong argument in favor of this view is put forward by Zhu Xie. See Pan Yong 1987, 30–31.

45. Needham 1971, 269–70, 306–308; Pan Yong 1987, 8–9; Liu Xiwei 1986, 169–86.

46. Pan Yong 1987, 34. Zhang Kunhe (1937, 207–209), while emphasizing the navigability of both routes, essentially argues in favor of the shortcut theory. Another argument holds that the canal merged into the Huan 渙 (Hui 濊) River near Songcheng before entering the Huai. See Pan Yong and Wang Yongqian 1986, 45.

47. For example, Han Longfu 1992, 177.

48. *ZZTJ* 606.5624.

49. Yangdi received the governor of Dongping while on his tour. See *SuS* 65.1538.

50. Weng Junxiong 1995, 533–34.

51. *ZZTJ* 180.5618.

52. Pan Yong 1987, 38–39; Zhang Kunhe 1937, 209; Kaochadui 1985, 73–74.

53. Pan Yong 1987, 40–41.

54. *ZZTJ* (181.5652) places the record after an entry about an event that took place in the twelfth month of 610. Apparently, *ZZTJ* dates it to 610 without specifying the month. See also *DYZJ*.5b; Twitchett 1970, 188; Zhang Kunhe 1937, 209–210.

55. *ZZTJ* 181.5653; *SuS* 3.75.

56. *ZZTJ* 181.5636, commentary; Zhang Kunhe 1937, 210–211; Twitchett 1970, 188–89.

57. On the Yongji Canal, see *ZZTJ* 181.5636; *SuS* 3.70; *DYZJ*.5a–5b; Pan Yong 1987, 46–50; Wright 1978, 179; Tan Qixiang 1982–1987, vol. 5, 17–18, (7)4–6. On Koguryŏ, see *ZZTJ* 181.5653; *SuS* 68.1595.

58. *ZZTJ* (181.5653) records the distance from Zhuo to Jiangdu as 3,000 *li*, which is likely an underestimate.

59. Quan Hansheng 1976b, 269–81; Pan Yong 1987, 17–28.

60. The Qi River was to the south of Anyang, Henan. It emptied into the Yongji Canal. See *SuS* 25.847. Here the Bian River refers to the Tongji Canal. See Tan Qixiang 1982–1987, vol. 5, 15–16, (7)1–2.

61. In the fifth month of 607, Yangdi mobilized adult males from more than ten commanderies to cut through the Taihang Mountains in order to create a throughway to Bing Prefecture. See *SuS* 3.68.

62. These were nine legendary rivers of predynastic China. See *SJ* 2.54, and 2.55, note 2.

63. *QTW* 797.8363b.

# Chapter 5

1. *SuS* 4.94; *BS* 12.471.

2. See Li Zefen 1989, 388–89. Li attributes all the palaces listed here to Yangdi. However, there is no evidence for the attribution except for Hongnong. Changchun 長春 in Chaoyi 朝邑 (east of Dali, Shaanxi), another palace Li attributes to Yangdi, existed in Wendi's time (*SuS* 2.41). On palaces along the canals, see *ZZTJ* 180.5618–19. On Guanzhong palaces, see *SuS* 29.808–809. On west Henan palaces, see *SuS* 30.834–35. Note: The Tang Shangyang Palace was located immediately west of the Imperial City of Luoyang. See *TLJCFK* 5.141–42; *HNZ*.220.

3. *HNZ* (136) treats Fanghua as a Tang name. But both *SuS* (15.381) and *ZZTJ* (180.5626) treat Fanghua as a Sui name. Cf. *TLJCFK* 5.143.

4. *TLJCFK* 5.143.

5. *TLD* 7.222; *HNZ*.217.

6. *HNZ*.111; *TPYL* 183.7. *ZZTJ* 180.5620 records 200 *li* as the circumference in Sui times. The actual total length of the four sides in Tang times is 130 *li*, not 126 *li* as recorded. A variant edition of *TLJCFK* (5.143) offers different measurements, which allows the numbers to add up: 120 *li* for the circumference and 29 *li* for the south side.

7. *HNZ*.136.

8. *HNZ*.198, 101.

9. *HNZ*.107–108.

10. *HNZ*.111–15.

11. The newly added Tang palaces include: Hebi 合璧, Gaoshan 高山, Longlin 龍鱗, Suyu 宿羽, Wangchun 望春, and Huangnü. 黃女. See *TLD* 7.222; *TLJCFK* 5.144–45.

12. *HNZ*.111–13.

13. *ZZTJ* 180.5620.

14. *TLJCFK* 5.144. On the acrobatic show, see chapter 10.

15. Tan Qixiang 1982–1987, vol. 5, 5–6, (12)19; *SJZ* 15.1306; *ZZTJ* 180.5618.

16. *TLJCFK* 5.144; *HNZ*.114, 138.

17. *HNZ*.115.

18. On Jinhua's location, see *YH* 158.26; *HNZ*.139; *TLJCFK* 5.145. On Yangdi's 616 trip there, see *ZZTJ* 183.5703; *SuS* 4.90. *ZGZY* (6.22.198) cites a similar firefly-catching event that took place at the Ganquan Palace in Hu County in Guanzhong. On Sui Ganquan, see *SuS* 29.808.

19. *HNZ*.114–15.

20. *HNZ*.115–16.

21. It was obviously inspired by "Preface to the Orchid Pavilion" by the calligrapher Wang Xizhi 王羲之 (Eastern Jin), in which Wang and his friends played the game of setting wine cups afloat a winding water course at the Orchid Pavilion. See "Quan Jin wen" 26.1609b in *QSQHSL*.

22. On Duliang, see *TPHYJ* 16.5. *TPHYJ* (16.10–11) dates the relay palace to Kaihuang 6 (586). Obviously, the palace served as a way station for the imperial progress along the Grand Canal, which was not yet built. It must have been an error for Daye 6 (610). In that year, on his visit to the south, Yangdi set up a relay palace along the Jiangnan Canal as well. See *ZZTJ* 181.5652.

23. On Jinyang, see *ZZTJ* 180.5634, 253.8214. On Fenyang, see *ZZTJ* 181.5639. On the Ten Palaces, see *TPYL* 173.848. On the aura of a Son of Heaven, see *DTCYQJZ* 1.5.

24. *SuS* 29.813; 3.70. On Yulin, see *XTS* 37.975. On the Ordos, see Waldron 1990, 61–64.

25. *ZZTJ* 181.5654.

26. *ZZTJ* 181.5655; *SuS* 3.76. On Chuluo as leader of the Abo branch of Eastern Tujue, see chapter 10.

27. *SuS* 30.858; Tan Qixiang 1982–1987, vol. 5, 15–16, (3)7.

28. On the palace built under the Sui, see *CFYG* 14.24; on its structures, see *ZZTJ* 185.5775.

29. *RTQFXL* 1.44.

30. Jiang Zhongyi 1990, 39, 44, note 5. *Jian* was apparently named after the Jian constellation.

31. *ZZTJ* 183.5702 (Piling), 185.5776 (Danyang); *SuS* 31.876. Other Sui palaces include: Chongye 崇業 in Weinan 渭南, and Taiping 太平 and Ganquan 甘泉 in Hu County 鄠縣 (present-day Hu County, Shaanxi). See *XTS* 37.962–63. Cen Zhongmian (1982, 40) attributes all of these palaces to Yangdi without giving any documentary evidence.

32. *ZZTJ* 183.5702.

33. *ZZTJ* 181.5639.

34. According to *SJ* (6.256), the First Emperor built three hundred palaces within Guanzhong and more than four hundred palaces without. Most of them are not confirmable. *YH* (158.25–27) lists forty Sui palaces, but only five Qin palaces.

35. *SJ* 6.247–48.

36. *SJ* 6.239; Wu Hung 1995, 108–109.

# Chapter 6

1. Wang Zhongluo 1979a *juan* 1–7; Tanigawa 1971, 332–36; Pearce 2001, 149–78.

2. *SuS* 26.720.

3. Miyazaki (1956, 498) provides some analysis on the reasons for Wendi's reforms.

4. Chen Yinke 1977, 84–92.

5. On the Sui-Tang Three Departments, see Yuan Gang 1994b; Lei Wen 2003, 68–76 (*shangshu sheng*); Ye Wei 2003, 119–130 (*menxia sheng*); Liu Houbin 2003, 146–148 (*neishi sheng*).

6. *SuS* 28.785; Yan Gengwang 1991, 436–79; Yamazaki 1956, 26–44; Wright 1979, 81–84.

7. *SuS* 48.1288.

8. Yamazaki 1956, 12–26; Lei Jiaji 1995, 160–65.

9. *SuS* 28.793.

10. *SuS* 48.1291–92.

11. The Sui Six Boards were officially known as the Six Sections (*liucao* 六曹). See *SuS* 28.774, 794.

12. On the Six Boards and the Nine Courts, see *SuS* 28.774–75, 785–86; *SuS* 28.794; Yan Gengwang 1991, 436–79 (in the Tang period). On *shilang*, see *TD* 22.607. In 583, *duguan* and *duzhi* were renamed *xingbu* and *minbu*, respectively. See *TLD* 6.179; 3.63.

13. Hucker 1985, 403, 451, 578. Note: Hucker claims these Terraces were set up around 604/605. According to *SuS* 28.793, the correct date is 607.

14. *SuS* 28.793, 801–802.

15. For the shepherd analogy, see *TD* 33.907, text and commentary. See also *SuS* 75.1721, Liu Xuan's comment.

16. Cen Zhongmian (1974, 40–41) lists a total of 200 prefectures at the founding of the Sui. It is smaller than the Northern Zhou number of 211 (*SuS* 29.807) at 580, and the Sui number of 310 provided by *TD* (33.907).

17. *SuS* 46.1253; 29.807.

18. Cen Zhongmian 1982, 5; 1974, 54–57. Note: Cen (p. 54) claims that the number of added Southern prefectures under Wendi is sixty. But in the table (p. 56), the number is sixty-one. I follow the table.

19. For tables of added and abolished counties under Wendi, see Cen Zhongmian 1974, 56–57.

20. *SuS* 29.807. *TD* (171.4468) records 1,024 for the total number of Northern Zhou counties. There seems to have been no effort on the part of Wendi to reduce the number of counties.

21. *TD* 171.4469; *SuS* 29.807–808.

22. Cen Zhongmian 1982, 5.

23. *SuS* 28.797.

24. *SuS* 28.785, 28.802; Xu Zhengwen 1994.

25. *SuS* 28.802–803.

26. On *fubing*, see Rotours 1947, XIII–XXII; Pulleyblank 1955, 61–63; Wright 1979, 96–102. A *fubing* soldier also differed from a typical 'militiaman' in light of the long-term service he had to provide and the professional training he received. See Graff 2002, 190.

27. On the Sui *tuan*, see *SuS* 8.160.

28. *XTS* 50.1324–25; *TLD* 25.644–45; *TD* 29.809–10; *TLSY* 16.304; *THY* 72.1298; Gu Jiguang 1978, 158–63.

29. *TD* 29.809; *SuS* 54.1369; Gu Jiguang 1978, 112–13.

30. On the Twelve Guards, see *SuS* 28.793–94; *SuS* 28.778–79; *XTS* 50.1324; Gu Jiguang 1978, 107–108, 116–118.

31. *SuS* 28.785–86, 800.

32. *SuS* 3.62. For a listing of Sui *zongguan* according to the *Sui shu*, see Cen Zhongmian 1974, 60–62.

33. On *da zongguan*, see chapter 1; *SuS* 28.789.

34. *SuS* 47.1267; Yan Gengwang 1972, 22–54; Kikuchi 1992b, 547–48.

35. Yi Yicheng 1991, 141–55; Kegasawa 1986, 444–81.

36. On Chen's thesis, see Chen Yinke 1982, 14ff. For criticisms of the thesis, see Yan Gengwang 1991, 619. See also Wechsler 1973; Lei Jiaji 1995, 8–25. On choronym, see Johnson 1977, 92.

37. The position of a de facto chief minister is confirmed by such expressions as *canyu chaozheng* 參預朝政, *canzhang* 參掌 *chaozheng*, *canjue junguo zhengshi* 參決軍國政事, etc. See *TLD* 9.274 for similar terms for de facto chief ministers under the Tang. For an inclusive list of Sui chief ministers, including deputy and honorary ones, see Yuan Gang 1994a, 207–209.

38. *SuS* 43.1216.

39. Eberhard 1949, 364–65.

40. Estimated. In 610, Su Wei was appointed leader of the Chancellery.

41. On this lineage, see Eberhard 1949, 61.

42. On Zhou Luohou, see *SuS* 65 and *BS* 76; on Mai Tiezhang, see *SuS* 64 and *BS* 78; on Yuan Ziwen, see *XTS* 74b.3166; on Lai Huer, see *SuS* 64 and *BS* 76. Note, Yuan Ziwen's date of appointment has not survived in history. His son Yuan Shizheng 袁士政 served as prefect of Nanzhou 南州 under the Tang, and his uncle Yuan Chong 袁充 died in 618 at seventy-five (seventy-four) (*SuS* 69.1610–13). It is likely that Ziwen was appointed under Yangdi.

43. Huang Yongnian 1996, 179–95; Han Sheng 1998, 259, 286–87.

44. *SuS* 26.720.

45. *SuS* 28.803.

46. See "Yangdi's Edict on Building Luoyang" in chapter 4.

47. For example, Cen Zhongmian 1982, 209–210.

## CHAPTER 7

1. See, for example, Tang Chengye 1967, 125–57.

2. On the Nine Ranks system, see Miyazaki 1956, 8–13. For the remark on birth and rank, see *TD* 14.328, commentary. On 587 as its possible date of abolition, see Gao Mingshi 1999, 55–58. On the examination system, see Miyazaki 1956, 517–22; Wright 1979, 89–93.

3. On *gongshi*, see *ZZTJ* 176.5488; Cen Zhongmian 1964, 4; Miyazaki 1956, 63–65; Gao Mingshi 1999, 12–16, 25. For Wendi's edict, see *SuS* 1.25. On *bingong* and *jinshi*, see Gao Mingshi 1992, 208–211; Gao Mingshi 1999, 45–51.

4. For Wendi's first edict, see *SuS* 2.46–47. On his second edict, see *FZTJ* 39.361a; Wright 1957, 100–101. On the perception that Wendi was against Confucianism, see *SuS* 75.1706; Yamazaki 1967, 18–22.

5. On Yangdi's pledge to support education, see *SuS* 3.62, 64; Wright 1975, 167. On the Confucian scholars, see *SuS* 75.1707. On Confucius' descendants, see *SuS* 3.72. On Yangdi's revival of Confucianism, see Yamazaki 1967, 22–23.

6. On *jinshi* under Yangdi, see *JTS* 101.3138; *BS* 26.962. For speculations that *jinshi* appeared under Wendi, see Miyazaki (1956, 64–65); Cen Zhongmian 1964, 4; Han Guopan 1979b, 296–97. On Early Tang degrees, see *TZY* 15.159. For Gao's speculation, see Gao Mingshi 1999, 43–52. On the rise of *jinshi* in Tang, see Miyazaki 1956, 64, 70.

7. *BS* 26.961–62; Gao Mingshi 1999, 40–43.

8. On *xiucai*, see Miyazaki 1956, 135.

9. *SuS* 2.47.

10. Lan Jifu 1993, 19–21; Wright 1957, 87–93.

11. Gao Mingshi 1999, 58–59.

12. On ritual theory, see Wechsler 1985, 20–36. For Wendi's comment on ritual, see *SuS* 2.48.

13. *SuS* 12.253, 14.345, 10.200; Chen Yinke 1977, 1–2; *SuS* 6.107.

14. On the five categories, see *TD* 41.1121–22; *TLD* 4.120; Wechsler 1985, 49–50; Xiong 1996, 261–63. On the sacrifices, see *SuS* 6.117. On *xingchen*, see *SuS* 6.116. On the chronograms, see Schafer 1977, 5. On *wusi* see *TPYL* 529.1–2. On *siwang*, see *SuS* 6.109–10. For their definitions, see *TPYL* 529.2–5.

15. *SuS* 6.116–17, 119. For definitions of Chinese ritual terms, see Xiong 2000, 154. Note: The Taiyang Gate, known alternatively as the Mingde Gate 明德門, was the southern main entrance of the city. See Xin Deyong 1991, 8.

16. On Taizu, see *SuS* 1.13; on the sacrifices to Ganshengdi and Divine Land (*shenzhou*), see *SuS* 6.117; on ritual changes introduced by Yangdi, see *SuS* 6.119. On the *mingtang* debate, see *SuS* 6.121–22.

17. For names of Sui royal ancestors, see *SuS* 1.1.

18. On the *tiao* convention, see *SuS* 3.69, 7.135–39; *TD* 47.1310–12.

19. On the Luoyang Ancestral Temple, see *SuS* 7.139.

20. On Mount Tai and the sacred mountains, see Wechsler 1985, 170–76; Kroll 1983. On Wendi's visit to Mount Tai, see *SuS* 7.140; 2.39; *ZZTJ* 178.5548. On Yangdi's visits to Mount Heng and Mount Hua, see *SuS* 7.140; see also Wechsler 1985, 175–76.

21. *Lei* refers to prayer ceremonies to the Lord on High, performed for a variety of events. The *yi* ceremony is conducted to honor the God of Soil (She). *Zao* means "to reach," specifically, "to reach the temple of one's father and grandfather." *Ma* is a military ceremony for the Horse God conducted at the battlefield. For a listing of Sui ritual categories, see *TD* 76.2061.

22. *SuS* 8.159–62 dates these events to 611 in error. See *SuS* 4.79ff.; *ZZTJ* 181.5659–60. Yangdi, as a prince, had conducted a similar ceremony in 600. *SuS* 8.162.

23. *SuS* 8.167–68.

24. On the carriage system, see *SuS* 10.200. For Chen's argument, see Chen Yinke 1977, 53–54.

25. *SuS* 10.200–12; *TD* 64.1794.

26. *SuS* 10.200.

27. *SuS* 10.203–12.

28. *SuS* 10.205. *Wei zhi* is the Cao-Wei part of the *Sanguo zhi* (*SGZ*) (History of the Three Kingdoms).

29. On the Southern cases cited, see *SuS* 10.206, 10.208.

30. *SuS* 10.207; *TD* 64.1794.

31. *SuS* 10.205. Elsewhere, *SuS* (10.203) records that Wendi ordered the reform of the five carriages and their companion vehicles. But there is no indication he ever used the latter.

32. *SuS* 10.205.

33. *SuS* 12.253–54.

34. On Yangdi's reform, see *SuS* 12.262–63. On the six regalia, see *ZLZS* 21.143; *LJSL* 12.352–53.

35. *SuS* 12.263–65.

36. On *kuzhe*'s origin, see Wang Guowei 1959, 22.1074–81. On *rongyi*, see *SuS* 12.279.

37. On *wubian*, see *SuS* 12.265–66. On *mao*, see *SuS* 12.266–67. Note: The passage does not give the timeframe of the adoption of the white gauze cap. However, the expression *jin* 今 (today) in the context clearly refers to the time when the above-cited panel appointed by Yangdi was active. Cf. *TD* 57.1621.

38. For information on these ornamental pieces, see *SuS* 12, 273–74; *JTS* 44.1944–45; for their illustrations, see Zhou Xibao 1984, 44.

39. It seems that these ornamental pieces were in use under Wendi before he abolished them. See *SuS* 12.271; 12.273–74.

40. *SuS* 12.271.

41. The *xiezhi* is a mythological animal with a single horn similar to a *lin* 麟 (unicorn), capable of going against the unjust.

42. *SuS* 12.271–72; 12.258. Apart from the censors, the other group of officials who wore the *xiezhi* cap were the *sili* 司隸 (inspectors) of the Terrace of Inspectors. On *quefei* and *xiezhi* caps in Han times, see *Xu Han shu* 30.3669, 30.3667 in *HHS*.

43. *SuS* 12.268–69.

44. *SuS* 12.279; *ZZTJ* 280.5627. On Qimin's relationship with Yangdi, see chapter 10.

45. The most important source for Sui laws is *SuS* 25.695–718, "Xingfa zhi" (Treatise on punishment and law). On the values and limitations of this source, see

Balazs 1954, 1–6. For a judicious translation of the same with ample annotation, see Balazs 1954, 28–184.

46. *TLD* 6.184–85. On the Sui statutes, see Gao Mingshi 1991, 379. On *ge* and *shi*, see Xiong 1997, 118; Ishida 1988, 225, 228–29.

47. Here *wushi* 五十 (fifty) is probably a scribal error for *liushi* 六十 (sixty). See *TLD* 6.185, *zhangxing*.

48. On the punishments, see *SuS* 25.710–11; Balazs 1954, 210–11.

49. *SuS* 25.711. Translation follows Johnson 1979, 17. Cf. Balazs 1954, 75.

50. *SuS* 25.710–11. On the *dengwen gu* institution, see *Sus* 25.712; Balazs 1954, 169; Xiong 2000, 59.

51. Chen Yinke 1977, 100–15; Cheng Shude 1963, 425–26; Balazs 1954, 207–08; Ishida 1988, 220–24; Gao Mingshi 1991, 385. Wright (1978, 116) emphasizes the influence of the Southern Dynasties, especially that of the Liang, but offers no textual evidence.

52. Translation follows Johnson 1979, and 1997. See also Balazs 1954, 79.

53. On the *Kaihuang Code* and its revision, see *SuS* 25.712; Balazs 1954, 73–89.

54. *SuS* 25.713–14; *ZZTJ* 177.5528–29; Balazs 1954, 81–83.

55. *SuS* 25.714. Note: In the relevant passage, the character *tong* 桶 in the term *cui tong* 榱桶 should be a substitute for *dong* 棟.

56. *SuS* 25.710–16; Balazs 1954, 85. For a brief coverage of Wendi's code and statutes, see Wright 1979, 103–106.

57. *SuS* 25.716.

58. Gao Mingshi 1991, 368–69.

59. On the *Daye Code*, see Gao Mingshi 1991, 368–69. Cf. Wright 1979, 106.

60. For the legal definition of *qingqiu*, see *TLSY* 11.217; Johnson 1997, 106.

61. *SuS* 25.716–17. Translation is loosely based on Balazs 1954, 91–92.

62. For a study of the origins of the *Daye Code*, see Ishida 1988, 225–28; Gao Mingshi 1991, 373–74.

63. *SuS* 25.716–17; *TLSY* 1.6; Cheng Shude 1963, 444.

64. Nunome 1980, 90–93.

65. Gao Mingshi (1997, 105–107) deals succinctly with this view.

66. *TLSY* 1.8; Johnson 1979, 65–66.

67. On discord, see *TLSY* 1.14; Johnson 1979, 78. On incest, see *TLSY* 1.16; Johnson 1979, 82.

68. *SuS* 25.716–17; *TD* 164.4233. On the *Daye Code*, see Balazs 1954, 89–93.

69. The *Daye Code* is listed in the "Jingji zhi" of the *Jiu Tang shu* (*JTS* 46.2010) and the "Yiwen zhi" of the *Xin Tang shu* (*XTS* 58.1494), but not in the "Yiwen zhi" of the *Song shi* (*SoS* 204.5137).

# Chapter 8

1. *FZTJ* 39.360a; *SuS* 76.1754. Cf. Jan Yün-hua 1966, 13.

2. On the Seven Luminaries, see *SuS* 20. 554–60.

3. Confucianism is also considered a "diffused religion" in the sense that it is diffused into secular institutions and has virtually no independent existence (C. K. Yang 1970, 294–95; C. K. Yang 1957, 281–82). This concept, although widely accepted, is not without its skeptics.

4. Yamazaki 1967, 18–23.

5. On Wendi's contempt for certain Daoists, see *SuS* 35.1094. On the three Daoists, see *SuS* 78.1774. On Sun Simiao, see *YJQQ* 113b.782b. In Sui-Tang Daoist literature, Kaihuang or opening sovereign was the fourth of the four kalpa cycles. See *SuS* 35.1091; *DJYS* "Xu" 803a–b; Yamazaki 1967, 25.

6. On Wang Qian, see *SuS* 1.4.

7. On *daochang*, see Benn 2000, 319–20.

8. On the crushing of the rebellion, see *YJQQ* 120.833b–c.

9. For the edict, see *SuS* 2.45.

10. On the penalty against anti-Daoist vandalism, see *SuS* 2.46. On Wendi's Daoist abbeys, see Xiong 2000, 243–44. For Du Guangting's record, see *LDCDJ*.1c.

11. On Liang Chen, see *ZXBJ*.543–45. On Louguan, see Chen Guofu 1963, 261–63; Kohn 2000, 285–87; Kohn 1997, 83–140. Yamazaki (1967, 26–28) uses "Xuandu Abbey" to refer to the predominant Northern school in Sui times. However, the clergy of Xuandu were transferred in toto from the Tongdao Abbey, which was dominated by Daoist adepts from the Lou Abbey.

12. Sunayama 1990, 136.

13. On Wang Yan, see *YJQQ* 85.602–603; Kohn 2000, 287. On Xuandu, see Xiong 2000, 250. On the popularity of Louguan, see Chen Guofu 1963, 261–63.

14. On Yangdi's abbeys, see *LDCDJ* 1.1–2. On the *si daochang*, see Yamazaki 1952.

15. On the cataloging of the scriptures, see *SuS* 32.908.

16. The Four White-headed Elders (*sihao* 四皓 ) were four Qin loyalists who later abandoned their pledge not to serve the Han court. See *SJ* 55.2045. The Eight Lords (*bagong* 八公) were eight transcendents who, because of their wrinkled and wizened faces, failed to obtain an audience with Prince of Huainan 淮南王 Liu An 劉安 in the early Western Han. Liu An eventually received them when they rejuvenated their appearances. See *LYJ* 1.857b–c.

17. *SuS* 77.1758–59; *BS* 88.2915–16.

18. On Shangqing as a more appropriate name for this school, see Robinet 2000, 197.

19. Jiao Kuang was considered a Louguan master as well because of his association with Mount Hua.

20. *YJQQ* 85.602b–c. On Jiao Kuang, see *XYBZ* xia.39c–40a (*DZ* 11). On the early history of the Shangqing/Maoshan school, see Robinet 1997, 114–124; Robinet 2000, 196–200.

21. Qing Xitai 1996, vol. 2, 28–29. On the origin of Yuanshi Tianzun, see Yamada 2000, 244.

22. *SuS* 35.1092; Qing Xitai 1996, vol. 2, 30.

23. Although the death of Tao (536) and the death of Wang (635) were separated by ninety-nine years, Wang's acquaintance with Tao may be explained by Wang's longevity. Wang died at the age of one hundred and twenty-six (one hundred and twenty-five). See *MSZ* 5.600c–601a.

24. *JTS* 192.5125; *YJQQ* 5.29a–b; *LSZXTDTJ* 25.244b; *TPGJ* 23.153.

25. *LSZXTDTJ* 25.245b–c, 25.246b–c. On Pan Shizheng, see Kohn and Kirland 2000, 342. On Sima Chengzhen, see Kohn and Kirkland 2000, 346–47.

26. *MSZ* (6.600–601) records that Wang Yuanzhi was born in 528 and died in 635 at age one hundred and twenty-six (one hundred and twenty-five). If his recorded age at death is true, he should have been born in 510. See Jiang Liangfu 1965, 100.

27. On Song Yuquan and Kong Daomao, see *SuS* 77.1760; *BS* 88.2916. On Xue Yi, see *JTS* 191.5089. On the *jiao* rite, see Schafer 1980, 42–43; Xiong 1996, 293–95. On Wang Yan, see *YJQQ* 85.602c–603a. On Zhou Yinyao, see *TPGJ* 6.42.

28. On the Daoists adepts, see *SuS* 35.1094. On Daoshu, see *YHNZ* 1.6a; *TLJCFK* 5.152. On Huiri, see *XGSZ* 25.652a, 652c–653a. Yamazaki 1967, 108.

29. On Cui Shanying, see *TPGJ* 120.847–48. *SuS* 59.1436. On the aura of a Son of Heaven, see *DTCYQJZ* 1.5; *TPGJ* 135.970. On the Fenyang Palace, see chapter 5.

30. *ZZTJ* 181.5658–59. Yuan Gang (2001, 386) suspects that the account contains fictitious elements. It seems to me that although this record is not found in the standard histories, it may have come from a nonfiction Daoist source.

31. On abbey supervisors, see *SuS* 28.802–803. For the Buddhist record, see *GHMJ* 25.281a.

32. The following part is in part based on Xiong 2002.

33. Tang Yongtong 1955, 470–72, 480–82.

34. On Taiwudi, see Tang Yongtong 1955, 493–96; Ch'en 1964, 147–51. On Wudi, see Tsukamoto 1948, 1949, 1950; Tang Yongtong 1955, 538–45; Ch'en 1964, 184–194; Ch'en 1954, 261–73.

35. On Zhang Bin, see *FZTJ* 38.358c. On the proscription of Daoism, see *GHMJ* 8.136b.

36. On Xuandi, see Tsukamoto 1949, 5–7. On Jingdi and his edict, see *ZS* 8.132; *FZTJ* 38.359a; *XGSZ* 2.436c. On Wendi, see *ZS* 8.131; Tsukamoto 1949, 16–31.

37. *FZTJ* 39.359b. On *nārāyaṇa*, see Mochizuki 1954–1971, vol. 4, 4012a–13a; Soothill and Hodous 1937, 248.

38. *SuS* 1.1; Chen Yinke 1980, 141; Lan Jifu 1993, 1–6. On Wang Shao, see *JGJFDLH* yi.379a; *SuS* 69.1601ff. Note: *JGJFDLH* reads Shao 邵 for Shao 劭. Shao is criticized by traditional scholars for overemphasis on oral accounts and vulgarity of language in his histories. But this should not detract from the importance of the court diary he kept. On court diaries, see Twitchett 1992, 35–42.

39. *FZTJ* 39.360b–c.

40. *LDSBJ* 12.108a. Cf. Wright 1957, 99–100.

41. On Daxingshan, see Yamazaki 1967, 45–47; Ono 1989 *Shiryō hen*, 14–48, *Kaisetsu hen*, 8–20. On its possible connection with ancestral worship, see Xiong 2000, 253–54.

42. For Wendi's remark, see *FZTJ* 39.359c; *BSL* 3.590b. On Wendi's favoritism to Lingzang, see *XGSZ* 21.610b–c. For a later criticism of Wendi, see *BSL* 3.590b. Wright (1959, 68) claims that Lingzang's appointment was intended to control and discipline the clergy.

43. *FZTJ* 39.360a.

44. *BZL* 3.503, 509.

45. Lan Jifu 1993, 88–90; Weinstein 1987, 9–10. On the Northern Qi *shitong*, see *BSL* 3.590b.

46. *XGSZ* 23.631a.

47. Lingyu 靈裕, for example, repeatedly turned down the appointment. See *XGSZ* 9.496.

48. Ono 1989 *Kaisetsu hen*, 9.

49. Wright (1957, 95; 360, note 118) seems to overplay the controlling aspect of the *datong*.

50. *LDSBJ* 12.108a.

51. *XGSZ* 12.516b. Cf. Hurvitz 1960–1962, 149.

52. Tsukamoto (1953, 5) overemphasizes the damage done by this unfavorable policy.

53. For Wendi's edict, see *LDSBJ* 12.105c, commentary. On the Three Stages school, see Yabuki 1927; Demiéville 1986, 858–59; Lan Jifu 1993, 167–70.

54. Cf. Wright 1957.

55. Ch'en 1964, 199–201.

56. Yamazaki 1942, 288–89, 351–53; Lan Jifu 1993, 21–27.

57. *ZZTJ* 177.5532.

58. *XGSZ* 17.568c. For the epigraphic information, see Zhao Wanli 1956 "Jishi" 8.84, plate 388.

59. For the biography of Huiyun (Zhiyun 智雲), see *XGSZ* 30.701c. Note: Here, "Zhiyun" is an error for Huiyun. See Zhao Wanli 1956 "Jishi" 8.84.

60. On Huiri in Jiangdu, see *XGSZ* 24.633b; Yamazaki 1967, 100–104. On Riyan, see *CAZ* 8.13.

61 *FYZL* (100.26) attributes two Chanding monasteries to Yangdi. The east one was actually built by Wendi in 603. See *LJXJ*.196a; Xiong 2000, 256–57. *CAZ* (10.10–11) dates the building of West Chanding to 607.

62. The Jingyun (Guangyun 廣運) Gate was within the palace grounds. See *TLJCFK* 5.134.

63. *SuS* 35.1099. On the identification of the *nei daochang* as Huiri in Luoyang, see Yamazaki 1952.

64. *XGSZ* 2.435c; *SGSZ* 3.724c; Mochizuki 1954–1971, vol. 4, 3542.

65. Lan Jifu 1993, 244–45.

66. Wang Guangzhao 2001, 1–17.

67. *BZL* 3.509c.

68. On spirit mediums, see Teiser 1988, 140–47. On Fan'an, see *XGSZ* 25.651c; *FYZL* 28.26.

69. *SGSZ* 18.821a–b; *TPGJ* 91.603–4.

70. On the *yiseng*, see *XGSZ* 25.652a, 653a; *FYZL* 28.26. On Faji, see *XGSZ* 25.652a–b.

71. *XGSZ* 29.692a–b.

72. *XGSZ* 25.644c–645a; *SuS* 3.72–74.

73. On Yangdi's relationship with Zhiyi, see Tsukamoto 1953, 8–12; Yamazaki 1967, 117–22.

74. Hurvitz 1960–1962, 145; Mochizuki 1954–1971, vol. 3, 2426b–c, vol. 5, 4711–12; Tang Yongtong 1955, 827–28; Soothill and Hodous 1937, 354; Janousch 1999, 112ff.

75. On Yangdi's promotion of Buddhism in the South, see *FZTJ* 39.361–62; Jan Yün-hua 1966, 18–19; Tang Yongtong 1982, 6. For Yangdi's acceptance letter, see *GQBL* 2.803b; *XGSZ* 17.566b–c; *GHMJ* 27.305c.

76. The *huacheng* 化城 or "transformed city" is the illusory city in the *Lotus Sūtra*, which embodies imperfect nirvana, especially that of Hinayāna.

77. The *kaishi* 開士 or "those who open the way to enlightenment" is often used to refer to monks or bodhisattvas.

78. *GQBL* 2.803b.

79. Soothill and Hodous 1937, 284b, 461b.

80. *GHMJ* 27.305c. According to the Dunhuang document *Chujiaren shou pusajie fa* 出家人受菩薩戒法 (Rules on monks who receive the bodhisattva commandments), a *zhizhe* was selected to preside over the ritual. See Janousch 1999, 115–16.

81. Yamazaki 1942, 292–96.

82. On Zhiyi and the Chen court, see Guo Peng 1980, 106–109. On Wendi's letter, see *GQBL* 2.802c; Hurvitz 1960–1962, 140.

83. On Sui policy towards Buddhism, see Wright 1957, 98–100.

84. On Yang Jun and his request to become a monk, see *SuS* 45.1239.

85. Wright provides 591 as the date of his departure. But *ZZTJ* (177.5532) gives 590 as the date of his posting.

86. The *SuS* (45.1231) expression "before his return to Yangzhou" 臨還揚州 clearly suggests that Yangdi had already been posted to the South. Cf. Wright 1975, 164.

87. *XGSZ* 19.584a–b; *FZTJ* 39.361a–c.

88. For Zhiyi's will, see *GQBL* 3.809a–810. For Yangdi's reply, see *GQBL* 3.810c–811. Modern suspicion of foul play in Zhiyi's death is based on flimsy evidence. See Yuan Gang 2001, 147–49.

89. On Yangdi and Tiantai, see Tsukamoto 1953, 12–16. On Guanding's visit to Yangdi, see *FZTJ* 39.361a. On Guanding in Daxingcheng, see *XGSZ* 19.584c.

90. On Yangdi's visit and Zhizao, see *FZTJ* 39.361b. On the death of Zhiyi, see *GQBL* 4.823c. On the Vegetarian Feast, see *FZTJ* 39.361b–c. On Yangdi's meeting with Guanding, see *XGSZ* 19.584c.

91. Ajātaśatru, who killed his father to occupy the throne of Magadha, was later converted to Buddhism.

92. The sūtra refers to the *Guan wuliangshoufo jing shu* 觀無量壽佛經疏 with Zhiyi's commentary. See Chen Yinke 1980, 143; Mochizuki 1954–1971, vol. 1, 826–27.

93. Ajātaśatru's father attempted to kill him as an ill-omened son. See Soothill and Hodous 1937, 293b.

94. Vipaśyin is the first of the Seven Buddhas of antiquity.

95. *FZTJ* 39.360a–b.

96. Chen Yinke 1980, 143–44. For a critical assessment of Chen's view, see Lan Jifu 1993, 44–45.

97. *FZTJ* 39.361b, text and commentary.

98. *BSL* 3.590c.

99. *XGSZ* 24.641a–b.

100. On Maitreya-inspired rebellions under Yangdi, see Lan Jifu 1993, 222–25.

101. *FZLDTZ* 10.562a; *FZTJ* 39.361c. According to *FZTJ*, the date of the event is 606. In the account in the *GHMJ* (280c–281a), the date is 609; Zhouwu 周武 is incorrectly replaced by Songwu 宋武; and Yangdi issued four rescripts before he finally gave up.

102. For example, Wendi treated the Vinaya master Lingzang as his equal in religion. *BSL* 3.590b.

103. For a detailed treatment of this issue in Tang times, see Weinstein 1987, 32–34.

104. *FZTJ* 39.362a; *FYZL* 17.16.

105. *FZTJ* 39.362a. See also *XGSZ* 27.682b–c.

106. Lan Jifu 1993, 39.

107. Yamazaki made a list of the monasteries closed in 611, in which he included twenty-one entities, leaving out Xingdao Monastery. See *TLJCFK* 3.69; cf. Yamazaki 1967, 136–37.

108. *TLJCFK* 2.34, commentary.

109. Yamazaki 1967, 137.

110. *SuS* 24.687.

111. Under Wendi, a total of two hundred thirty thousand people were ordained to become Buddhist clerics. It is likely that the size of the Buddhist community under Yangdi was in that range. By contrast, Yangdi's first Liaodong campaign alone deployed an army of more than one million with more than two million laborers for logistical support.

112. Sunayama 1990, 163, 180–84.

113. On Yangdi's model behavior, see *SuS* 45.1231.

114. *BZL* 3.509c. Cf. Tsukamoto 1953.

## CHAPTER 9

1. On the monetary situation of Six Dynasties China, see Quan Hansheng 1976a, 29–46.

2. On the *yongtong wanguo* coin and the *wuxing* large spade-coin, see Balazs 1953, 238.

3. The weight measure *jin* for the Sui *wuzhu* coins is that of the pre-607 system, under which, 1 *jin* is equal to 668.19 g. Under the post-607 system adopted by Yangdi, 1 *jin* is one third in weight or about 222.73 g. Since 1 *liang* is 1/16 of a *jin*, 1 pre-607 *liang* is about 41.76 g, and 1 post-607 *liang* is about 13.92 g. See Liang Fangzhong 1980, 545; *SuS* 16. 412; *TD* 9.198; Balazs 1953, 239. Here, "cash" is used to translate *qian* 錢 (coin), which was also the standard currency unit.

4. *SuS* 24.691–92.

5. *TD* 9.198–99; *SuS* 24.691–92; Quan Hansheng 1976b, 145–48; Peng Xinwei 1994, 231–32; Balazs 1953, 179–81. On currency debasement in the Early Tang, see *YH* 180.3306b.

6. On Sui and pre-Sui standards, see *SuS* 16.411–12. On the continued use of Wendi's length measure under Yangdi, see *SuS* 16.405. On the equivalency rates between Sui and earlier measures, see Liang Fangzhong 1980, 543–46; Wu Chengluo

1937, 64–76. The metric equivalents of Sui *mu* are calculated based on the following formulas:

1 post-607 *mu* = 0.2355 m (length of 1 *chi*) × 0.2355 × 6 × 6 × 240 [*bu*] = 479 m²;
1 pre-607 *mu* = 0.2951 m × 0.2951 × 6 × 6 × 240 [*bu*] = 752 m².

    7. *SuS* 3.67. In medieval China, there existed two types of closely related length measures, one for market use, and the other for musical instruments. They seem to have parted company by Sui times. See *SuS* 16.392.

    8. On the typology of Tang granaries, see *TD* 12.291–94; Zhang Gong 1985, 1.

    9. *SuS* 24.683; *TD* 10.220; Balazs 1953, 159; 220–21, note 152; Bingham 1941, 14–15. Note: Most of these place names were in use during Wendi's time. Yangdi changed a majority of them

    10. *ZZTJ* 175.5461.

    11. *SuS* 24.683–84; Balazs 1953, 159–60.

    12. *ZZTJ* 180.5626; *SuS* 24.686.

    13. Tonami, 1980. The term "capital granary" is a translation of *jingcang* 京倉. In the sources, *jingcang* refers only to the capital granary in Daxingcheng.

    14. *TLD* 19.526–27.

    15. *TD* 7.157, commentary.

    16. *YHNZ* 3.20b; *DYZJ*.2a; *TLJCFK* 5.140.

    17. On its capacity, see *TD* 7.157. On its archaeological evidence, see Luoyang-shi Bowuguan and Henansheng Bowuguan 1972; Luoyangshi Wenwu Gongzuodui 1992; Yu Fuwei and He Guanbao 1982, 33–34; Zhang Gong 1985; 68–73; Tonami 1980.

    18. *TLD* 19.526–527.

    19. On *changping cang*, see *SuS* 24.683; *TLD* 20.547; *TD* 12.289; *CFYG* 502.6019b; Balazs 1953, 159.

    20. *SuS* 24.684; 46.1254; Balazs 1953, 161–62. On *shecang* and *yicang*, see Zhou Yiliang 1998, 29–49; *CFYG* 502.6019b–6020a; *TD* 12.289–291. On Tang *yicang*, see *TD* 12.294.

    21. *SuS* 24.685; *TD* 12.289–90; Balazs 1953, 163; Zhang Gong 1985, 125–27. On *she* (community), see *SuS* 7.141; *RZL* 22.985–86.

    22. *THY* 88.1612; *TD* 12.290. Note: *SuS* 25.689 records that granaries were still full of grains by the end of the Sui. Here, they should refer to major official granaries.

    23. Zhang Gong (1985, 1–3) has attempted to trace regular granaries to the Qin dynasty. A 629 record (*CFYG* 502.6020) on the establishment of prefectural and county charitable granaries mentions existing regular granaries, which may have been carry-overs from the Sui.

    24. Zhang Gong 1985, 79–80. On *tuncang*, see *YHJXTZ* 4.110; *WS* 54.1201; *BS* 34.1257.

25. *ZZTJ* 184.5752.

26. *SuS* 24.688–89; Balazs 1953, 172, 230, note 206.

27. *ZZTJ* 183.5720; *SuS* 70.1628.

28. *ZZTJ* 183.5727.

29. *SuS* 24.689; *ZZTJ* 184.5754; Balazs 1953, 231, note 208. On Guanzhong, see *ZZTJ* 184.5749.

30. Weng Junxiong 1984; Zhao Yunqi 1993; Wu Jianguo 1992, 109–14.

31. *SuS* 24.680–81; *TD* 7.154; *CFYG* 486.5808b (date of the edict); Balazs 1953, 152, 215.

32. *SuS* 24.680; Balazs 1953, 151–52. On Tang "Taxation Statutes," see Twitchett 1970, 140. Note: One *qing* is equal to 100 *mu*.

33. For a criticism of the 582 rule, see Weng Junxiong 1984, 168. On land grants, see *SuS* 24.677.

34. Wu Jianguo 1992, 88–90.

35. *SuS* 24.677; Balazs 1953, 144.

36. *SuS* 24.682; *TD* 2.29; Balazs 1953, 157.

37. Although the 564 statutes of the Northern Qi record 20 *mu* as the quota of inheritable lands for a *ding* 丁 (adult male or adult), in the context of the Sui *juntian* system, that quota should apply to married adult males only. Unmarried adult males, taxed at a much lower rate, were probably entitled to smaller land grants.

38. Nos. 1, 2, 3, and 6 follow Weng Junxiong 1984, 168–69. On the Wude statutes, see Niida 1989, 22.540, *art.* 3a. Note: The Wude statues also stipulate that an additional 20 *mu* should be granted to the head of the household. On tax reduction for single male adults, see *SuS* 24.680.

39. Niida 1989, 22.540, *art.* 3a.

40. *SuS* 24.682; *TD* 2.29; Balazs 1953, 157.

41. *XTS* 37.960. *TD* 2.32 records a slightly different figure for the Tianbao period (742–756).

42. Zhao Gang and Chen Zhongyi 1982, 109.

43. For the Sui figures, see *TD* 2.28–29. Note: Here, "5 *qing*" is probably an error for "6 *qing*."

44. *Yichuang* was a Northern Qi term, meaning "the full tax responsibility of a man married to a woman." See *TD* 5.95. In Tang times, 1 *pi* 疋 was equal to 4 *zhang* in length and 1 *duan* 端 was equal to 5 *zhang* (*TD* 6.107–108; *JTS* 48.2090). The Sui standards should be the same. Traditionally, 1 *duan* 端 was equal to 2 *zhang* or half a *pi*. In Northern Wei times, 1 *duan* was equal to 6 *zhang*. See *ZZTJ* 148.4636.

45. *SuS* 24.680–81; Balazs 1953, 152. The following calculation is based on the land grants of a married couple.

46. *ZZTJ* 175.5461; *SuS* 24.681.

47. Niida 1989, 23.601, *art. 7*.

48. The metric equivalent of a Tang *mu* is calculated based on the following formula: 0.311 m (length of 1 Tang *chi*) × 0.311 × 5 × 5 × 240 = 580 m². On Tang commodity prices in the Tianbao reign, see Han Guopan 1979a, 224 (per *mu* yield), 215, 220 (silk), 219 (millet [*su* 粟] price); Zhang Zexian 1995, 362–365. One pre-607 *liang* was about 41.76 g, and 1 Tang *liang* was about 90% of that amount. One post-607 *liang* was about 1/3 of the pre-607 amount. I have not converted the Tang *liang* into the pre-607 *liang*, because the difference is miniscule.

49. *SuS* 24.680; Balazs 1953, 152.

50. *SuS* 24.677; Balazs 1953, 144.

51. Niida 1989, 133–36.

52. *SuS* 24.680–81, 686; *TD* 7.154; *CFYG* 486.5808b; Balazs 1953, 152, 215.

53. *SuS* 24.680–81; Balazs 1953, 153.

54. Niida 1989, 23.597–98, *art. 4*.

55. On a similar household classification system based on assets under the Tang, see Niida 1989, 151; *TD* 6.106; Tang Geng'ou 1981, 185–93.

56. *SuS* 24.685; Balazs 1953, 223, note 167; Tang Geng'ou 1981, 193–206.

57. *SuS* 24.672; Balazs 1953, 132.

58. *SuS* 24.684–85; *TD* 5.96–97; Balazs 1953, 162.

59. On the tax reduction, see *SuS* 24.686. In Early Tang, *ke* and *yi* 役 (corvée) were treated as separate impositions. Here *ke* seems to refer to taxes. See *THY* 85.1558. For a discussion on *ke*, see Twitchett 1970, 249. For the 606 edict, see *SuS* 3.66; *ZZTJ* 180.5624.

60. See for example, *SuS* 24.672, 24.681–82; Balazs 1953, 151–53.

61. On the harsh treatment of male laborers, see *SuS* 24.683; Balazs 1953, 158. On *jinding*, see *SuS* 24.685; Balazs 1953, 164.

62. On the trenches, see *SuS* 3.60. On Luoyang, see *SuS* 24.686; Balazs 1953, 165. On Tongji, see *SuS* 3.63. On corvée labor in Liaoxi, see *SuS* 24.687–88; Balazs 1953, 170–72.

63. *SuS* 24.686. On *ke*, see above.

64. On the use of female labor, see *SuS* 3.63 (605); *SuS* 24.687; *TD* 7.148 (608).

65. Horse prices were bid up to 100,000 cash per head (*ZZTJ* 181.5653), and donkey prices to 10,000 cash per head (*SuS* 24.687–88; Balazs 1953, 170–72). No doubt, the authors who entered these data intended to use them to indicate the significant rise in horse and donkey prices even though they did not provide the normal price ranges of these animals at the time. Later data show that Tang horses sold for 20,000 plus to 100,000 plus cash per head (*TPGJ* 452.3695; 436.3541). In one Tang record, a donkey was sold for around 5,000 cash (*TPGJ* 436.3549).

66. *ZZTJ* 181.5655–56; *SuS* 24.688.

67. *ZS* 6.93 (Northern Zhou); *SuS* 2.31 (Sui conquest of Chen); *SuS* 4.81 (Liaodong campaign).

68. *QTW* 794.7, Sun Qiao, "Fu fosi zou."

69. *SuS* 29.808.

70. *SuS* 24.686; Balazs 1953, 166.

71. The reference is to Luofu 羅敷, daughter of the Qin clan in Handan 邯鄲, in the State of Zhao during the Warring States period. Luofu was married to one Wang Ren 王仁. The King of Zhao took a fancy to her when he saw her picking mulberry leaves. See *WX* 28.12.

72. It refers to Su Hui 蘇蕙, wife of Dou Tao, prefect of Qinzhou 秦州 under Fu Jian 符堅. After Dou Tao was exiled, Su pined for a reunion with him, and sent him a silk embroidery she wove herself with a long series of poems and pictorial patterns. See *JS* 96.2523.

73. "Xixi Yan" is a tune pattern for Music Bureau style poetry. See *WYYH* 287.1461; You Guoen et al. 1979, vol. 2, 18–19.

74. Balazs 1953, 218, note 139.

75. On the debate concerning the authenticity of the 583 record, see Appendix 2. Note: *ZZTJ* (176.5481) places this event in a 585 entry. But the record is preceded by the word *chu* (earlier).

76. *ZZTJ* (181.5646–47) gives *minbu shilang* 民部侍郎 (vice president of the Court of Revenue) as his title, which had a more direct bearing on censuses.

77. *SuS* 67.1574–75; *BS* 74.2552.

78. *ZZTJ* 181.5647; *SuS* 67.1575.

79. Ikeda 1984, 161.

80. *ZS* 23.382.

81. Some scholars believe that the 547 document contains both tax and household registers. See Ikeda 1984, 105–111.

82. Niida 1989, 148. Translation by Ikeda 1973, 125.

83. Niida 1989, 149.

84. Niida 1989, 151. The twelve years in an earthly branch cycle are grouped as follows:

| yr. | *hai* 亥 | *zi* 子 | *chou* 丑 | *yin* 寅 | *mao* 卯 | *chen* 辰 | *si* 巳 | *wu* 午 | *wei* 未 | *shen* 申 | *you* 酉 | *xu* 戌 |
|---|---|---|---|---|---|---|---|---|---|---|---|---|
| no. | 12 | 1 | 2 | 3 | 4 | 5 | 6 | 7 | 8 | 9 | 10 | 11 |
| triennium | 1 | | | 2 | | | 3 | | | 4 | | |

85. Ikeda 1984, 169–74, 1973, 124–27; Twitchett 1970, 330–31; Song Jiayu 1988, 164–65. Note: The tax registers went to the Bureau of General Accounts (*duzhi* 度支) under the Board of Revenue (*hubu* 戶部). See *XTS* 51.1343; *TLD* 3.79–80 (*duzhi*).

86. Xiong 1999.

87. *TCTWS*, vol. 4, 71–72.

88. *THY* 85.1559, *jiuzhi*, commentary.

89. See appendix 2 for the calculation of these figures.

90. *SuS* 29.808.

91. *TD* 7.147.

92. *TLD* 3.73.

93. Liang Fangzhong 1980, 4, 6.

94. *JTS* 38.1384.

95. For the precise number of Sui households in 609, see *SuS* 29.808; for the estimate of the Early Tang population, see *TD* 7.148.

96. Bielenstein (1947 and 1987) made the claim that that certain figures of total national households in the sources, especially those of 280 and 627–649, were, based on, tax lists. This claim is not convincing. For example, the 652 figure of 3.8 million cited here, which falls under Bielenstein's tax list category, was reported by President of the Board of Revenue Gao Lüxing 高履行 (*TD* 7.148; *JTS* 4.70) to the court as the total number of registered households, not just that of taxpaying households. For a rebuttal of Bielenstein 1947, see Pulleyblank (1961, 292–93).

97. *SuS* 24.672; Balazs 1953, 131–33.

# Chapter 10

1. Zhenla or Chinrap means "Chinese Vanquished." See Schafer 1963, 5; *DYZL* Zhenla, 71–75.

2. *DYZL* Zhancheng.56–57, note 1.

3. *SuS* 82.1831–32. On the mortuary customs of the subcontinent at the time, see *DTXYJ* 2.208.

4. On Li Fozi, see *SuS* 2.48; *ZZTJ* 179.5598. On Liu Fang's mission, see Lü Simian 1980, 21. *ZZTJ* 180.5619; *CFYG* 984.11562; *SuS* 82.1832–33. On the creation of prefectures, see *SuS* 31.886.

5. Chitu means "Red Land." It is probably located in Province Wellesley opposite to the island of Penang (see Schafer 1963, 157; Fang Hao 1983, 226–28) or in Sumantra (see Chen Bisheng 1990). For variants, see Bingham 1941, 23.

6. *SuS* 82.1833–34; Schafer 1963, 3.

7. One *duan*ᵃ 段 is equal to half of a *pi* or 2 *zhang*. Sometimes *duan*ᵃ is used interchangeably with *duan* 端.

8. On the first and second Chitu missions, see *SuS* 3.71–72; *CFYG* 970.11395b. On Chang Jun's mission, see *SuS* 3.71, 82.1835; *ZZTJ* 181.5638–39; *CFYG* 970.11396a. *SuS* (82.1834) dates it to 607. On Chitu's third mission, see *SuS* 3.75. *SuS* (82.1835) records that Yangdi received Nayejia in Hongnong in the spring of 610. The record is not corroborated by other evidence.

9. *SuS* 81. The Korean state of Koguryŏ will be dealt with in a separate section.

10. Liang Chia-pin 1983–1984; Wright 1979, 138–39.

11. *SuS* 81.1823–24.

12. On Zhu Kuan, see Fang Hao 1983, 225–26; *SuS* 3.67. Zhu's post was *yuqiwei* 羽騎尉 (commandant of plumed cavalry; rank 9b). See *SuS* 28.792. On Chen Leng, see *SuS* 3.74, 81.1825; *ZZTJ* 181.5650; *CFYG* 984.11562b. Note: *SuS* 81.1825 records a smaller number of captives (several thousand).

13. *SuS* 81.1826–27.

14. On the 607 mission, see *SuS* 81.1827. The 608 mission is recorded in *SuS* 3.71. Note: Hori (1993, 207) suspects that the record is an interpolation. But his argument is not entirely convincing. The mission is also recorded in *CFYG* 970.11395b; *BS* 12.450. The 610 mission arrived either in the first month (*SuS* 3.74; *BS* 12.454), or in the third month (*CFYG* 970.11396a).

15. For the Japanese records, see Wang Xiangrong and Xia Yingyuan 1984, 50–55. On the debates concerning these missions, see Gao Mingshi 1993, 91.

16. *SuS* 81.1826. Inoue (1993, 168) identifies the Yamato sovereign here with Suiko Tennō. It is widely accepted that the 600 mission to Sui China was a diplomatic move aimed at Silla, which was then under attack by a Japanese expedition army. See Mori Katsumi 1955, 2–3, 5–6.

17. Tōno 1995, 41. Another view believes that the "Bodhisattva Son of Heaven" refers to Wendi. See Mori Katsumi 1955, 6–7.

18. *SuS* 81.1827; *CFYG* 997.11703a; Gao Mingshi 1993, 102, note 8.

19. At that time, Paekche, a tributary to Yamato, was interested in helping the Sui attack Koguryŏ. See Xu Xianyao 1992, 522, 546–47; Inoue 1993, 182–83; Ikeda 1971.

20. *SuS* 81.1827–28; *BS* 94.3137. Note: *SuS* reads Pei Qing for Pei Shiqing.

21. Wang Xiangrong and Xia Yingyuan 1984, 50–51. On *tairei*, see Xu Xianyao 1992, 541.

22. Gao Mingshi 1993, 91, 98.

23. Here I adopt a broad definition of Central Asia that include Xinjiang and Tibet in addition to the Central Asian republics of the former Soviet Union.

24. *SuS* 83.

25. *SuS* 67.1578–80. On Pei Ju, see Wright 1978, 169–71; Pan Yihong 1997, 116–18.

26. Zhang Xinglang 1977–1979, vol. 1, 61–62, vol. 4, 74–196; Fang Hao 1983, 230–38; Chavannes 1969, Troisième partie, IIA. On Yanqi, see Franke 1961, Band III, 206, note 394. On Fulin, see Franke 1961, Band III, 208–212, note 400; Zhang Xinglang 1977–1979, vol. 1, 79–85.

27. On Pei's vision, see *SuS* 67.1580. On Tuyuhun, see *SuS* 83.1842.

28. On Sui's attacks on Tuyuhun, see *SuS* 83.1844–45, 3.71; *ZZTJ* 181.5641. On Xue Shixiong, see *ZZTJ* 181.5642; *SuS* 65.1533–34. On Qu Boya and the tutun she, see *ZZTJ* 181.5644–45; *SuS* 3.73. On Gaochang and Yiwu, see Tan Qixiang 1982–1987, vol. 5, 30–31, (3)10–11.

29. On the state farms, see *SuS* 63.1504. On Hexi, see *ZZTJ* 181.5645; Tan Qixiang 1982–1987, vol. 5, 9–10. On Fuyun, see *ZZTJ* 181.5641–45; *SuS* 67.1580–81; 83.1844–45; Franke 1961, Band II, 332–35; Wright 1978, 170; Molè 1970, xvi–xviii, 43–45, 148–150, note 377; Pan Yihong 1997, 118–20.

30. *ZZTJ* 181.5662.

31. *TD* 174.4558.

32. *SuS* 83.1846–48; *BS* 97.3215–16.

33. Key studies of the Tujue include Chavannes 1969; Cen Zhongmian 1958; Liu Mau-tsai 1958 (Eastern Tujue); Grousset 1970, 80–90. More recent studies include Haneda 1978, 1–4; Sinor 1990, 285–308; Barfield 1989, 131–39; Liu Jianming 1997; Wu Yugui 1998, 81–146.

34. Cen Zongmian 1958, 15–16; Sinor 1990, 187–97; Wu Yugui 1998, 6–21.

35. Wu Yugui 1998, 22. Note: The editors of *SuS* (84.1864) read "*sheteqin*" for "*she, teqin*" in error.

36. *BS* (99.3288) records: "[They] carve numbers on a piece of wood, which, together with an arrow tipped with gold, is sealed with wax and serves as a contract."

37. Both *ZS* (50.910) and *BS* (99.3288) record the custom of "circling the tent seven times."

38. *SuS* 84.1864. See also *ZS* 50.909–10; *BS* 99.3285–3302; *TD* 197.5401–5407. For an incomplete translation of the *Zhou shu* passage, see Grousset 1970, 86–87. Note: For *tian* (Heaven) *ZS* 50.910 and *BS* 99.3288 read *tianshen* 天神 (Celestial God).

39. Xue Zongzheng 1992, 6–7, 710–11. On the early language of Tujue, *ZS* 50.910 records: "Their written language is similar to that of Hu 胡." In the sources, Hu (barbarians) is often used as a generic term for barbarian ethnic groups in the North and the Northwest. In Sui-Tang times, it increasingly referred to barbarians west of China, especially the Sogdians.

40. *SJ* 110.2879; *HS* 94.3834.

41. *BS* 99.3288; *ZS* 50.910.

42. On the founding of the first Tujue empire after the defeat of the Rouran, see Sinor 1990, 291–301. Although the official division of the Tujue is often dated to 583, Eastern and Western Tujue had existed much earlier. See Chavannes 1969, 219–21.

43. On the Tujue's victories over the Rouran and Ephthalites, see Chavannes 1969, 221–29.

44. *BS* 99.3290; *SuS* 84.1865; *ZS* 50.911; Cen Zhongmian 1958, 8–9. Cf. *ZZTJ* 171.5314.

45. Liu Mau-tsai 1958, Band I, 392–95. Wu Yugui (1998, 86–88) argues that here "my two sons" does not necessarily suggest the dominant position of Tujue.

46. On Tujue raids in early Sui times, see Liu Mau-tsai 1958, Band I, 433.

47. The infighting among the five qaghans is mentioned in an edict by Wendi. See *SuS* 84.1866. See also *SuS* 84.1854; *ZZTJ* 175.5449–50, 5456.

48. *ZZTJ* 175.5450–51; Wu Yugui 1998, 97–105; Pan Yihong 1997, 100–102.

49. *ZZTJ* 175.5462–63; Liu Jianming 1999, 197–206.

50. *ZZTJ* 175.5450; Pan Yihong 1997, 102–103. On Princess Qianjin, see *CFYG* 978.11493b.

51. *SuS* 84.1876, 1868, 1873; *ZZTJ* 175.5465; *BS* 99.3292–93, 3296–97. Both *SuS* (84.1876) and *ZZTJ* (176.5482) trace the east-west split to the war between Shabolue and Abo in 583. However, at that time, a separate western branch had been in existence under Datou. Supporting Abo against Shabolue, this western branch evolved into an independent Western Tujue empire. As for Abo and his line of successors, I follow Wu Yugui (1998, 18–32, 38–48) in treating them as a branch of Eastern Tujue. On different views concerning the split, see Liu Jianming 1999, 217–18; Lin Gan 1979, 132; Sinor 1990, 306; Franke 1961, II. Band, 248; Chavannes 1969, 219; Cen Zhongmian 1982, 19; Xue Zongzheng 1992, 178ff.

52. *SuS* 84.1870; *ZZTJ* 176.5482–83; Nunome 1979, 289–96; Xue Zongzheng 1992, 146–51.

53. *SuS* 84.1865–66.

54. The *Sui shu* (*SuS* 84.1872) assertion that Tuli (Rangan) was Shabolue's son is the result of textual corruption. See *SuS* 84.1885, note 6; Chavannes 1969, 49–50, note on Jen-kan (Rangan), Tou-li (Tuli), and Tch'ou-lo-heou (Chuluohou). Cf. Lu Junling and Lin Gan 1980, 580.

55. *SuS* 84.1874, 1876; Chavannes 1969, 4; Sinor 1990, 306. Although treated as a Western Tujue qaghan in the sources, Nili was an Eastern qaghan of the Abo (Apa) branch. See below and Wu Yugui 1998, 440.

56. Lü Simian 1980, 13; *SuS* 51.1332–33.

57. A second *Sui shu* account, which suffers textual corruption and is less credible, emphasizes Tuli's role in Qianjin's death. I follow Lü Simian (1980, 13) in rejecting this account. Cf. *SuS* 84.1871–72; *BS* 99.3296; *CFYG* 978.11494b; Pan Yihong 1997, 104–105.

58. *SuS* 2.44.

59. *SuS* 84.1872; *ZZTJ* 178.5564.

60. *ZZTJ* 178.5568.

61. *SuS* 84.1872–73; *BS* 99.3296–97; *ZZTJ* 180.5632; Cen Zhongmian 1958, 771–75, 513; Pan Yihong 1997, 105–106.

62. *ZZTJ* 178.5568–69; *SuS* 84.1872–73; *BS* 99.3296–97; Franke 1961, II. Band, 311–13.

63. *ZZTJ* 179.5590; Cen Zhongmian 1958, 83–84.

64. For example, in 601, ninety thousand Tujue people migrated into Sui territory. See *ZZTJ* 179.5588.

65. Cen Zhongmian 1958, 662–78; Wu Yugui 1998, 28.

66. *ZZTJ* 179.5600; *SuS* 84.1873–74; 51.1335.

67. Fanghua was an alternate name for the Western Park. See chapter 5.

68. The fish dragon acrobatic show embodied a long-standing tradition. See for example, *Xu Han Shu* in *HHS* 5.3131, note 4. It is believed that *sheli* were performers from the Kingdom of Sillah on the Irrawaddy. See Knechtges 1982, 232.

69. *SuS* 15.381; *ZZTJ* 180.5626–27.

70. On Yangdi's 607 tour and his meeting with Qimin, see chapter 2.

71. Jilusai 雞鹿塞 is west of Hanggin Houqi on the west edge of the Ulan Buh Desert, Inner Mongolia. It was a strategic frontier town in Han times. See *HS* 94.xia.3798–99; Tan Qixiang 1982–1987, vol. 2, 17–18, (2)4.

72. The Dragon Court (*longting* 龍庭) had been a place where the Xiongnu gathered to worship the Celestial God. See *HHS* 23.816, note 11. The carriage with green plumage (*lünian* 綠輦) was an imperial carriage decorated with green feathers.

73. The felt tent refers to the headquarters of Xiongnu's chanyu (khan).

74. The domed hut was the typical dwelling of the Xiongnu.

75. Huhanye chanyu, a Xiongnu leader, paid homage to the Han emperor in 51 BC. See *HS* 94.xia.3798; *ZZTJ* 27.887.

76. Tuqi means worthy and is often used as part of the title *xianwang* 賢王 or worthy king. It is also a personal name. Here Tuqi refers to Tuqi chanyu, who was defeated by his rival Huhanye in 56 BC. See *SJ* 110.2890; *HS* 94.xia.3796; *ZZTJ* 27.871.

77. Both "braided-hair" and "leather arm covers" are instances of metonymy.

78. Wudi mounted the platform in 110 BC. See *HS* 6.189; *ZZTJ* 20.676.

79. *SuS* 84.1875; *BS* 99.3299; *CFYG* 974.9.

80. *SuS* 84.1875; *BS* 99.3299; *ZZTJ* 181.5652.

81. *ZZTJ* 180.5627, 5632.

82. Sometimes, Qimin provided the Sui with cavalrymen for military operation, as, for example, in the case of the 605 campaign against the Qidan (*ZZTJ* 180.5621).

83. The death of Qimin is traditionally dated to 609, which is an error. Qimin was still alive in 610 (*SuS* 15.381). I follow Wu Yugui (1998, 174–76) in placing his death in 611. Cf. *ZZTJ* 181.5647; *CFYG* 978.11495a; Bingham 1941, 47. For variants

of Shibi's name, see *SuS* 84.1876 (Duojishi); *ZZTJ* 181.5647 (Duoji); and *BS* 99.3299 (Tuji).

84. Wu Yugui 1998, 38–48. Cf. *SuS* 84.1876–79.

85. *SuS* 84.1876–79; *BS* 99.3299–302; *ZZTJ* 180.5622–23, 181.5636–37, 181.5654–55.

86. *ZZTJ* 181.5658.

87. *SuS* 84.1876–79; *BS* 99.3299–302; *ZZTJ* 180.5622–23, 181.5636–37, 181.5654–55, 181.5658; Chavannes 1969, 13–20; Franke 1961, II. Band, 335–37; Wright 1978, 188–89. On Shegui qaghan, see Grousset 1970, 89.

88. *SuS* 67.1582.

89. *ZZTJ* (182.5697) places this event in the chronicles of 615. However, the record starts with the expression *chu* 初 (earlier), which suggests the event took place in an earlier time.

90. *SuS* 67.1581; *ZZTJ* 181.5652–53, Pei Ju's statement.

91. *SJ* 38.1620.

92. *HS* 95.3867.

93. On the founding of Koguryŏ, see Han Woo-keun 1970, 26.

94. Han Woo-keun 1970, 26, 41–47. Note; The term Liaodong has a number of meanings: (1) the southern part of Manchuria east of the Liao River under Koguryŏ; (2) the Chinese commandery with Wuliluo 武厲邏 as its seat (northwest of Shenyang); (3) the Koguryŏ city at present-day Liaoyang. See Tan Qixiang 1982–1987, vol. 5, 19–20, (5)4.

95. *WS* 100.2214–15; *BQS* 5.75; *SuS* 81.1813–14.

96. *SuS* 81.1814–15.

97. *JTS* 199a.5320.

98. *SuS* 81.1814.

99. For recent scholarship on Sui-Koguryŏ relations, see Liu Jianming 1999, 281–82; Hori 1979, 113–37; Han Sheng 1995, 351–72; Kikuchi 1992a, 1–35. Cf. Jin Baoxiang et al. 1989, 3–4.

100. *SuS* 81.1815.

101. On Wendi's campaign, see chapter 1 and Han Woo-keun 1970, 75–76. Yuan Gang (2001, 537) suggests that the Koguryŏ's real aim was probably to punish a branch of the Qidan that had been under their control for going over to the Sui.

102. *SuS* 81.1816; *BS* 94.3117; *ZZTJ* 178.5559–62. On Sui-Koguryŏ relations under Wendi, see Pan Yihong 1997, 108–111.

103. Liu Jianming 1999, 301–302; Liu Jianming 1995, 208–211; Yamazaki 1953, 1–10; Bingham 1941, 37–43.

104. *SuS* 67.1581–82; *ZZTJ* 181.5652. Xu Xianyao (1992, 506–507, 510) classifies foreign states in Sui times into two types: those with primarily tributary trade rela-

tions with the Sui, and those with complex cultural, religious and institutional relations. The latter may be regarded as civilized or borderline civilized states.

105. *SuS* 67.1581; *ZZTJ* 181.5652–53.

106. *ZZTJ* 181.5653; *SuS* 84.1875, 3.70; *BS* 99.3299; Pan Yihong 1997, 121–22. *SuS* 3.70 places the event in the eighth month. *ZZTJ* places the event in 610 in error. See Liu Jianming 1995, 209–211.

107. *SuS* 81.1817; *ZZTJ* 181.5662, 5666.

108. The translation is based on Legge 1960, vol. 3, 142–47, with modifications. This scheme, allegedly that of the semilegendary sovereign Yu 禹, is somewhat different from the nine *fu* system of the Zhou. But the basic concept is the same. See Karlgren 1970, 159–61.

109. *SSZY* 6.153a–b, text and commentary. On the origins of the concept of the Chinese world order, see Fairbank 1968, 4–8. The Yugong system also appears in "Xia benji" 夏本紀 in the *Shi ji*; "Zhouyu" 周語 in the *Guoyu*; and "Zhenglun" 正論 in the *Xunzi*. The system recorded in the *Guoyu* and *Xunzi* is slightly different from the Yugong model. See Hori 1993, 53–54.

110. Nishijima Sadao has advanced the thesis of the Sinitic cultural sphere for this period, composed of such elements as the Chinese written script, Confucianism, Buddhism based on sūtras in Chinese translation, and legal codes and statutes. It is challenged by other scholars on socioeconomic grounds. See Kikuchi 1979, 9–42.

111. On Tujue raids, see Cen Zhongmian 1958, 45–114; on major Sui counterattacks, see Cen Zhongmian 1958, 50, 54–55, 60, 62, 70, 80.

112. Other factors might include the unsettling situation on the Korean Peninsula and Yamato's low priority in the Sui court's international agenda. See Gao Mingshi 1993, 96–99.

113. *ZZTJ* 181.5641–45; *SuS* 67.1580–81, 83.1844–45.

114. On the settlement of Tujue people under Qimin, see Liu Mau-tsai 1958, Band I, 398–99.

115. *SuS* 81.1817; *ZZTJ* 181.5662, 5666.

116. *SuS* 83.1846–48. On the Tang conquest of Gaochang, see Chavannes 1969, 7–8.

117. On the influence of the Chinese legal codes and statutes, see Hori 1993, 250–56.

## CHAPTER 11

1. On St. Augustine's schemes, see Breisach 1983, 84–88.

2. Fogel 1984, 210.

3. Fogel 1984, 168–210; Miyakawa 1955, 537–43; Naitō 1967, vol. 5.

4. For the *Sui shu* record, see *SuS* 33.990. On the Guanlong bloc, see Chen Yinke 1982, 1–49.

5. Huang Yongnian 1998, 26–27.

6. *SuS* 37.1578–80.

7. *ZZTJ* 180.5615. There was a Tuoba ruler posthumously known as Yangdi as well, but he reigned in a predynastic age, thus does not qualify as a dynast. See *WS* 1.10.

8. *JTS* 1.8; *ZZTJ*. 186.5815, 180.5615. On the stereotyping of Yangdi, see Wright 1975, 158–87. An earlier posthumous title, *ming* 明 (bright), had been given to Yangdi by his grandson Yang Tong 楊侗. However, his short-lived regime is not recognized by historians nor is the posthumous title he authorized. See *SuS* 59.1438.

9. *SuS* 35.1617; *BS* 41.1518.

10. *ZZTJ* 185.5781.

11. *SuS* 4.95–96; Wechsler 1974, 117. The "Four Standards" refer to "ritual, righteousness, honesty, and a sense of shame." The concept was originally attributed to Guanzi 管子. See *SJ* 62.2132–33, text and note 5. The "Five Disfigurements" refer to five extreme corporal punishments in ancient times that involved disfigurement, allegedly invented by the sovereign of a legendary people known as Sanmiao 三苗. See *SSZY* 19.135c, text and commentary.

Shuofang was a commandery in Yangdi's time that lay in Jingbian, et al., north Shaanxi, and Uxin Qi, Inner Mongolia, with its seat at Yanlü 岩綠 (northeast of Baichengzi, Shaanxi). See Tan Qixiang vol. 5:7–8, (4)5.

12. See, for example, Han Guopan 1957, 92–93; Wang Zhongluo 1988–90, 91.

13. In one of Li Tong's edicts, he highlights territorial aggrandizement as one of Yangdi's major achievements. This was probably the prevailing view at the time as well. See *SuS* 59.1439.

14. Noticing that the sources have only recorded five children of Yangdi, Yuan Gang (2001, 441) argues that as sovereign he did not deserve the bad reputation for sexual excesses. However, Yuan fails to account for children (by his concubines) that he gave away. See *SuS* 4.94; 45.1231.

15. *ZZTJ* 182.5684.

16. For Chen Yinke (1982, 50–51), the geopolitical importance of Guanzhong was reflected in the successful implementation of the "primacy of Guanzhong policy."

17. *ZZTJ* 185.5791; *JTS* 1.6; *XTS* 1.6. On the Li Yuan rebellion, see Nunome 1968d, 101–49; Wang Zhongluo 1988–1990, 116–20.

# Appendix 2

1. *SuS* 24.681. "The third degree of mourning" (*dagong* 大功), which requires a mourning period of nine months, refers to the relationship between two men whose fathers are blood brothers.

2. For an excellent summary of the controversy regarding *maoyue* under the Sui, see Ikeda 1984, 157–62. See also Dong Guodong 1988, 109–121.

3. In Chinese, the figure at C1 looks even more suspicious when compared with D8. Here the last six characters are identical:

九百萬九千六百四 (C1)
三百九十九萬九千六百四 (D8)

Note, Bielenstein (1947, 155–56) speculates that the Northern Zhou figure (9 million) was only that of the taxpaying population. But that number would be too high. According to the *Tong dian* (*TD* 7.153), for example, under the Tang, there were about 8.2 million taxpayers out of a registered population of close to 53 million in 755; and about 2.37 million taxpayers out of a registered population of close to 17 million in 760.

4. Cf. Ikeda 1984, 164–65, note 12.

5. For a discussion of population growth rates in premodern China, see Kang Chao 1986, 30–31.

6. The process of the calculation is as follows:

$$[(20,000,000 + A) \times 1.127 + 2,000,000] \times 1.22 = 46,000,000$$

$$(20,000,000 + A) \times 1.127 + 2,000,000 = \frac{46,000,000}{1.22}$$

$$(20,000,000 + A) \times 1.127 = \frac{46,000,000}{1.22} - 2,000,000$$

$$20,000,000 + A = \frac{\dfrac{46,000,000}{1.22} - 2,000,000}{1.127}$$

$$A = \frac{\dfrac{46,000,000}{1.22} - 2,000,000}{1.127} - 20,000,000$$

$$A = 11,681,382$$

7. The number of households in the South at 589 (500,000) may have been greatly underestimated. Tao Wenniu (1993) raises it to 35% of the national total, and boosts the population under Wendi to well over 60 million. But Tao's calculation is too speculative. Pulleyblank (1961, 295–97) suggests that the Sui government simply took over the inadequate figure from the Chen. But the number 500,000 is not really out of whack when compared with 578,000 (see Liang Fangzhong 1980, 77), the house-

hold number for 609 in the Yangzhou area, an area that roughly corresponded to the former Chen territory. If we use the standard annual growth rate of 1%, after 20 years, 500,000 would become 610,000 ($500,000 \times 1.01^{20}$), which is even slightly higher than 578,000.

# Bibliography

An Jiayao 安家瑤, and Li Chunlin 李春林. "Tang Daming gong Hanyuan dian yizhi 1995–1996 nian fajue bagao" 唐大明宮含元殿遺址 1995–1996 年發掘報告. *Kaogu xuebao* 考古學報 (1997):3, 341–406, plates 1–32.

Aoyama Sadao 青山定雄. "Tō-Sō benka kō" 唐宋汴河考. *Tōhō gakuhō* 東方學報 (Tokyo) 2 (1931), 1–49.

Asami Naoichirō 淺見直一郎. "Yōdai no dai ichi ji Kōkuri enseigun: sono kibo to heishu" 煬帝の第一次高句麗遠征軍—その規模と兵種. *Tōyōshi kenkyū* 東洋史研究 44:1 (1985), 23–44.

Balazs, Étienne, trans. *Le Traité économique du "Souei-chou."* Leiden: E. J. Brill, 1953.

———, trans. *Le Traité juridique du "Souei-chou."* Leiden: E. J. Brill, 1954.

Barfield, Thomas J. *The Perilous Frontier: Nomadic Empires and China.* Cambridge, Massachusetts and Oxford, UK: Basil Blackwell, 1989.

Benn, Charles. "Daoist Ordinations and *Zhai* Rituals in Medieval China." In *Daoism Handbook* edited by Livia Kohn, 309–39. Leiden: E. J. Brill, 2000.

Bielenstein, Hans. "The Census of China during the Period 2–742 A.D." *Bulletin of the Museum of Far Eastern Antiquities* (Stockholm) 19 (1947), 125–63.

———. "Chinese Historical Demography: A.D. 2–1982." *Bulletin of the Museum of Far Eastern Antiquities* (Stockholm) 59 (1987), 1–288.

Bingham, Woodbridge. *The Founding of the T'ang Dynasty: The Fall of Sui and Rise of T'ang.* Baltimore: Waverly Press, 1941.

Boodberg, Peter A. "Marginalia to the Histories of the Northern Dynasties," 3–6. *Harvard Journal of Asiatic Studies* 3:3/4 (1939a), 230–83.

———. "The Rise and Fall of the House of the Yang." *Harvard Journal of Asiatic Studies* 4 (1939b), 253–70, 282–83.

*BQS. Bei Qi shu* 北齊書. Li Baiyao 李百藥 (Tang). Beijing: Zhonghua shuju, 1972.

Breisach, Ernst. *Historiography.* Chicago: University of Chicago Press, 1983.

*BS. Bei shi* 北史. Li Yanshou 李延壽 (Tang). Beijing: Zhonghua shuju, 1974.

*BSL. Beishan lu* 北山錄. Shenqing 神清 (Tang). *Taishō*, vol. 52, no. 2113.

307

*BZL. Bianzheng lun* 辯正論. Falin 法琳 (Tang). *Taishō*, vol. 52, no. 2110.

*CAZ. Chang'an zhi* 長安志. Song Minqiu 宋敏求 (Northern Song). In Hiraoka Takeo 平岡武夫. *Chōan to Rakuyō* 長安と洛陽, "Texts Volume." Kyoto: Kyōto daigaku jinbunkagaku kenkyūjo, 1956.

Cen Zhongmian 岑仲勉. *Huanghe bianqian shi* 黃河變遷史. Beijing: Renmin chubanshe, 1957.

——. *Tujue jishi* 突厥集史, 2 vols. Beijing: Zhonghua shuju, 1958.

——. *Tongjian Sui-Tang ji bishi zhiyi* 通鑑隋唐紀比事質疑. Beijing: Zhonghua shuju, 1964.

——. *Sui shu qiushi* 隋書求是. Taipei: Shixue chubanshe, 1974.

——. *Sui Tang shi* 隋唐史. Beijing: Zhonghua shuju, 1982.

Chao, Kang (Zhao Gang). *Man and Land in Chinese History: An Economic Analysis*. Stanford, CA: Stanford University Press, 1986.

Chavannes, Edouard. *Documents sur les Tou-kiue [Turcs] occidentaux*. Paris: A. Maisonneuve, 1903. Reprint, Taipei: Ch'eng Wen Publishing, 1969.

*CFYG. Cefu yuangui* 冊府元龜. Wang Qinruo 王欽若 et al. (Northern Song), comps. Beijing: Zhonghua shuju, 1960.

Chen Bisheng 陳碧笙. "*Sui shu* Chituguo jiu zai hechu" 隋書赤土國究在何處. *Zhong-guo shi yanjiu* 中國史研究 (1990):4.

Chen Guofu 陳國符. *Daozang yuanliu kao* 道藏源流考. Beijing: Zhonghua shuju, 1963.

Chen Jiuheng 隋久恆. "'Sui-Tang Dongdu chengzhi de kancha he fajue' xuji" 隋唐東都城址的勘查和發掘續記. *Kaogu* 考古 (1978):6, 361–79.

Chen Yinke 陳寅恪. Dongjin Nanchao zhi Wuyu" 東晉南朝之吳語. *Zhongyang yan-jiuyuan lishi yuyan yanjiusuo jikan* 中央研究院歷史語言研究所集刊 7 (1936), 1–4.

——. *Sui-Tang zhidu yuanyuan luelun gao* 隋唐制度淵源略論稿. 1963. Reprint, Beijing: Zhonghua shuju, 1977.

——. "Wu Zhao yu fojiao" 武曌與佛教. In Chen Yinke, *Jinmingguan conggao erbian* 金明館叢稿二編, 137–55. Shanghai: Shanghai guji chubanshe, 1980.

——. *Tangdai zhengzhi shi shulun gao* 唐代政治史述論稿. Shanghai: Shanghai guji chubanshe, 1982.

——. *Wei-Jin Nanbeichao shi jiangyan lu* 魏晉南北朝史講演錄. Edited by Wan Sheng-nan 萬繩楠. Taipei: Longyun chubanshe, 1995.

Ch'en, Kenneth K. S. "Some Factors Responsible for the Anti-Buddhist Persecution under the Pei-ch'ao." *Harvard Journal of Asiatic Studies* 17:1/2 (1954), 261–73.

——. *Buddhism in China: A Historical Survey*. Princeton: Princeton University Press, 1964.

Cheng Shude 程樹德. *Jiuchao lü kao* 九朝律考. Beijing: Zhonghua shuju, 1963.

*CS. Chen shu* 陳書. Yao Silian 姚思廉 (Tang). Beijing: Zhonghua shuju, 1972.

*Daozang* 道藏, 36 vols. Beijing: Wenwu chubanshe et al., 1987.

Demiéville, Paul. "Philosophy and Religion from Han to Sui." In *The Cambridge History of China*, volume 1, *The Ch'in and Han Empires, 221 B.C.–A.D. 220*, edited by Denis Twitchett and Michael Loewe, 808–72. Cambridge: Cambridge University Press, 1986.

Deng Ruiquan 鄧瑞全, and Wang Guanying 王冠英, eds. *Zhongguo weishu zongkao* 中國偽書綜考 Hefei, Anhui: Huangshan chubanshe, 1998.

Dien, Albert E. "The Role of the Military in the Western Wei/Northern Chou State." In *State and Society in Early Medieval China*, edited by Albert E. Dien, 331–68. Stanford: Stanford University Press, 1990.

*DJYS. Daojiao yishu* 道教義樞. Meng Anpai 孟安排 (Tang). *Daozang,* vol. 24.

Dong Guodong 凍國棟. "Suidai renkou de ruogan wenti guanjian" 隋代人口的若干問題管見. *Wei Jin Nanbeichao Sui-Tang shi ziliao* 魏晉南北朝隋唐史資料 9–10 (1988), 109–21.

*DTCYQJZ. Da Tang chuangye qiju zhu* 大唐創業起居注. Wen Daya 溫大雅 (Tang). Shanghai: Shanghai guji chubanshe, 1983.

*DTXYJ. Da Tang Xiyu ji* 大唐西域記. Xuanzang 玄奘 and Bianji 辯機 (Tang). References are to *Da Tang Xiyu ji jiaozhu* 校注, edited and annotated by Ji Xianlin 季羨林 et al. Beijing: Zhonghua shuju, 1985.

*DYSYJ. Daye shiyi ji* 大業拾遺記. (Song). *Shuofu* 説郛 edition.

*DYZJ. Daye zaji* 大業雜記. Liu Yiqing 劉義慶 (Southern Song). In *Wuchao xiaoshuo daguan* 五朝小説大觀, vol. 3. Shanghai: Saoyeshan Fang 掃葉山房 edition.

*DYZL. Daoyi zhilue* 島夷誌略. Wang Dayuan 汪大淵 (Yuan). References are to *Daoyi zhilue jiaoshi* 校釋, Su Jiqing 蘇繼廎, ed. and annotator. Beijing: Zhonghua shuju, 1981.

Eberhard, Wolfram. *Das Toba-Reich Nord Chinas*. Leiden: E. J. Brill, 1949.

Fairbank, John King, ed. *Chinese Thought and Institutions*. Chicago: The University of Chicago Press, 1957.

——. "A Preliminary Framework." In *The Chinese World Order: Traditional China's Foreign Relations*, edited by John King Fairbank, 1–19. Cambridge, MA: Harvard University Press, 1968.

Fang Hao 方豪. *Zhong Xi jiaotong shi* 中西交通史. Taipei: Zhongguo wenhua daxue, 1983.

Fogel, Joshua A. *Politics and Sinology: The Case of Naitō Konan (1866–1934)*. Cambridge, Mass.: Council on East Asian Studies, Harvard University, 1984.

Franke, Otto. "Das *Tse tschi t'ung kien* und das *T'ung kien kang-mu*: ihr Wesen, ihr Verhältnis zueinander und ihr Quellenwert." *Sitzungsberichte der Preussischen Akademie der Wissenschaften: Phil.-Hist. Klasse* (Berlin) (1930), 103–44.

———. *Geschichte des Chinesischen Reiches*, I.–IV. Bande. Berlin: Walter de Gruyter, 1961.

*FYZL. Fayuan zhulin* 法苑竹林. Daoshi 道世 (Tang). Beijing: Zhongguo shudian, 1991.

*FZLDTZ. Fozu lidai tongzai* 佛祖歷代通載. Nianchang 念常 (Yuan), comp. *Taishō*, vol. 49, no. 2036.

*FZTJ. Fozu tongji* 佛祖統紀. Zhipan 志磐 (Song). *Taishō*, vol. 49, no. 2035.

Gao Min 高敏. "Tang liangjing chengfang kao Dongdu bufen zhiyi" 唐兩京城坊考東京部分質疑. In *Zhonghua wenshi luncong* 中華文史論叢 (1980):3, 175–80.

———. "Guanyu Sui Yangdi qiandu Luoyang de yuanyin" 關於隋煬帝遷都洛陽的原因. In *Wei-Jin Sui-Tang shi lunji* 魏晉隋唐史論集, vol. 2, edited by Lishi Yanjiusuo 歷史研究所, Zhongguo Shehui Kexueyuan 中國社會科學院, 254–68. Beijing: Zhongguo shehui kexue chubanshe, 1983.

Gao Mingshi 高明士. "Cong lüling zhidu lun Suidai de zhiguo zhengce" 從律令制度論隋代的治國政策. In *Tangdai wenhua yantaohui lunwenji* 唐代文化研討會論文集, edited by Zhongguo Tangdai Xuehui Bianji Weiyuanhui 中國唐代學會編輯委員會, 359–96. Taipei: Wenshizhe chubanshe, 1991.

———. "Suidai de jiaoyu yu gongju" 隋代的教育與貢舉. In *Tangdai yanjiu lunji* 唐代研究論集, vol.4, edited by Zhongguo Tangdai Xuehui 中國唐代學會, 177–252. Taipei: Xinwenfeng chuban gongsi, 1992.

———. "Lun Wo gei Sui de 'wuli' guoshu shijian—jian shi Suidai de tianxia zhixu" 論倭給隋的 '無禮' 國書事件—兼釋隋代的天下秩序. In *Zhongguo yu Yazhou guojia guanxi shi xueshu yantao hui lunwen ji* 中國與亞洲國家關係史學術研討會論文集, edited by Zheng Liangsheng 鄭樑生, 73–106. Taipei: Tanjiang daxue lishixuexi, 1993.

———. "Suidai Zhongguo de tongyi—jianshu lishi fazhan de biranxing yu ouranxing" 隋代中國的統一—兼述歷史發展的必然性與偶然性. In *Zhongguo lishi shang de fen yu he xueshu yantaohui lunwenji* 中國歷史上的分與合學術研討會論文集. Taipei: Lianhebao wenhua jijinhui, 1995.

———. "Cong lülingzhi lun Kaihuang, Daye, Wude, Zhenguan de jishou guanxi" 從律令制論開皇、大業、武德、貞觀的繼受關係. In Zhongguo Tangdai Xuehui Bianji Weiyuanhui 中國唐代學會編輯委員會 *Disanjie Zhongguo Tangdai wenhua xueshu yantaohui lunwenji* 第三屆中國唐代文化學術研討會論文集, 91–111. Taipei: Zhongguo Tangdai xuehui, 1997.

———. *Sui-Tang gongju zhidu* 隋唐貢舉制度. Taipei: Wenjin chubanshe, 1999.

Gardner, Charles S. *Chinese Traditional Historiography*. Cambridge, Mass.: Harvard University Press, 1961.

Gardiner, Kenneth H. "Standard Histories, Han to Sui." In *Essays on the Sources for Chinese History*, edited by Donald Leslie, Colin Mackerras, and Wang Gungwu, 42–52. Columbia, SC: University of South Carolina Press, 1975.

*GHMJ. Guang Hongming ji* 廣弘明集. Daoxuan 道宣 (Tang). *Taishō*, vol. 52, no. 2103.

*GQBL. Guoqing bailu* 國清百錄. Guanding 灌頂 (Sui). *Taishō*, vol. 46, no. 1934.

Graff, David A. *Medieval Chinese Warfare: 300–900*. London and New York: Routledge, 2002.

Grousset, Rene. *The Empire of the Steppes*. Trans. from the French by Naomi Walford. New Brunswick, NJ: Rutgers University Press, 1970.

Gu Jiguang 谷霽光. *Fubing zhidu kaoshi* 府兵制度考釋. Shanghai: Shanghai renmin chubanshe, 1978.

Guo Peng 郭朋. *Sui-Tang Fojiao* 隋唐佛教. Jinan: Qilu chubanshe, 1980.

Han Guopan 韓國磐. *Sui Yangdi* 隋煬帝. Wuhan: Hubei renmin chubanshe, 1957.

———. "Tang Tianbao shi nongmin shenghuo zhi yipie" 唐天寶時農民生活之一瞥. In *Sui-Tang wudai shi lunji* 隋唐五代史論集, Han Guopan, 214–33. Beijing: Sanlian shudian, 1979a.

———. "Guanyu keju zhidu chuangzhi de liangdian xiaokao" 關於科舉制度創置的兩點小考. In *Sui-Tang wudai shi lunji* 隋唐五代史論集, Han Guopan, 294–97. Beijing: Sanlian shudian, 1979b.

Han Longfu 韓隆福. *Sui Yangdi pingzhuan* 隋煬帝評傳. Wuhan: Wuhan daxue chubanshe, 1992.

Han Sheng 韓昇. *Sui Wendi zhuan* 隋文帝傳. Beijing: Renmin chubanshe, 1998.

———. "Zui to Kōkuri no kokusai seiji kankei o megutte" 隋と高句麗の國際政治関係をめぐって. In *Hori Toshikazu sensei koki kinen—Chūgoku kodai no kokka to minshū* 堀敏一先生古稀記念—中國古代の國家と民眾, 351–72. Tokyo: Kyūko shoin, 1995.

Han Woo-keun. *The History of Korea*. Seoul: Eul-Yoo, 1970.

Haneda Akira 羽田明. "Introduction." *Acta Asiatica* 34 (1978), 1–21.

He Dezhang 何德章. "Sui Wendi dui jiangnan de kongzhi ji shice" 隋文帝對江南的控制及失策. *Xinan shifan daxue xuebao* 西南師範大學學報 (1993):2, 73–88.

*HHS. Hou Han shu* 後漢書. Fan Ye 范曄 (Liu-Song). Beijing: Zhonghua shuju, 1965.

Hiraoka Takeo 平岡武夫. *Chōan to Rakuyō* 長安と洛陽, "Texts Volume," "Map Volume," and "Index Volume." Kyoto: Kyōto daigaku jinbunkagaku kenkyūjo, 1956.

*HNZ. Henan zhi* 河南志. Xu Song 徐松 (Qing), comp. Beijing: Zhonghua shuju, 1994.

Hori Toshikazu 堀敏一. "Zuidai Higashi Ajia no kokusai kankei" 隋代東アジアの國際関係. In *Zui-Tō teikoku to Higashi Ajia sekai* 隋唐帝國と東アジア世界, edited by Tōdaishi Kenkyūkai 唐代史研究會, 113–37. Tokyo: Kyūko shoin, 1979.

———. *Chūgoku to kodai Higashi sekai* 中國と古代東アジア世界. Tokyo: Iwanami shoten, 1993.

*HS. Han shu* 漢書. By Ban Gu 班固 (Eastern Han). Beijing: Zhonghua shuju, 1962.

Hu Ji 胡戟. *Sui Yangdi xin zhuan* 隋煬帝新傳. Shanghai: Shanghai renmin chubanshe, 1995.

Huang Yongnian 黃永年. "Cong Yang-Sui zhongshu zhengquan kan Guanlong jituan de kaishi jieti" 從楊隋中樞政權看關隴集團的開始解體. *Xueshu jilin* 學術集林 9, 179–95. Shanghai: Yuandong chubanshe, 1996.

——. "Lun Wude Zhenguan shi tongzhi jituan de neibu maodun he douzheng" 論武德貞觀時統治集團的內部矛盾和鬥爭. In *Tangdai shishi kaoshi* 唐代史事 考釋, Huang Yongnian, 3–35. Taipei: Lianjing chuban shiye gongsi, 1998.

Hucker, Charles O. *A Dictionary of Official Titles in Imperial China*. Stanford: Stanford University Press, 1985.

Hurvitz, Leon. "Chih-i (538–597): An Introduction to the Life and Ideas of a Chinese Buddhist Monk." *Mélanges chinois at bouddhiques* vol. 12. Bruxelles: Imprimerie Sainte-Catherine, S.A., 1960–1962.

Ikeda On 池田温. "Hai Seisei to Kō Hyōjin: Zui-Tō to Yamato no kōshyō no ichimen" 裴世清と高表仁—— 隋唐と倭交渉の一面. *Nihon rekishi* 日本歷史 280 (1971), 1–16.

——. "T'ang Household Registers and Related Documents." In *Perspectives on the T'ang*, edited by Arthur Wright and Denis Twitchett, 121–50. New Haven: Yale University Press, 1973.

——. *Chūgoku kodai sekichō kenkyū: gaikan, rokubun* 中國古代籍帳研究：概觀、錄文 (Tokyo: 1979). Gong Zexian 龔澤銑, trans. Beijing: Zhonghua shuju, 1984.

Inoue, Mitsusada, with Delmer M. Brown. "The Century of Reform." In *The Cambridge History of Japan*, vol. 1, *Ancient Japan*, edited by Delmer M. Brown, 163–220. Cambridge: Cambridge University Press, 1993.

Ishida Yūsaku 石田勇作. "Zui kaikō ritsuryō kara butoku ritsuryō e—ritsuryō hensen katei no seiri (1)" 隋開皇律令から武德律令へ—— 律令變遷過程の整理 (1). In *Chūgoku kodai no hō to shakai—Kurihara Masuo sensei koki kinen ronshū* 中國古代の法 と社會——栗原益男先生古稀記念論集, edited by Hori Toshikazu 堀敏一 et al., 219–43. Tokyo: Kyūko shoten, 1988.

Jan Yün-hua, trans. *A Chronicle of Buddhism in China, 581–960 A.D.: Translations from Monk Chih-p'an's "Fo-tsu T'ung-chi."* Santiniketan: Visva-Bharati University, 1966.

Janousch, Andreas. "The Emperor as Bodhisattva: The Bodhisattva Ordination and Ritual Assemblies of Emperor Wu of the Liang Dynasty." In *State and Court Ritual in China*, edited by Joseph McDermott, 112–49. Cambridge: Cambridge University Press, 1999.

*JGJFDLH*. *Ji gujin fo dao lunheng* 集古今佛道論衡. Daoxuan 道宣 (Tang). *Taishō*, vol. 52, no. 2104.

Jiang Liangfu 姜亮夫. *Lidai renwu nianli beizhuan zongbiao* 歷代人物年里碑傳綜表, revised edition. Beijing: Zhonghua shuju, 1965.

Jiang Zhongyi 蔣忠義. "Yangzhoucheng kaogu gongzuo jianbao" 揚州城考古工作簡 報. *Kaogu* 考古 (1990):1, 36–44.

Jin Baoxiang 金寶祥 et al. *Sui shi xintan* 隋史新探. Lanzhou: Lanzhou daxue chuban-she, 1989.

Johnson, David. *The Medieval Chinese Oligarchy*. Boulder, CO: Westview Press, 1977.

Johnson, Wallace, trans. *The T'ang Code*, Volume I: *General Principles*. Princeton: Princeton University Press, 1979.

——. *The T'ang Code*, Volume II: *Specific Articles*. Princeton: Princeton University Press, 1997.

*JTS. Jiu Tang shu* 舊唐書. Liu Xu 劉昫 et al. (Wudai). Beijing: Zhonghua shuju, 1975.

Kakehata Minoru 欠端寬. "Zuitai no sōkan ni tsuite" 隋代の總管について. *Reitaku daigaku kiyō* 麗澤大學紀要 43 (1986), 93–107.

Kaochadui (Zhongguo Tangshi Xuehui Tang-Song Yunhe Kaochadui 中國唐史學會唐宋運河考察隊). *Tang-Song yunhe kaocha ji* 唐宋運河考察記. Xi'an: Shaanxisheng shehui kexueyuan, 1985.

Karlgren, Bernhard. *Glosses on the Book of Documents*. 1949. Reprint, Stockholm: Museum of Far Eastern Antiquities, 1970.

Kegasawa Yasunori 氣賀澤保規, ed. "Zuimatsu Tōsho no sho hanran" 隋末唐初の諸叛亂. In *Chūgoku minshū hanran shi* 中国民衆叛亂史, 4 vols, edited by Tanigawa Michio 谷川道雄 and Mori Masao 森正夫, 1978–83. Tokyo: Heibonsha, 1978.

——. "Zui Yōdai ki no fuheisei o meguru ichi kōsatsu" 隋煬帝期の府兵制をめぐる一考察. In *Ritsureisei—Chūgoku Chōsen no hō to kokka* 律令制—中國朝鮮の法と國家. Tokyo: Kyūko shoin, 1986.

*KHJ. Kai he ji* 開河記. Unknown author (Song). *Shuo fu* 説郛 edition.

Kikuchi Hideo 菊池英夫. "Sōsetsu" 總説. In *Zui-Tō teikoku to Higashi Ajia sekai* 隋唐帝國と東アジア世界, edited by Tōdaishi Kenkyūkai 唐代史研究會, 1–84. Tokyo: Kyūko shoin, 1979.

——. "Zuichō no tai Kōkuri sensō no hottan ni tsuite 隋朝の對高句麗戰爭の發端について. *Chūō daigaku Ajia shi kenkyū* 中央大學アジア史研究 16:3 (1992a), 1–35.

——. "Tangdai zhechongfu fenbu wenti yanjiu" 唐代折衝府分佈問題研究. Trans. by Han Sheng 韓昇. In *Riben xuezhe yanjiu Zhongguo shi lunzhu xuanyi* 日本學者研究中國史論著選譯, vol. 4: *Liuchao Sui-Tang* 六朝隋唐, edited by Liu Junwen 劉俊文, 514–56. Beijing: Zhonghua shuju, 1992b.

Knechtges, David R., trans. and annotator. *Wen xuan or Selections of Refined Literature*, volume 1: *Rhapsodies on Metropolises and Capitals*. Princeton: Princeton University Press, 1982.

Kohn, Livia. "Yin Xi: The Master at the Beginning of the Scripture." *Journal of Chinese Religions* 25 (1997), 83–140.

——. "The Northern Celestial Masters." In *Daoism Handbook*, edited by Livia Kohn, 283–308. Leiden: E. J. Brill, 2000.

Kohn, Livia, and Russell Kirkland. "Daoism in the Tang (618–907)." In *Daoism Handbook*, edited by Livia Kohn, 339–83. Leiden: E. J. Brill, 2000.

Kroll, Paul. "Verses from High: The Ascent of T'ai Shan." *T'oung Pao* 69:4/5 (1983), 223–60.

Lan Jifu 藍吉富. *Suidai fojiao shi shulun* 隋代佛教史述論. Taipei: Taiwan shangwu yinshuguan, 1993.

*LDCDJ*. *Lidai chongdao ji* 歷代崇道記. Du Guangting 杜光庭 (Tang). *Daozang*, vol. 11.

*LDSBJ*. *Lidai sanbao ji* 歷代三寶紀. Fei Zhangfang 費長房 (Sui). *Taishō*, vol. 49, no. 2034.

Legge, James, trans. *The Chinese Classics*, volume III: *The Shoo King*. Hong Kong: Hong Kong University Press, 1960.

Lei Jiaji 雷家驥. *Sui-Tang zhongyang quanli jiegou jiqi yanjin* 隋唐中央權力結構及其演進. Taipei: Dongda tushu gongsi, 1995.

Lei Wen 雷聞. "Sui yu Tang qianqi de shangshu sheng" 隋與唐前期的尚書省. In *Sheng Tang zhengzhi zhidu yanjiu* 盛唐政治制度研究, edited by Wu Zongguo 吳宗國, 68–118. Shanghai: Shanghai cishu chubanshe, 2003.

Li Chunmin 李春民. "Sui Xiao Yang muzhi kao" 隋蕭瑒墓誌考. *Kaogu yu wenwu* 考古與文物 (1996):1.

Li Shutong 李樹桐. "Li-Tang Taiyuan qiyi kaoshi" 李唐太原起義考實. In *Tangshi kaobian* 唐史考辨, Li Shutong, 1–42. Taipei: Taiwan Zhonghua shuju, 1985.

Li Zefen 李則芬. *Sui-Tang Wudai lishi lunwen ji* 隋唐五代歷史論文集. Taipei: Taipei shangwu yinshu guan, 1989.

Li Zhuomin 李卓敏. *Lishi Zhongwen da zidian* 李氏中文大字典. Shanghai: Xuelin chubanshe, 1981.

Liang Chia-pin. "An Examination of the Accounts of Liu-ch'iu Kuo in the Sui-shu." *Chinese Studies in History* 17:2 (1983–1984), 63–74.

Liang Fangzhong 梁方仲. *Zhongguo lidai hukou tiandi tianfu tongji* 中國歷代戶口、田地、田賦統計. Shanghai: Shanghai renmin chubanshe, 1980.

Lin Gan 林幹 et al. *Zhongguo gudai beifang gezu jianshi* 中國古代北方各族簡史. Hohhot, Inner Mongolia: Neimenggu renmin chubanshe, 1979.

Liu Houbin 劉後濱. "Sui yu Tang qianqi de zhongshu sheng" 隋與唐前期的中書省. In *Sheng Tang zhengzhi zhidu yanjiu* 盛唐政治制度研究, edited by Wu Zongguo 吳宗國, 146–175. Shanghai: Shanghai cishu chubanshe, 2003.

Liu Jianming 劉健明. "Yichang qiu buzhan ersheng de gongzhan—Sui Yangdi zheng Gaoli shixi" 一場求不戰而勝的攻戰—隋煬帝征高麗試析. *Tang yanjiu* 唐研究 1 (1995), 207–225.

———. "Sui Jiangdu shibian kaoshi" 隋江都事變考釋. *Tang yanjiu* 唐研究 2 (1996), 265–93.

———. "Suichao dui Tujue de zhengce (chugao)" 隋朝對突厥的政策 (初稿). In *Tangdai de lishi yu shehui* 唐代的歷史與社會, 45–58. Wuhan: Wuhan daxue chubanshe, 1997.

———. *Suidai zhengzhi yu duiwai zhengce* 隋代政治與對外政策. Taipei: Wenjin chubanshe, 1999.

Liu, Mau-tsai. *Die Chinesischen Nachrichten zur Geschichte der Ost-Türken (T'u-küe)*, I.–II. Bande. Wiesbaden: Otto Harrassowitz, 1958.

Liu Shufen 劉淑芬. "Sui Yangdi de nanfang zhengce" 隋煬帝的南方政策. *Shiyuan* 史原 8 (1978), 61–95.

———. "Suidai nanfang zhengce de yingxiang" 隋代南方政策的影響. *Shiyuan* 史原 10 (1980), 59–80.

Liu Xiwei 劉希為. "Sui Tongji qu liujing luxian bianxi" 隋通濟渠流經路線辨析. In *Yunhe fanggu* 運河訪古, edited by Tang-Song Yunhe Kaochadui 唐宋運河考察隊, 169–86. Shanghai: Shanghai renmin chubanshe, 1986.

*LJSL. Li jing shili* 禮經釋例. Ling Tingkan 淩廷堪 (Qing). *Congshu jicheng chubian* edition.

*LJXJ. Liangjing xinji* 兩京新記. Wei Shu 韋述 (Tang). With *Liangjing xinji jiben* 兩京新記集本, and *Liangjing xinji xushi* 兩京新記續拾. In *Chōan to Rakuō* 長安と洛陽, "Texts Volume," Hiraoka Takeo 平岡武夫. Kyoto: Kyōto daigaku jinbunkagaku kenkyūjo, 1956.

*LNL. Lai nan lu* 來南錄. Li Ao 李翱 (Tang). *Shuo fu* 説郛 edition.

*LS. Liang shu* 梁書. Yao Silian 姚思廉 (Tang). Beijing: Zhonghua shuju, 1973.

*LSZXTDTJ. Lishi zhenxian tidao tongjian* 歷世真仙體道通鑑. Zhao Daoyi 趙道一 (Yuan). *Daozang*, vol. 5.

Lu Junling 陸峻嶺 and Lin Gan 林幹. *Zhongguo lidai gezu jinian biao* 中國歷代各族紀年表. Hohhot, Inner Mongolia: Neimenggu renmin chubanshe, 1980.

Luoyangshi Bowuguan 洛陽市博物館 and Henansheng Bowuguan 河南省博物館. "Luoyang Sui-Tang Hanjia cang de fajue" 洛陽隋唐含嘉倉的發掘. *Wenwu* 文物 (1972):3.

Luoyangshi Wenwu Gongzuodui 洛陽市文物工作隊. "Luoyang Hanjia cang 1988 nian fajue jianbao" 洛陽含嘉倉1988年發掘簡報. *Wenwu* 文物 (1992):3, 9–14.

Lü Chunsheng 呂春盛. "Guanyu Yang Jian xingqi beijing de kaocha" 關於楊堅興起背景的考察. *Hanxue yanjiu* 漢學研究 18:2 (2000), 167–96.

Lü Simian 呂思勉. *Sui-Tang Wudai shi* 隋唐五代史. Hong Kong: Taiping shuju, 1980.

———. *Lü Simian dushi zhaji* 呂思勉讀史扎記. Shanghai: Shanghai guji chubanshe, 1982.

*LYJ. Lu yi ji* 錄異記. Du Guangting 杜光庭 (Tang). *Daozang*, vol. 10.

Ma Zhenglin 馬正林. "Tang-Song yunhe shulun" 唐宋運河述論. In *Yunhe fanggu* 運河訪古, edited by Tang-Song Yunhe Kaochadui 唐宋運河考察隊, 1–32. Shanghai: Shanghai renmin chubanshe, 1986.

Mao Hanguang 毛漢光. *Zhongguo zhonggu shehui shi lun* 中國中古社會史論. Taipei: Lianjing chuban shiye gongsi, 1988.

Marney, John. "Kung-t'i shih." In *The Indiana Companion to Traditional Chinese Literature*, edited by William Nienhauser, Jr., et al., 516–18. Bloomington: Indiana University Press. 1986.

Miyakawa, Hisayuki. "An Outline of the Naito Hypothesis and Its Effects on Japanese Studies of China." *Far Eastern Quarterly*, 14:4 (1955), 533–52.

Miyazaki Ichisada 宮崎市定. *Kyūhin kanjin hō no kenkyū: Kakyo zenshi* 九品官人法の研究—科舉前史. Kyoto: Tōyōshi kenkyūkai, 1956.

———. *Zui no Yōdai* 隋の煬帝. Tokyo: Jinbutsu ōraisha, 1965.

———. *Ajiashi kenkyū* アジア史研究. Kyoto: Dōhōsha, 1978.

———. *Dai-Tō teikoku* 大唐帝国. Tokyo: Kawade shobō shinsha, 1989.

*MLZMYW. Mangluo zhongmu yiwen, xubian, sanbian, sibian* 芒洛塚墓遺文、續編、三編、四編. Luo Zhenyu 羅振玉, comp. 1917. Reprint. *Lidai beizhi congshu* 歷代碑誌叢書, vol. 14. Nanjing: Jiangsu guji chubanshe, 1998.

Mochizuki Shinkō 望月信亨. *Bukkyō dai jiten* 佛教大辭典, third edition, 10 vols. Kyoto: Sekai seiten kankō kyōkai, 1954–1971.

Molè, Gabriella. *The T'u-yü-hun from the Northern Wei to the Time of the Five Dynasties*. Roma: Istituto Italiano per il Medio ed Estremo Oriente, 1970.

Mori Katsumi 森克己. *Kentōshi* 遣唐使. Tokyo: Shibundō, 1955.

Mori Shikazō 森鹿三. "Hoku-Gi Rakuyōjō no kibo ni tsuite" 北魏洛陽城の規模について. *Tōyōgaku kenkyū—Rekishi chiri hen* 東洋學研究——歷史地理篇, Mori Shikazō. Tokyo: Tōyōgaku kenkyūkai, 1970.

*MSZ. Maoshan zhi* 茅山志. Probably by Zhang Yu 張雨 (Yuan). Prefaced by Liu Dabin 劉大彬 (Yuan). *Daozang*, vol. 5.

*MSZY. Maoshi zhengyi* 毛詩正義. Kong Yingda 孔穎達 (Tang), subcommentator. *Shisanjing zhushu* edition.

Naitō Konan 內藤湖南. *Naitō Konan zenshū* 內藤湖南全集, vol. 5. Tokyo: Chikuma shobō, 1967.

Needham, Joseph, with Wang Ling. *Science and Civilisation in China*, vol. 1: *Introductory Orientations*. Cambridge: Cambridge University, 1954.

Needham, Joseph, with Wang Ling and Lu Gwei-djen. *Science and Civilisation in China*, vol. 4: *Physics and Physical Technology*, Part 3: *Civil Engineering and Nautics*. Cambridge: Cambridge University, 1971.

Niida Noboru 仁井田陞. *Tōryō shūi* 唐令拾遺. Li Jing 栗勁 et al., trans. Changchun: Changchun chubanshe, 1989.

Nishijima Tadao 西嶋定生. *Chūgoku kodai kokka to Higashi Ajia sekai* 中國古代國家と東アジア世界. Tokyo: Tōkyō daigaku shuppansha, 1983.

*NS. Nan shi* 南史. Li Yanshou 李延壽 (Tang). Beijing: Zhonghua shuju, 1975.

Nunome Chōfū 布目潮渢. *Zui Tō shi kenkyū: Tōchō seiken no keisei* 隋唐史研究—唐朝政權の形成. Kyoto: Tōyōshi kenkyūkai, 1968a.

———. "Yō Genkan no hanran" 楊玄感の叛亂. In *Zui Tō shi kenkyū: Tōchō seiken no keisei*, Nunome Chōfū, 19–52. Kyoto: Tōyōshi kenkyūkai, 1968b.

———. "Ri Mitsu no hanran" 李密の叛亂. In *Zui Tō shi kenkyū: Tōchō seiken no keisei*, Nunome Chōfū, 55–100. Kyoto: Tōyōshi kenkyūkai, 1968c.

———. "Ri En no kigi" 李淵の起義. In *Zui Tō shi kenkyū: Tōchō seiken no keisei*, Nunome Chōfū, 101–149. Kyoto: Tōyōshi kenkyūkai, 1968d.

———. "Zui no Taigi kōshu ni tsuite" 隋の大義公主について. In *Zui-Tō teikoku to Higashi Ajia sekai* 隋唐帝國と東アジア世界, edited by Tōdaishi Kenkyūkai 唐代史研究會, 279–303. Tokyo: Kyūko shoin, 1979.

———. *Zui no Yōdai to Tō no Taisō: Tsukurareta bōkun to meikun* 隋の煬帝と唐の太宗：つくられた暴君と明君. Tokyo: Seisui shoin, 1980.

Nunome Chōfū 布目潮渢 and Kirihara Masuo 栗原益男. *Chūgoku no rekishi 4: Zui-Tō teikoku* 中國の歴史 4: 隋唐帝國. Tokyo: Kōdansha, 1974.

Ono Katsutoshi 小野勝年. *Chūgoku Zui-Tō Chōan jiin shiryō shūsei* 中國隋唐長安寺院史料集成. *Shiryōhen* 史料篇 and *Kaisetsu hen* 解説篇. Kyoto: Hōzōkan, 1989.

Pan Yihong. *Son of Heaven and Heavenly Qaghan: Sui-Tang China and Its Neighbors*. Bellingham, Wash.: Center for East Asian Studies, Western Washington University, 1997.

Pan Yong 潘鏞 and Wang Yongqian 王永謙. "Sui-Tang yunhe yu zhongwan Tang caoyun" 隋唐運河與中晚唐漕運. In *Yunhe fanggu* 運河訪古, edited by Tang-Song Yunhe Kaochadui 唐宋運河考察隊, 43–59. Shanghai: Shanghai renmin chubanshe, 1986.

Pan Yong 潘鏞. *Sui-Tang shiqi de yunhe he caoyun* 隋唐時期的運河和漕運. Xi'an: Sanqin chubanshe, 1987.

Pearce, Scott. "Form and Matter: Archaizing Reform in Sixth-Century China." In *Culture and Power in the Reconstitution of the Chinese Realm, 200–600*, edited by Scott Pearce et al., 149–178. Cambridge, Mass.: The Harvard University Asia Center, 2001.

Peng Xinwei. *A Monetary History of China*. Trans. by Edward H. Kaplan. Bellingham, WA: Center For East Asian Studies, Western Washington University, 1994.

Pulleyblank, Edwin G. *The Background of the Rebellion of An Lushan*. London: Oxford University Press, 1955.

———. "Registration of Population in China in the Sui and Tang Periods." *Journal of the Economic and Social History of the Orient* 4 (1961), 289–301.

Qi Xia 漆俠. "Youguan Suimo nongmin qiyi de jige wenti" 有關隋末農民起義的幾個問題. In *Zhongguo nongmin qiyi lunji* 中國農民起義論集, edited by Li Guangbi 李光璧 et al., 97–118. Beijing: Sanlian shudian, 1958.

Qing Xitai 卿希泰, ed. *Zhongguo Daojiao shi* 中國道教史. Chengdu: Sichuan renmin chubanshe, 1996.

*QSQHSL*. *Quan Shanggu Sandai Qin-Han Sanguo Liuchao wen* 全上古三代秦漢三國六朝文, 4 vols. Yan Kejun 嚴可均 (Qing), comp. Beijing: Zhonghua shuju, 1958.

*QTS*. *Quan Tang shi* 全唐詩, 25 vols. Peng Dingqiu 彭定求 et al. (Qing), comps. Beijing: Zhonghua shuju, 1960.

*QTW*. *Quan Tang wen* 全唐文, 11 vols. Dong Gao 董誥 et al. (Qing), comps. With Lu Xinyuan 陸心源, *Tangwen shiyi* 唐文拾遺, and *Tangwen xushi* 唐文續拾. Beijing: Zhonghua shuju, 1983.

Qu Tuiyuan 瞿蛻園. "Lidai zhiguan jianshi" 歷代職官簡釋. In *Lidai zhiguan biao* 歷代職官表, Huang Benji 黃本驥 (Qing), 1–210. Shanghai: Zhonghua shuju, 1965.

Quan Hansheng 全漢昇. "Zhonggu ziran jingji." 中古自然經濟. In *Zhongguo jingji shi yanjiu* 中國經濟史研究, Quan Hansheng, 1–142. Hong Kong: Xinya yanjiusuo, 1976a.

———. "Tang-Song diguo yu yunhe" 唐宋帝國與運河. In *Zhongguo jingji shi yanjiu* 中國經濟史研究, Quan Hansheng, 265–395. Hong Kong: Xinya yanjiusuo, 1976b.

Ren Jiyu 任繼愈, ed. *Zhongguo daojiao shi* 中國道教史. Shanghai: Shanghai renmin chubanshe, 1990.

Robinet, Isabelle. *Taoism: Growth of a Religion*. Trans. by Phyllis Brooks. Stanford: Stanford University Press, 1997.

———. "Shangqing—Highest Clarity." In *Daoism Handbook*, edited by Livia Kohn, 196–224. Leiden: E. J. Brill, 2000.

*RTQFXL*. *Ru Tang qiufa xunli xingji* 入唐求法巡禮行記. Ennin 圓仁 (Heian/Tang). From *Nit-Tō guhō junrei gyōki no kenkyū* 入唐求法巡禮行記の研究, vols. 1–4, Ono Katsutoshi 小野勝年, trans., ed., and annotator. Tokyo: Suzuki gakujutsu zaidan, 1964–1969. Translated into Chinese by Bai Huawen 白化文 et al. as *Ru Tang qiufa xunli xingji jiaozhu* 入唐求法巡禮行記校注. Shijiazhuang: Huashan wenyi chubanshe, 1992.

*RZL*. *Rizhi lu* 日知錄. Gu Yanwu 顧炎武 (Qing). References are to Huang Rucheng 黃汝成, *Rizhi lu jishi* 日知錄集釋. Shijiazhuang: Huashan wenyi chubanshe, 1990.

Rotours, Robert des. *Traité des fonctionnaires et traité de l'armée*. Leiden: E. J. Brill, 1947.

Schafer, Edward. *The Golden Peaches of Samarkand*. Berkeley: University of California Press, 1963.

———. *Pacing the Void: T'ang Approaches to the Stars*. Berkeley: University of California Press, 1977.

———. *Mao Shan in T'ang Times*. Boulder, Colorado: Societey of Chinese Religions, Monograph 1, 1980.

*SGSZ*. *Song Gaoseng zhuan* 宋高僧傳. Zanning 贊寧 (Northern Song). *Taishō*, vol. 50, no. 2061.

*SGZ. Sanguo zhi* 三國志. Chen Shou 陳壽 (Western Jin). Beijing: Zhonghua shuju, 1959.

Sinor, Denis. "The Establishment and Dissolution of the Türk Empire." In *The Cambridge History of Early Inner Asia*, edited by Denis Sinor, 285–316. Cambridge: Cambridge University Press, 1990.

*SJ. Shi ji* 史記. Sima Qian 司馬遷 (Western Han). Beijing: Zhonghua shuju, 1959.

*SJZ. Shui jing zhu* 水經注. Li Daoyuan 酈道元 (Northern Wei), commentator; Yang Shoujing 楊守敬 and Xiong Huizhen 熊會貞 (Qing), subcommentators. References are to *Shui jing zhu shu* 水經註疏, 3 vols., edited by Duan Xizhong 段熙仲 and Chen Qiaoyi 陳橋驛. Nanjing: Jiangsu guji chubanshe, 1989.

*SKTY. Siku quanshu zongmu tiyao* 四庫全書總目提要 or *Siku quanshu zongmu*, 2 vols. Yong Rong 永瑢 et al. (Qing). Beijing: Zhonghua shuju, 1965.

Somers, Robert M. "The Sui Legacy." In *Sui Dynasty*, Arthur Wright, 198–206. New York: Knopf, 1978.

Song Jiayu 宋家鈺. *Tangchao huji fa yu juntian zhi yanjiu* 唐朝戶籍法與均田制研究. Zhengzhou, Henan: Zhongzhou guji chubanshe, 1988.

Soothill, Wiliam Edward, and Lewis Hodous. *A Dictionary of Chinese Buddhist Terms*. London: Kegan Paul, Trench, Trubner, 1937.

*SoS. Song shi* 宋史. Tuotuo 脱脱 et al. (Yuan). Beijing: Zhonghua shuju, 1977.

*SS. Song shu* 宋書. Shen Yue 沈約 (Liang). Beijing: Zhonghua shuju, 1974.

*SSD. Suishi duan* 隋史斷. Nangong Jingyi 南宮靖一 (Song). *Congshu jicheng chubian* edition.

*SSZY. Shangshu zhengyi* 尚書正義. Kong Yingda 孔穎達 et al. (Tang), subcommentors. *Shisanjing zhushu* edition.

*ST. Shi tong* 史通. Liu Zhiji 劉知幾 (Tang). References are to Pu Qilong 浦起龍 (Qing), *Shi tong tongshi* 史通通釋. Shanghai: Shanghai guji chubanshe, 1978.

*STJH. Sui-Tang jiahua* 隋唐嘉話. Liu Su 劉餗 (Tang). In *Sui-Tang jiahua, Chaoye qianzai* 隋唐嘉話、朝野僉載. Beijing: Zhonghua shuju, 1979.

Su Bai 宿白. "Sui-Tang Chang'an cheng he Luoyang cheng" 隋唐長安城和洛陽城. *Kaogu* 考古 (1978):6, 409–25.

Sunayama Minoru 砂山稔. *Zui-Tō Dōkyō shisōshi kenkyū* 隋唐道教思想史研究. Tokyo: Hirakawa shuppansha, 1990.

*SuS. Sui shu* 隋書. Wei Zheng 魏徵 et al. (Tang). Beijing: Zhonghua shuju, 1973.

*Taishō. Taishō shinshū daizōkyō* 大正新修大藏經. Tokyo: Taishō issaikyō kankōkai, 1924–1932.

Tan Qixiang 譚其驤, ed. *Zhongguo lishi ditu ji* 中國歷史地圖集, vols. 1–8. Beijing: Ditu chubanshe, 1982–1987.

Tanaka Tan 田中淡. "Zuichō kenchikuka no sekkei to kōshō" 隋朝建築家の設計と考証. In *Chūgoku no kagaku to kagakusha* 中國の科學と科學者, edited by Yamada Keiji 山田慶兒, 209–306. Kyoto: Kyōto daigaku jinbunkagaku kenkyūjo, 1978.

Tang Chengye 湯承業. *Sui Wendi zhengzhi shigong zhi yanjiu* 隋文帝政治事功之研究. Taipei: Taiwan shangwu yinshuguan, 1967.

Tang Geng'ou 唐耕藕. "Tangdai qianqi de hudeng yu zuyongdiao de guanxi" 唐代前期的戶等與租庸調的關係. In *Wei-Jin Sui-Tang shi lunji* 魏晉隋唐史論集, vol. 1, edited by Huang Lie 黃烈, 185–209. Beijing: Zhongguo shehui kexue chubanshe, 1981.

Tang Yongtong 湯用彤. *Han-Wei Liang-Jin Nanbeichao fojiao shi* 漢魏兩晉南北朝佛教史. Beijing: Zhonghua shuju, 1955.

———. *Sui-Tang fojiao shigao* 隋唐佛教史稿. Beijing: Zhonghua shuju, 1982.

Tang-Song Yunhe Kaochadui 唐宋運河考察隊, ed. *Yunhe fanggu* 運河訪古. Shanghai: Shanghai renmin chubanshe, 1986.

Tanigawa Michio 谷川道雄. *Zui Tō teikoku keisei shiron* 隋唐帝國形成史論. Tokyo: Chikuma shobō 築摩書房, 1971.

———. "Zuimatsu no nairan to minshū" 隋末の內亂と民眾. *Tōyōshi kenkyū* 東洋史研究 53:4 (1995), 55–81.

Tao Wenniu 陶文牛. "Suidai renkou de nanbei fenbu" 隋代人口的南北分佈. *Jinyang xuekan* 晉陽學刊 (1993):2, 48–53.

*TCTWS. Tulufan chutu wenshu* 吐魯番出土文書, 10 vols. Guojia Wenwuju Guwenxian Yanjiushi 國家文物局古文獻研究室 et al., ed. Beijing: Wenwu chubanshe, 1981–1987.

*TD. Tong dian* 通典. Du You 杜佑 (Tang). Wang Wenjin 王文錦 et al., eds., and punctuators. Beijing: Zhonghua shuju, 1988.

*TDZLJ. Tang da zhaoling ji* 唐大詔令集. Song Minqiu 宋敏求 (Northern Song), comp. Shanghai: Xuelin chubanshe, 1992.

Teiser, Stephen F. *The Ghost Festival in Medieval China.* Princeton: Princeton University Press, 1988.

Teng, Ssu-yü, trans. and annotator. *Family Instructions for the Yen Clan: Yen-shih Chia-hsün.* Leiden, E. J. Brill, 1968.

*THY. Tang huiyao* 唐會要. Wang Pu 王溥 (Wudai and Northern Song), comp. Beijing: Zhonghua shuju, 1955.

*TLD. Tang liudian* 唐六典. Li Linfu 李林甫 et al. (Tang). Chen Zhongfu 陳仲夫, ed. and punctuator. Beijing: Zhonghua shuju, 1992.

*TLJCFK. Tang liangjing chengfang kao* 唐兩京城坊考. Xu Song 徐松 (Qing). Fang Yan 方嚴, ed. and punctuator. Beijing: Zhonghua shuju, 1985.

*TLSY. Tanglü shuyi* 唐律疏義. Zhangsun Wuji 長孫無忌 et al. (Tang). Beijing: Zhonghua shuju, 1983.

Tōdaishi Kenkyūkai 唐代史研究會, ed. *Zui-Tō teikoku to Higashi Ajia sekai* 隋唐帝國と東アジア世界. Tokyo: Kyūko shoin, 1979.

Tonami Mamoru 礪波護. "Zui-Tō jidai no taisō to gankasō" 隋唐時代の太倉と含嘉倉. *Tōhō gakuhō* 東方學報 52 (1980).

Tōno Haruyuki 東野治之. "Japanese Embassies to T'ang China and Their Ships." *Acta Asiatica* 69 (1995), 39–62.

TPGJ. *Taiping guangji* 太平廣記, 10 vols. Li Fang 李昉 et al. (Northern Song), comps. Beijing: Zhonghua shuju, 1961.

TPHYJ. *Taiping huanyu ji* 太平寰宇記, 4 vols. Yue Shi 樂史 (Northern Song). Taipei xian: Wenhai chubanshe, 1993.

TPYL. *Taiping yulan* 太平御覽, 4 vols. Li Fang 李昉 et al. (Northern Song), comps. Beijing: Zhonghua shuju, 1960.

Tsukamoto Zenryū 塚本善隆. "Hokushū no haibutsu ni tsuite" 北周の廢佛に就いて. *Tōhō gakuhō* 東方學報 (Kyoto) 16 (1948), 29–101.

——. "Hokushū no shūkyō haiki seisaku no hōkai" 北周の宗教廢毀政策の崩壊. *Bukkyō shigaku* 佛教史學 1 (1949), 3–31.

——. "Hokushū no haibutsu ni tsuite 2" 北周の廢佛に就いて, 2. *Tōhō gakuhō* 東方學報 (Kyoto) 18 (1950), 78–111.

——. "Zui no kōnan seifuku to bukkyō" 隋の江南征服と佛教. *Bukkyō bunka kenkyū* 佛教文化研究 3 (1953), 1–24.

Twitchett, Denis. "Chinese Biographical Writing." In *Historians of China and Japan*, edited by W. G. Beasley and E. G. Pulleyblank, 95–114. London: Oxford University Press, 1961.

——. *Financial Administration Under the T'ang Dynasty.* Cambridge: Cambridge University Press, 1970.

——, ed. *The Cambridge History of China*, vol. 3, *Sui and T'ang China, 589–906*, Part I. Cambridge: Cambridge University Press, 1979a.

——. "Introduction." In *The Cambridge History of China*, vol. 3, *Sui and T'ang China, 589–906*, Part I, edited by Denis Twitchett, 1–47. Cambridge: Cambridge University Press, 1979b.

——. *The Writing of Official History under the T'ang.* Cambridge: Cambridge University Press, 1992.

TZY. *Tang zhiyan* 唐摭言. Wang Dingbao 王定保 (Wudai). Shanghai: Shanghai guji chubanshe, 1978.

Waldron, Arthur. *The Great Wall of China: From History to Myth.* Cambridge: Cambridge University Press, 1990.

Wang Guangzhao 王光照. "Sui Wendi zhi si shulun" 隋文帝之死述論. *Zhongguo shi yanjiu* 中國史研究 (1993):2, 98–107.

——. "Sui Jinwang Yang Guang 'Baotai jingzang' jianzhi shulun" 隋晉王楊廣 "寶臺經藏" 建置述論. *Tang yanjiu* 唐研究 7 (2001), 1–17.

Wang Guowei 王國維. *Guantang jilin* 觀堂集林, 4 vols. Beijing: Zhonghua shuju, 1959.

Wang Jian 汪籛. "Tang Taizong" 唐太宗. In *Wang Jian Sui-Tang shi lungao* 汪籛隋唐史論稿, Wang Jian, 70–117. Beijing: Zhongguo shehui kexue chubanshe, 1981.

Wang Sanbei 王三北 and Zhao Hongbo 趙宏勃. "Sui Yangdi minzu zhengce xinlun" 隋煬帝民族政策新論. *Xibei daxue xuebao* 西北大學學報 (1996):5.

Wang Xiangrong 汪向榮 and Xia Yingyuan 夏應元, comps. *Zhong-Ri guanxi shi ziliao huibian* 中日關係史資料彙編. Beijing: Zhonghua shuju, 1984.

Wang Zhongluo 王仲犖. *Beizhou liudian* 北周六典. Beijing: Zhonghua shuju, 1979a.

———. *Wei Jin Nanbeichao shi* 魏晉南北朝史. Shanghai: Shanghai renmin chubanshe, 1979b.

———. *Sui-Tang Wudai shi* 隋唐五代史, 2 vols. Shanghai: Shanghai renmin chubanshe, 1988–1990.

Wechsler, Howard J. "Factionalism in Early T'ang Government." In *Perspectives on the T'ang*, edited by Arthur Wright and Denis Twitchett, 87–120. New Haven: Yale University Press, 1973.

———. *Mirror to the Son of Heaven: Wei Cheng at the Court of T'ang T'ai-tsung*. New Haven: Yale University Press, 1974.

———. "The Founding of the T'ang Dynasty: Kao-tsu (reign 618–26)." In *The Cambridge History of China*, vol. 3, *Sui and T'ang China, 589–906*, Part I, edited by Denis Twitchett, 150–87. Cambridge: Cambridge University Press, 1979.

———. *Offerings of Jade and Silk*. New Haven: Yale University Press, 1985.

Weinstein, Stanley. *Buddhism under the T'ang*. Cambridge: Cambridge University Press, 1987.

Weng Junxiong 翁俊雄. "Suidai juntian zhi yanjiu" 隋代均田制研究. *Lishi yanjiu* 歷史研究 (1984):4, 167–76.

———. *Tangdai renkou yu quyu jingji* 唐代人口與區域經濟. Taipei: Xinwenfeng chubanshe, 1995.

Wong, Joseph. "Unfought Korean Wars: Prelude to the Korean Wars of the Seventh Century." *Papers on Far Eastern History* 22 (September, 1980), 122–58.

Wright, Arthur. "The Formation of Sui Ideology." In *Chinese Thought and Institutions*, edited by John King Fairbank, 71–104. Chicago: The University of Chicago Press, 1957.

———. *Buddhism in Chinese History*. Stanford: Stanford University, 1959.

———. "Sui Yang-ti: Personality and Stereotype." In *Confucianism and Chinese Civilization*, edited by Arthur Wright, 158–87. Stanford: Stanford University Press, 1975.

———. *Sui Dynasty*. New York: Knopf, 1978.

———. "Sui Dynasty." In *Cambridge History of China*, vol. 3, *Sui and T'ang China, 589–960*, Part I, edited by Denis Twitchett, 48–149. Cambridge: Cambridge University Press, 1979.

Wu Chengluo 吳承洛. *Zhongguo duliangheng shi* 中國度量衡史. Shanghai: Shangwu yinshuguan, 1937.

Wu Gang 吳剛, ed. *Sui Tang Wudai muzhi huibian* 隋唐五代墓誌滙編, *Shaanxi juan* 陝西卷. vol. 3. Tianjin: Tianjin guji chubanshe, 1991.

Wu Hung. *Monumentality in Early Chinese Art and Architecture*. Stanford: Stanford University Press, 1995.

Wu Jianguo 吳建國. *Juntian zhi yanjiu* 均田制研究. Kunming: Yunnan renmin chubanshe, 1992.

Wu Yugui 吳玉貴. *Tujue hanguo yu Sui-Tang guanxi shi yanjiu* 突厥汗國與隋唐關係史研究. Beijing: Zhongguo shehui kexue chubanshe, 1998.

Wu Zongguo 吳宗國. *Sheng Tang zhengzhi zhidu yanjiu* 盛唐政治制度研究. Shanghai: Shanghai cishu chubanshe, 2003.

*WX. Wen xuan* 文選, 3 vols. Xiao Tong 蕭統 (Liang), comp; Li Shan 李善 (Tang), commentator. Beijing: Zhonghua shuju, 1977.

*WYYH. Wenyuan yinghua* 文苑英華, 6 vols. Li Fang 李昉 et al. (Northern Song), comps. Beijing: Zhonghua shuju, 1966.

*XGSZ. Xu gaoseng zhuan* 續高僧傳. Daoxuan 道宣 (Tang). *Taishō*, vol. 50, no. 2060.

Xin Deyong 辛德勇. *Sui-Tang liangjing congkao* 隋唐兩京叢考. Xi'an: Sanqin chubanshe, 1991.

Xiong, Victor Cunrui. "Sui Yangdi and the Building of Sui-Tang Luoyang." *Journal of Asian Studies* 52:1 (1993), 66–89.

———. "Ritual Innovations and Taoism under Tang Xuanzong." *T'oung Pao* 82 (1996), 258–316.

———. Book Review of Wallace Johnson, trans., *The T'ang Code*, Volume II: *Specific Articles. Early Medieval China* 3 (1997), 117–21.

———. "The Land-tenure System of Tang China: A Study of the Equal-field System and the Turfan Documents." *T'oung Pao* 85 (1999), 328–90.

———. *Sui-Tang Chang'an (583–904): A Study in the Urban History of Medieval China.* Ann Arbor: Center for Chinese Studies, University of Michigan, 2000.

———. "Sui-Yangdi and Buddhism." *Zhongguo shehui lishi pinglun* 中國社會歷史評論 4 (2002), 345–367.

*XTS. Xin Tang shu* 新唐書. Ouyang Xiu 歐陽修 and Song Qi 宋祁 (Northern Song). Beijing: Zhonghua shuju, 1975.

Xu Xianyao 徐先堯. "Sui-Wo bangjiao xinkao" 隋倭邦交新考. In *Tangdai yanjiu lunji* 唐代研究論集, vol. 1, edited by Zhongguo Tangdai Xuehui 中國唐代學會, 497–554. Taipei: Xinwenfeng chuban gongsi, 1992.

Xu Zhengwen 許正文. "Suidai zhou jun zhengqu de zhengdun gaige" 隋代州郡政區的整頓改革. *Shaanxi shida xuebao* 陝西師大學報 (1994):2.

Xue Zongzheng 薛宗正. *Tujue shi* 突厥史. Beijing: Zhongguo sheke chubanshe, 1992.

*XYBZ. Xianyuan bianzhu* 仙苑編珠. Wang Songnian 王松年 (Wudai). *Daozang*, vol. 11.

Yabuki Keiki 矢吹慶輝. *Sangaikyō no kenkyū* 三階教の研究. Tokyo: Iwanami shoten, 1927.

Yamada Toshiaki. "The Lingbao School." In *Daoism Handbook*, edited by Livia Kohn, 225–55. Leiden: E. J. Brill 2000.

Yamazaki Hiroshi 山崎宏. *Shina chūsei bukkyō no tenkai* 支那中世佛教の展開. Tokyo: Seisui shoten, 1942.

———. "Yōdai no shidōjō" 煬帝の四道場. *Tōyō gakuhō* 東洋学報 34 (1952), 22–35.

———. "Zui no Kōkuri ensei to bukkyō" 隋の高句麗遠征と佛教. *Shichō* 史潮 49 (1953), 1–10.

———. "Zuichō kanryō no seikaku" 隋朝官僚の性格. *Tōkyō kyōiku daigaku bungakubu kiyō* 東京教育大學文學部記要 6 (1956), 1–59.

———. *Zui-Tō bukkyō no kenkyū* 隋唐佛教の研究. Kyoto: Hōzōkan, 1967.

Yan Gengwang 嚴耕望. "Suidai zongguanfu kao" 隋代總管府考. *Chūgokugaku shi* 中國學誌 (Tokyo: Taizan bunbutsusha) 6 (1972), 23–54.

———. "Tangdai shangshu sheng zhi zhiquan yu diwei" 唐代尚書省之職權與地位. In *Yan Gengwang shixue lunwen xuanji* 嚴耕望史學論文選集, Yan Gengwang, 431–508. Taipei: Lianjing chuban shiye gongsi, 1991.

Yang, C. K. "The Functional Relationship Between Confucian Thought and Chinese Religion." In *Chinese Thought and Institutions*, edited by John King Fairbank, 269–90. Chicago: The University of Chicago Press, 1957.

———. *Religion in Chinese Society*. Berkeley: University of California Press, 1970.

Yao Shuangnian 姚雙年. "Yang Su muzhi chukao" 楊素墓誌初考. *Kaogu yu wenwu* 考古與文物 (1991):2, 88–93.

Ye Wei 葉煒. "Sui yu Tang qianqi de menxia sheng" 隋與唐前期的門下省. In *Sheng Tang zhengzhi zhidu yanjiu* 盛唐政治制度研究, edited by Wu Zongguo 吳宗國, 119–45. Shanghai: Shanghai cishu chubanshe, 2003.

*YH*. *Yuhai* 玉海, 6 vols. Wang Yinglin 王應麟 (Southern Song). Nanjing: Jiangsu guji chubanshe, and Shanghai: Shanghai shudian, 1987.

*YHJXTZ*. *Yuanhe junxian tuzhi* 元和郡縣圖志. Li Jifu 李吉甫 (Tang). Beijing: Zhonghua shuju, 1983.

*YHNZ*. *Yuan Henan zhi* 元河南志 (Yuan). Ouxianglingshi 藕香零拾 edition. Reprint. In *Chōan to Rakuyō* 長安と洛陽, "Texts Volume," Hiraoka Takeo 平岡武夫. Kyoto: Kyōto daigaku jinbunkagaku kenkyūjo, 1956.

*YHXZ*. *Yuanhe xingzuan* 元和姓纂. Lin Bao 林寶 (Tang); Cen Zhongmian 岑仲勉, ed. Beijing: Zhonghua shuju, 1994.

Yi Yicheng 易毅成. "Sui-Tang zhiji Guanzhong anquan de zhanlue gouxiang yu shixing" 隋唐之際關中安全的戰略構想與施行. In *Tangdai wenhua yantaohui lunwenji* 唐代文化研討會論文集, edited by Zhongguo Tangdai Xuehui Bianji Weiyuanhui 中國唐代學會編輯委員會, 141–67. Taipei: Wenshizhe chubanshe, 1991.

*YJQQ*. *Yunji qiqian* 雲笈七籤. Zhang Junfang 張君房 (Song). *Daozang*, vol. 22.

You Guoen 遊國恩 et al. *Zhongguo wenxue shi* 中國文學史, 4 vols. Beijing: Renmin wenxue chubanshe, 1979.

*YSJX. Yanshi jiaxun* 顏氏家訓. Yan Zhitui 顏之推 (Northern Qi). References are to Wang Liqi 王利器, annotator, *Yanshi jiaxun jijie* 顏氏家訓集解. Shanghai: Shanghai guji chubanshe, 1980.

Yu Fuwei 余扶危 and He Guanbao 賀官保. *Sui-Tang Dongdu Hanjia cang* 隋唐東都含嘉倉. Beijing: Wenwu chubanshe, 1982.

Yu Haomin 俞灝敏. *Fengshui tanjiu* 風水探究. Hong Kong: Zhonghua shuju, 1991.

Yuan Gang 袁剛. *Sui-Tang zhongshu tizhi de fazhan yanbian* 隋唐中樞體制的發展演變. Taipei: Wenjin chubanshe, 1994a.

———. "Sui-Tang sansheng tizhi xilun" 隋唐三省體制析論. *Beijing daxue xuebao* 北京大學學報 (1994b):1, 97–107.

———. *Sui Yangdi zhuan* 隋煬帝傳. Beijing: Renmin chubanshe, 2001.

*YWLJ. Yiwen leiju* 藝文類聚. Ouyang Xun 歐陽詢 (Tang), comp. Shanghai: Shanghai guji chubanshe, 1965.

*ZGZY. Zhenguan zhengyao* 貞觀政要. Wu Jing 吳競 (Tang). Shanghai: Shanghai guji chubanshe, 1978.

Zhang Gong 張弓. *Tangchao canglin zhidu chutan* 唐朝倉廩制度初探. Beijing: Zhonghua shuju, 1985.

Zhang Kunhe 張崑河. "Sui yunhe kao" 隋運河考. *Yugong* 禹貢 7:1–3 (1937), 201–11.

Zhang Yuhuan 張馭寰 et al., eds. *Zhongguo gudai jianzhu jishu shi* 中國古代建築技術史. Beijing: Kexue chubanshe, 1990.

Zhang Xinglang 張星烺. *Zhongxi jiaotong shiliao huibian* 中西交通史料彙編. Beijing: Zhonghua shuju, 1977–1979.

Zhang Zexian 張澤咸. *Tangdai gongshang ye* 唐代工商業. Beijing: Zhongguo sheke chubanshe, 1995.

Zhao Gang 趙岡 (Chao Kang) and Chen Zhongyi 陳鐘毅. *Zhongguo tudi zhidu shi* 中國土地制度史. Taipei: Lianjing chuban shiye gongsi, 1982.

Zhao Wanli 趙萬里. *Han Wei Nanbeichao muzhi jishi* 漢魏南北朝墓誌集釋. Beijing: Kexue chubanshe, 1956.

Zhao Yunqi 趙雲旗. "Suidai juntian zhi shishi tantao" 隋代均田制實施探討. *Zhongguo shehui jingji shi yanjiu* 中國社會經濟史研究 (1993):3.

Zhou Shaoliang 周紹良 and Zhao Chao 趙超. *Tangdai muzhi huibian* 唐代墓誌彙編. Shanghai: Shanghai guji chubanshe, 1992.

Zhou Xibao 周錫保. *Zhongguo gudai fushi shi* 中國古代服飾史. Beijing: Zhongguo xiju chubanshe, 1984.

Zhou Yiliang 周一良. "Sui-Tang shidai zhi yicang" 隋唐時代之義倉. In *Zhou Yiliang ji* 周一良集, vol. 5, Zhou Yiliang, 29–49. Shenyang: Liaoning jiaoyu chubanshe, 1998.

*ZLZS. Zhou li zhushu* 周禮注疏. Jia Gongyan 賈公彥 (Tang), subcommentator. *Shisanjing zhushu* edition.

*ZS. Zhou shu* 周書. Linghu Defen 令狐德棻 et al. (Tang). Beijing: Zhonghua shuju, 1971.

*ZXBJ. Zhenxian beiji* (*Zhongnan shan shuojingtai lidai zhenxian beiji* 終南山説經臺歷代真仙碑記). Zhu Xiangxian 朱象仙 (Yuan). *Daozang,* vol.19.

*ZYZY. Zhouyi zhengyi* 周易正義. Kong Yingda 孔穎達 (Tang), subcommentator. *Shisanjing zhushu* edition.

*ZZTJ. Zizhi tongjian* 資治通鑑. Sima Guang 司馬光 et al. (Northern Song). Beijing: Zhonghua shuju, 1956.

# Index